Fodor's

SAN ANTONIO, AUSTIN & THE TEXAS HILL COUNTRY

Welcome to San Antonio, Austin, and the Texas Hill Country

In a state as big and bold as Texas, the possibilities for adventures are endless, but there's something about the cities of San Antonio and Austin, and the Texas Hill Country region that lies between them, that beckons visitors. San Antonio is filled to the brim with history and culture, especially along its famous River Walk, while Austin is widely considered one of the best cities in the country for dining, nightlife, and live music. Escape the urban whirlwind by heading out to the Hill Country, awash in wineries and wildflowers. This book was produced in the middle of the COVID-19 pandemic. As you plan your upcoming travels to Texas, please confirm that places are still open and let us know when we need to make updates by writing to us at editors@fodors.com.

TOP REASONS TO GO

- **History:** Remember the Alamo and learn more unique Texas history in museums and missions alike.
- **Food:** Barbecue and Tex-Mex reign here, but the region's diverse food scene continues to impress.
- **Live Music:** From famous music festivals to honky tonk dancehalls, this is the place for music lovers.
- **Small Town Charm:** Step into a slower way of life by retreating to the likes of Fredericksburg, Guerne, and more.
- **The Great Outdoors:** Whether it's river adventures, natural springs, or limestone caves, you'll find plenty of ways to stay active.

Contents

1 **EXPERIENCE SAN ANTONIO, AUSTIN, AND THE TEXAS HILL COUNTRY** 6

20 Ultimate Experiences 8
What's Where 16
Texas Today 18
What to Eat and Drink in Texas 20
What to Buy in Texas 22
Texas History 24
What to Read and Watch 27

2 **TRAVEL SMART** 29

Know Before You Go 30
Getting Here and Around 32
Essentials 36
On the Calendar 38
Great Itineraries 40
Contacts 44

3 **SAN ANTONIO** 45

Welcome to San Antonio 46
Planning 49
Downtown and the River Walk 53
The Pearl District 76
King William Historic District 83
Alamo Heights and Brackenridge Park 89
Southside and the Missions 98
North and Northwest 104

4 **AUSTIN** 113

Welcome to Austin 114
Planning 116
Downtown with Sixth Street and Rainey Street 125
Central Austin and the University of Texas 143
West Austin and Zilker Park 153
South Austin and South Congress District 163
East Austin 177
North Austin 188
Greater Austin 197

5 **THE TEXAS HILL COUNTRY** 205

Welcome to the Texas Hill Country 206
Planning 208
Fredericksburg 210
Luckenbach 223
Johnson City 224
Kerrville 227
Comfort 229
Bandera 231
Boerne 234

New Braunfels 239
Gruene 242
San Marcos 244
Lockhart 246
Wimberley 248
Dripping Springs 251
Marble Falls 253
Burnet 255
Llano 256
Mason 258

INDEX **260**

ABOUT OUR WRITERS **272**

MAPS

Downtown and the River Walk 54–55
The Pearl District 78
King William Historic District 84
Alamo Heights and Brackenridge Park 90–91
Southside and the Missions 100
North and Northwest 106–107
Downtown with Sixth Street and Rainey Street 128–129
Central Austin and the University of Texas 146–147
West Austin and Zilker Park 156–157
South Austin and South Congress District 166–167
East Austin 180–181
North Austin 190–191
Greater Austin 198–199
Fredericksburg 212–213

Chapter 1

EXPERIENCE SAN ANTONIO, AUSTIN, AND THE TEXAS HILL COUNTRY

1 The River Walk

Winding just beneath San Antonio's lively streets, the colorful River Walk pulses with touring boats and water taxis and strolling locals and tourists as well as a multitude of restaurants, shops, hotels, and attractions. (Ch. 3)

2 Austin's Sixth Street

This spirited stretch of pavement in downtown Austin is frequented by those in search of live music, good eats, and some of the best barhopping in the country. (Ch. 4)

3 Barbecue

What's a more perfect Texas lunch than slow-cooked beef brisket, baked beans, mac 'n' cheese, and corn on the cob followed by a slice of pecan pie? (Ch. 3–5)

4 Bluebonnet Season

Springtime in the Hill Country is the loveliest time of year, thanks to the abundance of wildflowers that pop onto the scene, particularly the iconic Texas bluebonnet. (Ch. 5)

5 San Antonio Museum of Art

With artwork that spans 5,000 years, including one of the biggest collections of Latin American art in the country, the SAMA is a must for art-lovers. (Ch. 3)

6 Tex-Mex

Enchiladas, chili con queso, tacos, chimichangas, burritos, and fajitas—all with lots of cheese—are staples on Tex-Mex menus and a must-eat for any Texas trip. (Ch. 3–5)

7 Enchanted Rock State Natural Area

Standing 425 feet tall and 1,825 feet above sea level, the large pink granite dome at this 624-acre park near Fredericksburg draws rock climbers as well as hikers, bird-watchers, campers, and stargazers. (Ch. 5)

8 The Alamo

Step into the most visited historic site in Texas and reflect on how frontiersmen Davy Crockett, James Bowie, and 185 others died fighting for Texas's independence. (Ch. 3)

9 Mount Bonnell

Take in some incredible views day or night of Austin and Lake Austin from atop Mount Bonnell. The many stone steps to the top are worth it for the stunning vistas. (Ch. 4)

10 Texas State Capitol

Taller than the U.S. Capitol, Texas's State Capitol in Austin is beautiful to behold both inside and out. (Ch. 4)

11 Congress Avenue Bridge Bats

This bridge in downtown Austin is home to North America's largest bat colony, and at dusk from late March to October, thousands of bats rush out from underneath the bridge. (Ch. 4)

12 Fredericksburg

Touristy Fredericksburg is one of the most popular towns in the Hill Country, thanks to its charming German heritage and antiques shops, plus the delicious offerings of its restaurants and vineyards. (Ch. 5)

13 Blanton Museum of Art

One of Austin's top cultural attractions, the Blanton showcases European paintings, ancient Greek pottery, Latin American art, and more from the 19,000 works in its permanent collection. (Ch. 4)

14 Barton Springs

Natural springs fill up this popular Austin swimming hole in Zilker Park. The outdoor pool delights swimmers with its average 69°F temperatures year-round. (Ch. 4)

15 San Antonio Missions National Historic Park

A glimpse into 18th-century San Antonio, these four Spanish colonial missions were originally established as Catholic missions by Spanish priests. (Ch. 3)

16 San Antonio Stock Show and Rodeo

Each February, get ready for steer wrestling, barrel racing, mutton busting, and more at the San Antonio Stock Show and Rodeo, a tribute to the state's Western heritage and modern-day ranching. (Ch. 3)

17 Texas Wine Trail

Tour one or more of the dozens of vineyards and wineries throughout the Texas Hill Country, where you can enjoy live music and wine pairings with delicious meals. (Ch. 5)

18 Music Festivals

From Austin City Limits in the fall to South by Southwest in the spring (and plenty of smaller ones throughout the year), Austin knows how to do music festivals. (Ch. 4)

19 Natural Bridge Caverns

Here, guided tours will take you through underground tunnels that twist and turn through whimsical formations of limestone created by water and time. (Ch. 3)

20 Football

Whether it's a local high school game or the University of Texas at Austin Longhorns, attending a football game gives you a true glimpse of Texas culture. (Ch. 3–5)

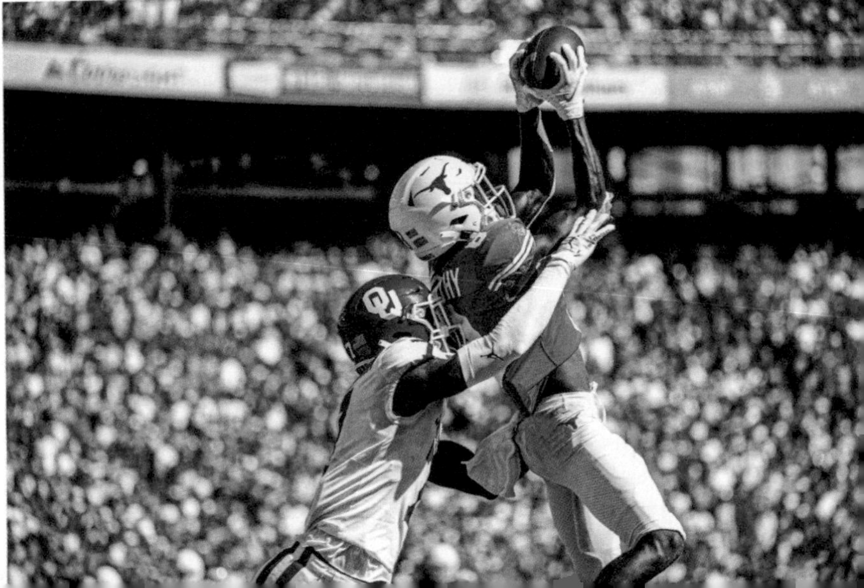

WHAT'S WHERE

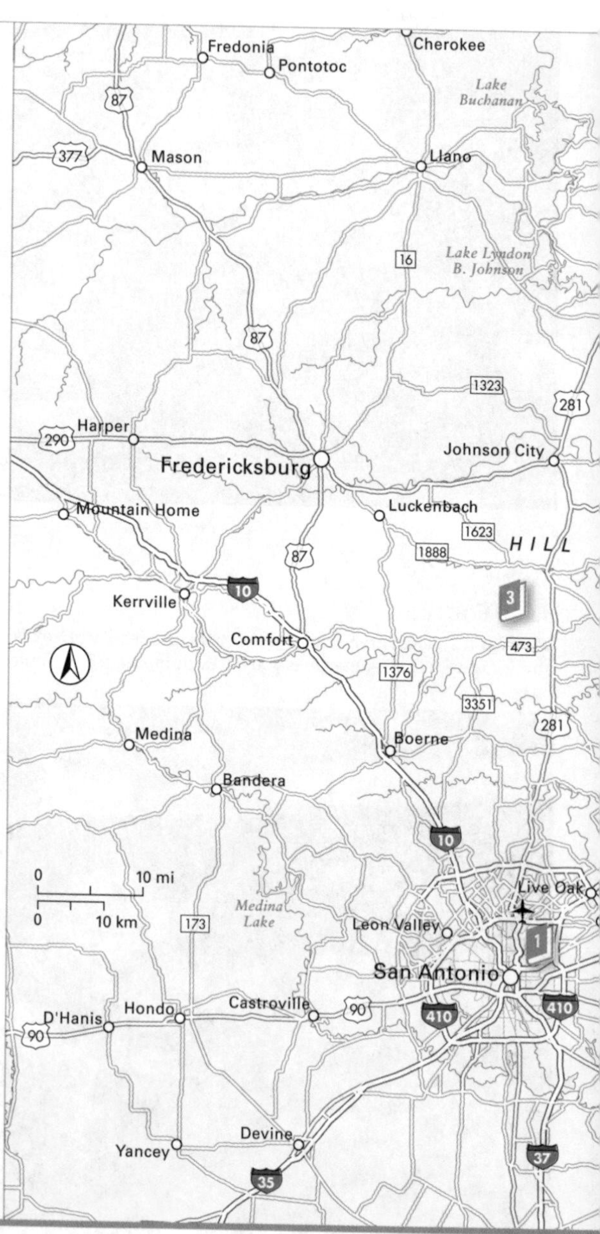

1 San Antonio. Remember the Alamo? That famous landmark is here, along with other historic buildings, though they sometimes get lost amid the charm of the ever-popular River Walk, a shady pedestrian walkway along the San Antonio River that snakes its way through town. Tourists gravitate to the scores of shops, hotels, and restaurants hugging the river's shore. If they're not at the River Walk, they might be exploring the city's many cultural offerings, taking in a Spurs game, or making their way to the Pearl District or Market Square to enjoy some Tex-Mex or the real thing, with fresh guacamole made tableside.

2 Austin. Keep it weird, y'all. That motto and a smallish-city feel have always been part of Austin's appeal, but today Texas's capital is one of the fastest growing cities in the country. Austin is home to the University of Texas campus and energetic Sixth Street—where music thumps into the wee hours of the night—as

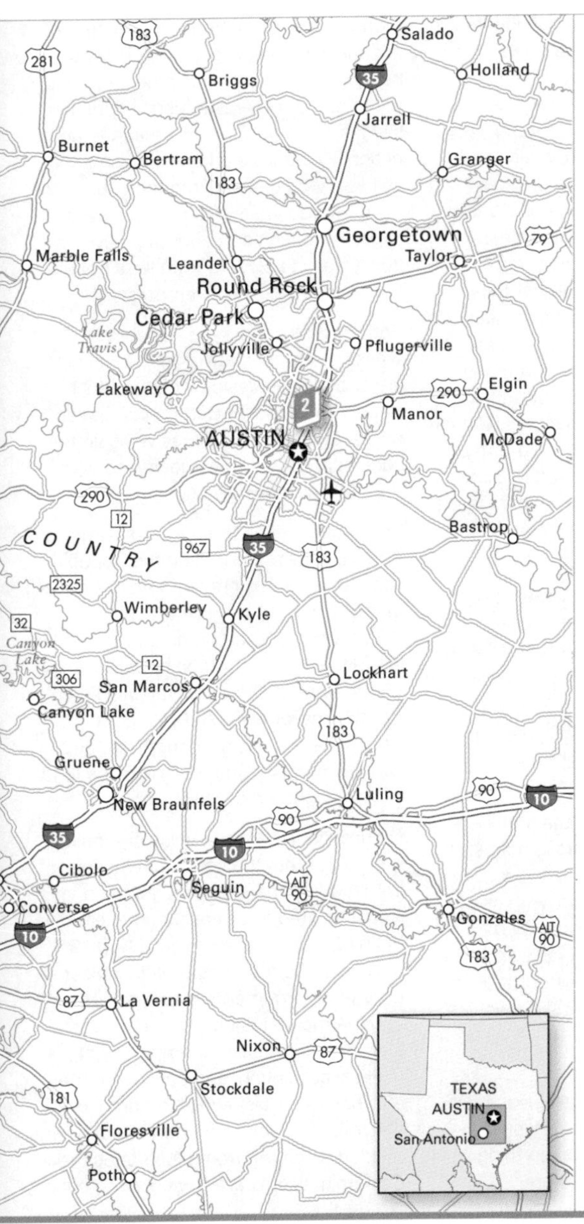

well as treasures like the Bullock Texas State History Museum, a repository for exhibits about the Lone Star State. Austin also has an outdoorsy side, with bicyclists, hikers, and yoga practitioners easily spotted on pathways and parks throughout town, but the city has gone high-tech as well, with Tesla now setting up shop in the capital and Dell Technologies headquartered in nearby Round Rock.

3 The Hill Country. Wineries, German-flavored Fredericksburg, sprawling ranches, antiques shops, lakes, and hills comprise the Texas Hill Country, a region west of Austin and north and northwest of San Antonio. Scenic drives are popular here, as are fresh finds and homemade pies from farmers' markets. The best time of year to visit without a doubt is springtime, when bluebonnets—Texas's state flower—arrive on the scene, coloring the landscape with their vibrant violet-blue hues.

Texas Today

THE PEOPLE

The people who call the Lone Star State home are a lot more multifaceted than meets the eye. Yes, they have a spirit of independence about them and deep pride in their state, and many also unite over sports, especially football; barbecue and any red meat, really; and a love of country, family, and religion. But demographically they are as diverse as America itself. Of the state's nearly 30 million residents, the percentage of non-Hispanic whites is almost the same as the Hispanic population—each about 40%. Black people make up about 13% of the state population and those of Asian descent about 5%, with the remainder Native Pacific Islanders, Native Americans, and others. Since 2010, the state population has increased by almost 4 million, and nearly 50% of that increase has been Hispanics. In San Antonio, 65% of the population is Hispanic.

There are large-scale Mexican-American neighborhoods in Texas's large cities; in Dallas, Houston, and San Antonio, there are also sizable communities of African Americans; and in small towns there are pockets of German and Czech communities, the descendants of 19th-century European settlers.

There is great affluence in the state—37 billionaires on the 2021 *Forbes* richest 400 Americans list live in Texas—and there is great inequality, too, with nearly 16% of the state's population living below the poverty line; until 2020 that percentage had been consistently falling since its high of 18.5% in 2011, reaching 13.6% in 2019.

THE POLITICS

Texas is a red state, but again, like most of America these days, that doesn't mean everyone agrees on everything politically—far from it. There are conservatives and there are liberals, and within these groups there's a range of thought, too. But when it comes to the national vote, Texas goes red. There's been talk that it's turning blue, or purple, some say, but then surprises happen, like the town of McAllen—made famous nationally with the photos showing children who crossed into the country from Mexico waiting to be processed, in cages—electing a Republican mayor in 2021, despite 58% of McAllen's population being registered Democrats.

Both Texas senators are Republican, while its representatives in the House are of both persuasions, currently 23 Republicans and 13 Democrats. Based on the 2020 Census, Texas will gain two additional House seats beginning with the 2022 midterm elections.

At the state level, the governor, Greg Abbott, is Republican, and the Republicans have the majority of both chambers of the Texas state legislature. Locally, the mayors of Texas's four largest cities—Houston, San Antonio, Dallas, and Austin—are all Democrats, while Fort Worth's mayor is Republican. Local city councils are officially nonpartisan, but council members in the large cities tend to be progressives.

Political hot buttons in Texas perennially revolve around border security and immigration, the economy, abortion, and issues related to diversity and tolerance. In 2020, health safety over COVID-19 moved to the top of statewide concerns (as well as arguments over mask and vaccine mandates), and there was an increased interest in unemployment, political corruption, and education. There also has been growing alarm among native Texans about the number of new residents coming from blue states like California. Texans are a welcoming bunch, but when those from the West Coast bring their politics and culture with them, locals call it the Californication of Texas.

WESTERN HERITAGE

People in Texas are proud of their Western roots, but if you're hoping to see everyone walking around in Stetsons and cowboy boots every day, you'll be disappointed. More likely you'll see this Western heritage's influence in more subtle forms, like the many pickup trucks on the busy city streets and thoroughfares and the country music playing on radio stations and in shops and restaurants. If you want to surround yourself with those dressed in Western attire, head to a honky-tonk, which is another name for a country-Western dance hall, or attend one of the state's many rodeos, a Western institution that is alive and well in the Lone Star State. Alternatively, opt for a stay at a dude ranch and you can have your own Billy Crystal city-slicker moment.

THE INFRASTRUCTURE

What do Texans all concur about when they complain? The traffic, of course. They may not agree on what to do about it, as proposed solutions vary, but they agree it's a problem. It seems one highway or another—or several—are being worked on at any given time in any given city. As the population continues to grow, infrastructure continues to be an issue. A lack of roads isn't so much the problem; controlling the traffic on said roads is. Heavily traveled Interstate 35, for example, which runs north and south through the state, has major congestion, extremely so in some areas, and the Texas Department of Transportation has proposed making it 20 lanes across at the bottleneck around Austin. While larger cities have buses and commuter trains, they're not highly used or highly convenient.

Texas is first and foremost a driving state. Over the years—decades, actually—there has been talk of building a high-speed train between Dallas and Houston, and it looks like a 240-mile high-speed rail with trains zipping across in 90 minutes (compared to a four-hour drive) is finally set to open in 2026.

THE ECONOMY

If Texas were its own nation, it would be the ninth largest economy in the world. It is a business-friendly state, with no corporate or personal income tax and not a lot of state or local government intrusion on how companies run their businesses. The state has led the nation in job growth for the past decade.

Energy, particularly oil and gas, has long been a top sector in the state economy, but other industries that drive GDP growth in Texas are health care, information and technology, trade and transportation, professional services, banking and financial services, education, manufacturing, construction, and tourism.

SPORTS

A ball game of some type is almost always happening somewhere in Texas, home to dozens of college sports teams, 11 professional men's sports teams, and two professional women's sports teams. Houston (Rockets), San Antonio (Spurs), and Dallas (Mavericks) all have NBA teams, and Dallas also a WNBA team, the Dallas Wings. Dallas (Cowboys, Rangers) and Houston (Texans, Astros) both have NFL and MLB teams. Austin (Austin Football Club), Dallas (Football Club Dallas), and Houston (Dynamo Football Club) play in Major League Soccer, and Houston (Dash) also plays in the National Women's Soccer League. Dallas has the state's one NHL team, the Dallas Stars.

What to Eat and Drink in Texas

BARBECUE

Smoked brisket is king here, but pulled pork, chicken, and spicy sausage are other meats frequently slow cooked in a barbecue pit. The wood used for the fire might be mesquite, which leaves a strong smoky undertone; oak, for a medium-to-strong flavor; or pecan, which produces a sweeter taste.

TEX-MEX

Using lots of shredded cheese, beans, spices, flour tortillas, and, of course, meat (beef, pork, or chicken), Tex-Mex is Texas's take on south-of-the-border fare, influenced by American, Mexican, and Spanish cuisines. Common Tex-Mex menu items are chili con queso, burritos, fajitas, tacos (especially breakfast tacos), enchiladas, and chimichangas.

CHILI AND FRITO PIE

Texas chili is made simply with meat and a flavorful chili paste that is created from dried peppers or chiles and spices. Enjoyed just fine by itself, Texas chili can also be the base for another Southwestern favorite: Frito pie. This messy dish consists of Fritos corn chips covered with chili, mounds of cheese, and a mix of onions, jalapeños, salsa, sour cream, and guacamole.

WHATABURGER

Easily recognized by its bright-orange flying W logo, Whataburger began in 1950 as a family-run burger stand in Corpus Christi and grew into a fast-food chain with hundreds of restaurants across the state. The menu is centered on the item Texans are most passionate about: red meat. Burgers are normally served with mustard, though they can be dressed up in many possible ways.

PECANS

Texas competes with Georgia as the largest pecan producer in the country. The Texas town of San Saba is the Pecan Capital of the World thanks to the native pecan trees that flourish around the San Saba and Colorado Rivers. Pecan harvesting is from October to early December. The pecan often stars in one of Texans' favorite desserts: pie.

BLUE BELL ICE CREAM

Made in Brenham, Texas, since 1907, Blue Bell ice cream is a statewide favorite and comes in multiple flavors. You'll find the ice cream in cartons in shops throughout the state or you can visit the "Little Creamery" headquarters in Brenham.

TEXAS WINE

Texas has several hundred wineries, and the Texas Hill Country alone is home to more than a hundred of them. The 50-plus varieties of grapes grown in the state include Cabernet Sauvignon, Zinfandel, Chardonnay, Tempranillo, Tannat, Mourvèdre, Blanc du Bois, and Sangiovese.

KOLACHES

Found in some of the state's Old World European communities, these round-shaped pastries originally from the Moravia region of the Czech Republic are traditionally filled with fruit—cherries, apples, lemons, apricots, or prunes—or even with poppy seeds.

CHICKEN-FRIED STEAK

Country cooking is widely popular in Texas, which means you can get cozy with a hearty serving of chicken-fried steak (or chicken-fried chicken if you prefer) with mashed potatoes, both smothered in creamy white (country) gravy. Chicken-fried steak or chicken is breaded, tenderized meat made by pounding the meat (usually round or cubed steak), dipping it in egg and seasoned flour, and then frying it to tasty perfection.

AUTHENTIC MEXICAN CUISINE

For Mexican dishes actually eaten south of the border, be on the lookout for authentic tamales. Wrapped in corn husks (remove before eating), this corn-based goodie might be chicken, beef, or cheese.

What to Buy in Texas

WESTERN WEAR

Great Western wear finds can be found throughout the state, from cowboy hats and cowboy boots to big decorative belt buckles.

TEXAS-SHAPED ITEMS

For a classic souvenir, you can find just about anything shaped like the state of Texas: magnets, earrings, cookie cutters, cake pans, keychains, waffle irons, ice maker trays, cutting boards, and even bottles of tequila and jars of hot sauce.

CHRISTMAS DECORATIONS IN FREDERICKSBURG

Ornaments, nutcrackers, snow globes, nativity scenes, and more are sold at the famous Christmas Store on Fredericksburg's Main Street.

SALSA

Pick up a jar of green or red salsa to take home a bit of Texas kick. Variations include ones with fire-roasted garlic, a hint of mango, or habanero.

BBQ SAUCE AND HOT SAUCE

Austin's Salt Lick barbecue chain makes bottles of barbecue sauce you can buy. Other Texas brands include Austin's Own, Mark's Good Stuff, and Terry Black's. For something spicier, these made-in-Texas hot sauces will bring it: Aztexan Pepper Company Habanero Supreme Pepper Sauce, Big Daddy's Hot Sauces, Hotline Pepper Products' Garlicky Greengo Hot Sauce, Suckle-Busters Texas Heat Original Pepper Sauce, Tex Sauce, Winston's Hot Pepper Sauce, and Yellowbird Habanero Sauce.

PEACHES

Peaches are the state's number-one seasonal fruit crop, and their sweet aroma draws people to fruit stands and farmers' markets. In the Hill Country, the Fredericksburg-Stonewall area is known as the Peach Capital of Texas and hosts an annual peach jamboree. Peach season runs from May through July.

HOMEMADE JAMS AND JELLIES

Using produce from Texas's farms and gardens, mom-and-pop stores throughout the state sell jams, jellies, butters, relishes, mustards, and more that they have made and canned themselves.

Cowboy hats

Some uniquely Texas flavors include Hill Country peach preserve, cactus sangria jelly, peach pecan butter, apple jalapeño jelly, raspberry chipotle pepper jam, prickly pear habanero jelly, and tequila marmalade.

BLUEBONNET-THEME SOUVENIRS
The Texas state flower—the beautiful bluebonnet—pops up on a number of items, from tote bags and pillows to postcards and journals to mugs and coasters to clothing and jewelry.

ANTIQUES
Hidden treasures from yesteryear fill stores in small towns in the Hill Country. You can find anything from vintage records to old-fashioned lighting to handcrafted furniture.

FUDGE AND CHOCOLATE
Your sweet tooth will love the Hill Country, home to multiple fudge shops. Try Texas Drop Fudge in Leakey; Fredericksburg Fudge Company and Lone Star Candy Bar in Fredericksburg; and Dutchman's Hidden Valley in Hamilton.

LAMMES CANDIES
Texas Chewie Pecan Pralines and Longhorns (chocolate-covered pecans and caramel) are two of the super-popular sweets made by Austin-based candy company Lammes. You can pick up a box to go around the state, or stop in at one of the four Austin candy shops.

Texas History

Most Texans are prone to boasting that their state was once a separate nation, but the Texans who achieved that distinction desired annexation to the United States, not nationhood. Here's a recap of how Texas moved from a Spanish colony to become its own nation, then state, along with tips on where you can see things in the state related to its history or where to go to learn more.

PRE-EUROPEAN SETTLEMENT

Long before Europeans arrived to colonize what is today Texas, the original occupants of the land included the semi-nomadic Atakapa, Karankawa, Mariame, and Akokisa tribes, who fished and hunted near the Texas coast, as well as farming and trading tribes, such as the Caddo in East Texas and the Jumano in West Texas. The first colonizers from Spain arrived in 1519, and by the 1530s Spaniards and voyagers from Cuba had traveled inland, followed by Francisco Vázquez de Coronado in the 1540s.

The non-nomadic tribes often offered help to the Europeans. The Jumano even asked the Spanish missionaries for religious instruction, leading priests to live with them for a time near San Angelo. The monotheistic Caddo tribe went so far as asking that a Spanish priest set up a mission to teach members of their tribe about their faith. However, with no immunity to European diseases, the Caddo fell ill with influenza and smallpox, many dying, and they then blamed the religion for bringing the epidemics. The mission languished and eventually closed.

Native tribes in what is now New Mexico fought against the invasion of their land and the push for natives to convert to Catholicism, so they drove Spaniards wanting to settle there to Texas instead. These Spaniards set up Texas's first permanent European settlement in 1681 in present-day El Paso. That area of Texas was occupied by the Ysleta Pueblos, who kept to the north bank of the Rio Grande.

In other instances, it was the Europeans who were pushing the native tribes south. Hunting tribes, such as the Apache and Comanche, were forced out of the northern plain states, so they made their way to Texas.

Learn More: The Bullock Museum in Austin tells some of the stories of the many native tribes who have inhabited Texas, some who were here before Texas's first European settlers and some who came to the state later after being driven away from their lands in other states.

SPANISH COLONIAL ERA

Though the first Spanish settlers in Texas had requests from some tribes for religious instruction, their first attempts to convert Native Americans to Christianity and to colonize this new-to-them world were tepid at best. Scattered settlements arose in West, Central, South, and East Texas, but none were populous, wildly prosperous, or able to defend themselves from outside hostility. The Apache wiped out dozens of them, crops failed when rain didn't come, hurricanes blew them away, and plagues brought down their populations. The French, led by René-Robert Cavalier, Sieur de La Salle, also established a settlement in Texas, but they were driven out or killed by native tribes.

Against the backdrop of building missions, Spanish missionaries were among the state's first ranchers, as cattle ranching had spread north into Texas from the Mexican states of Querétaro, Nuevo León, and Coahuila. The first cowhands were known as *vaqueros* ("vaca" is cow in Spanish), and they were usually from lower castes in Mexican society based on their race—African and Native American, as well as Spaniards with mixed heritage who became grouped by their new combined ancestry: *mulatto* (Spanish with African) and *mestizo* (Spanish with Native American).

Learn More: San Antonio Missions National Historic Park in San Antonio sheds light on Spain's role in the colonizing of Texas.

UNREST AND REBELLION

The Spanish lost what little control they had over Texas in 1821, when their empire lost the land to newly independent Mexico. At the time, Mexico was too involved in its own central and southern intrigues to turn attention to its sparsely populated northern areas, including Texas. Had it not been for the land hunger of the neighboring United States, the 19th century in Texas might have faded away as unnoticed as it had opened. But in 1819, a gang of American freebooters, known to historians as the Long Expedition, captured the Spanish settlement at Nacogdoches and declared the independence of Texas. The uprising failed, but it heralded a momentum that would ultimately lead to success.

The British immigrants and Americans from other states who began settling in Texas in 1821 favored Anglo-American jurisprudence, Protestantism, decentralism, and slavery—none of which the Catholic and centralized Spanish and Mexican governments allowed. Despite Mexico's intolerance for slavery, there were an estimated 5,000 slaves in Texas by 1836, and nearly 200,000 by the time of the Civil War. Most of them were forced to work on cotton plantations in East Texas, while others toiled as cowhands on ranches. Some ran away to Mexico.

The Mexican constitution of 1824 was in tune with the political idealism sweeping the North American continent—a belief that more egalitarian and democratic societies would take root and European corruption and authoritarianism could be discarded. Yet the new Mexican president was soon overthrown. When the charismatic Antonio López de Santa Anna challenged him, Anglo colonists prepared a new state constitution for Texas, which Stephen F. Austin brought to Mexico City. Santa Anna approved it, but Austin was arrested as he traveled back toward Texas and was imprisoned in Mexico City for treasonous words found in an intercepted letter. While Austin was imprisoned, Texans went ahead with implementing their new state constitution, until Santa Anna declared one-man rule, suspended the 11-year-old Mexican constitution, and made himself the dictator of Mexico.

Learn More: View a statue of Stephen F. Austin, "the Father of Texas," in the Texas State Capitol in Austin. About 50 miles west of Houston, the San Felipe de Austin State Historic Site marks the location of the colony begun by Austin in 1823.

THE BATTLE OF THE ALAMO

The colony rebelled, and Santa Anna set out from Mexico City to reconquer it. When he arrived in San Antonio in February 1836, he found about 189 Texas revolutionaries holed up in a former Spanish mission complex, San Antonio de Valero, better known today as the Alamo.

Santa Anna demanded the mission's surrender. The Texans answered with a cannon shot. Santa Anna ran up the red flag—no quarter, no surrender, no mercy—from atop San Fernando Cathedral and began a 13-day attack in what would come to be called the Battle of the Alamo. On the list of defenders were Davy Crockett, James Bowie, and William

Barret Travis. The revolutionaries fought from the walls and, when these were breached, hand to hand until, as legend has it, all were dead. (There is some evidence that a half-dozen men surrendered and were immediately executed.)

Santa Anna won the battle, but not the war. While Anna's troops were laying siege to the Alamo, Texas delegates were signing their Declaration of Independence in Washington-on-the-Brazos and naming Sam Houston commander of the Texas army. On April 21, Houston and his men attacked Santa Anna at San Jacinto and defeated the Mexican army there.

Learn More: Relive this fight for Texas independence at the Alamo in downtown San Antonio; the Washington-on-the-Brazos State Historic Site in Washington, Texas; and the San Jacinto Battleground State Historic Site, about 25 miles from Houston.

THE REPUBLIC OF TEXAS

Fearful of Santa Anna's pursuit to wipe out remaining Texas forces, Sam Houston led settlers in a retreat to Louisiana (known as the Runaway Scrape), but they met up with Santa Anna's troops on Vince's Bayou, near present-day Houston. With the rallying cry "Remember the Alamo," the Texans charged ahead. In 18 minutes, the Mexicans were defeated.

After its victory against Mexico, Texas became a republic, not because its leaders or people favored the move—the majority wanted to be one of the states in the United States—but largely because political arrangements at the time in Washington did not allow for a new slave-holding state. The nine-year history of the Republic of Texas was marked mainly by factional fights and penury, and most of the population was gratified when, in December 1845, Texas was allowed to join the United States.

A war between the U.S. and Mexico soon followed over a dispute about the boundary line between Texas and Mexico; that war concluded in 1848, but not before the United States conquered its neighbor to the south, extracting nearly half of Mexico's land area (all of present-day California, Nevada, and Utah, as well as parts of New Mexico, Arizona, Colorado, and Wyoming) as the price for peace—and setting the current borders for the State of Texas.

On the eve of the Civil War, there were over 182,500 enslaved people in Texas, nearly 30% of the population. Texas opted to secede from the Union on February 1, 1861, and formally joined the Confederate States on March 2. More than 90,000 soldiers from Texas fought for the Confederacy, and Waco produced six Confederate generals. On June 19, 1865, it was all over when Union forces stepped foot one last time in Texas. On that day they officially freed the slaves in the Lone Star State. June 19 has long since been recognized and celebrated each year by black Americans as Juneteenth; in 2021, the U.S. Congress made it an official federal holiday.

Learn More: See where the Republic of Texas's first governor lived at the Sam Houston Memorial Museum in Huntsville, Texas, a complex sited on part of the general's homestead. The Star of the Republic Museum in Washington, Texas, is a repository for all things related to Texas's era as its own nation.

What to Read and Watch

THE ALAMO
Playing Davy Crockett, John Wayne leads a team of volunteer Texans in a fight for Texas's independence only to be met with a bloody and fatal defeat at the Alamo in 1836. The movie set for this 1960 film was erected near Brackettville, Texas.

BIG WONDERFUL THING: A HISTORY OF TEXAS BY STEPHEN HARRIGAN
In this lengthy account of the Lone Star State's history, *Texas Monthly* contributor Stephen Harrigan captures the passion Texans feel for the state, while also countering the elements of pride and awe with some of the hard truths and many struggles Texas has faced since its early days.

FRIDAY NIGHT LIGHTS
The 2004 film follows the 1988 Permian High School football team in Odessa, Texas, as they try to make it to the state championship, with Billy Bob Thornton playing the head coach. In 2006, a spin-off of the movie debuted on NBC, becoming a beloved classic. The TV drama starring Kyle Chandler and Connie Britton centered on the passion West Texans have for high school football and the power of the catchphrase "clear eyes, full hearts, can't lose." It was filmed in Austin and Pflugerville.

GIANT
Filmed near Marfa, Texas, this 1956 movie features three classic stars of the big screen—Elizabeth Taylor, Rock Hudson, and James Dean. The sweeping Western portrays conflict and social discrimination between a wealthy Texas family and the Mexican workers they employ at their ranch near the Texas border beginning in the 1920s, as well as the clash between Taylor's cultured character and her rugged sister-in-law and between her two love interests.

GO DOWN TOGETHER: THE TRUE, UNTOLD STORY OF BONNIE AND CLYDE BY JEFF GUINN
While there are many books about Bonnie Parker and Clyde Barrow, the pair of native Texas outlaws who met in Dallas in 1930 ,this one looks beyond the mythology of the legendary duo as portrayed in the 1967 movie with Faye Dunaway and Warren Beatty. The pages of Guinn's hefty book capture their love for each other while always being on the run from the law.

KING OF THE HILL
While this animated TV sitcom takes place in fictional Arlen, Texas, the show's creator, Mike Judge, who is from Garland, a suburb of Dallas, says Arlen is inspired by actual Texas suburbs and small towns. The show ran on Fox for 13 seasons and often had storylines related to political humor.

LONESOME DOVE BY LARRY MCMURTY
This 1985 novel, which won the Pulitzer Prize for fiction, follows cowboys on their trail drive from Texas to Montana. Texas local McMurty followed it with a sequel, *The Streets of Laredo,* and two prequels, *Dead Man's Walk* and *Comanche Moon.* All four books inspired TV scripts, including the *Lonesome Dove* miniseries featuring Tommy Lee Jones and Robert Duvall.

NO COUNTRY FOR OLD MEN
Both a novel and a movie, *No Country for Old Men* is about a drug deal gone wrong near the Texas-Mexico border in 1980. Screenwriters Joel and Ethan Coen adapted author Cormac McCarthy's 2005 book into a movie, which they also directed. Released in 2007, the film starred Tommy Lee Jones, Javier Bardem, and Josh Brolin, and won several Academy Awards, including Best Picture.

What to Read and Watch

SELENA

The 1997 movie tells the true story of famous Texas-born Tejano singer Selena Quintanilla-Peréz, played by Jennifer Lopez, as she follows her dreams of singing and stardom, achieving a number-one album before she was murdered at age 23.

TEXAS BY JAMES MICHENER

A classic, this 1985 historical novel opens up a portal to the four-and-a-half centuries of Texas history with myriad stories weaving together fictional characters with real-life ones.

URBAN COWBOY

A pop culture favorite that left moviegoers in search of Western wear, the 1980 movie *Urban Cowboy* stars John Travolta and Debra Winger, who play characters Bud and Sissy. The two fall in love at a country-Western bar near Houston, where they dance the "Cotton-Eyed Joe" and Travolta's character famously rides a mechanical bull. The movie was inspired by a real-life honky-tonk named Gilley's in Pasadena, Texas, and two of its patrons, after their story appeared in an *Esquire*article.

THE PATH TO POWER: THE YEARS OF LYNDON JOHNSON BY ROBERT CARO

This book—part one of a multivolume biography about America's 36th president—does a deep dive on the Stonewall native's Texas roots while also providing a thorough look at his first few years in the political world.

Chapter 2

TRAVEL SMART

Updated by
Debbie Harmsen

★ STATE CAPITAL:
Austin

STATE POPULATION:
29.1 million

LANGUAGE:
English

$ CURRENCY:
U.S. Dollar

AREA CODES:
210, 830, and 726 (San Antonio); 512 and 737 (Austin); 512, 830, and 325 (Hill Country)

EMERGENCIES:
911

DRIVING:
On the right side of the road

ELECTRICITY:
120-240 v/60 cycles; plugs have two or three rectangular prongs

TIME:
1 hour behind New York

WEB RESOURCES:
www.austintexas.org
www.visitsanantonio.com
www.traveltexas.com/cities-and-regions/hill-country

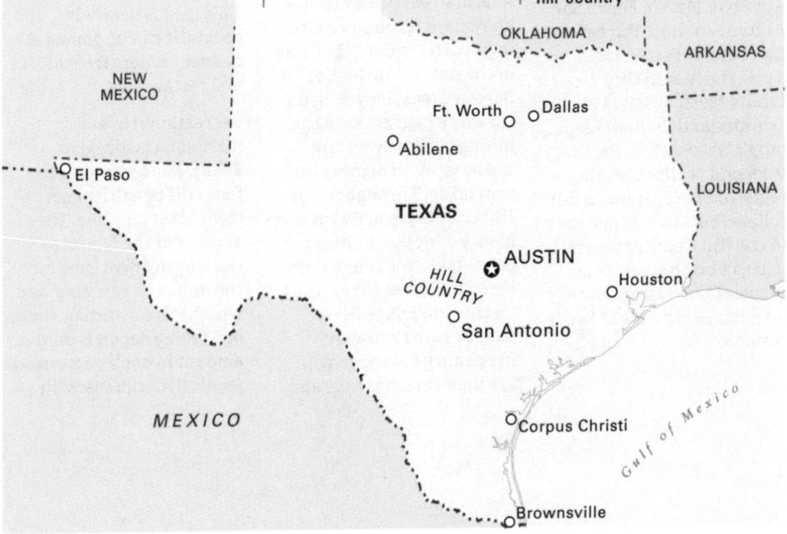

Know Before You Go

Among Texas's most popular destinations, San Antonio, Austin, and the Hill Country have dozens of notable attractions and things to do, and there's a lot of land to cover—so planning ahead is key. Here are some notes and tips to help you navigate your trip, whether it's your first time visiting this delightful part of Texas or your twentieth.

WHEN TO GO

With 300 days of sunshine per year, San Antonio, Austin, and the Texas Hill Country are year-round destinations. Fall and spring are the most pleasant times to visit, though it can rain much of May and November. Winter can be enjoyable, too, as it is often still shorts weather, while summers tend to be quite hot and humid. Some of the most popular festivals are in spring and fall, including South by Southwest in Austin in March, Fiesta San Antonio in April, Burnet's Bluebonnet Festival in April, the Austin City Limits Music Festival in October, and Fredericksburg's Oktoberfest the first weekend of October. The region doesn't get much fall foliage, but there is one spot in the Hill Country where you can catch some: Lost Maples State Natural Area, 90 miles northwest of San Antonio.

THE GREAT OUTDOORS

With 268,596 square miles comprising the state, Texas has a lot of land, and opportunities to explore the great outdoors are endless. The state has two national parks (Big Bend and Guadalupe), 80 state parks, 907 golf courses, and several thousand caverns, most concentrated west of Austin in the Texas Hill Country on the Edwards Plateau, which has a limestone bedrock that supports the growth of caves.

Austin in particular is known for its outdoor offerings, with residents bathing in the natural springs of Barton Creek, bicycling on the city's many bike paths, hiking in nearby nature preserves, and boating on area lakes. Throughout the Hill Country, you'll also find plenty of opportunities to get outside, including state parks and river adventures on the Guadalupe River. Just be sure to research in advance to ensure you are undertaking trails and activities that meet your fitness level and bring the necessary supplies with you.

HOURS OF OPERATION

Most businesses in central Texas operate during typical U.S. business hours, from 9 am to 5 pm, with shops usually open from 10 am to 8 pm (5 or 6 pm on Sunday). Restaurants, especially in Austin's touristy areas and on San Antonio's River Walk, generally stay open until 9 or 10 pm, and bars until 2 am.

ALCOHOL AND MARIJUANA

Effective September 2021, Texas law now allows beer and wine to be sold beginning at 10 am on Sunday. However, stores in Texas still cannot sell liquor on Sunday or after 9 pm on Saturday. Due to a new rule put in place during the COVID-19 pandemic that has since been made permanent, "alcohol to go" is now an option in Texas. This means beer, wine, and cocktails can be among the delivery orders from stores and restaurants.

Recreational use of marijuana is illegal in Texas. Those caught can face stiff penalties and significant jail time. The amount of the fine and the length of jail time for those caught can vary, and whether it's a misdemeanor or a felony depends on the amount in one's possession. Medical marijuana with up to 1% THC in dosages is legal under certain prescribed uses, including as a treatment for cancer and for veterans suffering from PTSD.

HOUSING ISSUES

Like several parts of the country, Austin has experienced a growing population of unhoused people, and groupings of tents downtown under interstate overpasses have become a common sight. In September 2021, Texas governor Greg Abbott signed into law a bill that prohibits these types of encampments in public areas of the state. It remains to be seen how much the ban will be enforced, but the largest camp in Austin was cleared out in October.

HEALTH AND SAFETY

Texas can get very hot and sticky in the summer, with the average temperature in the region in July and August a steamy 96°F with 65% humidity. Due to this stifling heat, sunstroke, heat exhaustion, and dehydration are ailments to watch out for when visiting that time of year. To protect yourself, wear a cap or hat and sunscreen, and always carry a bottle of water. If you're attending an outdoor event, try to sit or stand in the shade, and stay hydrated.

By law, Texans may carry handguns concealed or openly, provided they're in a holster.

SAVING MONEY

A great way to find deals in the region is to contact the visitors bureaus for Austin and San Antonio and the more general Texas Tourism. The staff and websites for these local and state tourism agencies will inform you about any packages available so you can bundle together lodging, attractions, and more for savings. They can also help you determine which lodging options include breakfast and parking in the overnight cost and which are within walking distance to key attractions so you spend less on gas.

In San Antonio, you might opt for the Go City Explorer Pass (🌐 *www.gocity.com/san-antonio/en-us*), which lets you experience the place in a more affordable way. The pass, which is stored on a downloadable app, allows you to select how many attractions you want to see (from two to five, from $77 to $129) and is good for 60 days once activated, within one year from the time of purchase. Attractions include SeaWorld San Antonio, Six Flags Fiesta Texas, the LBJ Ranch Tour, Natural Bridge Caverns, and the San Antonio Missions.

PACKING

When traveling to Texas in the summer, it may seem counterintuitive to pack a sweater, but a cardigan-style sweater or sweatshirt can come in quite handy. Remember that when it's blazing hot outside, the air-conditioning gets cranked up inside. And since Texas weather is unpredictable and A/C is sometimes needed even in November and February, it's practical to have a sweater handy any time of year that you visit. Also don't forget to pack your swimsuit, sunscreen, lip balm with SPF, sunglasses, and a cap or hat, as well as a compact umbrella. If you'll be driving a lot and need eyeglasses to drive, prescription sunglasses are quite useful. Oh, and save room in your luggage to bring home some Western wear.

Getting Here and Around

 Air

Located in the Central and South-Central part of Texas, Austin and San Antonio are easily reached via air from many U.S. destinations as well as several international ones. Flights from New York City reach Austin and San Antonio in about four hours, while Chicago, Los Angeles, and Miami are each a three-hour flight from either city. Visitors to the Hill Country can fly into either Austin or San Antonio.

AIRPORTS

About 80 miles apart from each other, San Antonio and Austin each have an airport, and those are the main airports in this region of Texas. San Antonio International Airport (SAT) is about 8 miles north of downtown in San Antonio's northeast quadrant, and it's the closer of the two airports to New Braunfels, Natural Bridge Caverns, and Fredericksburg, as well as towns in the southwest part of the Hill Country, such as Bandera, Boerne, Comfort, and Kerrville.

Austin-Bergstrom International Airport (AUS) is about 8 miles east of downtown Austin and is the closest commercial airport to Pedernales Falls State Park, LBJ State Park and Historic Site, and Longhorn Cavern State Park, as well as many towns in the Hill Country, including Dripping Springs, Marble Falls, and Johnson City.

Flying into Houston (IAH and HOU) or the Dallas–Fort Worth area (DFW and DAL) is not recommended for the region as Dallas and Houston are both about a three-to-five hour drive away from the Hill Country, depending on which town is your destination.

FLIGHTS

Seventeen airlines pass in and out of Austin-Bergstrom International Airport, while 13 airlines fly into and out of San Antonio International Airport. At both airports, Southwest Airlines is the busiest of the bunch, followed by American Airlines, two companies that are headquartered in North Texas in the Dallas–Fort Worth area. Both airports ranked in the top 10 for large airports in J. D. Power's 2021 North America Customer Satisfaction Study, and in 2019, Austin-Bergstrom International Airport was the runner-up for Best U.S. Airport in Fodor's Travel Awards.

AIRPORT TRANSFERS

VIA Metropolitan Transit has bus stops in both terminals A and B of the San Antonio International Airport. Take VIA bus route 5 to go downtown. Currently, it is $1.30 for the 30-minute ride from the airport to downtown.

In Austin, the Capital Metro airport bus runs every 30 minutes, leaving from baggage claim. The 30-minute ride from Austin-Bergstrom International Airport to downtown Austin costs $1.75 each way.

Cabs and ride-share services are also regularly available from the airports into the centers of Austin and San Antonio.

Bicycle

Wisconsin-based company BCycle runs Austin's and San Antonio's bike-share programs, though Austin has changed its name to MetroBike.

In Austin, MetroBike provides about 500 bicycles throughout central Austin for short-term rentals, with pickups and drop-offs at more than 70 spots. It costs $1 to unlock the bike, then 23 cents a minute for each minute of use. Various membership plans are also available.

In San Antonio, BCycle has traded its inventory of 650 bikes for all pedal-assist electric bikes, which can go up to 15 mph. They may be picked up and dropped off at 65 locations in San Antonio for a single-trip fee of $5 for every 30 minutes of use, with additional options for day passes and memberships.

Bike rental shops in Austin include Barton Springs Bike Rental (ideal for cycling around Zilker Park; $7.50 per hour/$22.50 per day for a beach cruiser, $11.50 per hour/$34.50 per day for a mountain bike or hybrid, and $14.50 per hour/$43.50 per day for road bikes and specialty bikes like tandems) and Mellow Johnny's ($30 to $50 per day, $150 to $260 per week). The organization Bike Austin has maps of area bike routes and organizes group rides. Barton Springs Bike Rental also offers bike tours.

Bike rental shops in San Antonio include Blue Star Bike Shop ($20 half-day/$28 full-day for a townie; $40 a day for a road/hybrid bike) and Bike World at the Pearl (rental rates range from $35 to $45 for half a day, $55 to $65 for a full day, and $230 to $260 for the week). Alamo Bike Shop and Ride Away Bicycles both organize group rides.

Bus

The major bus line that travels throughout Texas is Greyhound. Its 150 stops in Texas include San Antonio and Austin as well as a few towns in the Hill Country, including Fredericksburg. Other regional lines include Megabus, RedCoach, and Tornado Bus Company. Megabus provides trips from Dallas or Houston to both Austin and San Antonio. RedCoach travels to Austin from Dallas, Houston, and Waco. Tornado Bus Company departs from several cities in Texas to head to other Texas destinations; just note that the driver gives instructions and announcements in Spanish.

For information on city buses in San Antonio and Austin, please see those individual chapters.

Car

Texas is a driving state, and you will most likely need a car if you're planning to explore outside the cities. If you limit your time to only downtown Austin or the San Antonio River Walk area, you may find walking and using ride-shares works for you, but if you plan to visit both cities or make any excursions into the Hill Country, you'll want some wheels.

Interstate 35, which runs north and south through the state, connects Austin with San Antonio. Along that stretch of the interstate are San Marcos and New Braunfels.

To reach the Hill Country from Austin, travel northwest on U.S. Highway 71 toward Spicewood, Horseshoe Bay, and Llano, or travel west on Highway 190 to Dripping Springs, Johnson City, and Fredericksburg.

To reach the Hill Country from San Antonio, head north toward Marble Falls and Burnet on U.S. Highway 281, which runs all the way to Hico before connecting with Texas 220 and U.S. Highway 67, which snakes northeast through Glen Rose (home to fun dinosaur-related attractions) into just south of Fort Worth and Dallas. Alternatively, take TX 46 to Boerne and continue on TX 16 to Bandera

Getting Here and Around

and Kerrville, or take U.S. Highway 10 northwest to Comfort and switch to U.S. 87 to continue to Fredericksburg and then TX 16 to Llano. U.S. Highway 10 is the main thoroughfare that runs east and west through central Texas, with Houston on one end and El Paso on the other—a whopping 750 miles apart.

CAR RENTALS

All major Texas airports offer reliable rental car service through a selection of the major chains, with several classes of vehicles available. Operating out of Austin-Bergstrom International Airport are Advantage, Alamo, Avis, Budget, Enterprise, Hertz, Payless, and Thrifty. Running out of the San Antonio International Airport are Advantage, Alamo, Avis, Budget, Enterprise, Fox, and Hertz. Additionally, Enterprise has locations in Bastrop, Cedar Rock, Marble Falls, and Round Rock, as well as several nonairport Austin locations. Hertz has an office in Georgetown.

In addition to the major chains, Austin also has two alternative rental car companies. Austin is now headquarters to Tesla, and Elektrica Rentals can rent you a Tesla for your stay. Elektrica will deliver the car to you within 25 miles of Austin. Meanwhile, Avail rents cars that are owned by individual owners rather than the company itself, with all rentals fully insured by Allstate. No vehicles are more than 10 years old, and all have under 125,000 miles on their odometers.

Whenever you rent a car in the United States, ask about cancellation penalties, taxes, drop-off charges (if you're picking up and dropping off in different cities or locations), any surcharges (such as for an additional approved driver), any extras available (such as car seats, which Texas requires for children), and what any insurance offered by the rental company covers and doesn't cover. Also make sure that a confirmed reservation guarantees you a car because companies sometimes overbook. The minimum age requirement for most rentals is 18, though sometimes there is an extra charge for those not yet 25. You'll need a valid driver's license and a credit card to reserve and pay for the rental.

ROAD CONDITIONS

When it comes to driving on Texas roads, there are two C words you come to learn quickly: congestion and construction. Like all big U.S. cities, San Antonio and Austin get very congested around rush hour in the morning and afternoon, beginning when school lets out, without much (if any) pause before going right into the end of the work day. The most congested area in the state is Interstate 35 on Austin's east side between U.S. 290/TX 71/Ben White Boulevard and U.S. 290. During the morning rush hour, drivers on that stretch of Austin are going about 40 mph rather than the usual 60 mph, and from 4 pm to 6 pm they're averaging only 20 mph. That is true for both directions, though traffic going southbound is worse.

San Antonio's most congested roadway is U.S. 281 between Stone Oak Parkway and State Loop 1604, which gets backed up going northbound in the morning and going southbound in the late afternoon.

SPEED LIMIT

Outside of metropolitan areas, the speed limit on Texas highways is generally 75 mph. If you're pulled over for driving over the limit, a ticket could cost you around $200 to $300, depending on how much over you're going. If you're speeding in a work zone, it could go up to more than $350.

TOLL ROADS

Texas has several toll roads, and most use all-electronic toll tags. If you don't have a toll tag, you will be mailed a bill based on the address connected with your license plate. If you're renting a car, ask the rental car company how toll-tag fees should be handled.

Taxis and Ride-Sharing

Lyft and Uber are popular means of travel in Austin and San Antonio. Austin additionally has a local service called Ride-Austin, although it is currently suspended due to pandemic safety concerns.

In San Antonio, several taxi services are also available. In Austin, Austin Yellow Cab has been replaced with Austin zTrip. In a cost comparison of ride-share options between Austin-Bergstrom Airport and the Blanton Museum of Art, the RideAustin one-way fare was $22, while Lyft and Uber were both $23; between the San Antonio International Airport and the San Antonio Museum of Art, Lyft and Uber were $16, while a taxi was $27.

Train

Texas has limited train travel, but Amtrak does have stops in both Austin and San Antonio. Austin's train station is at 250 North Lamar Boulevard, while San Antonio's train station is at 350 Hoefgen Avenue.

Amtrak offers one train ride per day from San Antonio to Austin, departing San Antonio at 7 am and arriving in Austin at 9:23 am, before continuing on to the Dallas–Fort Worth area and then East Texas. Amtrak also offers one daily train ride the reverse direction, from Austin to San Antonio, departing Austin at 6:30 pm and arriving in San Antonio at 9:55 pm, before continuing east to Houston and Beaumont or west to El Paso. The price of coach between San Antonio and Austin is $8.

Stops between San Antonio and Dallas are San Marcos, Austin, Taylor, Temple, McGregor, Cleburne, and Fort Worth. Stops between San Antonio and El Paso are Del Rio, Sanderson, and Alpine.

Essentials

Activities

San Antonio, Austin, and the Texas Hill Country have an abundance of outdoor activities to enjoy, including state parks; local bike paths; theme parks, like Schlitterbahn Waterpark in New Braunsfels and SeaWorld San Antonio; and lots of sports. Locals cheer for the Spurs in San Antonio and the University of Texas Longhorns in Austin. A unique central Texas activity is exploring the region's many caverns.

Dining

Tex-Mex, barbecue, and steak are all popular items on Texas menus, as are hamburgers, chicken-fried steak, and seafood. And you'll find plenty of international options, especially in the big cities, particularly Middle Eastern, Asian, Italian, and German. In Austin, there are a number of restaurants catering to vegans and vegetarians, and in San Antonio, you can find many establishments serving authentic Mexican dishes. For dessert, pie is likely on the menu, particularly if you're in the Hill Country.

It's a good idea to make a reservation if you can, especially when you're in Austin, San Antonio, or Fredericksburg. Most establishments are laid-back in terms of dress code, though if you're unsure, or if you're going to brunch or lunch on a Sunday, you might want to go with a business-casual look to feel more at home, especially among the churchgoers who are stopping to eat after service.

Lodging

Hotels, bed-and-breakfasts, and home rentals through services like Airbnb and Vrbo are all accommodation options in Texas, plus there are places to camp in the great outdoors, whether you're setting up a tent or parking your RV. In the Hill Country, there's also the possibility of staying at a dude ranch, where you can learn what it's like to be a rancher. Book lodging in advance, especially if you're visiting during one of the area's big festivals.

Nightlife

Austin is called the Live Music Capital of the World, and music is easy to find at many venues here. When the sun goes down, Sixth Street and Rainey Street's entertainment district are the happening spots in town. Parking can be a challenge, so you may want to Uber from your hotel, which is always a good idea if your night entails drinking.

In San Antonio, the River Walk is the place to be. There also are comedy shows, fun hotel bars, theater offerings, and dance clubs, including country-Western dance halls.

While the nightlife scene isn't quite as happening in towns in the Hill Country, you can usually find one or two good bars, as well as some excellent wineries.

Performing Arts

Music, plays, dance, and more fill Texas stages and delight lovers of the performing arts. Among the top choices are San Antonio's symphony and dance company, and Austin's ballet.

Safety

Both Austin and San Antonio are relatively safe cities, although as with most cities, petty crimes like pickpocketing do happen. Always be alert and aware of your surroundings, especially in tourist-heavy areas, during the major festivals, and late at night.

COVID-19

Although COVID-19 brought travel to a virtual standstill for most of 2020 and into 2021, vaccinations have made travel possible and safe again. Remaining requirements and restrictions—including those for unvaccinated travelers—can, however, vary from one place (or even business) to the next. Also, in case travel is curtailed abruptly again, consider buying trip insurance. Just be sure to read the fine print: not all travel-insurance policies cover pandemic-related cancellations.

Visitor Information

A couple of great statewide resources are Texas Tourism and Texas Highways, the official travel magazine for the state. In San Antonio, the city's tourism website offers myriad ideas and helpful planning tips while Visit Austin breaks down things to do, events, where to go for live music, and more. The Office of the Texas Governor website gives information on what's happening in the state in regard to issues such as weather concerns (for example, hurricanes) and COVID-19 protocols and safety.

On the Calendar

January

Luckenbach Blues Festival. Bring a chair or blanket to sit outside (weather permitting) and enjoy an afternoon lineup of musicians at this Fredericksburg-area event. (🌐 *www.luckenbachtexas.com*)

February

Cowboy Mardi Gras. New Orleans meets the West at this event hosted by the 11th Street Cowboy Bar in Bandera, the Cowboy Capital of the World. (🌐 *www.11thstreetcowboybar.com*)

San Antonio Stock Show & Rodeo. About 1.5 million visitors come to the San Antonio fairgrounds to watch professional rodeo events as well as enjoy concerts, competitive events, and a carnival. (🌐 *www.sarodeo.com*)

March

South by Southwest. Featuring multiple festivals, Austin's largest event and indeed one of the world's largest live music events happens in venues throughout the capital each spring. (🌐 *www.sxsw.com*)

April

Bluebonnet Festival. Known as the Bluebonnet Capital of Texas, Burnet celebrates the star of the wildflower season with live music, food, arts and crafts booths, shows, and a carnival. (🌐 *www.bluebonnetfestival.org*)

Fiesta San Antonio. One of the best, most colorful events in Alamo City, the annual Fiesta features fireworks, shows, a parade, and more as it pays tribute to the city's history and diversity of cultures. (🌐 *www.fiestasanantonio.org)*

June

Hill Country Film Festival. Fredericksburg showcases nearly 100 indie films along with parties, panel discussions, and opportunities for networking. (🌐 *www.hillcountryff.com*)

Kerrville Folk Festival. Running for 18 days, this event at Quiet Valley Ranch has drawn tens of thousands of lovers of folk music, including songwriters, for 50 years. (🌐 *www.kerrvillefolkfestival.org*)

July

Spring Ho. This Lampasas event provides a week of fun, with family entertainment, fireworks, a parade, a carnival, arts and crafts booths, and a cook-off. (🌐 *springho.com*)

September

Bandera Round-Up. Cowboy-theme fun, from gunslinging shows to a longhorn-cattle parade, livens up Bandera over Labor Day weekend. (🌐 *www.banderaroundup.com*)

October

Austin City Limits Festival. With eight stages and more than 100 performances, Zilker Park rocks with bands for two weekends each fall in Austin. (🌐 *www.aclfestival.com*)

Octoberfest. All of Fredericksburg, the Polka Capital of Texas, gathers together in their lederhosen to yodel, dance, eat brats, raise a stein, and more at this fun celebration of all things German. (🌐 *www.oktoberfestinfbg.com*)

November

Austin Food + Wine Festival. This three-day affair pairs cooking demonstrations, delicious tacos, and mouthwatering barbecue with top wine, savory samples from area chefs, and much more. (🌐 *www.austinfoodandwinefestival.com*)

Fall Antiques Show. Boerne boasts a bounty of antiques at this weekend event at the Kendall Country Fairgrounds. (🌐 *www.texasantiqueshows.com/boerne-antique-shows.htm*)

Lightscape at San Antonio Botanical Garden. Thirty-eight acres of natural beauty light up for the holidays from mid-November through early January (daily except Thursday). Along with the impressive light displays, there's plenty of s'mores roasting. (🌐 *www.sabot.org/lightscape*)

Wurstfest. Celebrate New Braunfels's German heritage at this 10-day event with a carnival, music, and, of course, sausage and German beer. (🌐 *www.wurstfest.com*)

December

Christmas on the Square. Snow is guaranteed once a year in Burnet, where Santa, a parade, live entertainment, and fake snow galore bring seasonal merriment to the town square at this one-day event. (🌐 *www.burnetchamber.org*)

Luminations. Thousands of luminarias in the arboretum at the Lady Bird Johnson Wildflower Center are the highlight of this Austin event that runs from early December through late January. (🌐 *www.wildflower.org/luminations*)

Starry Starry Nights Lighted Christmas Park. Get into the festive spirit at Llano's Badu Park along the river, where light displays dazzle and hot chocolate awaits. Marble Falls has a similar event. (🌐 *www.llanos-tarrystarrynights.com*)

Great Itineraries

The Best of San Antonio, Austin, and the Hill Country

While you could easily spend a week each in Austin and San Antonio, if you have limited time in the area and want to see as much of the region as possible, a week-long road trip throughout the Texas Hill Country, with stops in both cities, is the perfect option. Texas Hill Country begins just north of San Antonio and stretches wide across the Edwards Plateau, where granite domes rise above grassy prairies of wildflowers as sparkling rivers ebb and flow along with the natural sway of the land. The pace of life is sweet and slow throughout this region, despite the vibrant energy and creativity from the eclectic mix of Anglo, German, and Spanish cultural influences.

DAY 1: NEW BRAUNFELS

Fly into Austin, and after picking up a rental car, hit the road to experience the scenic backgrounds of the "Devil's Backbone" (a limestone ridge that runs through parts of the Hill Country) as you head to the Hill Country town of New Braunfels. For lunch, the family recipes at **Salt Lick BBQ** were first tested over hot coals on a pit made with rocks during the wagon trains of the mid-1800s and have been perfected over a similar, impressively constructed permanent pit in Driftwood. The barbecue here is famous throughout Texas, and the outdoor picnic seating beneath the shade of Live Oak trees fills up quickly on sunny afternoons.

Just before you hit New Braunfels, make a pit stop in **Gruene**, a true Texan town. Depending on timing, you can grab an early dinner or a drink at the charming **Gristmill** or stop by for a quick show at the legendary **Gruene Hall**, the oldest continually operating dance hall in the state.

Taking its name from its German founder, Prince Carl of Solms-Braunfels, New Braunfels sits at the confluence of the Comal and Guadalupe Rivers, where visitors can float lazily down either waterway with rentals from countless local outfitters during warmer months or *próst* with the town at the annual Wurstfest in November. Cool down at **Schlitterbahn Waterpark** or stay dry with a retro movie-night out at the **Stars & Stripes Drive-In Theatre** after strolling the shops, museums, and restaurants of downtown New Braunfels.

For dinner, the atmosphere is lively and the schnitzel is crispy at **Krause's Café and Biergarten,** where the beer menu features both local craft brews and imported German beers. Afterward, grab a seat in the rock-and-roll piano bar **Moonshine & Ale** or grab a cocktail at **Sidecar.** You can stay at the **Lamb's Rest Inn** in town, or you can head back to Gruene for a night with the opulent accommodations at **Gruene Mansion Inn**.

DAY 2: SAN ANTONIO

On your second day, get an early start with breakfast in New Braunfels at **Naegelin's Bakery,** the oldest bakery in Texas and the best place in town to savor a hot cup of coffee and a handcrafted pastry. Afterward, hit the road for San Antonio, stopping on the way in Schertz, a town that winds its way from Randolph Air Force Base to the edge of the highway, where one of the largest flea markets in the United States is held on weekends: **Bussey's Flea Market.** Relax on the banks of Cibolo Creek or spend some time walking the trails at **Crescent Bend Nature Park.**

For lunch, stop at **Alamo Cafe** in Northwest San Antonio, where you can enjoy no-frills Mexican cuisine all made with fresh tortillas.

Once you reach San Antonio proper, follow the San Antonio River to see the key sites that make up this vibrant city, from the quaint pedestrian shops and restaurants of the **River Walk** to the five UNESCO missions in the city (including Mission San Antonio de Valero, better known as **The Alamo**). Alternatively, or with more time, visit the **San Antonio Museum of Art** or go to the top of the **Tower of the Americas** within Hemisfair Park.

For dinner, the River Walk is a popular option, but if you want something different, there's **Carnitas Lonjas,** where the carnitas tacos are slow-cooked to perfection and best enjoyed with a cold cerveza at any of the no-frills picnic tables surrounding the South Side taqueria. Overnight at **Hotel Emma.** Its chic quarters once housed a brewery, but now this riverfront hotel is home to 145 guestrooms and suites, as well as some of the top dining options in town. The hotel's location in the Pearl area provides easy access to the city's best restaurants, bars, cafes, and shops, not to mention the Pearl's twice-weekly farmers' market.

DAY 3: BOERNE

Enjoy breakfast at **La Panaderia,** a bakery and café with multiple locations in San Antonio, all selling exquisite pan dulces and handmade breads. This morning unwind for a few hours at north San Antonio's **La Cantera Resort & Spa,** where you can get a massage or play a round of golf. Then make the drive to Boerne, just 30 minutes away. Stop in for lunch at the **Flagstop Café** just outside the town. Its burgers are legendary in these parts, but you can't go wrong with anything fried.

In the afternoon, explore Boerne's historic side at the **Kuhlmann-King Historical Complex**—featuring an impressive 1880s home built by a German settler—or visit **The Dienger Trading Co.,** which now

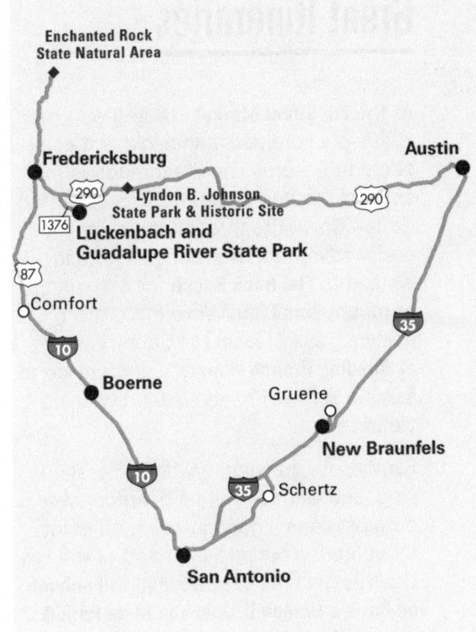

operates a boutique store, bakery, and bistro from its carefully restored 1884 building. Alternatively, soak in the sunshine at the **Cibolo Center for Conservation** nature center and farm, and create an urban scavenger hunt out of the town's Art al Fresco trails before heading underground at the **Cave Without a Name.**

For dinner, choose between **Peggy's on the Green,** which serves southern food with an upscale twist inside a historic 19th-century stagecoach stop, and **Compadres Hill Country Cocina,** which specializes in smoked meats and Tex-Mex eats.

DAY 4: FREDERICKSBURG

Set inside a historic building on Main Street, the **Boerne Grill** serves Hill Country coffee with local breakfast staples like smothered biscuits, *migas*, and breakfast tacos. Enjoy a bite and then make your way to Fredericksburg, stopping along the way for a break in Comfort for antiques shopping between the town's Front Street and High Street.

Great Itineraries

At the **8th Street Market** inside the former 1940s-era Ford dealership, old and unexpected treasures line the interior as the smell of roasted coffee from the Comfort Coffee Co. wafts through the air. If you prefer adventure over antiquing, head instead to **Flat Rock Ranch** for a morning of mountain biking. While in Comfort, enjoy a glass of local Hill Country wine at **Bending Branch Winery,** a great place to sample some of Texas's award-winning vintages.

Famous for its wine, wildflowers, shopping, and German heritage, Fredericksburg provides a good jumping-off point for venturing out into the heart of the Hill Country, with its easy access to **Enchanted Rock, Lyndon B. Johnson State Park & Historic Site,** and the trails at **Wildseed Farms** (the nation's largest working wildflower farm) so be sure to stay at least two nights here. After lunch, brush up on your World War II history at the **National Museum of the Pacific War,** shop around the boutiques of Main Street, pick your own peaches at **Jenschke Orchards,** and taste your way through the Hill Country at **Southold Farm + Cellar** and **Slate Mill Wine Collection.**

For dinner, feast on German-fare made with local ingredients at **Otto's German Bistro,** and stop in for samples at **Das Peach Haus,** home to Fischer & Wieser products like the locally beloved Original Roasted Raspberry Chipotle Sauce. Spend the next two nights in a private cottage at **Cotton Gin Village** or at the luxury bed-and-breakfast Hoffman Haus, which boasts 23 rooms, each with the distinctly Hill Country aesthetic of crisp white linens and lavender bath products.

DAY 5: LUCKENBACH AND GUADALUPE RIVER STATE PARK

Breakfasts at **Emma + Ollie** in Fredericksburg range from a build-your-own biscuit bar to a croissant egg sandwich. After that culinary experience, make your way to the quirky town of Luckenbach. Best known for its 1887 dance hall—which still hosts regular dances and concerts and has become a rite-of-passage for many Texas musicians—the original general store and "feed lot" food stand are both worthy of a visit before continuing on.

There are 13 miles of hiking and biking trails throughout **Guadalupe River State Park,** although most visitors are more focused on the 4 miles of river frontage. Toss a tube in the river for a peaceful float or hop in for a refreshing dip on a hot day. Or if you prefer, take a detour to **LBJ National Historic Park** in Stonewall. Afterward, head back to Fredericksburg for dinner at **Cabernet Grill** and then drinks at **Fredericksburg Brewing Company**.

DAY 6: AUSTIN

The next morning, make your way to Austin. With an average of more than 300 sunny days each year and live music venues that range from parks to patios, getting outside in Austin is the best way to soak in this capital city's vibe. But as soon as you arrive in Austin on your first day, get in line (like, a really long line) for the award-winning brisket at **Franklin Barbecue.** They sell out quickly, usually by 2 pm, so be sure to plan accordingly.

Afterward, see for yourself how Austin's reputation as the "Live Music Capital of the World" rings true with live performances from big name artists popping up everywhere from **Waterloo Records** to the **Cactus Café**. Head to the South

Congress (SoCo) District to see firsthand how local businesses strive to "Keep Austin Weird" through its quirky vintage stores, independent book shops, and funky eateries. Then spend the night bar-hopping along Sixth Street until you're ready to crash at the iconic Austin Motel. The former roadside motel has since become a playground for Austin's stylish set, where rooms feature retro-chic decor that vibes with the motel's mid-century modern look.

DAY 7: AUSTIN

Begin your day with another quintessential Austin dining experience, breakfast tacos. The handmade tacos at **Veracruz All Natural** have a spot on everyone's "taco top 10."

Afterward, walk the 10-mile urban trail around **Lady Bird Lake,** swim in the spring-fed waters of **Barton Springs**, and peruse the galleries at the **Jack S. Blanton Museum of Art** at the University of Texas at Austin before catching your flight home.

Fly back home out of the Austin the next morning.

Contacts

Air

AIRPORTS Austin-Bergstrom International Airport. *3600 Presidential Blvd., Austin* *512/530–2242* *austintexas.gov/airport.* **San Antonio International Airport.** *9800 Airport Blvd., San Antonio* *210/207–3411* *flysanantonio.com.*

AIRPORT TRANSFERS Via Metropolitan Transit. *1021 San Pedro Ave., Downtown* *210/362–2020* *www.viainfo.net.* **Capital Metro.** *2910 E. 5th St., East Austin* *512/474–1200* *www.capmetro.org.*

Bicycle

AUSTIN Barton Springs Bike Rentals. *1707 Barton Srings Rd., Austin* *512/480–0200* *www.bartonspringsbikerental.com.* **Bike Austin.** *Austin* *No phone* *www.bikeaustin.org.* **Mellow Johnny's.** *400 Nueces St., Austin* *512/473–0222* *www.mellow-johnnys.com.* **Metro Bike.** *512/474–1200* *www.capmetro.org/ourservices/metrobike.*

SAN ANTONIO San Antonio BCycle. *210/281–0101* *sanantonio.bcycle.com.* **Alamo Bike Shop.** *210/226–2453* *www.facebook.com/AlamoBike.* **Bike World Rentals.** *210/222–1969* *www.bikeworld.com.* **Ride Away Bicycles.** *210/495–2453* *www.rideawaybicycles.com.*

Bus

CONTACTS Greyhound Lines. *800/231–2222* *www.greyhound.com.* **Megabus.** *877/462–6342* *us.megabus.com.* **RedCoach.** *877/733–0724* *www.redcoachusa.com/texas.* **Tornado Bus Company.** *214/941–1878* *www.tornadobus.com.*

Car

CONTACTS Avail. *877/447–9403* *availcarsharing.com/locations/austin.* **Elektrica Rentals.** *512/236–5668* *www.elektricarentals.com.*

Taxi

CONTACTS Austin zTrip. *Austin* *512/452–9999* *www.ztrip.com/austin.* **San Antonio National Cab.** *San Antonio* *210/434–4444* *www.nationalcab.com.* **San Antonio Taxi.** *San Antonio* *210/571–7171* *sanantoniodispatchtaxi.business.site.* **San Antonio zTrip.** *San Antonio* *210/222–2222* *www.ztrip.com/san-antonio.*

Train

CONTACTS Amtrak. *800/872–7245* *www.amtrak.com.*

Visitor Information

CONTACTS The Office of the Texas Governor. *Austin* *gov.texas.gov.* **Texas Highways.** *www.texashighways.com.* **Texas Tourism.** *www.traveltexas.com.* **Visit Austin.** *Austin* *www.austintexas.org.* **Visit San Antonio.** *210/244–2000* *visitsanantonio.com.*

Chapter 3

SAN ANTONIO

3

Updated by
Julie Catalano

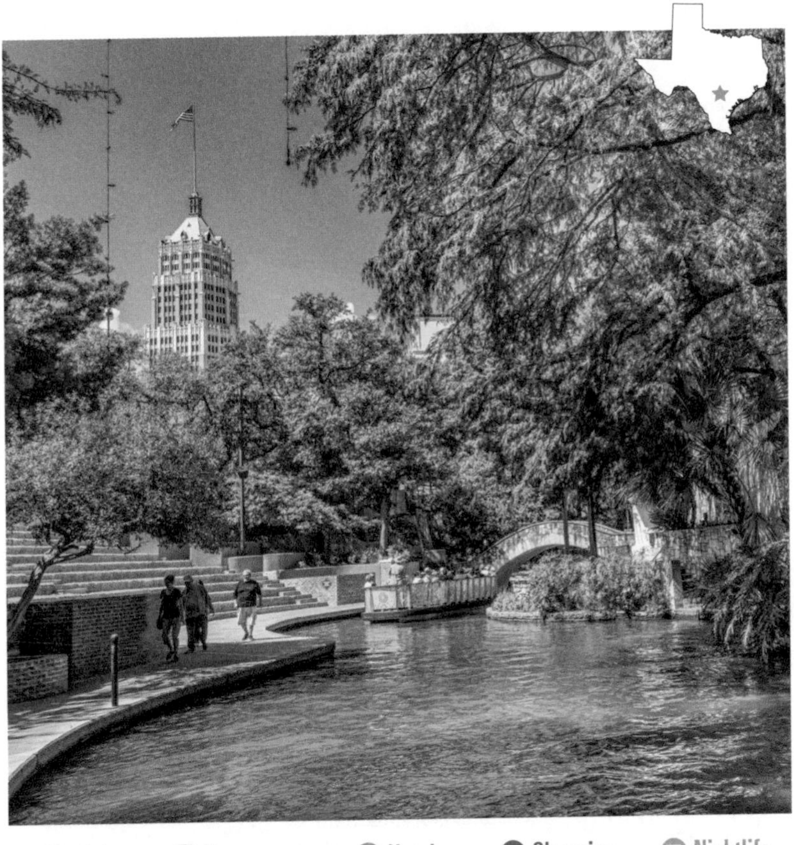

Sights ★★★★★

Restaurants ★★★★☆

Hotels ★★★★☆

Shopping ★★☆☆☆

Nightlife ★★★☆☆

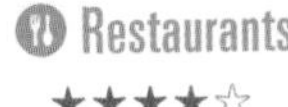

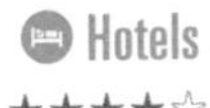

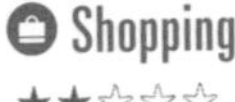

WELCOME TO SAN ANTONIO

TOP REASONS TO GO

★ **The River Walk:** Meandering from the heart of downtown south to the missions and north to the Pearl District, you can't miss the San Antonio River Walk. Take a stroll along its cypress-draped serenity for a relaxing stroll, or take a dinner cruise aboard a barge.

★ **Historic Missions:** Five missions from the 1700s, including the famous Alamo, are all within city limits. Follow the signs to find these exquisite buildings with Spanish-Colonial architecture.

★ **Artwork:** With museums, galleries, and a school devoted to arts education, the arts—and artists—are flourishing in San Antonio. Take in an exhibition while in town, or watch an artist at work.

★ **Mexican Culture:** From the institutes and museums focusing on Latinx arts to the shops, restaurants, and entertainment at Market Square, a Mexican sensibility saturates San Antonio.

1 Downtown and the River Walk. What can you say about the home of the top two attractions in Texas—the Alamo and the River Walk? This area is a jackpot of sights and sounds, with enough shops, dining, museums, nightlife, and festivals to fill any itinerary.

2 The Pearl District. The newest gem in an already impressive collection of neighborhoods, the Pearl District is a living testament to transformation, as a historic closed brewery has become the hottest of hot spots, with once abandoned buildings now hosting trendy restaurants and wide-open spaces now seeing lively, year-round happenings.

3 King William District. In a city filled with historic neighborhoods, the King William Cultural Arts District south of downtown stands high above the rest, thanks to German immigrants who built the stunning, late-19th-century structures that now serve as shining examples of historic preservation.

4 Alamo Heights and Brackenridge Park. One of the city's most affluent older neighborhoods, everything about Alamo Heights says location, location, location. Here you can enjoy top-flight restaurants, unique shopping, and the city's beloved 343-acre Brackenridge Park. You can also revisit San Antonio's "Gilded Age" (1890–1930) in the Monte Vista Historic District, where eminent oil and ranching families built their homes in a variety of styles within about 100 city blocks of quiet, tree-lined streets.

5 The Southside and the Missions. The most compelling Southside attraction is San Antonio Missions National Historical Park, the only UNESCO World Heritage site in Texas. The 8-mile Mission Reach section of the River Walk beckons nature lovers, hikers, bikers, and paddlers.

6 North and Northwest San Antonio. San Antonio never stops growing, and a big part of that growth is coming from the northern part of the city. Luxury resorts, fine dining, premier golf courses, upscale shopping centers, the main campus of the University of Texas San Antonio, and popular theme parks encourage visitors and locals alike to head north.

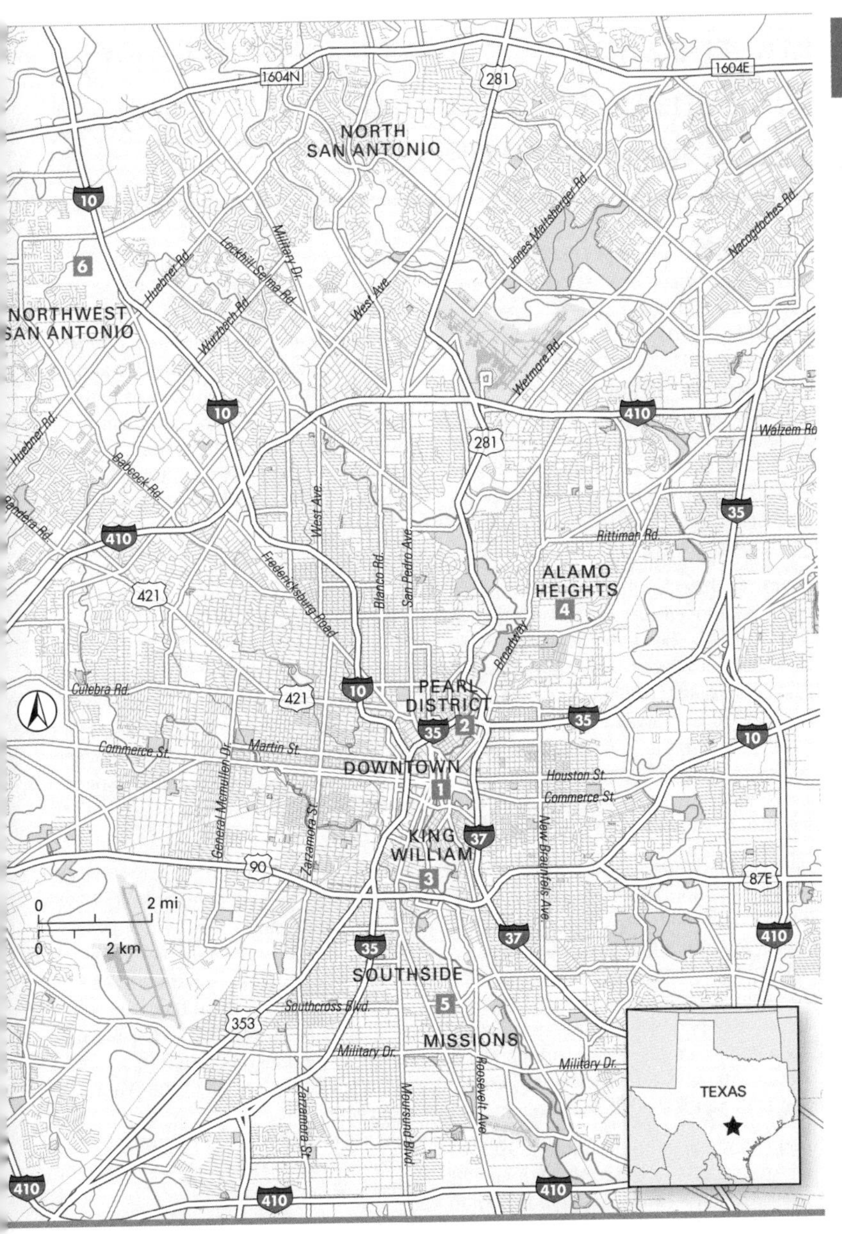

NORTH SAN ANTONIO
NORTHWEST SAN ANTONIO
ALAMO HEIGHTS
PEARL DISTRICT
DOWNTOWN
KING WILLIAM
SOUTHSIDE
MISSIONS
TEXAS
1604N
1604E
281
10
410
35
37
421
90
87E
353
Huebner Rd.
Lockhill Selma Rd.
Military Dr.
West Ave.
Wurzbach Rd.
Jones Maltsberger Rd.
Nacogdoches Rd.
Wetmore Rd.
Walzem Rd
Babcock Rd.
Bandera Rd.
Fredericksburg Road
Blanco Rd.
San Pedro Ave.
Broadway
Rittiman Rd.
Culebra Rd.
Commerce St.
Martin St.
General Mcmullen Dr.
Zarzamora St.
Houston St.
New Braunfels Ave.
Southcross Blvd.
Moursund Blvd.
Roosevelt Ave.
0
2 mi
2 km
1
2
3
4
5
6

Wake up in The Alamo City with the scent of huevos rancheros in the air, the sound of mariachis out your window, and the sight of barges winding down the San Antonio River, and you know you're somewhere special.

San Antonio is quite possibly Texas's most beautiful and atmospheric city, so it's no wonder it's the state's number-one tourist destination, welcoming an estimated 41 million visitors a year. Remember the Alamo? It's here, sitting in a plaza right downtown, within walking distance of many hotels. But while most visitors check out this famous symbol of Texas liberty when they come to town, the historic mission is by no means the only reason to visit.

In fact, the heart of the visitor area is the Paseo del Rio—the River Walk—a festive, almost magical place that winds through downtown at 20 feet below street level. Nestled in by tall buildings and cypress trees and tucked away from the noise of traffic above, the River Walk draws crowds to its high-rise and boutique hotels, specialty shops, and plethora of restaurants with alfresco dining.

Families are drawn to the big theme parks on the northwestern edge of town. SeaWorld San Antonio is the largest marine-adventure park in the SeaWorld chain and has what every kid wants in a park: animals, rides and roller coasters, plus a water park. Meanwhile, Six Flags Fiesta Texas also boasts a water park and roller coasters, in addition to many other rides and impressive musical shows.

Snuggled firmly in South-Central Texas, San Antonio also acts as the gateway to the Hill Country—a landscape punctuated with majestic live oaks, myriad lakes, and flush-with-wildflowers hills—as well as the beginning of South Texas, the huge triangular tip of the state that is home to the Rio Grande Valley and South Padre Island, favorite destinations for bird-watchers and beach-goers. San Antonio also isn't far from the Mexico–Texas border; it's between two and three hours to Del Rio to the west and Laredo to the south.

Given the city's close proximity to Mexico and its one-time position as the chief Mexican stronghold in Texas (prior to Texas's independence), it's not surprising that the rich tapestry of San Antonio's heritage has a good deal of Mexican culture woven into it. Visitors can peruse shops selling Mexican crafts and jewelry, dine on Tex-Mex food, and enjoy Spanish music and mariachi bands at Market Square.

If experiencing San Antonio's multifaceted diversity—including not only its Mexican side but also its German, French, African, and Asian influences—is of prime importance to you, then the best time to visit may well be during Fiesta each April. An event that began in the late 1800s to pay tribute to the soldiers who died in the Battles of the Alamo and San Jacinto, the 10-day city-wide celebration captures San Antonio's many cultures with music, food, fairs, parades, a carnival, and more.

Planning

When to Go

October and April are the prime months for a comfortable visit to San Antonio, though the spring (when it's not raining) is ideal for seeing the scenery if you're planning to visit the missions or take an excursion into the Hill Country. Also in the spring, a celebratory mood overtakes the town during the annual Fiesta event.

From June through September, intense heat bakes the city, with high humidity to boot. If you come then, you can escape the heat with well-air-conditioned inside attractions and at the popular water parks of SeaWorld and Six Flags Fiesta Texas.

Though not out of the question, winter snows are very rare, as are light ice storms. More likely are heavy spring rains, which can result in flash flooding in the Hill Country.

FESTIVALS

Ballet in the Park

Presented by Ballet San Antonio, Ballet in the Park is a program of dance under the stars performed by the artists of San Antonio's premier professional ballet company. Bring blankets, lawn chairs, and the family to downtown's Travis Park. ✉ *Travis Park, 301 E. Travis St., Downtown* ☎ *210/207–3677* 🌐 *www.travispark-sa.com.*

Fest of Tails Kite Festival & Dog Fair

Dog lovers and kite enthusiasts bring blankets and lawn chairs to enjoy the views of high-flying kites, live music, vendors, festival fare, a pooch parade, and a costume contest. It's great family fun for all ages. ✉ *McAllister Park, 13102 Jones Maltsberger Rd., North* ☎ *210/212–8423* 🌐 *www.saparksfoundation.org.*

Fiesta San Antonio

The city's biggest annual party launches 10 days of city-wide celebrations. Parades and performances are part of approximately 100 events that honor the heroes of the Alamo and the Battle of San Jacinto. ✉ *San Antonio* ☎ *210/227–5191 ticket information* 🌐 *www.fiestasan-antonio.org.*

Fourth of July Celebration at Woodlawn Lake Park

The Official City of San Antonio Fourth of July Celebration draws thousands every year to the beloved Woodlawn Lake Park neighborhood on the city's west side. The all-day, family-friendly event features food trucks, vendors, and live musical performances capped off by a spectacular fireworks extravaganza over the lake. ✉ *Woodlawn Lake Park, 1103 Cincinnati Ave.* ☎ *210/212–8423* 🌐 *www.saparks-foundation.org.*

Mardi Gras Festival & Parade

Colorfully festooned floats create a Mardi Gras spectacle each winter, turning the River Walk into a 2½-mile party. Arneson River Theatre comes alive with music and entertainment. ✉ *Arneson River Theatre, 418 Villita, River Walk* ☎ *210/227–4262* 🌐 *www.thesanantonioriverwalk.com.*

San Antonio Stock Show & Rodeo

The annual San Antonio Stock Show and Rodeo draws about 1.5 million visitors to the AT&T Center and Freeman Coliseum for 2½ weeks of dozens of events and attractions. Over more than 70 years, this event has grown to be one of the largest and most popular in the city—featuring top names in entertainment, plus a ranch rodeo, youth rodeo, livestock show, horse show, and carnival. ✉ *1 AT&T Center Parkway, Downtown* ☎ *210/225–5851* 🌐 *www.sarodeo.com.*

St. Patrick's Day River Parade & Festival

The San Antonio River is dyed green as the River Walk celebrates St. Patrick's Day with 14 decorated floats featuring

Irish entertainment, including bagpipes. This event started in 1968 and has since been organized by the San Antonio River Walk Association and the Harp & Shamrock Society of Texas to honor St. Patty and the city's Irish culture with musicians, artisans, and dancers. ✉ *Arneson River Theatre, 418 Villita, River Walk* ☎ *210/227–4262* 🌐 *www.thesanantonioriverwalk.com.*

Texas Folklife Festival
During this annual summertime event, more than 40 cultures exhibit their contributions to the history and heritage of Texas through music, food, dance, and folktales at the UTSA Institute of Texan Cultures at Hemisfair. ✉ *UTSA Institute of Texan Cultures, 801 E. César E. Chávez Blvd., Downtown* ☎ *210/458–2300* 🌐 *texancultures.utsa.edu/events/texas-folklife-festival/* 🎫 *$15.*

Texas Independence Day Celebration
The annual commemoration of Texas independence takes place every March in Alamo Plaza, marking the Texas Declaration of Independence that proclaimed freedom from Mexican rule on March 2, 1836. You'll find musical performances and day-long living-history exhibits. ✉ *The Alamo, 300 Alamo Plaza, Downtown* ☎ *210/225–1391* 🌐 *www.thealamo.org.*

Getting Here and Around

AIR
San Antonio International Airport (SAT) is in northeast San Antonio between Highway 281 and I–410, about 13 miles from the downtown River Walk area. The Pan Am Expressway leads from the airport to the central business district.

AIRPORTS San Antonio International Airport. ✉ *9800 Airport Blvd.* ☎ *210/207–3411* 🌐 *flysanantonio.com.*

BUS
Greyhound Bus connects San Antonio with Texas cities and beyond. The Greyhound station in downtown San Antonio is open 24 hours.

San Antonio has an extensive city bus system that serves virtually every part of the city with 6,851 bus stops along 96 bus lines, running seven days a week. They offer six categories of service: bus service, paratransit service for riders with disabilities, VIA Primo for high-frequency service, VIA-Link ridesharing service, Vanpool for commuters, and special event Park & Ride service.

VIA provides bus service throughout downtown and the cultural corridors, including route options such as routes 2, 9, 14, 8, and 42. VIA's Route 100 Primo Bus services as the downtown circulator connecting the VIA Centro Plaza Transit Center to the VIA Ellis Alley Transit Center. Regular bus fare is $1.30 and transfers are free. The VIA Day Pass is $2.75.

For information and help planning, visit the SA Visitor Center across from the Alamo, the VIA Bus Information Center across from City Hall, or the VIA Ellis Alley Transit Park & Ride. You can also go to the VIA website or download the free VIA goMobile+ app to help plan your trip.

CONTACTS Via Metropolitan Transit. ✉ *1021 San Pedro Ave., Downtown* ☎ *210/362–2020* 🌐 *www.viainfo.net.* **Greyhound Bus.** ✉ *500 N. Saint Mary's St., Downtown* ☎ *210/270–5868, 800/231–2222* 🌐 *www.greyhound.com.*

CAR
Three interstate highways converge in central San Antonio: I–35, which links San Antonio with Dallas and Austin to the north and Laredo and the Mexican border to the south; I–10, which connects San Antonio to Houston to the east and then veers northwest before heading to El Paso and the West Coast; and I–37,

which connects San Antonio to Corpus Christi on the Gulf of Mexico. A number of U.S. highways and Texas state roads also lead into the city, including U.S. 281 to the north and south and U.S. 90 to the east and west. Two other highways loop around the city; I–410 encircles the heart of San Antonio, and Texas Highway 1604 makes a wider circle that encompasses areas beyond the city limits.

In most cases, having a car in San Antonio is extremely helpful. Like most Texas locales, things are quite spread out. That being said, if you're focusing on the River Walk and the surrounding area, you'll probably want to park your car at your hotel and tackle sightseeing on foot or via the downtown VIA buses, namely VIA's Route 100 Primo bus, the downtown circulator.

TRAIN

Amtrak provides passenger service to and from San Antonio. Its Texas Eagle line arrives and departs daily, connecting San Antonio to Austin, Ft. Worth, Dallas, and other cities enroute north to Chicago. The Sunset Limited line serves San Antonio three times a week, running east–west across the country between New Orleans and Los Angeles and including stops in Tucson and Phoenix.

CONTACTS Amtrak. ✉ *Amtrak Train Station, 350 Hoefgen Ave., Downtown* ☎ *210/223–3226, 800/872–7245* 🌐 *www.amtrak.com.*

Restaurants

San Antonio is a terrific dining town. It's big enough and has enough demanding conventioneers to support the fine dining you'd usually find in much larger cities. But it still has a relaxed small-town feel that makes it easy to dine out almost anywhere without much fuss. You can count on one hand the number of restaurants requiring jackets; the dress codes at most other nice restaurants pretty much stop at "no shorts, please." Reservations and long waits are rare except at a few high-end restaurants and at peak times on the River Walk. But when a popular restaurant recommends reservations, it's best to follow their advice.Essentially, San Antonio cuisine is about two things: Mexican-inspired flavors and meat. Mexican, Tex-Mex, Latin, and a variety of other fusion variations crowd this bicultural town. You'll find wonderful Mexican breads and pastries and rich sauces with complex flavors heavy on the chiles, fresh peppers, and even chocolate. Margaritas and local beers, courtesy of the local German immigrant brewing tradition, remedy the occasional chili overdose (though not all Latin food here is spicy—far from it). If your idea of a perfect meal is a steak, ribs, or just a killer hamburger, this is your kind of town. But San Antonio isn't stuck remembering the Alamo at every meal: chef-driven restaurants with a wide range of cuisines, including Asian, German, French, and fusion, offer a break from beef and tortillas. Restaurants are often happy to accommodate dietary needs whether gluten-free, vegetarian, or vegan. Most restaurants, especially downtown and at the River Walk, are open seven days a week. Outside the downtown tourist area, restaurants generally close at around 10 on weekdays, 11 on weekends. River Walk restaurants and bars stay open later, generally until 2 am.

In 2017, UNESCO named San Antonio a Creative City of Gastronomy, only the second city in the United States to receive this designation.

Hotels

Many visitors choose to stay downtown to be close to the Alamo, River Walk, major museums, and other attractions. Once you're downtown, almost everything is accessible on foot or via river shuttle or VIA bus; a car isn't needed and parking can be expensive. The city has one shuttle service from the airport that serves all downtown hotels. It runs from 7 am to 11 pm right from the airport. Several national chain hotels are concentrated along the River Walk and adjacent to the convention center. In recent years several boutique hotels have opened, promoting spa weekends and indulgent getaways. Downtown has also seen the opening of some larger, value-oriented and extended-stay chains. Several full-service resorts within the city limits, most in the north/northwest area near SeaWorld San Antonio and Six Flags Fiesta Texas amusement park, offer golf, tennis, on-site water parks, children's activities, restaurants, spas, and the services you'd expect from a resort—a good option for families. Most major resorts are a 15- to 20-minute drive from downtown.Bed-and-breakfasts are concentrated in a few of the national historic districts, but still offer a variety of mid-range and pricier room options. Just keep in mind that only a few accept children younger than 12. San Antonio is also a major convention destination, so it can be feast or famine for hotel rooms certain times of the year; peak seasons are generally spring and late fall. At the right time you can get some great deals for top-quality accommodations, but during special events (Fiesta week, the NCAA Final Four tournament, major conventions) expect to pay top dollar and make reservations months in advance. Because of the city's appeal for business travelers, you can actually find lower rates on weekends at many hotels.

■TIP→ Hotel and restaurant reviews have been shortened. For full information, visit Fodors.com. Restaurant prices are per person for a main course at dinner or if dinner is not served, at lunch. Hotel prices are for two people in a standard double room in high season.

What It Costs

$	$$	$$$	$$$$
RESTAURANTS			
under $14	$14–$22	$23–$30	over $30
HOTELS			
under $125	$125–$225	$226–$325	over $325

Tours

GO RIO Cruises

This company provides daily narrated boat tours using a fleet of colorful, eco-friendly electric boats that regularly depart from River Walk docks. The informative tours cover San Antonio history and culture. Try to take your trip near twilight, when the sounds and light begin to soften. Private-event charters and dinner cruises are also available. In addition, GO RIO provides river shuttle service from downtown to the Museum Reach section of the River Walk, which ends at the Pearl District. Combo tickets are available to hop on, hop off the river shuttles for one day or multiple days. ✉ *202 E. Nueva St., River Walk* ☎ *210/227–4746* 🌐 *www.goriocruises.com* 🎟 *$14.*

Grey Line Tours—San Antonio

The longtime worldwide tour company chain offers half-day (four hours), full-day (eight hours), and seasonal tours in and around San Antonio, ranging from the Missions UNESCO World Heritage Site Tour, the Grand Historic City Tour, and a San Antonio craft brewery tour to the Texas Hill Country and LBJ Ranch Tour. A private, eight-hour Texas Hill Country Wine Excursion departing from San Antonio is also available. Or you can BYOT—Build Your Own Tour—for a group custom-sightseeing experience in or outside San Antonio in a private SUV or limo. For regular tours, the company offers free cancellation up to 24 hours prior to departure. ✉ *1343 Hallmark Dr.,*

Northeast ☎ 800/341–6000 🌐 www.graylinesa.com 🎫 $65.

Visitor Information

CONTACTS Visit San Antonio. ☎ *210/244–2000 🌐 visitsanantonio.com.*

Downtown and the River Walk

Coming from the northeast and heading southwest, I–35 slices through San Antonio, curving around its main downtown area, which is primarily composed of the region south and east of I–35, west of I–37, and north of I–10. The San Antonio River falls along the western part of downtown but makes a little loop into the downtown area around Market and Commerce Streets, producing the ideal conditions for a winding River Walk set a level below the main hubbub of traffic. That's not to say the River Walk is quiet. While the cars and horns are out of sight and earshot, the festive, largely developed River Walk is often bustling with people—both visitors and locals. All of San Antonio comes here to dine, shop, and eat with friends along the river's banks.

Four prime areas downtown are Alamo Plaza, Market Square, La Villita, and Hemisfair. Alamo Plaza is, of course, where the Alamo is located, but it also serves as a bit of a town square, with many hotels (like the famous Menger Hotel) and tourist traps (such as the Wax Museum) either off the plaza or nearby. Market Square is a vibrant taste of Old Mexico, and La Villita is a unique art village of shops and restaurants. Hemisfair, the site of the San Antonio World's Fair in 1968, is now undergoing massive renovation as a cultural and mixed-use district.

The River Walk, with its twisting way, is near all these areas and connects many of the main downtown attractions and hotels. If downtown is San Antonio's heart, the river's many arms are its arteries, bringing everyone to where the action is.

Sights

★ The Alamo

HISTORIC SIGHT | At the heart of San Antonio, this one-time Franciscan mission established in 1718 as Mission San Antonio de Valero stands as a revered repository of 300 years of Texas history. It is a monument to the 187 Texan and Tejano (Texans of Mexican descent) volunteers who fought and died here during a 13-day siege in February and March of 1836 led by Mexican dictator General Antonio López de Santa Anna. The Texan army lost, but the defeat inspired an April victory at the Battle of San Jacinto with the rallying cry "Remember the Alamo," spurring Texas toward independence from Mexico. Today the historic shrine (Alamo Church) and Long Barrack are the only structures remaining from the 1836 battle. Explore the serene gardens featuring a 16-pounder cannon exhibit, Living History Encampment, Statues of Heroes walk, and illustrated Wall of History. Admission to the Alamo Church is free but requires a timed ticket (reserve online) to keep the crowds at a minimum inside the shrine; with your timed ticket, you can upgrade to the Victory or Death 45-minute audio tour for $9, which also gives you entry to the Alamo Exhibit with its unique artifacts and historical documents. A one-hour Alamo Tour with an experienced Alamo history interpreter is $40. The Young Texans Tour for kids of all ages is $30. ✉ *300 Alamo Plaza, Downtown* ☎ *210/225–1391* 🌐 *www.thealamo.org* 🎫 *Free; audio tour and Alamo Exhibit $9; guided tours $40.*

Briscoe Western Art Museum

ART MUSEUM | **FAMILY** | This is a stunning museum that celebrates the art, history, and culture of the American West,

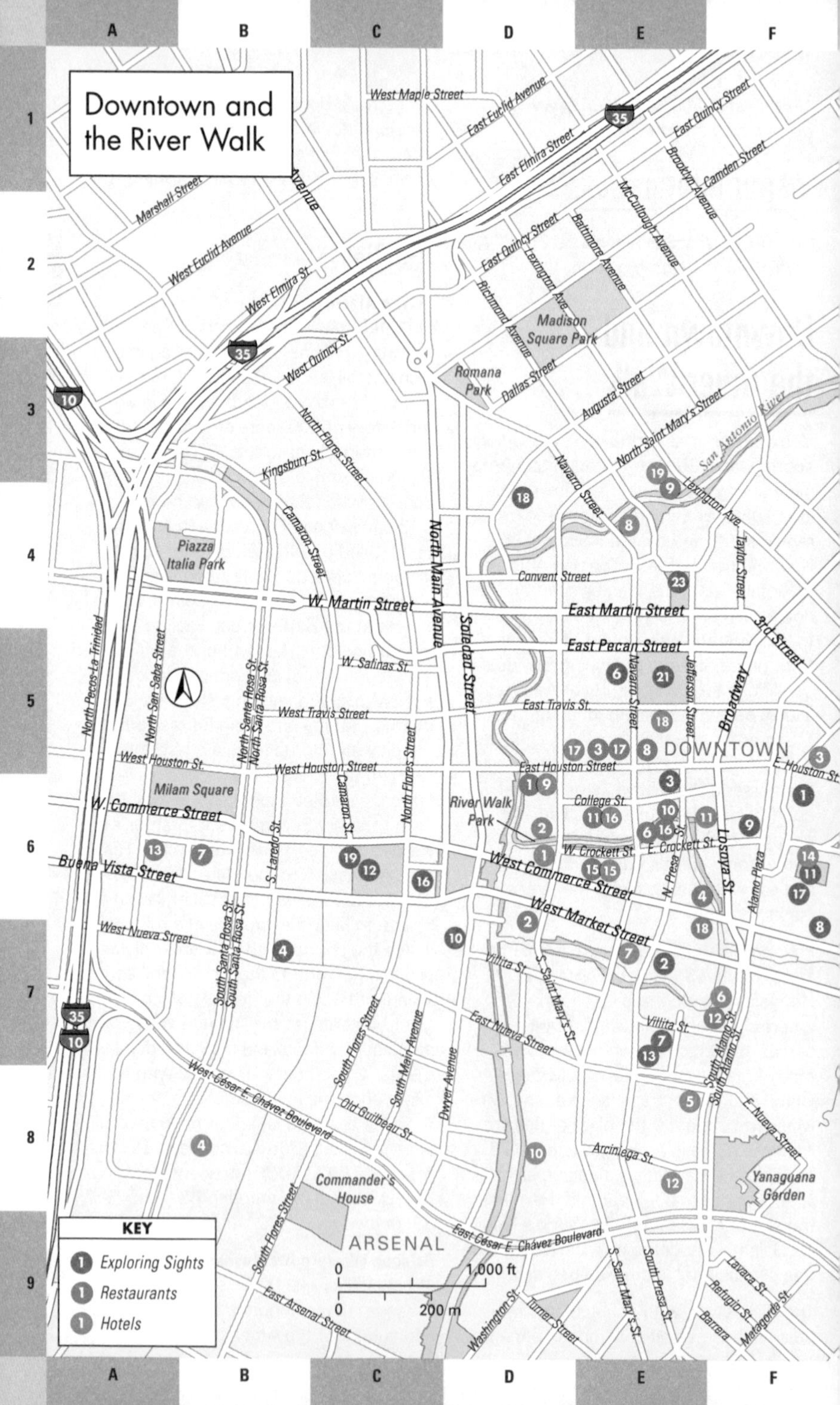

Downtown and the River Walk
A
B
C
D
E
F
West Maple Street
East Euclid Avenue
East Quincy Street
East Elmira Street
Brooklyn Avenue
Camden Street
McCullough Avenue
Marshall Street
Avenue
West Euclid Avenue
West Elmira St.
East Quincy Street
Lexington Ave.
Baltimore Avenue
Richmond Avenue
Madison Square Park
West Quincy St.
Romana Park
Dallas Street
Augusta Street
North Saint Mary's Street
San Antonio River
North Flores Street
Kingsbury St.
Navarro Street
Lexington Ave.
Camaron Street
Piazza Italia Park
North Main Avenue
Taylor Street
Convent Street
W. Martin Street
East Martin Street
Soledad Street
3rd Street
East Pecan Street
North Pecos-La Trinidad
North San Saba Street
North Santa Rosa St.
North Santa Rosa St.
W. Salinas St.
Navarro Street
Jefferson Street
Broadway
West Travis Street
East Travis St.
DOWNTOWN
West Houston St.
West Houston Street
East Houston Street
E. Houston St.
Milam Square
Camaron St.
North Flores Street
River Walk Park
College St.
W. Commerce Street
S. Laredo St.
W. Crockett St.
E. Crockett St.
N. Presa St.
Losoya St.
Alamo Plaza
Buena Vista Street
West Commerce Street
West Market Street
West Nueva Street
South Santa Rosa St.
South Santa Rosa St.
Villita St.
S. Saint Mary's St.
South Flores Street
South Main Avenue
East Nueva Street
Villita St.
South Alamo St.
South Alamo St.
West César E. Chávez Boulevard
Dwyer Avenue
Old Guilbeau St.
E. Nueva Street
Arciniega St.
Yanaguana Garden
Commander's House
ARSENAL
East César E. Chávez Boulevard
South Flores Street
S. Saint Mary's St.
South Presa St.
Lavaca St.
Refugio St.
Metagorda St.
Barrera
East Arsenal Street
Washington St.
Turner Street
0
1,000 ft
0
200 m
KEY
Exploring Sights
Restaurants
Hotels

Sights

1 The Alamo F6
2 Briscoe Western Art Museum E7
3 The Buckhorn Saloon & Museum and the Texas Ranger Museum E6
4 Casa Navarro State Historic Site B7
5 Hemisfair G8
6 Hopscotch E5
7 La Villita Historic Arts Village E7
8 LEGOLAND Discovery Center F7
9 Louis Tussaud's Waxworks & Ripley's Believe It or Not! Odditorium F6
10 Main Plaza D7
11 The Menger Hotel F6
12 Old Spanish Trail C6
13 San Antonio African American Community Archive and Museum E7
14 San Antonio Museum of Art (SAMA) H1
15 San Antonio River Walk G7
16 San Fernando Cathedral C6
17 Sea Life San Antonio F6
18 Southwest School of Art D4
19 Spanish Governor's Palace C6
20 Tower of the Americas G8
21 Travis Park E5
22 UTSA Institute of Texan Cultures H9
23 Vietnam Veterans Memorial E4

Restaurants

1 Ácenar D6
2 Biga on the Banks D7
3 Bohanan's Prime Steaks and Seafood E5
4 Boudro's E6
5 Chart House at the Tower of the Americas G8
6 The County Line E6
7 La Margarita Mexican Restaurant & Oyster Bar B6
8 La Panaderia E5
9 Landrace E4
10 Landry's Seafood House E6
11 Las Canarias E6
12 Little Rhein Prost Haus F7
13 Mi Tierra Cafe and Bakery A6
14 Morton's G6
15 Ostra Restaurant E6
16 Paesanos Riverwalk E6
17 The Palm Restaurant E5
18 Schilo's E6

Hotels

1 Canopy by Hilton San Antonio Riverwalk D6
2 Drury Inn & Suites San Antonio Riverwalk D6
3 The Emily Morgan Hotel F5
4 Fairfield Inn & Suites by Marriott San Antonio Downtown/ Market Square B8
5 The Fairmount E8
6 Hilton Palacio del Rio F7
7 Hotel Contessa E7
8 Hotel Havana E4
9 Hotel Valencia Riverwalk D6
10 Hyatt Place San Antonio/ Riverwalk D8
11 Hyatt Regency San Antonio E6
12 Marriott Plaza San Antonio E8
13 Marriott Rivercenter ... G7
14 Menger Hotel F6
15 Mokara Hotel & Spa E6
16 Omni La Mansión del Rio E6
17 Sheraton Gunter Hotel D5
18 St. Anthony, a Luxury Collection Hotel E5
19 Thompson San Antonio Riverwalk E3

located in a beautifully restored 1930s San Antonio Public Library building on the River Walk. The museum is named in honor of the late Texas governor Dolph Briscoe Jr. and his wife Janey Slaughter Briscoe. Highlights of the collection include a monumental bronze sculpture, John Coleman's *Visions of Change*, that represents both Native Americans and cowboys. Featured works include those by Frederic Remington, Allan Houser, Martin Grelle, Charles Marion Russell, W. Herbert Dunton, and more. There are 14 galleries on three levels, housing paintings, sculpture, photography, and artifacts reflecting Native American art, Spanish and Mexican colonial-era art, and Western folk art. The beautiful McNutt Sculpture Garden is free and open to the public, with access from the River Walk and an entrance on Market Street. ✉ *210 W. Market St., Downtown* ☎ *210/299–4499* 🌐 *www.briscoemuseum.org* 🎟 *$12* 🕑 *Closed Tues. and Wed.*

The Buckhorn Saloon & Museum and the Texas Ranger Museum

HISTORY MUSEUM | These are two museums for the price of one, and both add up to a 40,000-square-foot Texas history lesson and fun for the whole family. In 1881 the Buckhorn Saloon opened as a Texan watering hole, and future president Teddy Roosevelt and his Rough Riders are said to have been among its patrons, as were writer O. Henry and Mexican Revolution leader Francisco "Pancho" Villa. Primary customers after it opened were hunters and trappers, eager for a cold brew and to trade furs and horns. Saloon owner Albert Friedrich collected the horns, some of which his father made into horn chairs. Today the museum features a huge collection of taxidermy and animal displays, including, of course, tons of antlers. Famous artifacts (and they number in the thousands) include one of Gene Autry's saddles. In 2006, the Former Texas Rangers Association teamed up with the Buckhorn Saloon & Museum to open the Texas Ranger Museum, with exhibits that recount the stories of law enforcement in the Lone Star State from Stephen Austin on as well as displays of artifacts covering more than 100 years of Texas Ranger history. The café/saloon, with its original marble and cherry wood back-bar, serves brewed draft beer and a full menu of mostly American fare. ✉ *318 E. Houston St., Downtown* ☎ *210/247–4000* 🌐 *www.buckhornmuseum.com* 🎟 *$23.*

Casa Navarro State Historic Site

NOTABLE BUILDING | A signer of the Texas Declaration of Independence, lawyer, legislator, and Tejano civil rights advocate José Antonio Navarro built these three limestone, brick, and adobe buildings in the 1850s for his residence and law office. He had sold his ranch near Seguin and moved to San Antonio to be active on the city council. Open to visitors, the half-acre site in Old San Antonio's Laredito area is now a National Historic Landmark and features period furniture and copies of Navarro's writings—he wrote about the history of Texas from a Tejano's perspective and in the Spanish language. It is San Antonio's only historic site focused on the Mexican history and heritage of Texas from the viewpoint of a native Texan with Mexican ancestry. ✉ *228 S. Laredo St., Downtown* ☎ *210/226–4801* 🌐 *www.thc.texas.gov/historic-sites/casa-navarro-state-historic-site* 🎟 *$4.*

Hemisfair

CITY PARK | **FAMILY** | The site of the 1968 World's Fair, Hemisfair is in the process of being transformed into a 40-acre public space for the city. The site currently houses some of San Antonio's best-known attractions: the Tower of the Americas, the UTSA Institute of Texan Cultures, and the Mexican Cultural Institute, as well as the Yanaguana Playground and Splash Pad for children, which was recognized by the Urban Land Institute as an outstanding example of a vibrant, open urban space. Parts of the

The Alamo has persisted as a symbol of Texas pride and independence for almost 200 years.

park are currently under construction; the Mays Family Foundation donated $1 million to build a garden in their matriarch Peggy's honor, a 25,000-square-foot space near the remaining historic homes on the site. The park is open every day from 5 am to midnight, and almost any time of day or night you will see people on the walking paths, dog walkers (dogs must be on a leash), and residents and visitors enjoying community programming like free concerts and outdoor workouts. Hemisfair is also home to various annual festivals and city celebrations. Check their website for upcoming events. ✉ *4334 S. Alamo St., Downtown* ☎ *210/709–4750* 🌐 *www.hemisfair.org* 🎟 *Free.*

★ Hopscotch

ART GALLERY | This is a 20,000-square-foot space you must see to believe, as descriptions, or even images, don't really do it justice. It is a permanent and uniquely curated (to say the least) gallery of 14 distinctive, immersive, and interactive installations by 40 local, national, and international artists seeking to create high-impact works in sustainable and creative ways. A sample of exhibits includes Gaze, Quantum Space, VJ Yourself, Freefall, Matrix, Experiences Over Things, and many more. Exhibits are on a rotating basis, but it's guaranteed you will see something you like, and maybe something you don't, like any other art. The space also features a public-facing lounge, full bar, and a fun, quirky gift shop, as well as a large patio and food truck. It is highly recommended to purchase tickets in advance for the gallery; tickets are timed to avoid congestion in the hallways and rooms and give everyone a chance to fully enjoy each exhibit. ✉ *Travis Park Plaza Bldg., 711 Navarro St., Suite 100, Downtown* ☎ *No phone* 🌐 *www.letshopscotch.com* 🎟 *$24* 🕒 *Closed Mon.–Wed.*

La Villita Historic Arts Village

HISTORIC DISTRICT | Meaning "Little Village," La Villita is a prime place for shopping, dining, and entertainment and the host to more than 200 festive events each year. It was the original settlement in Old San Antonio and one of the city's first neighborhoods founded almost 300 years ago. Stroll among the adobe, brick, and stone structures in varying architectural styles. Enjoy browsing (and buying!) at about two dozen boutiques and galleries selling art, jewelry, and handmade items by local and regional artists, who occasionally present workshops and exhibitions on-site. La Villita Historic Arts Village is named on the National Register of Historic Places. Be sure to pick up a map so you don't miss anything in this charming hamlet. ✉ *418 Villita St., Downtown* ☎ *210/207–8614* 🌐 *www.lavillitasanantonio.com* 🎫 *Free.*

LEGOLAND Discovery Center

OTHER ATTRACTION | FAMILY | Built from more than 1.5 million LEGO bricks (50,000 for the Alamodome alone), just the sight of Miniland San Antonio is worth the price of admission. It's a stunning replica that includes some of the city's most popular landmarks, including the Alamo, River Walk, Tower of the Americas, and much more. The cars even obey traffic signals, and the river boats glide down the river. Designed for families with children ages 3–10 to play together, the bright, colorful space features themed play areas, LEGO-theme rides like Kingdom Quest and Merlin's Apprentice Ride, and creative workshops with LEGO Master Model Builders. There's also a 4D Cinema featuring short films with LEGO characters. During December, check out the LEGO Holiday Bricktacular. An expansive shop features LEGO kits to make your own, well, just about anything. ✉ *Shops at Rivercenter, 849 E. Commerce St., Downtown* ☎ *210/610–1150* 🌐 *www.legolanddiscoverycenter.com* 🎫 *$25* ☞ *Adults over 18 must be accompanied by children.*

Louis Tussaud's Waxworks & Ripley's Believe it or Not! Odditorium

OTHER ATTRACTION | Part of an entertainment complex across from the Alamo, these two spots are filled with Instagram-friendly selfie opportunities. More than 200 wax figures at Waxworks depict the famous and infamous along with superheroes, television and movie stars, sports figures, musicians, and more. Many wax figures are displayed against elaborate sets and backdrops. Ripley's Believe it or Not! has 18,000 square feet in its "Odditorium" that features unusual worldwide collections in 18 themed galleries, some including hands-on interactive exhibits. There is also a Ripley's Believe it or Not! 4D Motion Theatre attraction that features 3D short adventure films with moving seats. ✉ *307 Alamo Plaza, Downtown* ☎ *210/224–9299* 🌐 *www.ripleys.com* 🎫 *$25.*

Main Plaza

PLAZA/SQUARE | FAMILY | Downtown's Main Plaza welcomes all from far and near, whether they're looking to gather with others, attend a performance, or enjoy the space in solitude. Also known as Plaza de Las Islas Canarias, a nod to the Canary Island settlers in San Antonio, the area has been around since the early 18th century. After ups and downs due to growth and other factors, the plaza is now alive with performers and visitors thanks to the efforts of the Main Plaza Conservancy, a nonprofit dedicated to creating and developing a family-friendly plaza for all ages and promoting arts and culture in an open-air setting. Enjoy free musical concerts, dance performances, yoga, movies, seasonal and holiday events, and more. Check the online calendar to see upcoming and recurring events. The spectacular *San Antonio: The Saga* is a 24-minute art installation by renowned artist Xavier de Richemont, projected onto the facade of the San Fernando Cathedral. The show runs at multiple times every Tuesday, Friday, Saturday, and Sunday evening through 2024. ✉ *115 N. Main Ave., Downtown* ☎ *210/225–9800* 🌐 *www.mainplaza.org* 🎫 *Free.*

The Menger Hotel

HOTEL | You don't have to stay here to enjoy the ambience of San Antonio's most historic lodging. After you visit the Alamo, stop by this stunning 1859 property next door that offers a history book full of "who's whos" who have slept here. Famous guests include Civil War generals Robert E. Lee and William Sherman, Mount Rushmore sculptor Gutzon Borglum (who had a studio at the hotel), playwright Oscar Wilde, and author O. Henry, who mentioned the hotel in several of his short stories. As legend has it, William Menger built the Victorian hotel to accommodate the many carousers who frequented his brewery, which stood on the same site. Step inside the very cool Menger Bar to see its mahogany bar, a precise replica of one from a pub in London's House of Lords. Here cattlemen closed deals with a handshake over three fingers of rye, and Teddy Roosevelt supposedly recruited his Rough Riders—hard-living cowboys fresh from the Chisholm Trail. Note that the Buckhorn Saloon & Museum also makes the same claim; either someone's been playing too much poker and can't stop bluffing, or Teddy had to go recruiting more than once. Throughout the spacious lobby, hallways, and public areas, check out the fascinating historical mini-exhibits. The on-site Colonial Restaurant is also open to the public. ✉ *204 Alamo Plaza, Downtown* ☎ *210/223–4361* 🌐 *www.mengerhotel.com* 🎟 *Free.*

Old Spanish Trail

TRAIL | Consisting of some of the oldest roads in Texas, the Old Spanish Trail (OST) links cities of Spanish-conquest settlement from St. Augustine, Florida, to San Diego, California, and is commemorated by the 0-mile marker stone on the lawn of San Antonio's city hall. As the trail meanders through the city, a decorative stone bench recognizing the trail is at 3400 Fredericksburg Road. The Old Spanish Trail Centennial Celebration Association (OST100) was organized to promote and preserve the sights along the OST. They plan to end their decade-long celebration with a motorcade grand finale from St. Augustine to San Diego in 2029. ✉ *3600 Fredericksburg Rd.* ☎ *210/735–3503* 🌐 *www.oldspanishtrailcentennial.com* 🎟 *Free.*

★ **San Antonio African American Community Archive and Museum**

HISTORY MUSEUM | An important museum with an important mission, the goal of SAACAM (pronounced *say*-cam) is to preserve and share the history and culture of African Americans in San Antonio. It's a small place with a huge story, one that's told beautifully with well-organized exhibits and thoughtful events, like the Black History Film Series, book discussions, workshops, and activities. One permanent exhibit presents a timeline that illustrates black history in San Antonio through archival photographs and documents. Overall the museum uses timeline displays and digital archives to tell the story of African Americans in San Antonio dating from the 1500s to present day. There's even a kiosk for visitors to share their own stories. The small but striking gift shop features items only from San Antonio authors and artisans. The museum is also where you can book river tours on African American history in conjunction with GO RIO Cruises. ✉ *218 S. Presa St., Downtown* ☎ *210/734–3350* 🌐 *www.saaacam.org* 🎟 *Free.*

★ **San Antonio Museum of Art (SAMA)**

ART MUSEUM | Don't miss this magnificent global art museum right on the River Walk. Housed in the former historic Lone Star Brewery, the 69,500-square-foot museum is best known for its spectacular Nelson A. Rockefeller Center for Latin American Art, with thousands of works of Spanish colonial art, folk art, pre-Columbian art, and Latin American modern and contemporary art. There are also impressive collections of American Indian, African, Islamic, European, and Ancient Greek, Roman, and Egyptian art.

An extensive collection of Asian art is housed in its own Lenora and Walter F. Brown Asian Art wing, including pieces from the Ming and Ch'ing dynasties. Past exhibitions have included works by impressionists, Matisse, sculptor and designer Harry Bertoia, Carlos Mérida, Rodin, and many more. The museum offers a variety of tours, along with classes, workshops, and special events. The SAMA museum gift shop is one of the best, brimming with accessories, home decor, gifts, art prints, jewelry, seasonal items, and books, including guides to selected collections. ✉ *200 W. Jones Ave., Downtown* ☎ *210/978–8100* 🌐 *www.samuseum.org* 🎟 *$20* 🕒 *Closed Mon.*

★ San Antonio River Walk

PROMENADE | Built a full story below street level, the Paseo del Rio is the city's (and state's) leading tourist attraction, with the Downtown Reach section comprising about 3 miles of scenic stone pathways that line both San Antonio River banks as it flows through downtown, connecting many of the city's sights, hotels, and restaurants. In some places, the walk is peaceful and quiet; in others, it is a mad conglomeration of restaurants, bars, hotels, shops, and strolling mariachi bands, all of which can also be seen from GO RIO Cruises tour boats and river shuttles. To the north, the Museum Reach section of the River Walk extends roughly 4 miles from Lexington Street to Grayson Street. Boat tours do not travel to this section, but the river shuttles do, making their last stop at the Pearl District after a lock-and-dam experience at Brooklyn Street. The final section, the Mission Reach, extends south of downtown, uniquely encompassing 8 miles of riparian woodlands with native plants and an active aquatic habitat. No restaurants, hotels, shops, or river boats are on this stretch, but visitors can access the four missions at the San Antonio Missions National Historical Park via the walking path alongside the river. The fifth mission, the Alamo, is steps away from the Downtown Reach. The San Antonio River Walk and its three distinctive sections extend about 15 miles total. ✉ *849 E. Commerce St., Downtown* ☎ *210/227–4262* 🌐 *www.thesanantonioriverwalk.com* 🎟 *Free.*

San Fernando Cathedral

CHURCH | All are welcome at the oldest standing church building in Texas and the first church in San Antonio. Still an active parish (mass is held daily), San Fernando Cathedral was built in 1731 by the city's Canary Island colonists. Mexican general Santa Anna raised a blood-red flag of "no quarter" here before he stormed the Alamo in 1836, signifying to the Texans that he would take no prisoners. In 1873, following a fire after the Civil War, the chapel was replaced with the present-day construction. A small sarcophagus on display holds the ashes of unknown soldiers, presented as the remains of the defenders of the Alamo. However, some modern historians are skeptical because evidence of military uniforms was discovered, which the Texan army never wore. Special events are held here, including symphonies, singers, musicians, and televised specials. ✉ *115 Main Plaza, Downtown* ☎ *210/227–1297* 🌐 *www.sfcathedral.org* 🎟 *Free.*

Sea Life San Antonio

AQUARIUM | **FAMILY** | A fun and educational adventure for all ages, this aquarium boasts more than 250 species and 3,000 sea creatures in 160,000 gallons of water. It also has the city's only walk-through underwater ocean tunnel, where you can safely get up-close and personal with about 500 sea creatures. Stingray Bay has five different species of stingrays, while in the freshwater habitat, you'll see native-to-Texas creatures. One of the best features of Sea Life is the way the exhibits are constructed low enough to the ground so that even small kids can get a good look (and it saves family members from having to

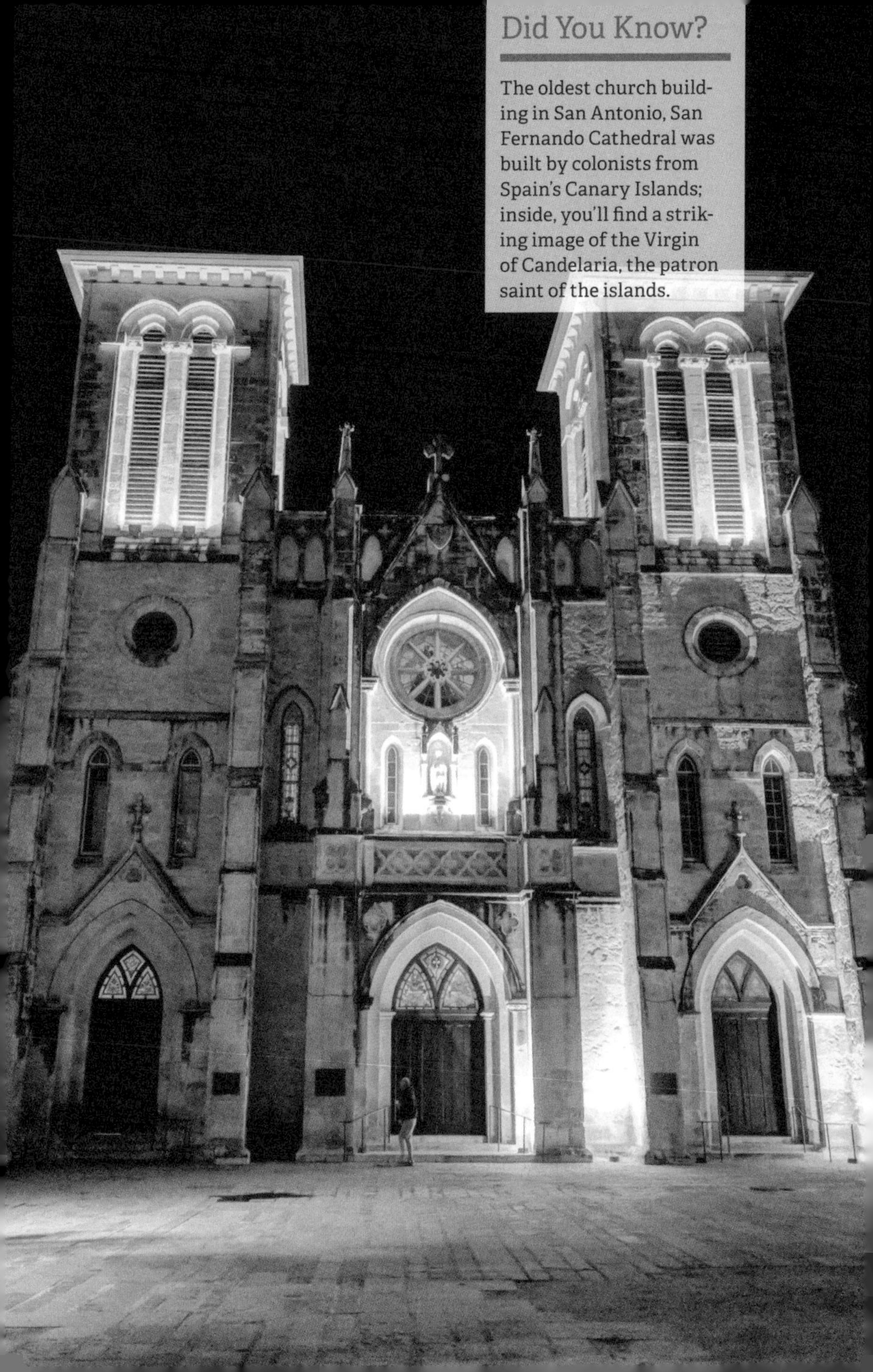

Did You Know?

The oldest church building in San Antonio, San Fernando Cathedral was built by colonists from Spain's Canary Islands; inside, you'll find a striking image of the Virgin of Candelaria, the patron saint of the islands.

The site of the 1968 World's Fair, Hemisfair is now a bustling city park home to the Tower of the Americas.

hoist them up). The interactive rock-pool is a kid-friendly favorite, with a Sea Life expert giving fun facts about the touchable creatures. The aquarium holds educational talks and feeding demonstrations throughout the day; be sure to ask about them as their timing may vary. ✉ *Shops at Rivercenter, 849 E. Commerce St., Downtown* ☎ *210/610–1160* 🌐 *www.visitsealife.com* 🎫 *$24.*

Southwest School of Art

COLLEGE | The only independent college of art in Texas, Southwest School of Art offers a Bachelor of Fine Arts degree (BFA) as well as classes and studio programs for thousands of adults and children. The school is housed in the former Ursuline Academy, which in 1851 became the first girls' school in the city. The long halls of the once busy dormitory are now filled with photography, jewelry, fibers, paper making, painting, and the like. The very popular annual Fiesta Arts Fair is held on the grounds each year during Fiesta Week. The Gallery Shop sells handcrafted items, including silver Southwestern jewelry, hand-painted plates, and wooden Christmas ornaments. Grab a sandwich, homemade soup, a salad, or homemade dessert at the school's Copper Kitchen Café, which was once the dining room for the old Ursuline Academy and is now a favorite of staff, students, and the public. ✉ *300 Augusta St., Downtown* ☎ *210/200–8200, 210/224–9337* 🌐 *www.swschool.org* 🎫 *Free.*

Spanish Governor's Palace

CASTLE/PALACE | Notice the expertly carved wooden doors at the entrance here: they tell the story of Spanish explorers in the New World, with the "baby face" representing America. San Antonio, then known as Presidio San Antonio de Béxar, was under Spanish rule from 1722 to 1821. This National Historic Landmark started as a one-room house built for the captain of the garrison in 1722. Walk through the self-guided tour with a map available at the entrance to see how and when the residence grew to 10 rooms, with period furnishings throughout and plaques that describe additions, such as the captain's office, an education room, dining room, kitchen, children's bedroom, and more. Relax on the cobblestone patio, enjoy the lovely courtyard, and make a wish at the wishing well. ✉ *105 Plaza de Armas, Downtown* ☎ *210/207–7527* 🌐 *www.spanishgovernorspalace.org* 🎫 *$5* 🕒 *Closed Mon.*

Tower of the Americas

OTHER ATTRACTION | **FAMILY** | At 750 feet tall, here you can take a glass-elevator ride traveling at 800 feet per minute, straight up, a very intense 43 seconds. Once the symbol of HemisFair '68, the 1968 World's Fair in San Antonio, locals now just call it "The Tower." Three elevators can carry almost 2,000 passengers an hour. There are also two observation decks, a café, a gift shop, a 4D movie theater, and the revolving Chart House, a steak-and-seafood restaurant at the top. One admission ticket covers the elevator ride, admission to the on-site Skies Over Texas 4D Theater (a multisensory movie experience), and access to the Flags Over Texas Observation Deck. ✉ *739 E. César E. Chávez Blvd., Downtown* ☎ *210/223–3101* 🌐 *www.toweroftheamericas.com* 🎫 *$15.*

Travis Park

CITY PARK | Since 1870, Travis Park has welcomed the community for gatherings, celebrations, concerts, holidays, and other special events. As one of the oldest municipal parks in the United States, this 2.6-acre green space is a destination all its own, especially for such popular events as Jazz'SAlive and the H-E-B Christmas Tree Lighting ceremony held the day after Thanksgiving. Other activities throughout the year include an ice rink, free movies, food trucks, fitness classes, Ballet in the Park, and live music. ✉ *301 E. Travis St., Downtown* ☎ *210/207–3677* 🌐 *www.travisparksa.com* 🎫 *Free.*

UTSA Institute of Texan Cultures

HISTORY MUSEUM | **FAMILY** | Located between the Alamodome and the Tower of the Americas, this fascinating museum features 65,000 square feet of exhibits that focus on the major cultural groups who made Texas what it is today. Exhibits explore the customs, traditions, food, music, and ways of life of the many people who came to define the Texan identity. Highlights include a re-created sharecropper's house, a cowboys and cattle drives exhibit, large-scale murals depicting Native American cultures, and an in-depth *Tejano* exhibit on the intersection of Spanish and Indigenous peoples that birthed a new culture. ✉ *801 E. César E. Chávez Blvd., Downtown* ☎ *210/458–2300* 🌐 *www.texancultures.utsa.edu* 🎫 *Suggested donation $12* 🕒 *Closed Mon.–Wed.*

Vietnam Veterans Memorial

MONUMENT | Combat artist Austin Deuel created *Hill-881 South,* the sculpture in front of the Tobin Center for the Performing Arts that graces Veterans Memorial Plaza, dedicated to the memory of those who served in the U.S. Armed Forces. The plaza was dedicated in 1986. ✉ *Veterans Memorial Plaza, 451 Jefferson St., Downtown* ☎ *210/207–7819* 🌐 *www.vietnamveteransmemorialofsanantonio.com* 🎫 *Free.*

Restaurants

Ácenar

$$ | **MEXICAN** | Big and bold contemporary design creates a lively atmosphere for this exciting collaboration by restaurateurs Lisa Wong of Rosario's fame and Pete Selig, known for Biga on the Banks. The nouvelle Tex-Mex spot sits astride a less-traveled section of the River Walk and offers excellent margaritas (many made from exotic ingredients, such as pear cactus), guacamole made tableside, and fresh ceviche. **Known for:** River Walk views; Mexican desserts; table-side chips and guac service. 💲 *Average main:*

$18 ✉ 146 E. Houston St., River Walk ☎ 210/222–2362 🌐 www.acenar.com ⏲ Closed Mon.

★ Biga on the Banks

$$$ | **AMERICAN** | One of the best restaurants in the city, the menu at Biga on the Banks is big and eclectic, and the dining atmosphere manages to be both larger than life and romantic. The choices change daily to take advantage of the freshest ingredients available, with dishes ranging from seared red-grouper grits to 11-spiced Axis venison chops. **Known for:** advance reservations a must; prix-fixe seasonal menu; sticky toffee pudding for dessert. 💲 *Average main: $27 ✉ 203 S. Saint Mary's St., River Walk ☎ 210/225–0722 🌐 www.biga.com ⏲ Closed Mon. No lunch.*

Bohanan's Prime Steaks and Seafood

$$$$ | **STEAKHOUSE** | At this elegant chef-driven restaurant, executive chef and owner Mark Bohanan dishes up prime-grade center-cut meat with exclusive selections of ultra-marbled, extraordinarily tender Japanese Akaushi beef (that means no growth hormones, ever). They also offer a tempting variety of fresh seafood, including wild Alaskan salmon, fresh Gulf red snapper, and Hawaiian big-eye sashimi tuna. **Known for:** Japanese Akaushi beef; mature Old World atmosphere; exceptional bar. 💲 *Average main: $55 ✉ 219 E. Houston St., Suite 205, Downtown ☎ 210/472–2600 restaurant, 210/472–2202 bar 🌐 www.bohanans.com ⏲ Closed Sun. and Mon. No lunch.*

Boudro's

$$$ | **AMERICAN** | This River Walk landmark serves a great variety of steaks and seafood. A little bit Gulf Coast, a little bit Mexican, and a whole lotta Texan, their something-for-everybody menu caters to almost every palette exceptionally well. **Known for:** excellent cuts of steak; River Walk dining; fresh Gulf Coast seafood. 💲 *Average main: $24 ✉ 421 E. Commerce St., River Walk ☎ 210/224–8484, 210/225–2839 🌐 www.boudros.com.*

Chart House at the Tower of the Americas

$$$$ | **SEAFOOD** | This steak house reigns over the San Antonio skyline, perched at the top of the Tower of the Americas and rotating slowly and smoothly. Its predecessor was primarily popular as a destination for drinks, but Chart House serves up some great steaks and seafood to keep you occupied for an entire night out while enjoying one-of-a-kind views of the city. **Known for:** spectacular views; creative cocktails; great weekday happy hour. 💲 *Average main: $35 ✉ Tower of the Americas, 739 E. César E. Chávez Blvd., Downtown ☎ 210/223–3101 🌐 www.chart-house.com.*

The County Line

$$ | **BARBECUE** | **FAMILY** | A household name in barbecue with several locations in Texas and one in Albuquerque, the Country Line is famous for its barbecued ribs, smoked brisket, and related fare. The barbecue here is dry-rubbed, with the sauce on the side, and the various combo platters and family-style options let you sample from smoked turkey and sausage, brisket, beef and pork ribs, and more. **Known for:** famous barbecue; River Walk patio dining; generous portions. 💲 *Average main: $17 ✉ 111 W. Crockett St., Suite 104, River Walk ☎ 210/229–1941 🌐 www.countyline.com.*

Landrace

$$$$ | **AMERICAN** | At this restaurant focused on Texas heritage and place—primarily sourcing its ingredients locally and regionally—renowned chef Steve McHugh creates an evolving menu that, naturally, changes with the seasons. As sleek, comfortable, and contemporary as the Thompson Hotel it's housed in, the restaurant has River Walk access where guests can stroll up directly from the river level without having to go through the hotel. **Known for:** regional and sustainable cuisine; Old Fashioned cocktails made

tableside; gladly accommodates special diets. *$ Average main: 45 ✉ Thompson San Antonio Riverwalk, 111 Lexington Ave., Downtown ☎ 210/942–6026 🌐 www.landracetx.com.*

Landry's Seafood House

$$$$ | SEAFOOD | FAMILY | Located in the thick of things right on the San Antonio River, this upscale national seafood chain is a pleasurable oasis from the area's hustle-and-bustle. A variety of fresh fish prepared in a number of ways include Chilean sea bass and almond-crusted mahimahi; top steak cuts appease those who prefer turf to surf. **Known for:** menu with chef recommendations; "the Alamo" lobster tail and filet mignon; River Walk patio seating. *$ Average main: $32 ✉ 517 N. Presa St., River Walk ☎ 210/229–1010 🌐 www.landrysseafood.com.*

La Margarita Restaurant & Oyster Bar

$$ | MEXICAN FUSION | FAMILY | In the heart of Market Square, here you can sample Mexican fare or oysters or both while surrounded by Spanish tile and light music. Try the fajitas, enchiladas, or puffy tacos, seated inside or on the patio under colorful umbrellas with a great view of the square. **Known for:** excellent margaritas; sizzling fajitas; great atmosphere. *$ Average main: $20 ✉ Market Sq., 120 Produce Row, Downtown ☎ 210/227–7140 🌐 www.lamargarita.com ⏲ Closed Tues. and Wed.*

★ La Panadería

$ | BAKERY | In a city filled with Mexican bakeries, brothers José and David Cáceres kicked the whole pan dulce (pastry) game up a notch with La Panadería. Their love for baking comes from selling their mama Doña Josefina's loaves of fresh-baked bread on the streets of Mexico City, and they've translated that passion into a winning combination of fresh, quality products available for only a limited amount of time each short day. **Known for:** freshly baked Mexican pastries that sell out quickly; unique Nutella cruffin (croissant-muffin); inexpensive brunch items. *$ Average main: 11 ✉ 301 E. Houston St., Downtown ☎ 210/592–6264 🌐 www.lapanaderia.com ⏲ No dinner.*

Las Canarias

$$$ | AMERICAN | River Walk dining at its most elegant and romantic, this three-level restaurant is known for its sophistication and romance and has one of the most relaxing and beautiful outdoor dining areas on the River Walk, with graceful palm trees and soothing views. The menu is a celebration of refined American cuisine that combines locally sourced ingredients in chef-inspired dishes. **Known for:** best margaritas on the River Walk; scenic patio dining; elegant ambience. *$ Average main: $30 ✉ Omni La Mansion del Rio, 112 College St., River Walk ☎ 210/518–1063 🌐 www.omnihotels.com.*

Little Rhein Prost Haus

$$ | GERMAN | Housed in a limestone structure built in 1847, this rustic restaurant was originally the residence and store of German immigrant Otto Bombach, and now it's a spot to enjoy traditional German fare and music in a historic River Walk setting. A highlight is the Bavarian Beer Room, an Opera Haus–style space with live entertainment at selected times. **Known for:** biergarten-style patio on River Walk; big selection of schnapps; homestyle German fare. *$ Average main: $16 ✉ 231 S. Alamo St., River Walk ☎ 210/890–2225 🌐 www.littlerheinprosthaus.com.*

★ Mi Tierra Cafe and Bakery

$$ | MEXICAN | The heart of Market Square boasts one of San Antonio's most venerable culinary landmarks, part of the notable Cortez Family of restaurants. Opened in 1941 as a three-table café for early-rising farmers to get breakfast, Mi Tierra ("my land") is a traditional Mexican restaurant, bakery, and bar that serves its hallmark breakfasts all day; the *chilaquiles famosas*—eggs scrambled with corn

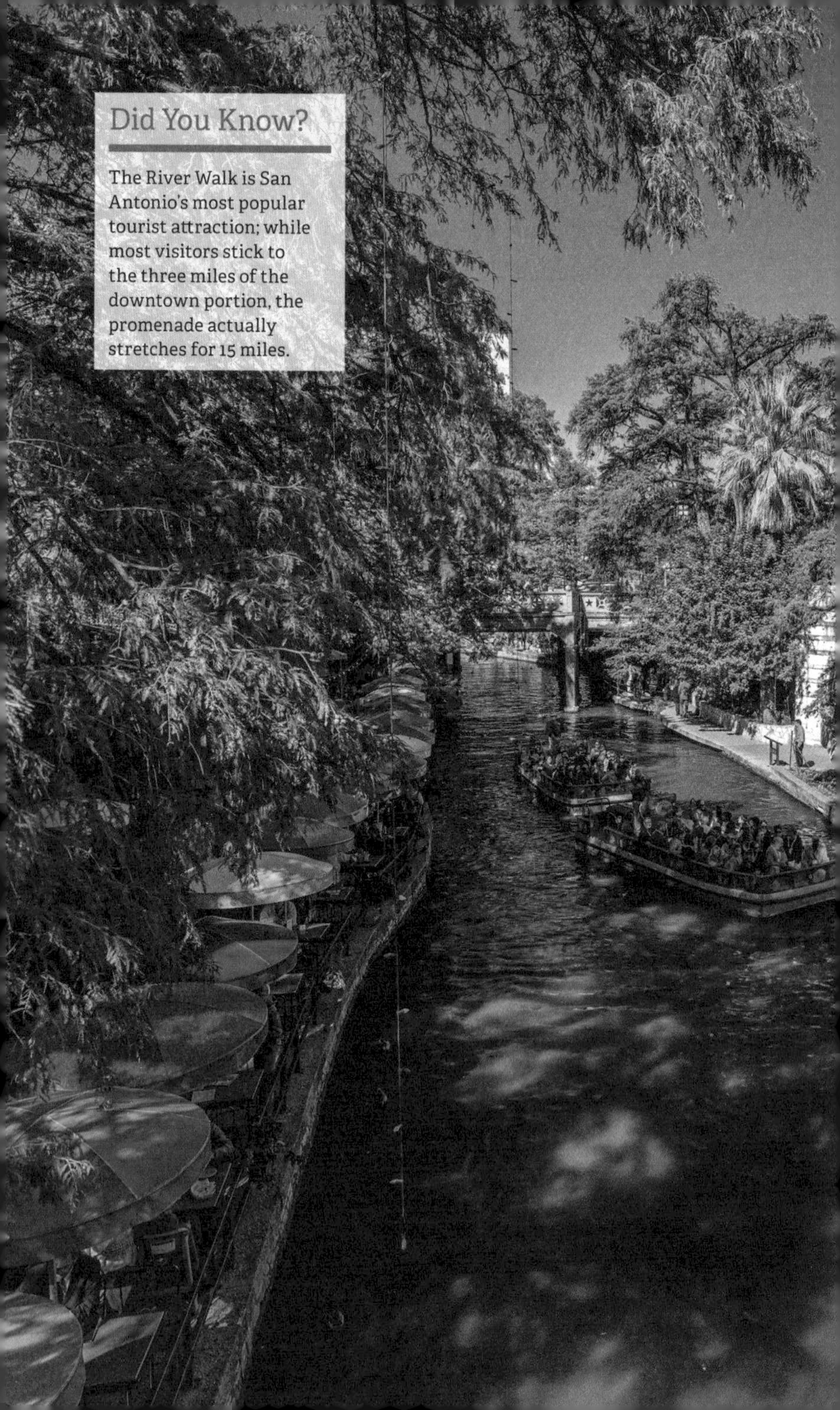

Did You Know?

The River Walk is San Antonio's most popular tourist attraction; while most visitors stick to the three miles of the downtown portion, the promenade actually stretches for 15 miles.

FIVE & DIME
DAVE & BUSTER'S
H&M

tortilla strips and topped with *ranchero* (mild tomato-based) sauce and cheese—are alone worth coming back for again and again. **Known for:** huge pan dulce (Mexican pastry) counter; margaritas, tequilas, and cocktails galore; colorful, unique atmosphere. *Average main: $20 218 Produce Row, Market Square 210/225–1262 www.mitierracafe.com.*

Morton's

$$$$ | **STEAKHOUSE** | **FAMILY** | Near the Alamo, the River Walk, and the Menger Hotel, this branch of the Morton's steakhouse chain is appropriately elegant and contemporary. Fabulous steaks, the selection and size of which are truly impressive, range from double-cut fillets to porterhouse to Cajun rib eye, and are matched with exquisite wines and service. **Known for:** chef's table meal kits to prepare at home; prime steaks and chops; extensive bar menu. *Average main: $39 Shops at Rivercenter, 300 E. Crockett St., River Walk 210/228–0700 www.mortons.com No lunch.*

Ostra Restaurant

$$$$ | **SEAFOOD** | **FAMILY** | Its name means oyster in Spanish, and you will find them plenty fresh here, chilled on the half shell and served with mignonette or chipotle cocktail sauce. The oyster bar also serves up clams, crabs, shrimp, and ceviche. **Known for:** prime River Walk location; premium seafood dishes; top oyster bar. *Average main: 36 Mokara Hotel & Spa, 212 W. Crockett St., Downtown 210/396–5817 www.omnihotels.com.*

Paesanos Riverwalk

$$$$ | **ITALIAN** | This deservedly popular spot at a bend on the River Walk melds fine Italian dining with a Mediterranean approach. The range of foodie-friendly dishes includes the signature shrimp *paesano* , a delicate and flavorful, lightly breaded and baked concoction accented with lemon, butter, and garlic, available as an appetizer or as an entrée. **Known for:** famous shrimp paesano; extensive wine list; River Walk patio dining. *Average main: $35 111 W. Crockett St., Suite 101, River Walk 210/227–2782 www.paesanosriverwalk.com No lunch.*

The Palm Restaurant

$$$$ | **STEAKHOUSE** | **FAMILY** | The San Antonio location of this classic New York–style steak house maintains the chain's efforts to bring back the supper clubs of decades past. Premium seafood, including jumbo Nova Scotia lobster, and Italian specialties add plenty of diversity to a menu populated by prime aged porterhouses, double-cut New York strip, and veal chops. **Known for:** Palm signature cocktails; retro supper club atmosphere; whimsical handprinted caricatures of famous past guests. *Average main: $40 233 E. Houston St., Suite 100, Downtown 210/226–7256 www.thepalm.com.*

★ Schilo's

$ | **GERMAN** | **FAMILY** | This venerable and popular downtown institution has been serving up hearty German soul food for breakfast (served all day), lunch, and dinner since Mama and Papa Schilo established their first location in 1917. The delicatessen moved to its current spot on East Commerce Street in 1942; Schilo's even lays claim to being the oldest operating restaurant in San Antonio and nobody has challenged them for the title. **Known for:** famous split-pea soup and hearty all-day breakfast; long waits during peak hours; homemade root beer (including a spiked option). *Average main: $10 424 E. Commerce St., Downtown 210/223–6692 www.schilos.com.*

Hotels

Canopy by Hilton San Antonio Riverwalk

$$$ | **HOTEL** | **FAMILY** | With a clean, contemporary design and excellent location, the Canopy by Hilton has almost everything you would want for a comfortable stay

right on the River Walk. **Pros:** good on-site dining and drinking; great location; friendly, attentive staff. **Cons:** no pool; possible noise from River Walk partiers; pricey valet parking. *Rooms from: 239* *123 N. St. Mary's St., Downtown* *210/404–7516* *www.hilton.com* *No Meals* *195 rooms.*

Drury Inn & Suites San Antonio Riverwalk

$$$ | **HOTEL** | One of the best values among River Walk hotels, the Drury Inn & Suites is located in the historic 1921 Petroleum Commerce Building. **Pros:** free nightly cocktail reception; great value for families and business travelers; premium location for sightseeing. **Cons:** some rooms can have bad views so be sure to ask; no airport shuttle service; rooms and decor nothing to write home about. *Rooms from: $246* *201 N. Saint Mary's St., River Walk* *210/212–5200* *www.druryhotels.com* *150 rooms* *Free Breakfast.*

The Emily Morgan Hotel

$$$ | **HOTEL** | Built in the 1920s and named for the woman who inspired the song "The Yellow Rose of Texas," this historic boutique hotel sits across from the Alamo on a triangular piece of land. **Pros:** nice marriage of modern amenities and classic features; so close to the Alamo, you can see it from some rooms; two blocks from the River Walk. **Cons:** room size can vary; no balconies; relatively expensive. *Rooms from: $239* *705 E. Houston St., Downtown* *210/225–5100* *www.emilymorganhotel.com* *177 rooms* *No Meals.*

Fairfield Inn & Suites by Marriott San Antonio Downtown/Market Square

$$ | **HOTEL** | This Fairfield Inn looks like every other in the chain, but it's clean and comfortable, with easy access to all of San Antonio's downtown sights. **Pros:** close to Market Square shops and restaurants; refreshingly straightforward atmosphere; inexpensive on-site parking lot. **Cons:** only one elevator; thin walls between rooms; cookie-cutter chain hotel with ho-hum decor. *Rooms from: $140* *620 S. Santa Rosa St., Downtown* *210/229–1000* *www.marriott.com* *110 rooms* *Free Breakfast.*

★ The Fairmount

$$$ | **HOTEL** | This eminent luxury three-story hotel made the *Guinness Book of World Records* when its 3.2-million-pound brick bulk was moved six blocks in 1985 to its present location; it's now the pinnacle of high-end boutique hotels in San Antonio. **Pros:** room service from fine dining on-site restaurants; dripping with European-style character and charm; luxuriously appointed rooms and suites. **Cons:** not exactly right in the thick of the River Walk/downtown action; occasional worn furnishings; expensive. *Rooms from: $300* *401 S. Alamo St., Downtown* *210/224–8800* *www.fairmountsa.com* *37 rooms* *No Meals.*

Hilton Palacio del Rio

$$$ | **HOTEL** | A towering complex with a central location on the busiest part of the River Walk, this Hilton is steps away from many top restaurants and attractions in the city. **Pros:** one block to convention center; superb location for sightseeing; every room has a private balcony. **Cons:** geared toward conventions, so not a lot of charm; busy intersection, so lower floors can be noisy; expensive, even for a nice Hilton. *Rooms from: $259* *200 S. Alamo St., River Walk* *210/222–1400* *www.hilton.com* *485 rooms* *No Meals.*

★ Hotel Contessa

$$$ | **HOTEL** | This exceptional boutique hotel is the only all-suites hotel on the River Walk. **Pros:** full-service spa; sophisticated, unique atmosphere; top-notch concierge. **Cons:** only valet parking on-site; per-night amenity fee; expensive. *Rooms from: $313* *306 W. Market St., River Walk* *210/229–9222* *www.thehotelcontessa.com* *265 rooms* *No Meals.*

★ Hotel Havana

$$$ | **HOTEL** | The hip Hotel Havana is a boutique oasis on the north end of the River Walk with colorful Cuban-inspired flair and bold artwork housed in its rather modest outward appearance. **Pros:** location on quiet part of the River Walk away from crowds; 24-hour bilingual staff; signature minibar stocked with local and international snacks and drinks. **Cons:** not exactly in the thick of downtown/River Walk happenings; room size can vary; very popular, so sometimes hard to book. *Rooms from: $226 ✉ 1015 Navarro St., Downtown ☎ 210/222–2008 🌐 www.havanasanantonio.com 27 rooms 🍽 No Meals.*

Hotel Valencia Riverwalk

$$ | **HOTEL** | The first boutique hotel in San Antonio, Hotel Valencia Riverwalk is renowned for its sleek and modern style, a captivating blend of Spanish colonial and modern Mediterranean design. **Pros:** great location on a quiet part of the river; hip, posh, and indulgent; range of accessible accommodations. **Cons:** pricey valet parking; no pets allowed; high demand can mean difficulty booking, especially at peak times. *Rooms from: $200 ✉ 150 E. Houston St., River Walk ☎ 210/227–9700 🌐 www.hotelvalencia-riverwalk.com 213 rooms.*

Hyatt Place San Antonio/Riverwalk

$$$ | **HOTEL** | Many all-suites and extended-stay hotels provide plenty of space but fall short on style, but this spot challenges the status quo with their customary and luxurious bedding and cozy and sleek furnishings in every room. **Pros:** tech-friendly; clean and modern design; spacious rooms. **Cons:** have to look elsewhere for fine dining options; only grab-and-go-style menu items near front desk; caters primarily to business travelers. *Rooms from: $234 ✉ 601 S. Saint Mary's St., River Walk ☎ 201/227–6854 🌐 sanantonioriverwalk.place.hyatt.com 132 rooms 🍽 Free Breakfast.*

Hyatt Regency San Antonio

$$$ | **HOTEL** | A steady stream of conventioneers, vacationers, and locals pass through the Hyatt's soaring 16-story atrium, following a water feature that takes them directly from the Alamo in front to the River Walk in the back, or up the Hyatt's famous glass elevators to their rooms and meeting spaces. **Pros:** unforgettable views; superb location between River Walk and Alamo; multiple on-site dining options. **Cons:** River Walk partying can sometimes be heard at night; crowded elevators at peak times; can get crowded on weekends. *Rooms from: $319 ✉ 123 Losoya St., Downtown ☎ 210/222–1234 🌐 www.hyatt.com 630 rooms 🍽 Free Breakfast.*

Marriott Plaza San Antonio

$$$ | **HOTEL** | Location is everything at this lush, 6-acre oasis in the middle of downtown San Antonio. **Pros:** attentive staff; superb location for sightseeing; beautifully manicured grounds. **Cons:** pricey on-site and valet parking; convention- and business-oriented; fees for high-speed Internet and video chat. *Rooms from: $259 ✉ 555 S. Alamo St., Downtown ☎ 210/229–1000 🌐 www.marriott.com 251 rooms 🍽 No Meals.*

Marriott Rivercenter

$$$ | **HOTEL** | With more than 1,000 rooms, more than 70,000 square feet of meeting space, and a 40,000-square-foot ballroom, this 38-story hotel (attached to sister hotel Marriott Riverwalk) has all the pluses—and minuses—of a very large hotel. **Pros:** friendly staff; on-site restaurant, bar, and café; great location. **Cons:** fees for in-room Wi-Fi and high-speed Internet; might feel too large for some; pricey on-site and valet parking. *Rooms from: $275 ✉ 101 Bowie St., River Walk ☎ 210/223–1000 🌐 www.marriott.com 1000 rooms 🍽 No Meals.*

Menger Hotel

$$ | **HOTEL** | Since its 1859 opening, the famous Menger has lodged the likes of Ulysses S. Grant, Theodore Roosevelt,

and Oscar Wilde, and today you'll still be the envy of many an overheated tourist strolling immediately across the street from the entrance to the Alamo into the cool lobby and up to your room (perhaps with a view of the Alamo). **Pros:** haven for history buffs; prime location next door to the Alamo; famous old-school bar. **Cons:** valet parking only; small business center; limited restaurant hours. *Rooms from: $219 204 Alamo Plaza, Downtown 210/223–4361 www.mengerhotel.com 316 rooms No Meals.*

★ Mokara Hotel & Spa
$$$$ | **HOTEL** | The ultimate spa getaway on the River Walk, luxury accommodations and services are offered at this hotel in the shell of the 19th-century L. Frank Saddlery Building. **Pros:** a true spa destination; everything a luxury award-winning hotel professes to be; River Walk rooms have private balconies. **Cons:** valet parking only at sister property Omni La Mansion del Rio; strict pet policy; pricey. *Rooms from: $379 212 W. Crockett St., River Walk 210/396–5800 www.omnihotels.com 99 rooms No Meals.*

Omni La Mansión del Rio
$$$ | **HOTEL** | Originally built as a school in 1852 and then converted to a hotel for the HemisFair, the 1968 World's Fair, today the Omni La Mansión del Rio is replete inside and out with Spanish tiles, archways, exposed beams, and soft, earthy tones. **Pros:** excellent on-site restaurant; beautiful, historic atmosphere; exceptional service. **Cons:** smallish desks; fee for Wi-Fi; pricey valet parking. *Rooms from: $325 112 College St., River Walk 210/518–1000 www.omnihotels.com 338 rooms No Meals.*

Sheraton Gunter Hotel
$$$ | **HOTEL** | Since 1909 this storied downtown hotel has been a favorite of ranchers and business travelers. **Pros:** definitely not a chain hotel; excellent location near theater and dining; lots of history. **Cons:** pricey valet parking; some areas need updating; no fine dining restaurant on-site. *Rooms from: $261 205 E. Houston St., Downtown 210/227–3241 www.marriott.com 322 rooms No Meals.*

St. Anthony, a Luxury Collection Hotel
$$$$ | **HOTEL** | You too can feel like royalty in one of the city's most historic places to stay: the opulent St. Anthony transports visitors to days gone by while offering modern amenities in a great downtown location. **Pros:** lots of history and famous guests; multiple on-site dining options; complimentary electric car–charging stations. **Cons:** pricey valet parking; can be noisy from nearby Travis Park public events; increased traffic from private events. *Rooms from: 358 300 E. Travis St., Downtown 210/227–4392 www.marriott.com No Meals 277 rooms.*

Thompson San Antonio Riverwalk
$$$$ | **HOTEL** | Located across the San Antonio River from the Tobin Center for the Performing Arts, at the Thompson you are in the heart of the arts district, and fairly close to major sights like the Alamo and the Pearl (both about a mile away). **Pros:** great location near arts district and the Pearl; exceptional on-site restaurant; chic, fuss-free room decor. **Cons:** expensive; pricey valet parking only; not exactly in the middle of downtown. *Rooms from: 369 115 Lexington Ave., Downtown 210/876–1234 www.hyatt.com No Meals 162 rooms.*

Nightlife

Bonham Exchange
DANCE CLUBS | If you're staying near the Alamo, this is a must-see LGBTQ club for the open-minded and those who aspire to be. Housed in the 20,000-square-foot classic 1892 Turner Hall, the Bonham Exchange is a testament to the tenacity of legendary downtown developer Arthur P. "Hap" Veltman, who scouted the

area in 1980 to replace his previous gay nightclub, the San Antonio Country. After a costly renovation, the club opened in 1981, and this amazing place has been going strong ever since. There are three levels of lively dance floors plus a bar area off the entrance. Multiple DJs spin every music genre you can imagine. Every year they throw an impossible-to-describe Halloween bash, and the club has a float in the Battle of Flowers parade during the annual Fiesta Week. Touring companies of Broadway shows have held their cast parties here, and at least one ghost hunter has scoured top to bottom for anybody who might have forgotten to (or didn't want to) leave the party. It has a friendly, welcoming atmosphere and great drink specials. Cover charges vary from nothing to $5 depending on days and times. ✉ *411 Bonham St., Downtown* ☎ *210/224–9219* 🌐 *www.bonhamexchange.com.*

Drink Texas

BARS | Across from Hotel Contessa, Drink Texas serves tapas and has a large variety of signature cocktails, wines by the bottle, and wines by the glass. They're also known for their long (2 pm to 9 pm) happy hour. ✉ *200 Navarro St., Downtown* ☎ *210/224–1031* 🌐 *www.drinktexas.com.*

★ Esquire Tavern

BARS | Originally opened in 1933 following the end of Prohibition, the Esquire Tavern has a storied past as the oldest riverfront bar on the River Walk. The legendary locale even claims to be the longest bar in Texas, at 100 feet. The sleek, dark 1930s interior blends well with an elevated pub-style menu. The evolving seasonal classic cocktail menu is a favorite of locals and visitors alike. The intimate Downstairs area is directly on the River Walk and is open Friday and Saturday from 7 pm to 2 am. ✉ *155 E. Commerce St., Downtown* ☎ *210/222–2521* 🌐 *www.esquiretavern-sa.com.*

Howl at the Moon

CABARET | Come here to have a dueling-piano bar and high-energy live show experience—and don't hesitate to sing along. They have a big selection of cocktails, shots, and beers. It's a great place for parties and group events. ✉ *111 W. Crockett St., #201, Downtown* ☎ *210/212–4770* 🌐 *www.howlatthemoon.com.*

★ Iron Cactus Mexican Grill and Margarita Bar

BARS | Choose from the extensive selection of tequilas and margaritas here as well as nearly 30 tequila flights for the indecisive. They also have domestic, imported, and Texas craft beers. ✉ *200 River Walk, Suite 100, Downtown* ☎ *210/224–9835* 🌐 *www.ironcactus.com.*

Mad Dogs British Pub

PUBS | Claiming to be an authentic British-theme pub, Mad Dogs offers a selection of imported beers and cocktails as well as entertainment that includes DJs, karaoke, and live acts. They also have a pub menu of fish and chips, Scotch eggs, bangers and mash, and more. Shows are "mostly" family-friendly, but no minors are admitted after 10 pm. ✉ *123 Losoya St., #19, Downtown* ☎ *210/222–0220* 🌐 *www.maddogs.net.*

★ Menger Bar

BARS | At this historic bar within the historic Menger Hotel (one of the city's great cultural treasures), listen to tales of how Teddy Roosevelt recruited his army of Rough Riders here. The bar was built in 1871, as a replica of London's House of Lords pub. It's a fun place to go with friends for a drink or to meet the locals. A small pub menu is served all day. ✉ *204 Alamo Plaza, Downtown* ☎ *210/223–4361* 🌐 *www.mengerhotel.com.*

Pat O'Brien's

BARS | The San Antonio outpost of New Orleans institution Pat O'Brien's serves the bar's wickedly strong Hurricanes, along with cocktails like the Cyclone

The Arneson River Theatre is one of the highlights of the River Walk.

and the Cat-5 Margarita. They have live music daily on the patio and a New Orleans–style menu. ✉ *121 Alamo Plaza, Downtown* ☎ *210/541–5940* 🌐 *www.patobriens.com.*

The Republic of Texas

BARS | After dinner, the Republic of Texas restaurant transforms into a nightclub. Enjoy one of the nightly drink specials or order the massive 42-ounce margarita served in a souvenir take-home glass. ✉ *526 River Walk, Downtown* ☎ *210/226–6256* 🌐 *www.therepublicoftexasrestaurant.com.*

Re:Rooted 210 Urban Winery & Tasting Room

WINE BARS | With this winemaking and tasting room facility in downtown San Antonio, this urban winery specializes in local wine education and serving only Texas wines. It usually features six wines on tap and dozens of bottles. ✉ *623 Hemisfair Blvd., Suite 106, Downtown* ☎ *254/661–2721* 🌐 *www.rerootedwine.com.*

Waxy O'Connor's Irish Pub

PUBS | Amazingly, this pub was built in County Monaghan, Ireland, and shipped to San Antonio, where it was reassembled. They are open for lunch and dinner daily (lots of Irish specials, naturally) and have live music every night. ✉ *234 River Walk* ☎ *210/229–9299* 🌐 *www.waxyoconnors.com.*

Performing Arts

MUSIC AND CONCERTS

Arneson River Theatre

THEATER | Erected in 1939, this unique outdoor music and performing arts venue in the heart of La Villita was designed by River Walk architect Robert H. H. Hugman and built by the WPA. Have a seat on the grass-covered steps on the river's edge and watch performers on the small stage across the water. In this open-air format, the river, not a curtain, separates performers from the audience. Some of San Antonio's top events take place here, including Fiesta Noche del Rio, a summer music and dance show

Head to the Historic Market Square for authentic eats and artisan crafts.

presented since 1957, making it the oldest outdoor performance of its kind in the United States. ✉ *418 Villita St., Downtown* ☎ *210/207–8614* 🌐 *www.lavillitasanantonio.com.*

Mexican Cultural Institute San Antonio
ARTS CENTERS | **FAMILY** | Since the time of HemisFair '68, this small but impressive two-story center has exhibited Mexican culture as depicted in film, dance, art, and more. ✉ *600 Hemisfair Plaza Way, Downtown* ☎ *210/227–0123* 🌐 *icm.sre.gob.mx.*

★ **Tobin Center for the Performing Arts**
ARTS CENTERS | The Tobin Center for the Performing Arts represents one of the most remarkable transformations in the history of San Antonio. After voters approved $100 million in construction bonds, the old and venerable Municipal Auditorium became a world-class performing arts venue. The H-E-B Performance Hall has 2,039 seats in a flat-floor configuration. Besides bringing in top acts in music and theater from around the world, the Tobin has resident companies that reflect the very best that the city has to offer: Ballet San Antonio, Classical Music Institute, OPERA San Antonio, The Children's Chorus of San Antonio, San Antonio Symphony, and Youth Orchestras of San Antonio. Free performances and activities are also held on the grounds on the Will Naylor Smith River Walk Plaza, including free movie nights and yoga and wellness programming. Ask about free scheduled tours of this impressive and important landmark. ✉ *100 Auditorium Cir., Downtown* ☎ *210/223–8624* 🌐 *www.tobincenter.org.*

THEATER

Carver Community Cultural Center
ARTS CENTERS | This community treasure is the cultural heart of the city's east side. Year-round performances, classes, and programming focus on their mission to celebrate the world's diverse cultures, with emphasis on African and African American heritage. Acts that have graced the stage at the Jo Long Theatre for the Performing Arts include top names in modern dance, ballet, music, poetry, and

theater. The Carver Gallery, in the theater lobby, presents visual artists in free exhibitions that change every few months. The building complex itself has a storied past, with the Little Carver venue housed in what was once a beloved neighborhood church and the Jo Long Theatre lobby once a city library designated only for black residents when segregation kept them out of other city library branches. ✉ *226 N. Hackberry St., Downtown* ☎ *210/207–7211* 🌐 *www.thecarver.org.*

Guadalupe Cultural Arts Center

ARTS CENTERS | Founded in 1980 to preserve and develop Chicano, Latino, and Native American arts and culture, the GCAC regularly stages dance, music, and theatrical performances. It also displays the art of emerging artists and holds classes in dance and music, with a unique summer theater day-camp for young aspiring playwrights, actors, and tech crew. Of the center's major annual events, the Tejano Conjunto Festival is a huge draw, bringing together more than 10,000 conjunto music lovers from all over. The annual CineFestival San Antonio presents five days of Latinx film. The GCAC is a national model that has inspired other community-based Latinx arts organizations nationwide. ✉ *723 S. Brazos St., Downtown* ☎ *210/271–3151* 🌐 *www.guadalupeculturalarts.org.*

★ **The Majestic Theatre**

THEATER | A masterpiece of baroque splendor with Spanish mission and Mediterranean-style influences, this 1929 movie and vaudeville theater once showcased talents like Jack Benny, Bob Hope, and George Burns. Today the fully restored, 2,311-seat theater presents the Majestic Broadway Series of top-notch touring companies of Broadway shows like *Hamilton, Waitress, Chicago,*and many more, along with concerts and comedy shows. No photography of any kind is allowed, so commit to memory the glittering "night sky," ornate architecture, and dazzling surroundings of one of the finest atmospheric theaters in existence. See a show here if you can get last-minute tickets—they sell same-day tickets immediately before each performance. ✉ *224 E. Houston St.* ☎ *210/226–5700* 🌐 *www.majesticempire.com.*

Shopping

★ **Historic Market Square**

CRAFTS | **FAMILY** | This is about as close you can get to Old Mexico without crossing the border. Market Square (*El Mercado*) has been a favorite of locals and visitors for generations for eating, drinking, shopping, and celebrating. The three-block space houses restaurants, shops, galleries, and working artisans crafting their wares in everything from silver to leather to woodwork. The Market Square outdoor plaza often has music and dance performances, especially during the holidays. Check the website calendar for upcoming programming. It's a fun, colorful outing, especially if you're dining at Mi Tierra Bakery and Café or La Margarita Restaurant & Oyster Bar and are up for a lively afternoon or evening. ✉ *514 W. Commerce St, Downtown* ☎ *210/207–8600* 🌐 *www.marketsquaresa.com.*

Activities

There's plenty for the sports lover in San Antonio. If you like to get outdoors, the city has several fantastic parks and natural areas within its borders, and many others are just beyond the city limits. There are also a number of great golf courses in and around San Antonio. If you'd rather watch a game, the San Diego Padres AA affiliate, the San Antonio Missions, plays baseball in "The Wolff" (Nelson Wolff Municipal Stadium), the jewel of the Texas League. The city is also home to an AHL hockey team, the San Antonio Rampage.

The hottest ticket in town, though, is definitely the NBA's San Antonio Spurs, who have won a total of five NBA championships. They play at the city's AT&T Center.

BASKETBALL

AT&T Center

BASKETBALL | The home of five-time NBA champions the San Antonio Spurs, the AT&T Center boasts two anchor tenants: the beloved Spurs and the popular San Antonio Stock Show & Rodeo. The Spurs host games here from October through April, with seats available in every price range; a seat in the rafters can be had for as little as $10, or you can sit courtside for about $1,000. Since its opening in 2002, the center has attracted millions of visitors for special events, including concerts by everyone from the Rolling Stones to Cirque du Soleil. ✉ *1 AT&T Center Pkwy., Downtown* ☎ *210/444–5000* 🌐 *www.attcenter.com.*

FOOTBALL

Alamodome

FOOTBALL | This 64,000-seat, $186-million sports arena is a busy place. Home of the Valero Alamo Bowl each December, featuring teams from the Pac-12 and Big 10 conferences, the site hosts other sporting events as well as concerts, trade shows, and conventions. The Alamodome is also the home of the UTSA football team, the Roadrunners. Club-level luxury suites provide a perfect view of the action on field, stage, or ice. The Alamodome is the only place in North America with two permanent Olympic-size ice rinks under the same roof. Event tickets can be purchased through Ticketmaster or at the Alamodome's southwest box office (closed weekends). Parking fees are determined on an event-by-event basis. ✉ *100 Montana St., Southside* ☎ *210/207–3663* 🌐 *www.alamodome.com.*

The Pearl District

The original 1880s Pearl Brewery—once the largest brewery in Texas—closed in 2001. By 2002, it was purchased by San Antonio company Silver Ventures, who developed a master plan for both revitalizing the 22-acre complex and preserving its historic structures. The food-focused mixed-use development continues to grow today, with new and buzzworthy venues regularly opening that highlight the best in dining, shopping, entertainment, residences, and work spaces.

The Pearl is a lively destination on the Museum Reach of the River Walk and home to some of the top restaurants and hippest, most fashionable shops in the city. Luxurious Hotel Emma has made virtually every best hotel list, with a spa nearby. Pearl Farmers Market draws crowds on weekend mornings and actually is a producers' market, where vendors grow, harvest, and raise every product they sell, all within a 150-mile radius of San Antonio. The Pearl is also a hub for BCycle, the first bike-share program in Texas.

Thousands of locals and visitors make the Pearl a regular part of their daily lives as they shop, dine, work and play in this exciting and unique piece of San Antonio.

Sights

Culinary Institute of America, San Antonio

COLLEGE | One of four branches of the country's most famous culinary school, the CIA Texas campus in San Antonio attracts food lovers and future chefs with a special interest in Latin American culture and cuisine. Associate and bachelor degrees in the culinary arts are offered here, but if you're just a foodie passing through, you can sign up for one-day classes that range from three to five hours on topics like Mexican desserts, live-fire grilling, holiday pies, and more. Or try a short session on Food and Wine

Originally a historic brewery, the Pearl District is now a bustling complex home to restaurants, bars, shops, and a weekly farmers' market.

Pairing 101. Longer, more intense boot camps are available on Mexican and Mediterranean cuisine and, of course, grilling and barbecue. If you would rather relax and watch someone else work, check out the one- to two-hour chef demonstrations on a variety of topics, with tastings and take-home recipes included. To skip work entirely, make reservations at Savor, the CIA restaurant, for a meal created and presented by advanced CIA students under the guidance of professional faculty. ✉ *312 Pearl Pkwy, Alamo Heights* ☎ *210/554–6400* 🌐 *www.ciachef.edu* 🎫 *Public tours $2; cooking classes and demonstrations vary* ⏲ *Closed weekends.*

Restaurants

Bakery Lorraine

$ | **BAKERY** | Here expertly crafted croissants, cookies, muffins, macarons, rolls, tarts, and danish pastries are as delicious as they come. Heartier breakfast fare includes quiche Lorraine, croque madame, Turkish eggs, and French toast, while lunch features Cuban roast pork loin sandwiches and other options on their homemade breads. **Known for:** classic French pastries; popular homemade bread; loyal following. [$] *Average main: $13* ✉ *306 Pearl Pkwy., Historic District* ☎ *210/862–5582* 🌐 *www.bakerylorraine.com* ⏲ *No dinner.*

Best Quality Daughter

$$ | **ASIAN FUSION** | **FAMILY** | Here excellent Asian-American fusion is served in a delightful, vibrant setting within the historic Mueller House. Chefs/owners Jennifer Hwa Dobbertin and Quealy Watson create an innovative and regularly changing all-day menu, plus lunch specials, always with a unique blend of Asian-American and South Texas influences, plus touches of other cuisines. **Known for:** artwork by Asian-American women; fusion menu that changes regularly; many vegan and vegetarian options. [$] *Average main: 16* ✉ *602 Avenue A, San Antonio* ☎ *210/819–2346* 🌐 *www.bestqualitydaughter.com.*

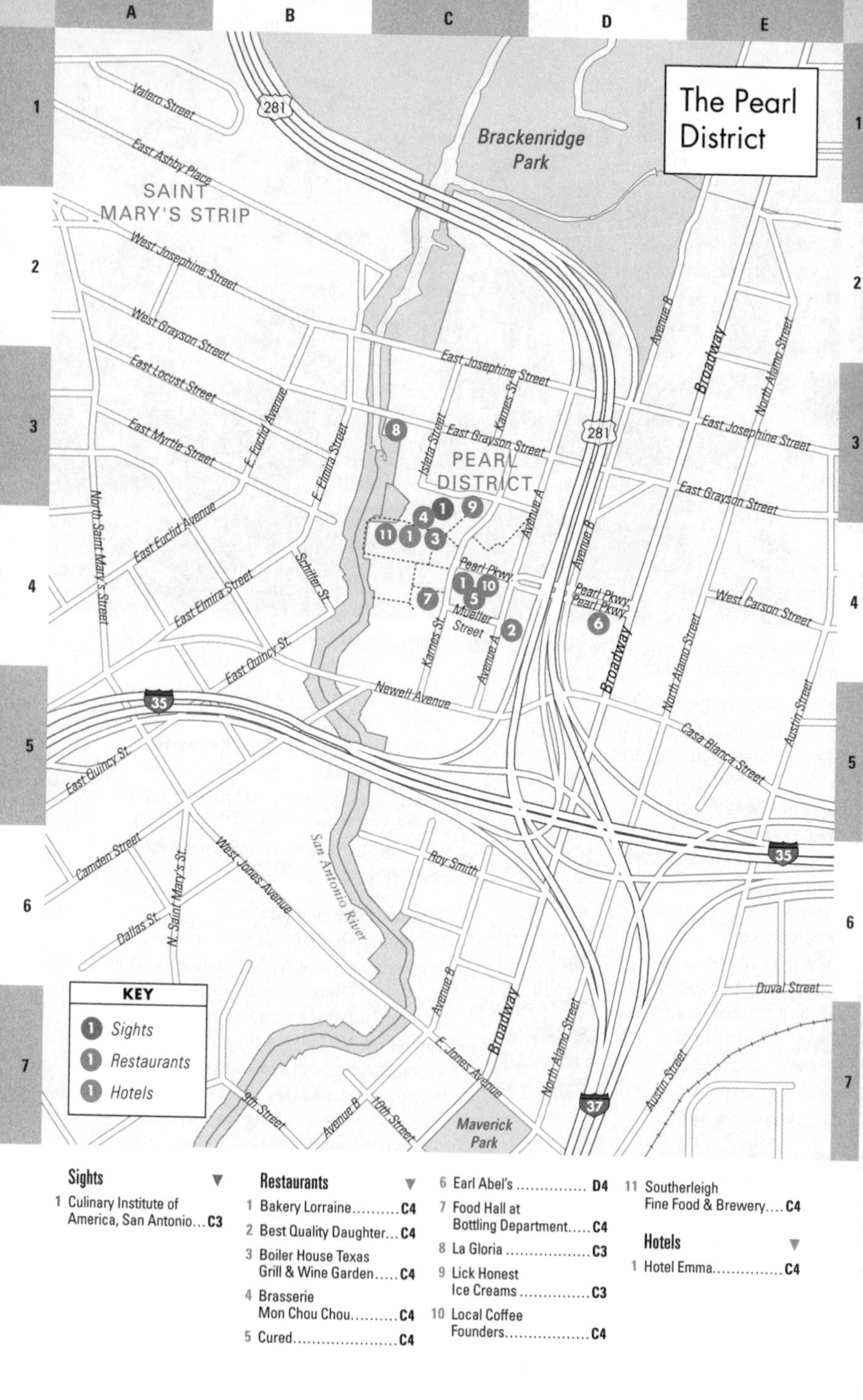

Sights

1 Culinary Institute of America, San Antonio... **C3**

Restaurants

1 Bakery Lorraine.......... **C4**

2 Best Quality Daughter... **C4**

3 Boiler House Texas Grill & Wine Garden..... **C4**

4 Brasserie Mon Chou Chou.......... **C4**

5 Cured....................... **C4**

6 Earl Abel's **D4**

7 Food Hall at Bottling Department..... **C4**

8 La Gloria **C3**

9 Lick Honest Ice Creams **C3**

10 Local Coffee Founders.................. **C4**

11 Southerleigh Fine Food & Brewery.... **C4**

Hotels

1 Hotel Emma............... **C4**

Boiler House Texas Grill & Wine Garden

$$$$ | **STEAKHOUSE** | **FAMILY** | Built within the 130-year-old renovated boiler house of the original Pearl Brewery, the Boiler House Texas Grill & Wine Garden is every bit as Texas-size in flavor as it is in its expansive two-level space. Sophisticated yet casual, it enjoys a loyal following, many of whom settle in at the long bar for signature and seasonal craft cocktails. **Known for:** prime steaks; historic atmosphere; sourcing from local farms and markets. *Average main: $31 ✉ 312 Pearl Pkwy., Historic District ☎ 210/354–4644 🌐 www.boilerhousesa.com.*

Brasserie Mon Chou Chou

$$$$ | **FRENCH** | Surprisingly, the concept of a French restaurant with Southern hospitality works well here. That was the dream of the three Frenchmen founders from different regions in France (Strasbourg, Chartres, and Lyon) who met up in San Antonio; some of the dishes are a tribute to their respective grandmothers and meals shared around family tables. **Known for:** French comfort food; stylish, unfussy ambience; indoor/outdoor dining. *Average main: 35 ✉ 312 Pearl Pkwy., Historic District ☎ 210/469–3743 🌐 www.brasseriemonchouchou.com.*

Cured

$$$$ | **AMERICAN** | Chef Steve McHugh brings his love of regional ingredients and organic methods to charcuterie-focused New American cuisine in a historic setting. Dishes change seasonally, but the primary theme is always meat (non-red-meat options include seafood, soups, and salads). **Known for:** all things charcuterie; pickled and cured groceries for sale; historic setting in the Pearl's most distinctive building. *Average main: 35 ✉ 306 Pearl Pkwy., Unit 101, Historic District ☎ 210/314–3929 🌐 www.curedatpearl.com ⏲ Closed Mon.*

★ **Earl Abel's**

$$ | **AMERICAN** | **FAMILY** | For almost 90 years now, Earl Abel's has managed to stay as hip as ever thanks to their classic homestyle menu and loyal fans that have followed them to a new location in the Pearl. The top-notch comfort food is made fresh daily and includes everything you would hope to see on your family table: classic breakfasts, soups and salads, hearty sandwiches, Abel's famous meat loaf, house-roasted turkey breast with cornbread stuffing, chicken-fried steak, garlic fried rice, and much more, with homemade pie and cake for dessert. **Known for:** famous fried chicken; homestyle comfort food; cakes and pies for dessert. *Average main: $15 ✉ 1639 Broadway, San Antonio ☎ 210/444–9424 🌐 www.earlabelssa.com.*

★ **Food Hall at Bottling Department**

$$ | **CONTEMPORARY** | This is the Pearl's reimagining of a food court, an eminently casual spot featuring chef-driven stands. Choose from six vendors: Chilaquil, serving Mexican street food and namesake chilaquiles; Fletcher's Hamburgers (which also sells hot dogs made with 100% organic Texas Akaushi beef); Kineapple, with healthy smoothies and snacks; Mi Roti, Caribbean street food built around roti, a Caribbean flatbread; Park Bar, a casual wine and beer bar with Texas beer and seasonal cocktails; and Tenko Ramen, a noodle-driven eatery with Japanese-style snacks. **Known for:** fun food hall atmosphere; diverse selection of cuisines; historic setting. *Average main: 15 ✉ 312 Pearl Pkwy., Bldg. 6, Historic District ☎ 210/564–9140 🌐 www.bottlingdepartment.com.*

★ **La Gloria**

$ | **MEXICAN** | **FAMILY** | You can't get too far in San Antonio without stumbling into a Tex-Mex restaurant, but when you need something that relays the authenticity of true Mexican cuisine, La Gloria is the place. Inspired by the street foods of Mexico, chef/owner Johnny Hernandez has created a vibrant taqueria-style restaurant celebrating the bold flavors and classic offerings you'd typically find with Mexican street vendors. **Known**

for: best Mexican street food in the city; colorful, lively setting; extensive cocktail menu. $ *Average main: $10* ✉ *100 E. Grayson St., Historic District* ☎ *210/267–9040* 🌐 *www.chefjohnnyhernandez.com/restaurants/la-gloria/.*

Lick Honest Ice Creams

$ | **ICE CREAM** | Staying true to their name, this company states that 73% of their ingredients come from local farmers and artisans, and they use as many organic ingredients as possible, making every single batch of ice cream by hand in Austin. Their everyday flavors are heavenly—think caramel salt lick, coffee with cream, dark chocolate with olive oil and sea salt, roasted beets with fresh mint, and more, while seasonal flavors include candied pecan-bourbon, Hazel's pumpkin pie, red velvet, and Too Hot Chocolate. **Known for:** homemade ice cream in unique flavors; dairy-free and vegan options; local and organic ingredients. $ *Average main: 6* ✉ *312 Pearl Pkwy., Suite 2101, Historic District* ☎ *210/314–8166* 🌐 *www.ilikelick.com.*

Local Coffee Founders

$ | **AMERICAN** | This is a pleasant hangout with excellent products and a good vibe. They have a great selection of coffees and teas and a small healthy food menu with selected pastries that come from Hotel Emma and Bakery Lorraine. **Known for:** friendly staff; outdoor seating; commitment to local sourcing. $ *Average main: 6* ✉ *302 Pearl Pkwy., Historic District* ☎ *210/530–1004* 🌐 *www.localcoffee.com.*

★ Southerleigh Fine Food & Brewery

$$ | **AMERICAN** | Galveston chef-owner Jeff Balfour serves up a Southern comfort–style all-day menu paired with 15 different craft beers brewed on-site in a custom-manufactured brewery designed by Portland Kettle Works, bringing brewing back to the Pearl. The menu changes seasonally, and if you can't decide, choose selections from the chef's For the Table menu to share—options usually include Southerleigh's famous fried snapper throats, deviled eggs, South Texas antelope tartare, fried frog legs, and Galveston Bay shrimp boil. **Known for:** fried snapper throats; historical and industrial atmosphere; 15 types of beers brewed on-site. $ *Average main: 19* ✉ *136 E. Grayson St., Suite 120, Historic District* ☎ *210/455–5701* 🌐 *www.southerleighatpearl.com.*

Hotels

★ Hotel Emma

$$$$ | **HOTEL** | There are no superlatives left to describe the wonder that is Hotel Emma, located in the original 1894 Pearl brewhouse and providing luxurious guest rooms and exemplary service. **Pros:** fine dining restaurant and luxe city bar on-site; ultimate in luxury and service; historic riverfront setting. **Cons:** tourists in lobby and venues; breakfast not included; very, very expensive. $ *Rooms from: 830* ✉ *136 E. Grayson St., Historic District* ☎ *210/448–8300* 🌐 *www.thehotelemma.com* 🍽 *No Meals* 🛏 *146 rooms.*

Nightlife

★ Blue Box Bar

BARS | A very cool bar with a friendly vibe and bright decor, Blue Box serves a good selection of house cocktails, house shots of pineapple serrano tequila and strawberry vodka, cigars, wine, and beer—including some good seasonal craft brews. The name comes from the blue box cooler that overnight "third shift" workers at the original Pearl Brewery would keep their beers in (brewery workers could drink on the job back then). Happy hour lasts all day on Sunday and Monday. ✉ *312 Pearl Pkwy., Historic District* ☎ *210/227–2583* 🌐 *www.blueboxbar.com.*

Jazz, TX

LIVE MUSIC | Book your table and seating times online for a visit to this favorite cool spot for live jazz and fine dining.

You'll find one of the city's most stunning boutique hotels, the Hotel Emma, in the Pearl District.

Jazz, TX is located in the basement of the Food Hall and Bottling Department, accessible by outside stairs or indoor elevator. With seven shows a week (two on Saturday and Sunday nights), they have quite the variety of live music performances: jazz, blues, big band, Texas swing, salsa, and Latin jazz. The atmosphere is very old-school supper club, with craft cocktails, wine, and beer being served. There's a pretty standard food menu, too. Weekend shows are $35 per person, while weekday shows run $20 to $25. ✉ *312 Pearl Pkwy., Historic District* ☎ *210/332–9386* 🌐 *www.jazztx.com.*

★ Sternewirth Tavern & Club Room
BARS | One of the most elegant spaces at the Pearl—no surprise since it's inside Hotel Emma—the bar is named for the Sternewirth Privilege, the 19th-century tradition of giving brewery employees free beer during the workday. The cool, dark, inviting space has a 25-foot vaulted ceiling over a collection of softly lit seats, a fireplace, and a beautiful bar serving signature cocktails, beer, and wine, along with satisfying bar bites. ✉ *136 E. Grayson St., Historic District* ☎ *210/223–7375* 🌐 *www.thehotelemma.com.*

Shopping

Adelante Boutique
WOMEN'S CLOTHING | A San Antonio fashion staple for more than 46 years, this family-owned business is now run by the third-generation owner. It's a beautiful store bursting with color and textures selling a brilliant array of women's fashions that reflect local flair and culture. Over the years the store has expanded into select home decor as well as jewelry, accessories, and gifts. The staff is welcoming and helpful, but it can get busy so plan on plenty of time to browse and take it all in. ✉ *303 Pearl Pkwy., Unit 107, Historic District* ☎ *210/826–6770* 🌐 *www.adelanteboutique.com.*

Dos Carolinas
MEN'S CLOTHING | How to explain a guayabera? Although it is traditionally known as a men's button-down pleated shirt

originating in Cuba, it has gained popularity in Puerto Rico, Mexico, the Caribbean, Central America, and here in South Texas where natural fabrics like cotton and linen breathe best in the heat. Designer Caroline Matthews has over 30 years of experience in fitting, designing, and creating custom guayaberas. The process starts with selecting a fabric, then you choose a style, sleeve length, color, and the kind of fit. Each shirt takes at least four to six weeks to complete. The shop does quite a bit of designing for weddings, where smartly tailored guayaberas are more relaxed than tuxedos. The store also carries a selection of ready-made guayaberas and other guayabera-wear, including robes and drawstring pajamas. ✉ *303 Pearl Pkwy., Suite 102, Historic District* ☎ *210/224–7000* 🌐 *www.doscarolinas.com.*

★ Feliz Modern POP

OTHER SPECIALTY STORE | One of the most fun shops at the Pearl, Feliz Modern POP is a cool and colorful collection of things for you, your home, your friends, your family, your pets, and everyone you know. Many items have a Southwestern or Latin flair, like the Revolutionary Women of Texas and Mexico coloring book or a catnip-taco cat toy. Co-owners Mario and Ginger Diaz have assembled quite a collection for gifting, entertaining, and celebrating the connections in our lives with global art, accessories, and home decor. There's candy and artisanal soda, too. Their flagship store, Feliz Modern, is at 110 W. Olmos in the Monte Vista Historic District. ✉ *303 Pearl Pkwy., Unit 104, San Antonio* ☎ *210/622–8364* 🌐 *www.felizmodern.com.*

Larder

MARKET | This little jewel is a combination market, café, and bakery tucked away on the first floor of Hotel Emma. Browse their eclectic stock of culinary luxuries and upscale staples as well as fresh flowers, freshly prepared food to take out or eat in, Merit coffee, fresh baked goods, and wine and beer. Their menu consists of breakfast and an all-day lunch menu of salads, soup of the day, and cold and warm sandwiches. They also have unique gift items and signature tote bags for both Hotel Emma and Larder. ✉ *Hotel Emma, 136 E. Grayson St., Historic District* ☎ *210/448–8355* 🌐 *www.larderatemma.com.*

Niche at Pearl

WOMEN'S CLOTHING | Stylish women's wear is just the beginning here. Niche carries an impressive collection of handbags, hats, loungewear, scarves, and bandanas as well as kids' clothing, swimwear, and blankets. For the home, pick up glassware, dish towels, home fragrances, cards, gifts, and tea-time items. The coolest part of the store is Stitch at Niche, a curated fabric shop and project space, where you can buy striking textiles by the yard, unique buttons and trims, and DIY kits for embroidery, tapestry weaving, and cross-stitch. ✉ *302 Pearl Pkwy., Suite 112, Historic District* ☎ *210/437–0239* 🌐 *www.nicheatpearl.com.*

Rancho Diaz

HOUSEWARES | You'll find vintage and modern pieces here from Texas, Mexico, and all over the world. Owners Ginger and Mario Diaz opened Rancho Diaz as an eclectic, artisan-inspired home decor store with unique handcrafted items for design enthusiasts. Categories include terra-cotta planters and vases, upscale pet items, Christmas and Day of the Dead decor, and greeting and note cards. An exciting aspect of the store is that it carries the Tex Mex Dance Party Collection, curated and collected by former folk arts administrator and native Texan Rose Reyes. Her home decor brand focuses on vintage handmade objects and art with a Texas/Mexican flair. ✉ *303 Pearl Pkwy., Suite 101, Historic District* ☎ *210/670–5509* 🌐 *www.ranchodiaz.com.*

Ten Thousand Villages

OTHER SPECIALTY STORE | This is one of those stores you visit when you can't seem to find the right gift. As part of a network of over 390 U.S. retail outlets, they showcase unique, fair-trade products from more than 130 artisan groups in about 38 countries. Their selection is staggering, and the categories seem endless: accessories, jewelry, indoor and outdoor home decor, textiles, baskets, stationery, drinkware, tabletop, linens, birdhouses, garden, bath and body, and gifts for everyone from the wellness guru to the foodie. ✉ *302 Pearl Pkwy., Suite 114, Historic District* ☎ *210/444–1393* 🌐 *www.tenthousandvillages.com.*

★ **The Twig Book Shop**

BOOKS | **FAMILY** | This longtime beloved independent bookstore has been part of San Antonio's literary world since 1972, residing in several neighborhoods before landing at the Pearl. The large and well-stocked store has thousands of books in all subjects as well as cards and gift items. It hosts regular author-signing events for local and national writers as well as a weekly children's story time. Ask the very helpful and knowledgeable staff about the latest and best independent and mainstream bestsellers. ✉ *306 Pearl Pkwy., Unit 106, San Antonio* ☎ *210/826–6411* 🌐 *www.thetwig.com.*

King William Historic District

In the late 19th century, leading German merchants settled in what is now the 25-block King William Historic District south of downtown. Today the area's Victorian mansions, set in a quiet, leafy neighborhood, are a pleasure to behold. Madison, Guenther, and King William Streets are particularly pretty for a stroll or drive. Architecture and history buffs from all over visit this area to tour the homes that have been converted to museums or are otherwise open to visitors. This district is part of Southtown, an emerging area gaining acclaim as an eclectic arts, dining, and entertainment center.

Sights

Blue Star Arts Complex

ARTS CENTER | **FAMILY** | At this popular and diverse arts center, you can enjoy several restaurants and bars and pay a visit to Blue Star Contemporary, the longest running contemporary art venue in San Antonio. The complex also houses individual galleries and art houses. You can bike or run along the river, too. Admission to the complex is free, but individual venues may charge a fee. ✉ *1414 S. Alamo St., King William Historic District* ☎ *210/354–3775* 🌐 *bluestarartscomplex.com.*

Steves Homestead

HISTORIC HOME | This 1876 Victorian home is one of the few in the King William Historic District open for touring. Not only was its eclectic architecture—a blend of French Second Empire and Italian Villa styles—copied by other well-to-do San Antonians, but the estate was the city's first to have a telephone (1881) and among the first to install electric lights (1894). Completed in 1876, the house, occupied by lumber magnate Edward Steves, also has a slate mansard roof and delicate floral stenciling on the ceilings. The home is set up as it would have looked at the time it was occupied, with the same fixtures. Admission includes a self-guided tour. ✉ *509 King William St., King William Historic District* ☎ *210/224–6163* 🌐 *www.saconservation.org* 🎟 *$10* 🕑 *Closed weekdays.*

Villa Finale Museum & Gardens

HISTORIC HOME | This former home of San Antonio preservationist and collector Walter Mathis (who is widely recognized as the catalyst for the revitalization of the King William neighborhood in the

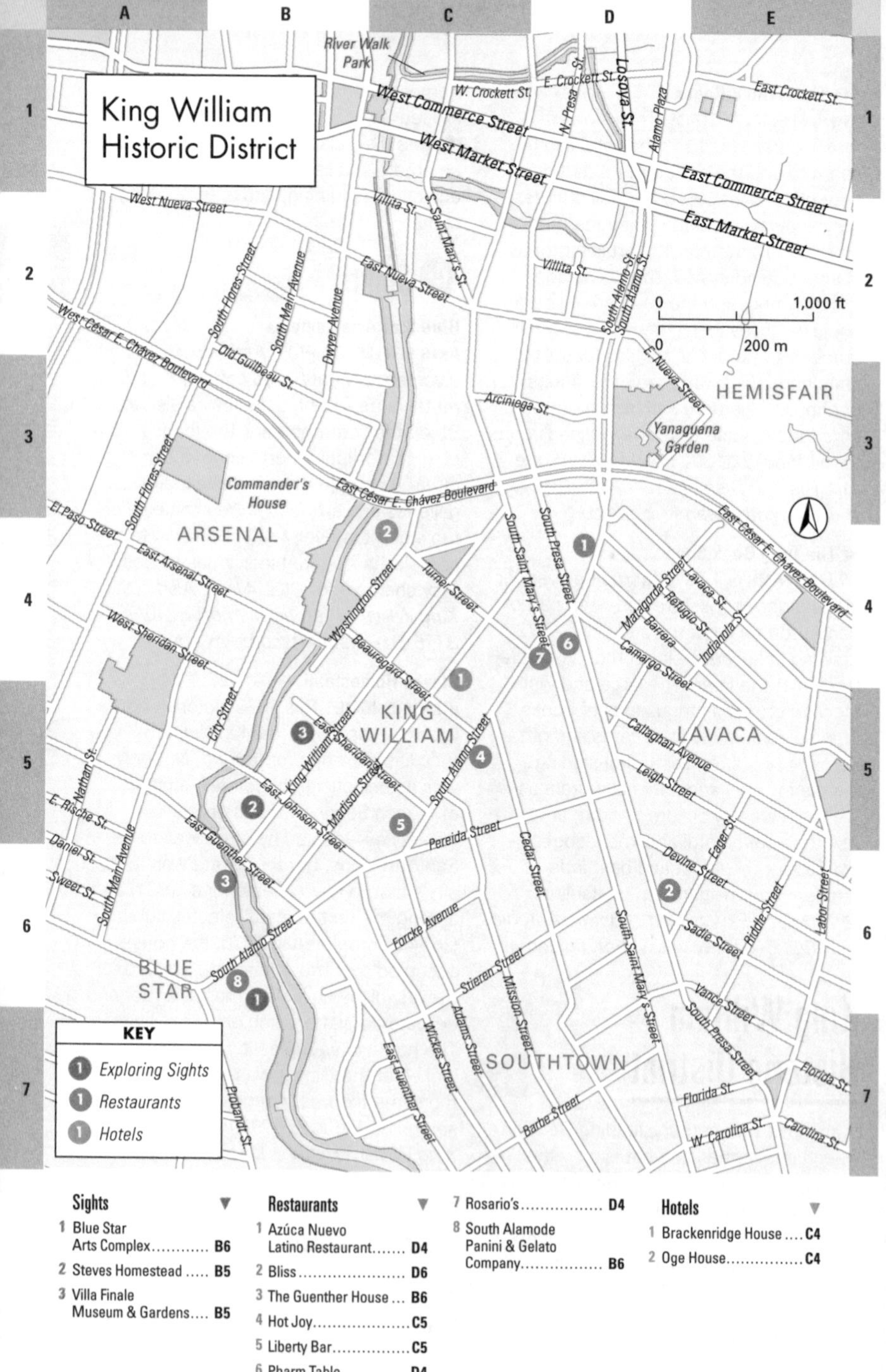

Sights

1 Blue Star Arts Complex **B6**

2 Steves Homestead **B5**

3 Villa Finale Museum & Gardens.... **B5**

Restaurants

1 Azúca Nuevo Latino Restaurant....... **D4**

2 Bliss **D6**

3 The Guenther House ... **B6**

4 Hot Joy.................... **C5**

5 Liberty Bar................ **C5**

6 Pharm Table **D4**

7 Rosario's................. **D4**

8 South Alamode Panini & Gelato Company................. **B6**

Hotels

1 Brackenridge House **C4**

2 Oge House................ **C4**

late 1960s) is not only a National Trust for Historic Preservation site but also a San Antonio treasure. Villa Finale is home to more than 13,000 pieces of fine and decorative art, including what is believed to be one of the most complete collections of Napoleonic materials. Museum admission includes a self-guided tour, and staff are available to answer questions. There is no fee to see the gardens. ✉ *401 King William St., King William Historic District* ☎ *210/223–9800* 🌐 *www.villafinale.org* 🎟 *$10* 🕑 *Closed Sun. and Mon.*

Restaurants

Azúca Nuevo Latino Restaurant

$$ | LATIN AMERICAN | FAMILY | If you want something different from San Antonio's usual Mexican or Tex-Mex offerings, venture south to find festive fare here hailing from the Caribbean, Spain, and South and Central America. Executive chef Rene Fernandez mixes up flavors and styles *con pasion*. Start with an appetizer sampler (five different apps) and move on to seed-crusted ahi tuna or meats basted with chimichurri , a tangy basil sauce. **Known for:** Authentic Latin cuisine; great bar selection; live music and dancing weekend nights. $ *Average main: 21* ✉ *709 S. Alamo St., King William Historic District* ☎ *210/225–5550* 🌐 *www.azuca.net* 🕑 *Closed Sun. No lunch.*

Bliss

$$$$ | AMERICAN | Chef-owner Mark Bliss and his wife Lisa opened this spot in a former filling station in 2012, and since then it has just gotten better. The cuisine is contemporary American, and that can mean custom charcuterie as well as delectable entrées of seafood (maybe scallops, monkfish, or halibut), game (quail or rabbit), and beef. **Known for:** true chef's table in the kitchen for up to 10 diners; regularly changing menu; exceptional service. $ *Average main: 42* ✉ *926 S. Presa St., King William Historic District* ☎ *210/225–2547* 🌐 *www.foodisbliss.com* 🕑 *Closed Sun. and Mon. No lunch.*

★ The Guenther House

$ | CAFÉ | FAMILY | This popular restaurant is housed in a stately 1860 home built by the founder of Pioneer Flour Mills. Breakfast is served all day, and options like fluffy Pioneer Brand biscuits, breakfast tacos, Southern sweet cream waffles, and delectable pastries are half the reason to eat here. **Known for:** beautiful historic setting with gorgeous decor; freshly baked pastries and biscuits; on-site store selling baking mixes and gift sets. $ *Average main: $13* ✉ *205 E. Guenther St., King William Historic District* ☎ *210/227–1061* 🌐 *www.guentherhouse.com* 🕑 *Closed Mon. and Tues. No dinner.*

★ Hot Joy

$$ | ASIAN FUSION | Nationally acclaimed Hot Joy has an eclectic menu that occasionally calls for an adventuresome spirit. You can try a Mexican twist on Asian fare like *migas* fried rice or pozole verde ramen, or go for the consistent standouts like the twice-fried crab wings—chicken wings fried in crab fat. **Known for:** stylish, vibrant decor; authentic Spam fried rice; cash-only policy. $ *Average main: 16* ✉ *1014 S. Alamo St., King William Historic District* ☎ *210/368–9324* 🌐 *www.hotjoysa.com* 🕑 *No lunch weekdays* 💳 *No credit cards.*

Liberty Bar

$$ | AMERICAN | FAMILY | Formerly a convent, this historic pink building now offers an eclectic, something-for-everyboy menu that includes sourdough pizzas, homemade fettuccini, and hearty entrees like pot roast and grilled salmon. The bar has seasonal cocktails, wines, and draft beer in bottles and cans. **Known for:** hip, funky, friendly vibe; housemade bread and pastries; fun weekend brunch. $ *Average main: $20* ✉ *1111 S. Alamo St., King William Historic District* ☎ *210/227–1187* 🌐 *www.liberty-bar.com* 🕑 *Closed Tues. and Wed.*

Did You Know?

While King William is filled with historic homes, most are still active residences, which means you can only visit a handful of them. The Steves Homestead is one such property; it was actually the city's first home to have a telephone.

Pharm Table

$$ | **VEGETARIAN** | **FAMILY** | On a mission to reinvent health food into something more flavorful and inspiring, Pharm Table's plant-forward cuisine uses locally sourced produce with no dairy, wheat, refined sugar, or processed foods anywhere on the menu. To that end, Pharm Table incorporates smaller portions of clean animal proteins with an emphasis on nutrient-dense foods. **Known for:** organic, local, and gluten-free dishes; emphais toward antiinflammatory eating; plant-forward menu. *Average main: 16* ✉ *611 S. Presa St., King William Historic District* ☎ *210/802–1860* 🌐 *www.pharmtable.com* ⏱ *Closed Mon. and Tues.*

Rosario's

$$ | **MEXICAN** | **FAMILY** | A fitting gateway to Southtown, this vibrant, colorful spot has contemporary decor enhanced by striking paintings from local artists. Since 1992, Rosario's has been serving authentic, crowd-pleasing Mexican favorites like chicken chipotle, enchiladas, and tender tips of beef tongue. **Known for:** lively, colorful setting; some of the best margaritas in the city (that you can even get to-go); extensive menu of Mexican classics. *Average main: $15* ✉ *910 S. Alamo St., King William Historic District* ☎ *210/223–1806* 🌐 *www.rosariossa.com* ⏱ *Closed Mon.*

South Alamode Panini & Gelato Company

$ | **ICE CREAM** | A cute place with top-notch gelato and panini, fresh and handmade are the best words to describe the items here, from the gelato to the pickles and mayonnaise. They import their meats and cheeses from Italy and so far have created more than 125 flavors of gelato, although they only rotate 20 flavors a day. **Known for:** delicious paninis; generous services of handmade gelato; inventive flavor combos. *Average main: 5* ✉ *Blue Star Arts Complex, 1420 S. Alamo St., King William Historic District* ☎ *210/788–8000* 🌐 *www.southalamodepaniniandgelato.com* ⏱ *Closed Mon.*

Hotels

Brackenridge House

$$ | **B&B/INN** | The first bed-and-breakfast in the King William Historic District, Brackenridge House has a two-story veranda overlooking a tree-lined street. **Pros:** beautiful decor; reasonably priced for a very sought-after spot; all rooms have mini-refrigerator. **Cons:** can be difficult to book, especially at peak tourist times; continental breakfast only; rooms are smallish. *Rooms from: $149* ✉ *230 Madison St., King William Historic District* ☎ *210/271–3442* 🌐 *www.brackenridgehouse.com* *6 rooms* *Free Breakfast.*

★ Oge House

$$ | **B&B/INN** | This gorgeous bed-and-breakfast sits on 1½ acres that back up to a quiet section of the river running through the King William Historic District. **Pros:** attentive staff; exquisitely decorated; perfect romantic getaway. **Cons:** River Walk and downtown area not within easy walking distance; historic decor not for everyone; only continental breakfast on-site for extra $7/person. *Rooms from: $189* ✉ *209 Washington St., King William Historic District* ☎ *210/223–2353* 🌐 *www.nobleinns.com/oge.html* *19 rooms* *No Meals.*

Nightlife

Azúca

BARS | On Friday and Saturday night, come to Azúca to put some salsa or merengue in your step. When you aren't dancing, you'll be sipping on a Latin or specialty cocktail. A full dinner menu and more than 15 types of mojitos are available, too. ✉ *709 S. Alamo St., King William Historic District* ☎ *210/225–5550* 🌐 *www.azuca.net.*

Within Brackenridge Park, you'll find plenty of top attractions like the serene Japanese Tea Garden.

Alamo Heights and Brackenridge Park

The area north of downtown (but south of the airport) is known as Alamo Heights, an incorporated city within San Antonio in Bexar County. This affluent residential neighborhood contains an abundance of restaurants, shops, and cultural establishments as well as the lush, locally loved (and much used) Brackenridge Park.

Northwest of downtown and southwest of Alamo Heights, the Monte Vista Historic District encompasses 100 blocks and features homes from the turn of the 19th century, when San Antonio's "Gilded Age" brought affluent residents to the area. Dozens of architectural styles define the homes; among them are beaux arts, Craftsman, Dutch Colonial, Georgian, Greek Revival, Italianate Renaissance, Mediterranean, Mission, Modern, Neoclassical, Prairie School, Pueblo Revival, Queen Anne, Ranch, Tudor, and Victorian. The entire district is on the National Register of Historic Places, and today shops and restaurants join residences on the quiet, tree-shaded streets.

Sights

★ Brackenridge Park

CITY PARK | FAMILY | Beloved Brackenridge Park has been a big part of San Antonians' lives for more than a century. The 343-acre riverside park makes an excellent setting for a picnic or a stroll, with about 3 miles of walking trails, public art, softball fields, a municipal golf course, concessions, and sights like the Japanese Tea Garden and the San Antonio Zoo. Take a 2-mile ride around the park on a miniature train that runs daily; buy tickets at the Train Depot. The mission of the Brackenridge Park Conservancy is to work as a steward of and an advocate for the park, enhancing and protecting its natural, historic, recreational, and educational resources. One of its

Alamo Heights and Brackenridge Park
A
B
C
D
E
F
1
2
3
4
5
6
7
8
9
Basse Road
McCullough Avenue
El Monte Boulevard
Lovera Boulevard
Blanco Road
West Hermine Boulevard
West Thorain Boulevard
281
McAllister Freeway
Devine Road
West Mandalay Drive
West Mariposa Drive
Beacon Avenue
San Pedro Avenue
Howard Street
OLMOS PARK
West Wildwood Drive
West Hermosa Drive
Clower Street
Alametos
Lee Hall Street
Edison Drive
Fresno Drive
McIlvaine St.
Parklane Drive
Stanford Drive
Luther Drive
Breeden Street
Camey Street
Belvidere Dr.
Primera Dr
Santa Monica St.
East Olmos Drive
West Olmos Drive
Westwood Drive
Melrose Place
East Melrose Dr.
Elmwood Drive
Thelma Drive
West Norwood Ct.
W. Norwood Ct.
West Ridgewood Ct.
W. Ridgewood Ct.
West Hildebrand Ave.
East Hildebrand Avenue
West Lullwood Ave.
Belknap Place
Shook Avenue
West Rosewood Ave.
West Hollywood Ave.
West Lynwood Ave.
Bushnell Ave.
West Elsmere Pl.
Fulton Avenue
West Gramercy Place
West Gramercy Pl.
West Kings Highway
West Summit Avenue
West Agarita Ave.
West Mulberry Ave.
West Huisache Ave.
North Main Ave.
Michigan Avenue
Grant Avenue
Ripley Avenue
North Flores Street
West Magnolia Ave.
West Mistletoe Ave.
Aganier Avenue
MIDTOWN
West Woodlawn Ave.
West Craig Place
West Russell Place
Fredericksburg Rd
West French Place
West Ashby Place
West Courtland Place
West Dewey Place
Ogden Street
San Pedro Springs Park
TOBIN HILL
E. Josephine St.
W. Myrtle St.
East Myrtle Street
East Park Avenue
East Evergreen Street
PEARL
KEY
Exploring Sights
Restaurants
2
6
9
10
11
13

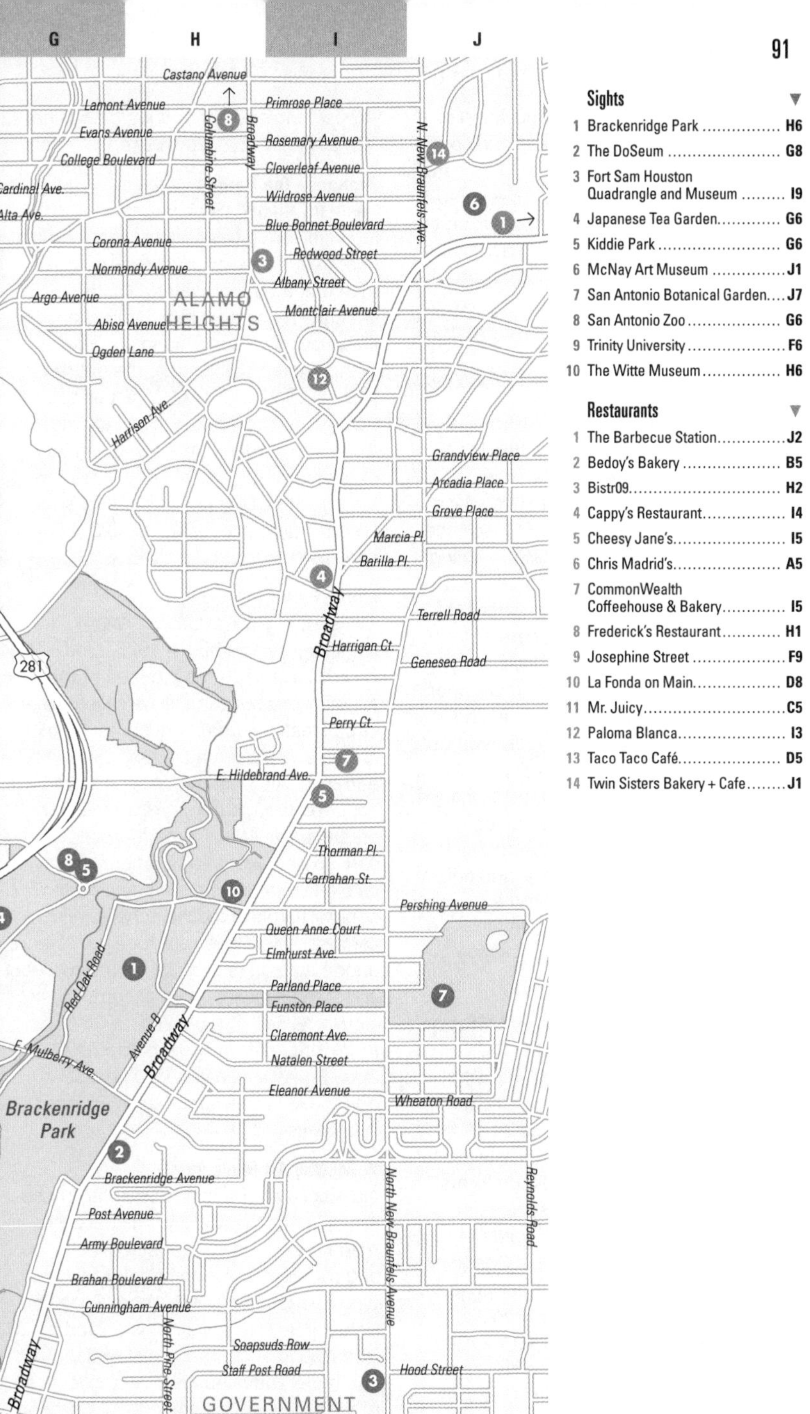

Sights

1 Brackenridge Park **H6**
2 The DoSeum **G8**
3 Fort Sam Houston Quadrangle and Museum **I9**
4 Japanese Tea Garden............. **G6**
5 Kiddie Park **G6**
6 McNay Art Museum **J1**
7 San Antonio Botanical Garden.... **J7**
8 San Antonio Zoo **G6**
9 Trinity University **F6**
10 The Witte Museum................ **H6**

Restaurants

1 The Barbecue Station..............**J2**
2 Bedoy's Bakery **B5**
3 Bistr09.............................. **H2**
4 Cappy's Restaurant................. **I4**
5 Cheesy Jane's....................... **I5**
6 Chris Madrid's...................... **A5**
7 CommonWealth Coffeehouse & Bakery............ **I5**
8 Frederick's Restaurant........... **H1**
9 Josephine Street **F9**
10 La Fonda on Main................. **D8**
11 Mr. Juicy.............................**C5**
12 Paloma Blanca...................... **I3**
13 Taco Taco Café..................... **D5**
14 Twin Sisters Bakery + Cafe........**J1**

numerous projects is the renovation of the Sunken Garden Theater, including the preservation of the historic amphitheater and its backstage facilities, redesigned landscaping, and more. The park is on the National Register of Historic Places and is a Texas State Antiquities Landmark. ✉ *3700 N. St. Mary's St., Alamo Heights* ☎ *210/207–7275* 🌐 *www.brackenridgepark.org* 🎫 *Free.*

The DoSeum

CHILDREN'S MUSEUM | FAMILY | If your kids are bored of the Alamo, head to the DoSeum, where they can explore 60,000 square feet of interactive space in galleries connected to STEM (science, technology, engineering, math) learning and discovery, along with the arts and literacy. Exhibits are geared to ages under 11, but even grown-ups will get a kick out of the Semmes Foundation Spy Academy and the beautiful Big Outdoors section, with Art Yard, Solar Tree, and WaterWorks. Visitors 18 or older without children are welcome, but will be asked at entry to present a valid driver's license and to submit to a brief automated background check. The DoSeum Store features apparel, books, gifts, and educational toys and games. ✉ *2800 Broadway, Alamo Heights* ☎ *210/212–4453* 🌐 *www.thedoseum.org* 🎫 *$14; free 1st Tues. of month 5:30–7:30 pm.*

Fort Sam Houston Quadrangle and Museum

MILITARY SIGHT | FAMILY | Visit this U.S. Army military history museum to learn the story of Fort Sam Houston from the late 19th century to the present. It's filled with exhibits about the site's early days, with displays that include old uniforms, firearms, vehicles, and personal papers, which you can see on a self-guided tour. The museum is located in the Quadrangle, which was once an outdoor prison and now where dozens of peacocks, deer, ducks, and other wildlife roam freely. Fort Sam Houston is a National Historic Landmark. ✉ *1405 E. Grayson St., Alamo Heights* ☎ *210/221–1886* 🌐 *quadrangle-fort-sam-houston.business.site* 🎫 *Free* 🕓 *Closed weekends.*

Japanese Tea Garden

GARDEN | FAMILY | Step into this lovely, lush, flowering oasis within Brackenridge Park that was originally a rock quarry. A man-made 60-foot waterfall is the focus, along with beautiful rock bridges and walkways over and around lily ponds with hundreds of koi fish. The entire place is filled with photo ops perfect for Instagram. The Jingu House café at the top of the garden offers a wide variety of teas and light lunch fare. ✉ *Brackenridge Park, 3853 N. Saint Mary's St., Alamo Heights* ☎ *210/212–8423* 🌐 *www.saparksfoundation.org* 🎫 *Free.*

Kiddie Park

AMUSEMENT PARK/CARNIVAL | FAMILY | Originally established in 1925, Kiddie Park is now located on the grounds of the San Antonio Zoo but can still be called America's oldest children's amusement park. It has a separate entrance next to the zoo's entrance. Although modern updates have occurred though the years, Kiddie Park preserves its 1920s style that made the park so popular for generations, like with its old-fashioned Ferris wheel and the popular hand-carved Herschell-Spillman carousel. Most rides are for ages 12 and under, but adults can ride on the carousel and flying saucers when accompanying a child. ✉ *San Antonio Zoo, 3903 N. St. Mary's St., Alamo Heights* ☎ *830/773–3603* 🌐 *www.kiddiepark.com* 🎫 *$3 per ride; $14 unlimited rides* 🕓 *Closed weekdays.*

★ McNay Art Museum

ART MUSEUM | The first modern art museum in Texas, the McNay was once the magnificent home of artist, collector, and oil heiress Marion Koogler McNay, who bequeathed her 24-room Spanish Colonial Revival–style mansion and its 23 landscaped acres to the city of San Antonio. It currently houses an art collection of works by Paul Gauguin, Paul Cézanne, Henri Matisse, Pablo Picasso, Vincent

The McNay Art Museum was the first modern art museum in Texas when it opened in 1954.

Van Gogh, and more, for a total of about 22,000 works. The museum also houses the Tobin Collection of Theatre Arts. Robert Tobin was a San Antonio philanthropist who assembled a world-renowned 12,000-item collection chronicling theater history. Custom tours are available for a variety of group sizes, ages, and interests. ✉ *6000 N. New Braunfels Ave., Alamo Heights* ☎ *210/824–5368* 🌐 *www.mcnayart.org* 🎫 *$20; free Thurs. 4–9 pm and 1st Sun. of every month noon–5 pm* ⏲ *Closed Mon. and Tues.*

San Antonio Botanical Garden

GARDEN | **FAMILY** | Step into 38 acres of formal gardens, wildflower-spangled meadows, native Texas vegetation, fascinating historical structures, and diverse sections designed to educate and delight nature lovers at the San Antonio Botanical Garden. Here you can walk on 11 acres of Texas native trails with more than 250 plant species representing three distinct regions of Texas. The stunning centerpiece of the garden is the Lucile Halsell Conservatory, a unique collection of five exhibit rooms. A self-guided tour of the climate-controlled conservatory takes visitors through plants and flowers found in different worldwide environments from the desert to the tropics. Other highlights include the Zachry Foundation Culinary Garden, which promotes healthy food choices and encourages visitors to participate in planting, harvesting, and preparing fresh fruits and vegetables. The Kumamoto En, a gift from San Antonio sister-city Kumamoto, is a serene, authentic Japanese garden with stone walks and water features. The Family Adventure Garden encourages kids to experience more than a dozen fun spaces to run, climb, and splash. ✉ *555 Funston Pl., Alamo Heights* ☎ *210/536–1400* 🌐 *www.sabot.org* 🎫 *$16.*

★ **San Antonio Zoo**

ZOO | One of San Antonio's most popular attractions, the 56 acres—34 of which are open to the public—of the San Antonio Zoo house approximately 15,000 animals representing more than 900

To discover the wide range of plant species found in Texas, head to the San Antonio Botanical Garden.

species. The Africa Live exhibit comes complete with special circulation and filtration systems for a state-of-the-art underwater hippo and crocodile habitat where visitors can observe them along with African fish. The Tiny Tots Nature Spot is the first zoo exhibit in the nation designed specifically for children under 5 and their families to engage in interactive experiences with nature and animals. Lory Landing is an Australian rain forest environment home to hundreds of brightly colored, active, and curious lorikeets that engage with zoo visitors; cups of nectar are available for purchase at the nearby Lory Café to feed these playful birds. Check the website for a description of other experiences, such as behind-the-scenes tours and feeding experiences available for an additional fee. Current conservation efforts at the zoo's Center for Conservation and Research focus on fish, amphibians, reptiles, crustaceans, and insects. ✉ *Brackenridge Park, 3903 N. Saint Mary's St., Alamo Heights* ☎ *210/734–7184* 🌐 *sazoo.org* 🎫 *$30.*

Trinity University

COLLEGE | Situated to the west of Brackenridge Park, this nationally recognized private institution of higher education is known for its lush campus dotted with redbrick buildings and sparkling fountains, along with sweeping views of downtown. Trinity's curriculum is rooted in the liberal arts and sciences, with more than 110 majors and minors, more than 115 clubs and organizations, and 18 varsity athletic teams. If the timing is right, attend a show at the Ruth Taylor Theater or attend the Distinguished Lecture Series at Laurie Auditorium. ✉ *1 Trinity Pl., Monte Vista Historic District* ☎ *210/999–7011* 🌐 *www.trinity.edu.*

★ The Witte Museum

HISTORY MUSEUM | FAMILY | A treasure trove of Texas and regional history, art, heritage, natural history, and science, the Witte is one of the city's best museums. As you enter, walk through the H-E-B Lantern, where a replica of a giant Quetzalcoatlus overhead ushers visitors into the beginning of their journey into Texas

Deep Time. The Kittie West Nelson Ferguson People of the Pecos Gallery spans the entire second floor and focuses on the prehistoric hunter-gatherers of Texas. Other demonstrations include encounters with native Texas animals that make the Witte their home and exhibits on how the People of the Pecos created rock art that has survived thousands of years. The Bolner Family Museum Store has exclusive items inspired by the museum's collections and exhibitions. ✉ *Brackenridge Park, 3801 Broadway St., San Antonio* ☎ *210/357–1900* 🌐 *www.wittemuseum.org* 🎟 *$14; free Tues. 3–6 pm.*

Restaurants

The Barbecue Station

$ | **BARBECUE** | **FAMILY** | Though its former filling station location is inconspicuous—apart from the line of hungry patrons—this family restaurant meets any barbecue hankerings. Mouthwatering, dry-rubbed beef brisket, smoked turkey, pork ribs, pulled pork, and sausages are served with tangy sauce (on the side), pickles, and slices of white bread. **Known for:** authentic vintage setting; wood-smoked barbecue; family-owned. [$] *Average main: $12* ✉ *1610 N.E. Loop 410, Alamo Heights* ☎ *210/824–9191* 🌐 *www.barbecuestation.com* 🕓 *Closed Sun.*

Bedoy's Bakery

$ | **BAKERY** | **FAMILY** | Pick up fresh Mexican pastries from this long-standing neighborhood *panaderia* (bakery) in Monte Vista. They make all the traditional pan dulce plus novelty cakes and frosted cookies. **Known for:** family-owned since 1961; long lines on weekend mornings; huge variety of pastries that often sell out. [$] *Average main: 5* ✉ *803 W. Hildebrand Ave., Monte Vista Historic District* ☎ *210/736–2253* 🌐 *bedoysbakery.com.*

Bistr09

$$$ | **FRENCH** | A chic, upscale brasserie in the heart of Alamo Heights, Bistr09 serves French favorites that include lobster risotto, *poulet roti*, and seared tuna salad Nicoise. Family-style offerings are paella and roasted chicken, and don't miss the flourless chocolate cake for dessert. **Known for:** exceptional service; good happy-hour menu; French cuisine done right. [$] *Average main: 26* ✉ *6106 Broadway, Alamo Heights* ☎ *210/245–8156* 🌐 *www.bistr09.com* 🕓 *No lunch.*

Cappy's Restaurant

$$$ | **AMERICAN** | **FAMILY** | An Alamo Heights casual but upscale staple since 1977, Cappy's features exceptional menus of innovative dishes against a warm, two-level modern backdrop of brick architecture, tall windows, and pleasant outdoor seating. Well-prepared and presented dinner entrées include potato-crusted halibut, Wild Isles salmon with lobster mashed potatoes, and beef tenderloin with roasted fingerlings. **Known for:** consistently excellent food; extensive bar selection; weekend brunch. [$] *Average main: $24* ✉ *5011 Broadway, Alamo Heights* ☎ *210/828–9669* 🌐 *www.cappysrestaurant.com* 🕓 *Closed Mon.*

Cheesy Jane's

$ | **FAST FOOD** | **FAMILY** | For a smallish place, Cheesy Jane's has a surprisingly varied menu, with big burgers, milk shakes and malts, and nostalgic decor dominating this throwback to old-time malt shops. Flavors for shakes and malts—made with Cheesy Jane's ice cream—include plain vanilla, peppermint, Dreamsicle, chocolate peanut butter, amaretto-espresso, and more. **Known for:** big shakes and malts; good menu selection of burgers and sandwiches; retro-style atmosphere. [$] *Average main: $10* ✉ *4200 Broadway, Alamo Heights* ☎ *210/826–0800* 🌐 *www.cheesyjanes.com* 🕓 *Closed Mon.*

Chris Madrid's

$ | **BURGER** | A San Antonio burger institution since 1977, Chris Madrid's is synonymous with burgers. The six varieties of hamburger—which locals and tourists alike consider among the best anywhere—come in two sizes: the regular quarter-pound and the Macho half-pound. **Known for:** excellent burgers; family-friendly atmosphere; notable community involvement. $ *Average main: $10* ✉ *1900 Blanco Rd., North* ☎ *210/735–3552* 🌐 *www.chrismadrids.com* ⏲ *Closed Sun.*

CommonWealth Coffeehouse & Bakery

$ | **AMERICAN** | A French twist on the usual coffeehouse scene, friendly staff here serve up freshly baked bread and pastries in a hip, stylish location within a beautifully renovated historic home in Alamo Heights. The weekday menu offers breakfast and lunch favorites like croissants béchamel and croque madames, while the robust beverage menu has signature and seasonal coffee flavors, teas, and smoothies. **Known for:** excellent French pastries; vintage, comfortable vibe; perfect Saturday brunch menu. $ *Average main: 10* ✉ *118 Davis Court, Alamo Heights* ☎ *210/560–2955* 🌐 *www.commonwealthcoffeehouse.com* ⏲ *No dinner.*

Frederick's Restauant

$$$$ | **FRENCH FUSION** | Chef-owner Frederick Costa marries French and Asian cuisine here to create some fantastic fusion dishes in relaxing, romantic surroundings. Seafood is a standout at both lunch and dinner, with options that include Scottish salmon with soy glaze and sweet Thai chili barbecue sauce or wild-caught Alaska halibut with lemon butter and fennel. **Known for:** excellent service; French-Asian fine dining; warm ambience. $ *Average main: $36* ✉ *Dijon Plaza East, 7701 Broadway St., Alamo Heights* ☎ *210/828–9050* 🌐 *www.fredericksrestaurantsa.com* ⏲ *Closed Sun.*

Josephine Street

$$ | **STEAKHOUSE** | This Texas roadhouse is famous for dishing up steaks and whisky since 1979. In an early 1900s building on the outskirts of downtown, "Jo Street" is decidedly casual and friendly. **Known for:** homestyle food like chicken-fried steak; delicious peach cobbler for dessert; Texas roadhouse atmosphere. $ *Average main: $20* ✉ *400 E. Josephine St., Downtown* ☎ *210/224–6169* 🌐 *www.josephinestreet.com.*

★ **La Fonda on Main**

$$ | **MEXICAN** | Laying claim as San Antonio's oldest Mexican restaurant, La Fonda opened in 1932 and has had an ardent following ever since. The robust menu offers traditional Tex-Mex plus some dishes from the interior of Mexico. **Known for:** great hacienda-like ambience; tres leches cake for dessert; excellent Tex-Mex. $ *Average main: $20* ✉ *2415 N. Main Ave., Monte Vista Historic District* ☎ *210/733–0621* 🌐 *www.lafondaonmain.com* ⏲ *Closed Mon.*

Mr. Juicy

$ | **FAST FOOD** | **FAMILY** | You'll know this drive-through spot by its lime-green structure that practically glows in the distance, guiding you to what some are saying is quite possibly the best burger they've ever had. The menu is wonderfully simple: burgers, fries, and shakes, but it does it all very well. **Known for:** steak au poivre sauce, for extra fee; big juicy burgers; hand-cut fries. $ *Average main: 10* ✉ *3315 San Pedro Ave., Monte Vista Historic District* ☎ *210/994–9838* ⏲ *Closed Mon.*

Paloma Blanca

$$ | **MEXICAN** | **FAMILY** | A warm, almost clubby atmosphere lets you know to expect more than the typical Tex-Mex fare at this Alamo Heights mainstay since 1997. Tempting offerings as varied as grilled fillet of red snapper, enchiladas verdes (covered in green tomatillo salsa), posole (shredded pork and hominy), tacos *de Cameron* (grilled shrimp), and *pollo con mole* (chicken breast in authentic mole *de xico* sauce) are sure to please. **Known for:** upscale Mexican cuisine; classy, comfortable ambience; tortillas and other ingredients for sale to take home. $ *Average main: $20* ✉ *Cambridge Shopping Center, 5800 Broadway*

St., Alamo Heights ☎ *210/822–6151* 🌐 *www.palomablanca.net.*

Taco Taco Café

$ | **MEXICAN** | **FAMILY** | If you've never had a breakfast taco, this is the place to try it in San Antonio. Newbies may pause at the number of possibilities, including chorizo and egg, chilaquiles, and *migas* (eggs scrambled with fried tortilla strips, cheese, and peppers), but first-timers really can't go wrong with a basic potato and egg taco. **Known for:** breakfast and all-day tacos; lengua de res (beef tongue); long lines in the morning that move fast. 💲 *Average main: $10* ✉ *145 E. Hildebrand Ave., Monte Vista Historic District* ☎ *210/822–9533* 🌐 *www.tacotacocafesa.com.*

Twin Sisters Bakery + Cafe

$ | **AMERICAN** | **FAMILY** | This Alamo Heights standard has served fresh, healthy food since 1981. Regulars and visitors love it because it's a neighborhood spot with a tempting bakery case and a varied menu for breakfast and lunch, including some Mexican favorites. **Known for:** tasty baked goods and Mexican breakfasts; great location with free parking; friendly, attentive staff. 💲 *Average main: 10* ✉ *Sunset Ridge Shopping Center, 6322 N. New Braunfels Ave., Alamo Heights* ☎ *210/822–2265* 🌐 *www.tsbandc.com* ⏲ *Closed Sun. No dinner.*

Nightlife

Bar du Mon Ami

BARS | This quiet, cozy neighborhood bar is a favorite go-to for area locals. You'll get a greeting from pleasant bartenders and, on certain days, from a very sweet dog. The space has a chill, intimate atmosphere that's dimly lit and perfect for conversation. Experienced bartenders serve craft cocktails, wine, and beer. They don't serve food, but there is a restaurant next door. ✉ *4901 Broadway, Alamo Heights* ☎ *210/421–8681.*

Broadway 50/50

BARS | Built in 1935, this fun, casual place has been a staple of the Alamo Heights community for so long that most people can't remember when it wasn't there. The crowd is eclectic, although it skews younger, and it's a great place to hang out, have a cold adult beverage, listen to live music or karaoke, and watch sports. There's also a lunch and dinner menu—the burgers alone have their own devout following. The weekend brunch serves breakfast plates, sandwiches, tacos, French toast, and omelets. ✉ *5050 Broadway, Alamo Heights* ☎ *210/832–0050* 🌐 *www.broadway5050.com.*

Shopping

Alamo Quarry Market

SHOPPING CENTER | **FAMILY** | Look for the distinctive smokestacks at this open-air shopping, dining, and entertainment center (the area was once a cement factory). Today, Alamo Quarry Market includes a Regal movie theater complex and many standard mall stores, such as Old Navy, Whole Foods, and Banana Republic. This entire area actually offers a huge array of shopping. Quarry Village is across from Quarry Market, and the Shops at Lincoln Heights are close by at the intersection of Broadway and East Base Road. ✉ *255 E. Basse Rd., Alamo Heights* ☎ *210/824–8886* 🌐 *www.quarry-market.com.*

Central Market

SUPERMARKET | If you think a supermarket can't be a destination, think again. The only location of the chain in San Antonio (there are nine others in Texas), Central Market is both a foodie heaven and a popular gourmet grocery store in Alamo Heights. Among the many offerings, you'll find scratch-made baked goods, chef-prepared meals, a great wine selection, a fresh seafood counter, and an on-site tortilleria for fresh tortillas. Top off your finds with a fresh flower arrangement from the well-stocked floral center up front. An in-house cooking school provides classes (for a fee) in such areas as afternoon tea, autumn in Italy, sushi and sake party, make and take tamales, wines, and many more. Their very popular Hatch Chile Fest takes place every August. ✉ *4821 Broadway, Alamo Heights* ☎ *210/368–8600* 🌐 *www.centralmarket.com.*

Sloan/Hall

WOMEN'S CLOTHING | Upscale boutiques, especially in tony neighborhoods like Alamo Heights, can be intimidating, but there's no such vibe in this jewel of a find in the Uptown Alamo Heights Center. It's cozy space, but the multicategory store is comfortably filled with a wide variety of designer offerings in women's high-end fashion, perfumes, limited edition books, greeting cards, home accessories, gifts, and antiques. The fine artisan jewelry is irresistible—whatever you choose for that perfect gift, you will absolutely want one for yourself. Everything is beautifully displayed, and customer service is attentive and helpful. ✉ *Uptown Alamo Heights Center, 5424 Broadway, Alamo Heights* ☎ *210/828–7738* 🌐 *www.sloan-hall.com.*

Sunset and Co.

OTHER SPECIALTY STORE | **FAMILY** | Previously known as Sunset Ridge Home and Hardware, the name Sunset & Co. may be new, but it's the same wonderful place to browse to your heart's content. The store seems endless, brimming as it is with gifts and accessories for him and her, jewelry, bath and body products, men's hats, travel bags, clothing and accessories for babies and kids, and more. There's plenty for the home and kitchen, too, as well as hardware and outdoor items, like Weber grills, grilling accessories, coolers, and tool sets. They also offer services for glass-cutting, key-cutting, Miele vacuum repair, screen repair, paint color matching, and custom monogramming. ✉ *Sunset Ridge Shopping Center, 6438 N. New Braunfels Ave., Alamo Heights* ☎ *210/930–1717* 🌐 *www.sunsetandco.com.*

Activities

Brackenridge Golf Course

GOLF | This historic course was the first inductee of the Texas Golf Hall of Fame and is the oldest 18-hole course in the state, at 6,243 yards, par 71. Located in San Antonio's Brackenridge Park, it first opened for play in 1916, and is also the oldest municipal course in the city. Green fees include the use of a cart. Clubs are available to rent. Check the website for various discounts on different days and times. ✉ *Brackenridge Park, 2315 Avenue B, Alamo Heights* ☎ *210/226–5612* 🌐 *www.alamocitygolftrail.com/brackenridge-park-golf-course/* 🎫 *From $69.*

The Quarry Golf Course

GOLF | The historic Quarry Golf Course is 18 holes, 6,740 yards, par 71. The front nine here plays like a links-style course, with no trees and an ever-present breeze to deal with. The back nine, however, is set in a 100-year-old limestone quarry with 100-foot perimeters. Green fees range from $45 to $125 depending on day and time. Fees include cart and range balls. ✉ *444 E. Basse Rd., Alamo Heights* ☎ *210/824–4500* 🌐 *www.quarrygolf.com* 🎫 *From $45.*

Southside and the Missions

Unquestionably, the jewel of the Southside is the San Antonio Missions National Historical Park, home to four of the city's five missions (the fifth is the downtown Alamo), and part of a UNESCO World Heritage Site. The Southside is also home to the Mission Reach section of the San Antonio River Walk in its most natural state. Walk, bike, or paddle the 8-mile stretch along the river bank ecosystem.

Did You Know?

Mission San José is the largest of the San Antonio missions, and 80% of its interior and exterior are still original.

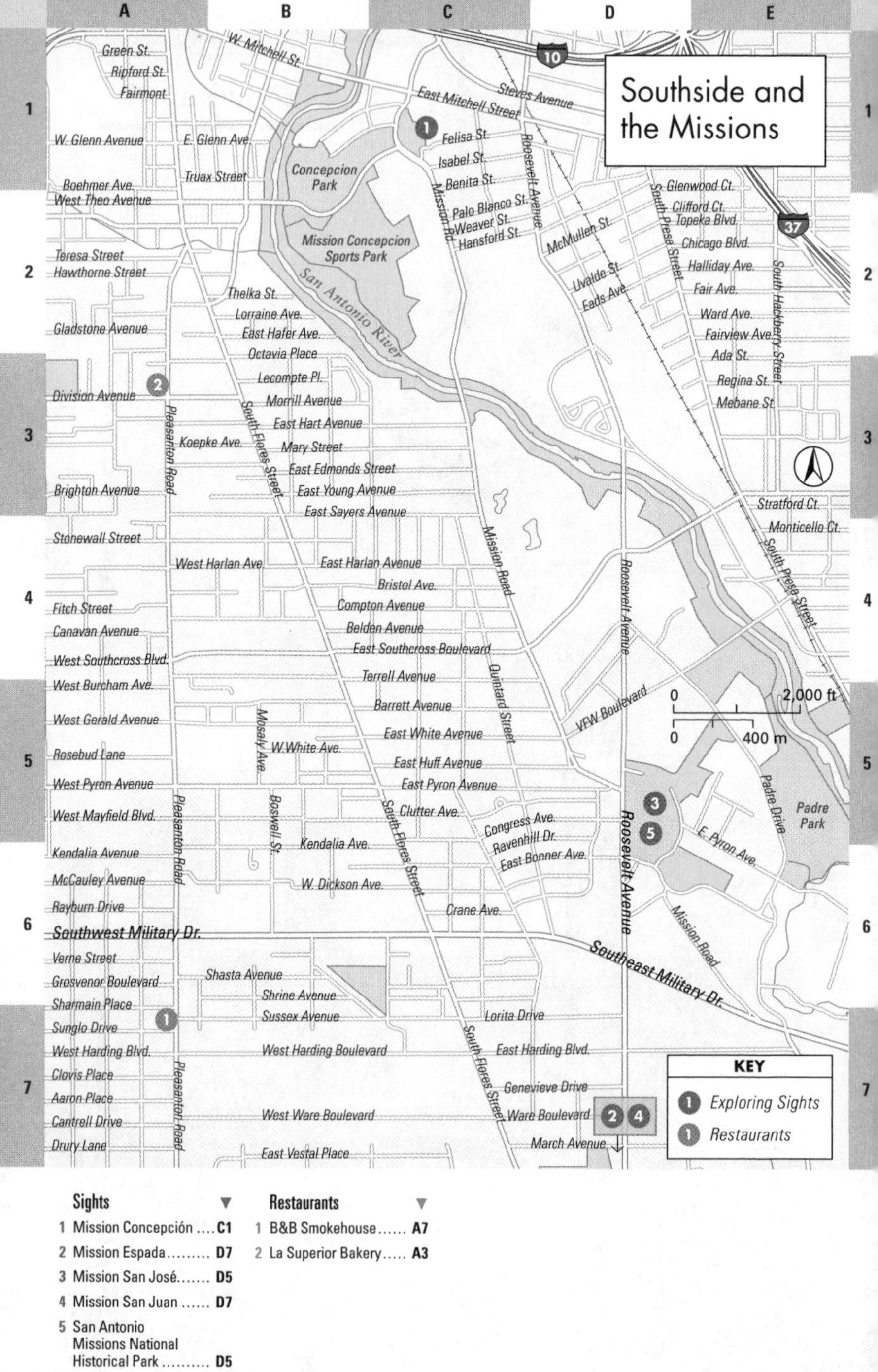

Sights

1 Mission Concepción **C1**
2 Mission Espada......... **D7**
3 Mission San José....... **D5**
4 Mission San Juan **D7**
5 San Antonio Missions National Historical Park **D5**

Restaurants

1 B&B Smokehouse...... **A7**
2 La Superior Bakery..... **A3**

Sights

★ San Antonio Missions National Historical Park

HISTORIC SIGHT | A National Park Service site and the only UNESCO World Heritage site in Texas, the San Antonio Missions National Historical Park is located on the Southside about 10 minutes south of downtown. Except for the Alamo, San Antonio's missions constitute the park and all four are active Catholic parishes to this day. Established along the San Antonio River in the 18th century by Franciscan friars, the missions stand as reminders of Spain's most successful attempt to extend its New World dominion northward from Mexico. The missions had the responsibility of converting the natives (primarily American Indians) to Catholicism. The missions were also centers of work, education, and trade. They represented the greatest concentration of Catholic missions in North America, and were the basis of the founding of San Antonio. The four missions from north to south are Mission Concepcion, Mission San Jose, Mission San Juan, and Mission Espada. They are roughly 2½ miles apart from one another, but driving between them is easy—they are connected by Mission Road and Mission Parkway—and there is free parking at each mission. Admission to all missions is free. The visitor center and store for the park district is at Mission San Jose. Pick up a map of the grounds there and ask about upcoming special programming; the park is regularly alive with community gatherings, artists working plein air, festivals, and more. ✉ *2202 Roosevelt Ave., Southside* ☎ *210/932–1001 visitor center* 🌐 *www.nps.gov/saan* 🎫 *Free.*

Mission Concepción

CHURCH | As the oldest unrestored stone church in the U.S., Mission Concepcion looks much like it did when it was dedicated in 1755. It is a fine example of Spanish Colonial architecture, and was known for its colorful frescoes, most of which are long gone. The most striking remaining fresco is the "Eye of God" on the ceiling of the library, a face from which rays of light emanate. ✉ *807 Mission Rd., Southside* ☎ *210/534–1540* 🌐 *www.nps.gov/saan* 🎫 *Free.*

Mission Espada

CHURCH | The southernmost mission, Acequia was named for St. Francis of Assisi, founder of the monastic order of Franciscans. The mission's full name is Mission San Francisco de la Espada. It includes an Arab-inspired aqueduct that was part of the missions' famous *acequia* water management system. ✉ *10040 Espada Rd.* ☎ *210/627–2021* 🌐 *www.nps.gov/saan* 🎫 *Free.*

★ Mission San José

CHURCH | At the center of the Mission Trail and the largest mission, Mission San Jose is known as the Queen of Missions. It's near the historical park's visitor center and it's the best place to catch a tour, led by a Texas Ranger or volunteer, because the history of San Jose is critical to understanding the story of the missions and San Antonio. The mission was founded in 1720 by Father Antonio Margil de Jesus, a prominent Franciscan missionary. The current church is 80% original as the outer wall, granary, convent, and Native American quarters were restored by the WPA in the 1930s. The Rose Window, sculpted in 1775, is located on the south wall of the church sacristy and considered one of the finest examples of Baroque architecture in North America. Start your tour at the stunning Mission San José, the "Queen of Missions." It's adjacent to the visitor's center, where a National Park Service ranger or docent illuminates the history of the missions. San José's outer wall, American Indian dwellings, granary, water mill, and workshops have been restored. Here you can pick up a driving map of the Mission Trail that connects San José with the other missions. ✉ *6701 San Jose Dr., Southside* ☎ *210/932–1001* 🌐 *wwwnps.gov/saan* 🎫 *Free.*

Did You Know?

The western entrance to the Mission Concepción was built to align with the sunset in a double illumination solar event close to or on August 15th, the feast day of the Assumption of Mary.

Mission San Juan

CHURCH | On a visit to Mission San Juan, you'll find a white exterior and Romanesque arches on on the outside while the inside has a serene chapel and a small museum. This mission once supplied all its own needs, from cloth to crops. The shaded Yanaguana Trail behind the mission winds along the low river-bottom land and provides a look at many indigenous plants along with wildlife like turtles, owls, and snakes. The San Antonio Food Bank has a partnership with the Farm at Mission San Juan to create a living demonstration farm fed by a historic *acequia* (community-operated water canal). ✉ *9101 Graf Rd., Southside* ☎ *210/534–0749* 🌐 *www.nps.gov/saan* 🎟 *Free.*

Restaurants

B & B Smokehouse

$ | **BARBECUE** | **FAMILY** | A continuation of a family-run Southside business since 1958, this version of B&B opened in 1984 and has a menu that goes beyond the usual barbecue fare. In addition to the typical brisket, smoked sausage, and pulled pork, they also offer burgers, club sandwiches, tacos, and a veggie chef salad that's fresh and flavorful. **Known for:** BBQ brisket, sausage, turkey, and pork; friendly, efficient service; dine-in or drive-thru options. $ *Average main: 13* ✉ *2619 Pleasanton Rd., Southside* ☎ *210/921–2745* 🌐 *www.bbsmokehouse.com* ⏲ *Closed Mon.*

La Superior Bakery

$ | **BAKERY** | **FAMILY** | This is a popular old-school neighborhood Mexican bakery. Their pastry-laden cases contain Mexican pan dulce staples like conchas, empanadas, and campechanas, plus cupcakes, cookies, donuts, apple fritters, pink cake, and fresh bread. **Known for:** neighborhood favorite; big selection of Mexican pastries that sell out quickly; good value. $ *Average main: 3* ✉ *519 Pleasanton Rd., Southside* ☎ *210/924–1616.*

Activities

Mitchell Lake Audobon Center

BIRD WATCHING | Bird-watchers worldwide come here to see the more than 300 species that visit each year. This 1,200-acre natural area is located on a natural migratory route and serves as a stopping point for thousands of birds annually. Purchase entry tickets on arrival or on the website. Tickets are also available for guided early-morning birding tours. The annual Migratory Bird Fest and Birdathon is celebrated every spring. The center has seasonal hours so call before visiting to verify they are open. ✉ *10750 Pleasanton Rd., Southside* ☎ *210/628–1639* 🌐 *mitchelllake.audubon.org* 🎟 *$5.*

North and Northwest

North and northwest San Antonio isn't just about luxury resorts and thrilling theme parks. There's a relaxing, bucolic feel to this side of town with natural wonders like Friedrich Wilderness Park and Government Canyon State Natural Area. Like all of San Antonio, it boasts every kind of restaurant, from mom-and-pop eateries to the finest of dining. For wildlife of another kind, there's championship shopping at The Shops at La Cantera and at The Rim.

Sights

★ **Morgan's Wonderland**

THEME PARK | **FAMILY** | The world's first theme park designed and built for individuals with special needs, 25-acre Morgan's Wonderland is completely wheelchair-accessible, with playgrounds, attractions, and rides specially built to accommodate wheelchairs, like the colorful carousel and the Whirling Wonder Ferris Wheel. Traditional swing areas also feature wheelchair swings. The Wonderland Express perimeter train ride gives an overview of Morgan's Wonderland and

Morgan's Inspiration Island, the latter with five tropic-themed splash pads and a Riverboat Adventure Ride that travels through a jungle setting. And because not everyone's wheelchair is suited for a watery environment, there are complimentary waterproof wheelchairs and protective accessories for guests. The inspiration for such an amazing place is Morgan Hartman, daughter of native San Antonian businessman and philanthropist Gordon Hartman and his wife Maggie. The Gordon Hartman Family Foundation pursues Gordon and Maggie's goal of helping people of all ages with special needs. Morgan Hartman is now 27 and is greeted like a rock-star when she visits her namesake park. Special needs children and adults are admitted to the park free of charge. Before planning a visit, call or check their website for seasonal hours and closings. ✉ *5223 David Edwards Dr., Northeast* ☎ *210/495–5888* 🌐 *www.morganswonderland.com* 🎫 *$19; free for anyone with special needs.*

★ Natural Bridge Caverns

CAVE | FAMILY | Thirty minutes north of downtown San Antonio, you can trek down 180 feet below the earth's surface for a half-mile walk through this beautiful, historic cavern system. Take the original Discovery Tour to explore the largest show cavern in Texas with its stalagmites, stalactites, flowstones, chandeliers, and soda-straw formations. The more adventurous (and physically fit) can take the Adventure Tour to get down and dirty (read: muddy) like a real spelunker. Caverns are cool with high humidity. Wear comfortable shoes with good traction. Trails can be wet, and climbing and descending stairs are involved. Tour prices can vary by date. Surface attractions include a four-level ropes course, seven zip rails, and climbing towers. Booking and buying ahead is recommended for cavern tours. ✉ *26495 Natural Bridge Caverns Rd., North* ☎ *210/651–6101, 210/651–6144* 🌐 *www.naturalbridgecaverns.com* 🎫 *$23.*

SeaWorld San Antonio

THEME PARK | The largest marine park in the United States, SeaWorld San Antonio consists of more than 250 acres where you can see shows and animal habitats and experience thrilling coasters and family-friendly rides. Shows include orcas, belugas, sea lions, otters, and Pacific white-sided dolphins, and there's also an immersive experience where you can get up close to belugas. The Aquatica water park (admission is separate from SeaWorld) offers a range of water rides and pools. The pricing structures for both parks vary seasonally and depend on if you purchase tickets in advance or at the entrance. Check the website or call for the latest prices. ✉ *10500 Sea World Dr., Northwest* ☎ *210/520–4732* 🌐 *www.seaworld.com* 🎫 *$79.*

★ Six Flags Fiesta Texas

AMUSEMENT PARK/CARNIVAL | FAMILY | Set within 100-foot-tall quarry walls, this amusement park features five themed sectors highlighting Texas's rich diversity, from the state's Mexican and German culture to its rip-roarin' Western past. Nine roller coasters are here, including Batman: The Ride, Boomerang Coast to Coaster, the hybrid wood/steel Iron Rattler, the spinning/twisting Pandemonium, the "spaghetti bowl" Poltergeist, the family-friendly Road Runner Express, Superman: Krypton Coaster (the largest steel coaster in Texas), and the Goliath, a 50-mph body-blasting suspended looping coaster. The Dare Devil Dive Flying Machines that imitate the maneuvers of acrobatic dogfights is the tallest ride of its kind in the world. There's also Scream, a 20-story tower-drop ride. The park has about 40 rides in all, and its Whitewater Bay water park is open seasonally. Rounding out the offerings are many excellent family-friendly live musical shows. ✉ *17000 W I–10, Northwest* ☎ *210/697–5050* 🌐 *www.sixflags.com/fiestatexas* 🎫 *$35.*

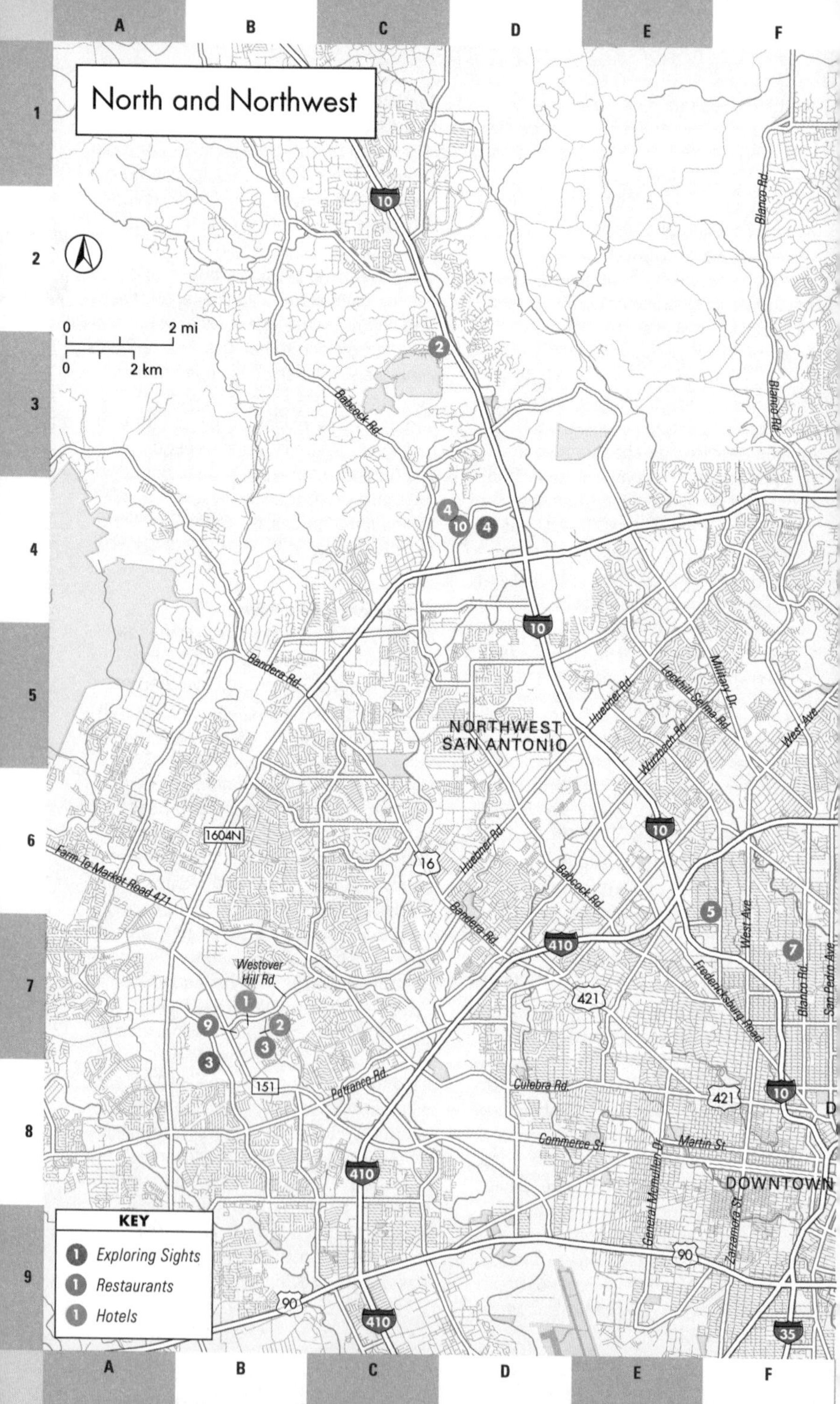

North and Northwest
A
B
C
D
E
F
1
2
3
4
5
6
7
8
9
0
2 mi
0
2 km
Babcock Rd.
Bandera Rd.
NORTHWEST
SAN ANTONIO
Huebner Rd.
Lockhill Selma Rd.
Military Dr.
Wurzbach Rd.
West Ave.
Blanco Rd.
1604N
Farm To Market Road 471
16
Babcock Rd.
Westover
Hill Rd.
421
151
Petranco Rd.
Culebra Rd.
Fredericksburg Road
San Pedro Ave.
Commerce St.
Martin St.
General Mcmullen Dr.
Zarzamora St.
DOWNTOWN
90
410
10
35
KEY
Exploring Sights
Restaurants
Hotels

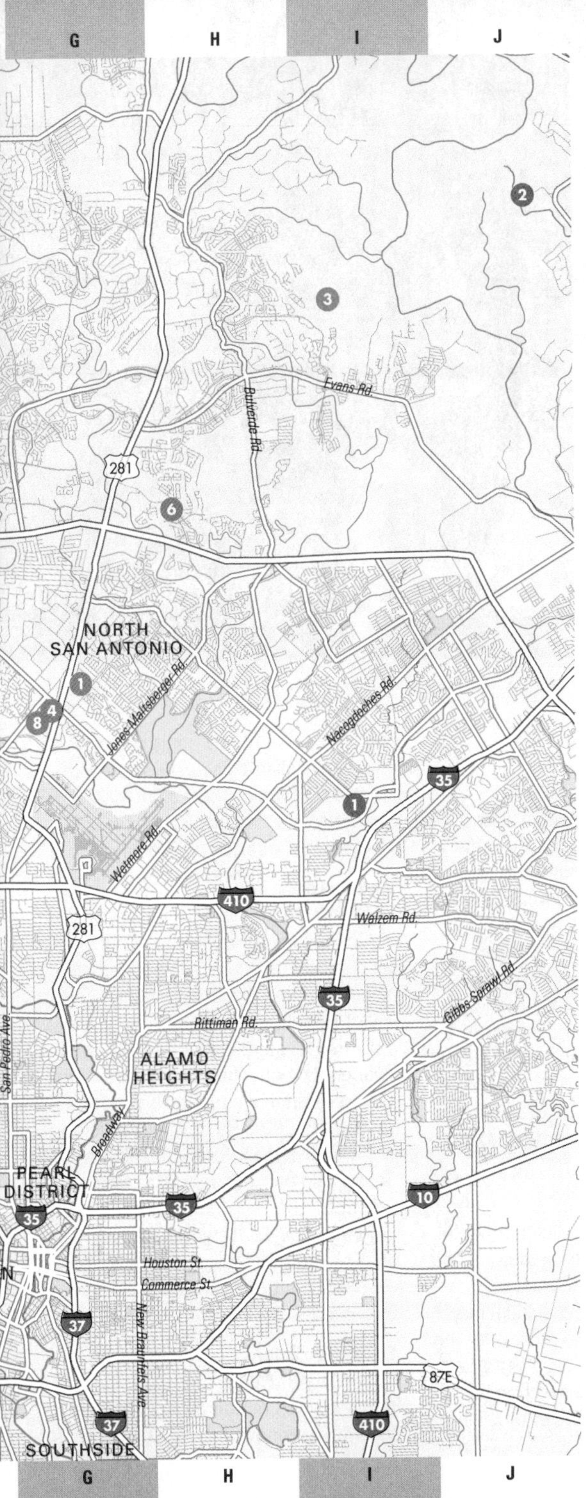

Sights

1 Morgan's Wonderland I5
2 Natural Bridge Caverns............ J1
3 SeaWorld San Antonio............ B8
4 Six Flags Fiesta Texas............. D4

Restaurants

1 Alamo Cafe G5
2 Aldo's Ristorante Italiano C3
3 Antlers Lodge B7
4 El Jarro de Arturo.................. G5
5 La Fogata Mexican Cuisine........ F6
6 La Hacienda de Los Barrios...... H3
7 Los Barrios F7
8 Magnolia Pancake Haus.......... G5
9 Rudy's Country Store & Bar-B-Q............................ B7
10 Signature D4

Hotels

1 Hilton San Antonio Hill Country Hotel.................. B7
2 Hyatt Regency Hill Country Resort and Spa..................... B7
3 JW Marriott San Antonio Hill Country Resort & Spa.......... I2
4 La Cantera Resort & Spa D4

Natural Bridge Caverns are the largest known caverns open to visitors in Texas.

Restaurants

Alamo Cafe

$$ | **MEXICAN** | **FAMILY** | A perennial favorite with locals, Alamo Cafe is far from the actual Alamo, but you'll still remember it for its fresh tortillas and no-frills approach to Mexican dishes. This is a good place to try fried jalapeño starters, sizzling fajitas, quesadillas, and puffy, soft, or crispy tacos. **Known for:** family-friendly atmosphere; vegetarian and gluten-free options; fajitas trio of beef, chicken, and shrimp. *Average main: $16 ✉ 14250 San Pedro Ave., Northwest ☎ 210/495–2233 🌐 www.alamocafe.com ⏲ Closed Mon.*

Aldo's Ristorante Italiano

$$$ | **ITALIAN** | **FAMILY** | Enjoy authentic Italian cuisine at this upscale restaurant. The warm and inviting space features a wide menu of appetizers, entrée salads, pasta, seafood, poultry, beef, and chops; try the salmon Pavarotti, the *quaglia all griglia* (quail), or the *brasato* (braised boneless prime short ribs). **Known for:** extensive wine list; nice happy hour; authentic northern Italian cuisine. *Average main: $28 ✉ Dominion Ridge Center, 22211 IH–10 W, Northwest ☎ 210/696–2536 🌐 www.aldossa.com ⏲ No lunch.*

Antlers Lodge

$$$$ | **AMERICAN** | Known for luxury takes on Texan fare—think venison posole, Texas charcuterie, and mole braised bison short rib—this elegant restaurant in the Hyatt Regency Hill Country Resort and Spa also has lighter options like Faroe Islands salmon. The centerpiece of the dining room is a huge chandelier with more than 500 sets of naturally shed antlers. **Known for:** exceptional service; Texas wild game; supporting farmers and artisans. *Average main: $42 ✉ Hyatt Regency Hill Country Resort and Spa, 9800 Hyatt Resort Dr., North/Northwest ☎ 210/520–4001 🌐 www.hyatt.com ⏲ Closed Sun. and Mon. No lunch.*

El Jarro de Arturo

$$ | **MEXICAN** | **FAMILY** | Since 1975, this family-owned restaurant has been a favorite for innovative Mexican cuisine.

It's tough to choose from the huge menu, with standout specials like mole enchiladas, tenderloin chipotle, and red snapper in a tequila sauce. **Known for:** huge food menu of Mexican classics; vegetarian-friendly items; popular lunch buffet. *Average main: $19* *San Pedro Sq., 13421 San Pedro Ave., North* *210/494–5084* *www.eljarro.com* *Closed Mon.*

La Fogata Mexican Cuisine

$$ | MEXICAN | FAMILY | The open and airy spaces of La Fogata's rambling, hacienda-style indoor dining areas plus its lush, tropical outdoor patio put you in the mood for the menu of authentic Mexican dishes to come. A top-shelf, hand-shaken margarita helps you relax and enjoy an enormous selection of options ranging from chicken mole to a rich, flavorful *calabacita con carne de puerco* (pork stew with fresh squash and corn). **Known for:** festive tropical atmosphere; extensive menu of traditional Mexican specialties; homemade tortillas. *Average main: $21* *2427 Vance Jackson Rd., Northwest* *210/340–1337* *www.lafogata.com.*

La Hacienda de Los Barrios

$$ | MEXICAN | FAMILY | It may feel like you're walking into a centuries-old hacienda at this enormous outpost just outside Texas Loop 1604, but the tacos, nachos, and enchiladas have a modern twist. If you can't decide what to choose, hedge your bets by going for the enchilada assortment—five delectable takes served with refried beans and guacamole salad. **Known for:** extensive homestyle Mexican menu; family-friendly atmosphere; margarita night on Wednesday. *Average main: $15* *18747 Redland Rd., North* *210/497–8000* *www.lahaciendabarrios.com* *Closed Mon.*

Los Barrios

$$ | MEXICAN | FAMILY | Chef Diana Barrios Treviño—a frequent guest on TV food and talk shows—oversees the kitchen at this family-run restaurant, known for its authentic gourmet Mexican dishes. Eat in the relaxed, casual patio dining atmosphere with lots of light. **Known for:** perfect chile relleno; homestyle Mexican comfort food; notable community involvement. *Average main: $20* *4223 Blanco Rd., North* *210/732–6017* *www.losbarriosrestaurant.com* *Closed Mon.*

Magnolia Pancake Haus

$ | AMERICAN | A much-loved breakfast institution, Magnolia prides itself on dishes made from fresh and wholesome ingredients. The fluffy buttermilk pancakes are a mainstay, but for something different, try the Bodega Bay omelet or Oma's puffed apple pancake made with Granny Smith apples and Haus secret spices, served with powdered sugar and European-style whipped cream. **Known for:** house-specialty Oma's puffed pancake; emphasis on fresh ingredients; long waits for breakfast. *Average main: $12* *606 Embassy Oaks, North* *210/496–0828* *www.magnoliapancakehaus.com* *No dinner.*

Rudy's Country Store & Bar-B-Q

$$ | BARBECUE | What looks like an old gas station is actually home to some of San Antonio's favorite barbecue. The wait to place your order is worth it once you bite into some tender brisket (their original "sause" is on the side) or smoked turkey dry-rubbed with flavor and cooked in wood-fired pits. **Known for:** vintage atmosphere; many barbecue meat options; tasty sides. *Average main: $14* *10623 Westover Hills Blvd., Northwest* *210/653–7839* *www.leonspringsbbq.com.*

★ **Signature**

$$$$ | FRENCH FUSION | South Texas meets the South of France doesn't sound like it should work, but it does, and beautifully, at chef Andrew Weissman's concept of a fine dining restaurant that blends French and Texan cuisines in seasonally sublime ways. Everything here is fresh, fresh, fresh, right down to the on-site garden of herbs and vegetables. **Known for:** menu that changes with the seasons; beautiful setting with great views; roasted pheasant hen-of-the-woods. *Average main: 38 ✉ La Cantera Resort & Spa, 16401 La Cantera Pkwy., Northwest ☎ 210/247–0176 🌐 www.signaturerestaurant.com ⏲ Closed Mon.*

Hotels

Hilton San Antonio Hill Country Hotel
$$ | **HOTEL** | A 15-minute drive northwest of downtown, you'll find this full-service resort at the base of Texas Hill Country; it's the official hotel of SeaWorld. **Pros:** good-size rooms; helpful staff; three outdoor pools. **Cons:** not close to downtown or the River Walk; no pets allowed; driving everywhere (except to SeaWorld) is a necessity. *Rooms from: $213 ✉ 9800 Westover Hills Blvd., Northwest ☎ 210/509–9800 🌐 www.hilton.com 227 rooms No Meals.*

★ Hyatt Regency Hill Country Resort and Spa
$$$ | **RESORT** | **FAMILY** | Step into relaxation at this sophisticated yet homey country resort with lots of shade—a key feature when the mercury soars during a San Antonio summer. **Pros:** multiple on-site dining options; good value for an expansive resort; very kid-friendly. **Cons:** possible highway noise; breakfast not included; not near downtown or the River Walk. *Rooms from: $319 ✉ 9800 Hyatt Resort Dr., Northwest ☎ 210/647–1234 🌐 www.hyatt.com 500 rooms No Meals.*

★ JW Marriott San Antonio Hill Country Resort & Spa
$$$$ | **RESORT** | **FAMILY** | Set among the bubbling streams and tree-covered hills of Cibolo Canyons, the JW Marriott San Antonio Resort & Spa is a magnificent family escape and a premier golf destination. **Pros:** excellent Lantana Spa; ; very family-friendly; two championship golf courses. **Cons:** parking lot a bit far from lobby; not close to downtown or the River Walk; daily resort fee charged per room. *Rooms from: $399 ✉ 23808 Resort Pkwy., Northwest ☎ 210/276–2500 🌐 www.marriott.com 1002 rooms No Meals.*

★ La Cantera Resort & Spa
$$$$ | **RESORT** | Make a list of the things you'd look for in a luxury, full-service resort, and chances are La Cantera has it. **Pros:** virtually every amenity you could ask for; the ultimate luxury retreat; superb Loma de Vida Spa. **Cons:** pricey valet parking; expensive; removed from downtown and the River Walk. *Rooms from: $449 ✉ 16641 La Cantera Pkwy., North ☎ 210/558–6500 🌐 www.lacanteraresort.com 496 rooms No Meals.*

Shopping

The Rim
MALL | A mixed-use lifestyle center of shops, dining, entertainment, and luxury residences, businesses at The Rim include Bass Pro Shops, Bakery Lorraine, Woodhouse Day Spa, Ulta Beauty, Nordstrom Rack, Panera Bread, and more. Find out current sales on the promotions tab of their website. *✉ 17703 La Cantera Pkwy., Northwest ☎ 210/641–1777 🌐 www.therimsa.com.*

The Shops at La Cantera
MALL | This upscale shopping center on La Cantera Parkway has something for everyone. Shop at standard mall stores, like Abercrombie & Fitch, 7 for All Mankind, Anthropologie, Apple, Banana Republic, and Barnes & Noble, as well as at higher-end retailers, such as Coach New York, Louis Vuitton, and Tiffany & Co. Plenty of dining options are here, too, from fast-casual on up. There are in-store cooking classes, pet nights with Santa, holiday showcases, and more. Find out about all their events on their website. *✉ 15900 La Cantera Pkwy., Northwest ☎ 210/582–6255 🌐 www.theshopsatlacantera.com.*

BASEBALL

Nelson W. Wolff Municipal Stadium

BASEBALL & SOFTBALL | FAMILY | Enjoy a night at the Nelson W. Wolff Municipal Stadium watching the San Antonio Missions, the Double-A affiliate of the San Diego Padres. The Missions play about 70 home games a year, from April through early September. As with any minor-league baseball team, expect lots of promotions, giveaways, and fun on-field activities during the game. Starting admission is $10 for a seat on the grassy "berm"; prices go up from there. Parking is $10. Look for weekday discounts on both tickets and parking. The Missions' mascot is Ballapeno (rhymes with jalapeño). Home to the Missions since 1994, "The Wolff" has a small-town ballpark feel with all the amenities. Concession stands serve up traditional ballpark fare like hot dogs, nachos, the Texas-born novelty Frito pie, and more, along with assorted beverages. The Fiesta Deck can be rented for groups, with buffet-style serving. Bleachers, individual seating, luxury suites, and the grassy berm in left field add up to a total of seating for 9,200. The Mission Team Shop sells caps, shirts, toys, and souvenirs. ✉ *Nelson W. Wolff Municipal Stadium, 5757 U.S. 90 W, Northwest* ☎ *210/675–7275* 🌐 *www.milb.com* 🎫 *$10.*

GOLF

Cedar Creek Golf Course

GOLF | Enjoy scenic views—and isn't that a big part of what golfing is all about?—while perfecting your swing at this beautifully designed course in the hills. Hazards include waterways and waterfalls. Standard green fees are $49 Monday through Thursday and $54 on weekends; the price includes a cart. Without a cart, the green fees are lower. Check the website for various discounts on different days of the week. This is an 18-hole regulation length course, range from 5,520 to 7,158 yards, par 72. ✉ *8250 Vista Colina, Northwest* ☎ *210/695–5050* 🌐 *www.alamocitygolftrail.com/cedar-creek-golf-course/* 🎫 *From $49.*

La Cantera Golf

GOLF | This golf resort offers 36 holes of championship golf at two outstanding courses: the 18-hole, 7,001-yard, par 72 Resort Course has scenic views of Six Flags Fiesta Texas and the Texas Hill Country. Designed by Jay Morrish and PGA tour pro Tom Weiskopf, it was a PGA tour stop for 15 years. The 18-hole, 6,926-yard, par 71 Arnold Palmer Course was designed by the legendary golfer, where the signature number 4 requires a long carry over a waterfall-fed lake at the lip of the green. Green fees range from $59 to $159. ✉ *La Cantera Resort & Spa, 16641 La Cantera Pkwy., North/Northwest* ☎ *210/558–4653* 🌐 *www.lacanteragolf-club.com* 🎫 *From $59.*

PARKS AND NATURAL PRESERVES

Friedrich Wilderness Park

NATURE PRESERVE | For locals, Friedrich Wilderness Park is a great close-to-home spot with more than 10 miles of hiking trails, a mere 20 miles from the Alamo on the northwest side of town near Six Flags Fiesta Texas. This 600-acre hilly haven for rare birds and orchids is a nesting site for two federally listed bird species: the black-capped vireo and the golden-cheeked warbler. As a protected area that minimizes impact on the environment, rollerblades, scooters, skateboards, and bicycles are not allowed. Bird-watchers from around the world are often spotted here. Some species are seasonal, such as blue jays (fall and winter), eastern meadowlarks (spring), red-winged blackbirds (spring and summer), scissor-tailed flycatchers (spring, summer, and fall), and double-crested cormorants (winter). You can see turkey vultures, finches, Carolina wrens, doves, northern woodpeckers, northern cardinals, mockingbirds, and more year-round. For trail conditions, check out their

Facebook or Twitter, call the park office, or go to Friends of San Antonio Natural Areas (🌐 *fosana.org*). ✉ *21395 Milsa Dr., North* ☎ *210/207–3780* 🌐 *www.sanantonio.gov* 🎫 *Free.*

Government Canyon State Natural Area
STATE/PROVINCIAL PARK | This 12,244-acre natural area about 26 miles from downtown is home to numerous varieties of trees and several species of rare birds, such as the golden-cheeked warbler. It also offers views of surrounding Bexar County and glimpses of San Antonio. Protected Habitat Area trails are open September through February, but other trails of varying difficulty are available year-round. There is a picnic area, a playground, camping, mountain-biking trails, nature/interpretive trails, and a visitor center/museum. The area is very popular, and reservations are recommended for both camping and day use. Reservations can be made online or by phone at the Texas State Parks Customer Service Center, 512/389–8900. ✉ *12861 Galm Rd., North* ☎ *210/688–9055, 512/389–8900 reservations* 🌐 *tpwd.texas.gov/state-parks/government-canyon* 🎫 *$6* 🕒 *Closed Tues.–Thurs.*

Chapter 4

AUSTIN

Updated by
Ramona Flume

Sights ★★★☆☆ | Restaurants ★★★★★ | Hotels ★★★★★ | Shopping ★★★★☆ | Nightlife ★★★★★

WELCOME TO AUSTIN

TOP REASONS TO GO

★ **Live Music:** Country, rock, punk, jazz, classical, pop, folk, and bluegrass—Austin is one of the best places in the country for live music, whether it's in one of its iconic music halls or famed festivals like Austin City Limits.

★ **Foodie Heaven:** Barbecue joints, Tex-Mex eateries, acclaimed international favorites, and more than 1,500 food trucks keep hunger at bay.

★ **The Great Outdoors:** A mild, sunny climate, lots of green space, miles of bike paths, and public swimming holes make it easy to stay active.

★ **Nightlife:** Whether you're looking to join the bachelor and bachelorette parties on Sixth Street or to explore the hip dives in east Austin, there are plenty of ways to keep the party going here.

1 Downtown with Sixth Street and Rainey Street. Located between Lady Bird Lake and the UT campus, Austin revolves around this vital axis of commerce, nightlife, history, and live music. The highly walkable area provides easy access to some of the best attractions in the capital.

2 Central Austin and the University of Texas. The main feature of this quaint area just north of downtown is the "Forty Acres" of the University of Texas, but there are heaps of classic neighborhood charms and hidden gems to be found off-campus.

3 West Austin and Zilker Park. Things seem to move a little bit slower in West Austin, whether it's at the sprawling, lakeside fields of Zilker Park, historic swimming holes like Barton Springs, or laid-back local foodie institutions that give travelers a true taste of Old Austin.

4 South Austin and South Congress District. Keeping it weird is a way of life just south of the Congress Bridge. The funky boutiques, high-end shops, music venues, famed restaurants, and pop-up art markets on iconic South Congress Avenue can easily take up a day, but there are plenty of hip hotels in the area that make it worthy of an extended stay.

5 East Austin. The city's fastest growing neighborhood continues to develop into a hot spot for food, culture, and music in Austin, but the community is also proud of its enduring Latinx and African American roots.

6 North Austin. This charming neck of the woods is home to Old Austin residents, funky vintage shops, and local businesses, plus a recent boom of award-winning eateries and the Domain's vast upscale shopping delights.

7 Greater Austin. Austin's wide appeal gets an added boost because of its prime proximity to the Texas Hill Country. Explore the bucolic beauty of the surrounding region at nearby state parks, swimming holes, wineries, breweries, and riverside retreats.

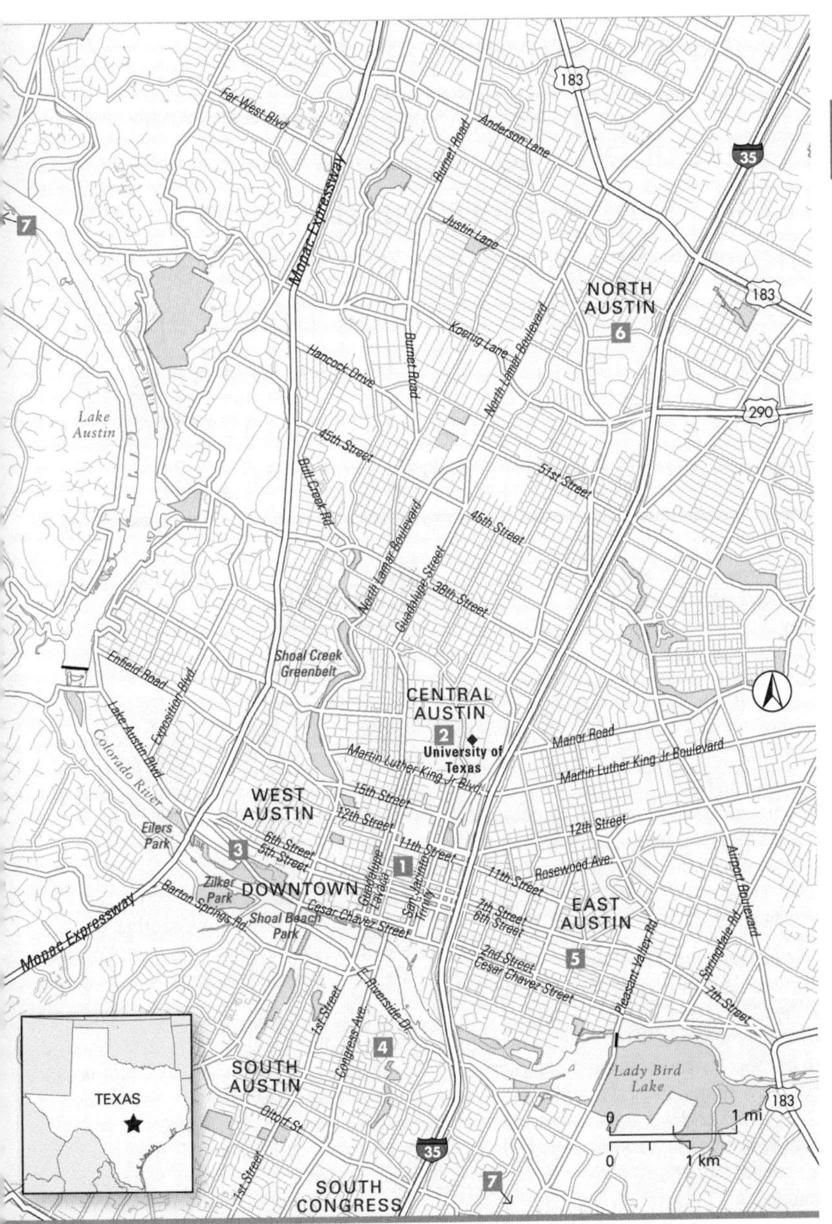
183
Far West Blvd
Anderson Lane
Burnet Road
35
7
Mopac Expressway
Justin Lane
NORTH AUSTIN
6
183
Koenig Lane
Hancock Drive
Burnet Road
North Lamar Boulevard
290
Lake Austin
45th Street
Bull Creek Rd.
51st Street
45th Street
North Lamar Boulevard
Guadalupe Street
38th Street
Shoal Creek Greenbelt
Enfield Road
Exposition Blvd
CENTRAL AUSTIN
2
University of Texas
Manor Road
Lake Austin Blvd
Colorado River
Martin Luther King Jr Blvd
Martin Luther King Jr Boulevard
15th Street
WEST AUSTIN
12th Street
12th Street
Eilers Park
6th Street
5th Street
3
11th Street
1
Rosewood Ave.
11th Street
Airport Boulevard
Zilker Park
DOWNTOWN
Guadalupe
Lavaca
San Jacinto
Trinity
EAST AUSTIN
7th Street
6th Street
Barton Springs Rd.
Shoal Beach Park
Cesar Chavez Street
Mopac Expressway
2nd Street
Cesar Chavez Street
5
Pleasant Valley Rd
Springdale Rd.
7th Street
E. Riverside Dr.
1st Street
Congress Ave.
4
SOUTH AUSTIN
Lady Bird Lake
183
TEXAS
0
1 mi
0
1 km
Oltorf St
35
1st Street
7
SOUTH CONGRESS

A city that's teeming with pride in its quirkiness, hipness, and weirdness, Austin has a near-universal appeal thanks to its diverse artistic and musical communities, eclectic food scene, academic and political pedigrees, and burgeoning entrepreneurial and tech industries. Each year, more than 30 million travelers visit the Texas capital, making it one of the fastest growing cities in the U.S. and a constant presence atop every "Best Cities to Live" poll.

Of course, it also lays claim to being the live music capital of the world, with flagship attractions like the annual SXSW Music Festival and the Austin City Limits Festival along with nearly 300 live music venues throughout the city. But it also has Matthew McConaughey cheering from the sidelines at UT football games games and transplants like Elon Musk championing the growing juggernaut of the local tech scene, ensuring that no matter what your assumptions of Austin are, you're bound to be surprised at what you find here.

The astounding growth of Austin hasn't stunted its Keep Austin Weird credentials either. The arts scene here, from public murals and interactive art installations to outdoor symphonies and stand-up comedy, keeps carving out niches for all things wild and wonderful. If everything is bigger in Texas, including the hype of its capital city, then Austin is not to be missed.

Planning

When to Go

Spring and autumn (namely February through April and September through November) are considered peak season and the best times to visit Austin. Temperatures hover in the 70s and 80s, and events like South by Southwest, the Austin City Limits Music Festival, and University of Texas home football games are in full swing. Of course, hotel prices are then at their peak as well.

The off-season is generally considered to be July, August, December, and January. Sweltering summers see temperatures pushing past 100°F. Luckily there are plenty of green spaces and swimming holes where you can cool off. Winter visits might limit access to some of the city's abundant outdoor offerings and annual festivals, but the weather in December and January is generally very mild and prices are usually pretty low outside of the holiday season.

Get the best bang for your buck in late spring and early summer (from May into June)—the weather is pleasant, UT students are heading home, and hotel prices are gentle.

FESTIVALS AND EVENTS

ABC Kite Fest

In March, head down to Zilker Park, nestled near downtown, for this beloved annual kite event. Be sure to bring the kids, a picnic basket, and even your furry friends to see the beautiful kite creations, competitions, and amazing aerial tricks. You can bring a kite yourself or just watch the festivities—and if the mood strikes, you can even purchase a kite on-site or attend a kite-building workshop. If you can take your eyes off the kites, the festival site is an ideal spot to take in the Austin skyline. ✉ *2100 Barton Springs Rd., Zilker Park* ☎ *512/837–9500* 🌐 *www.abckitefestival.org.*

Austin City Limits Music Festival

As much as Austinites love music, they love being outdoors even more. The result is this six-day fall music festival spanning two weekends in October; it's the unofficial farewell-to-summer shindig that takes over Zilker Park. Fans flock to hear more than 130 international, national, and local acts on eight stages. Featured headliners have included the likes of Bob Dylan, Miley Cyrus, Tom Petty, Björk, Phish, Willie Nelson, Radiohead, and Billie Eilish. ✉ *2100 Barton Springs Rd., Zilker Park* 🌐 *www.aclfestival.com.*

Clyde Littlefield Texas Relays

One of the top track and field events in the United States, the Texas Relays are held in early April at Mike A. Myers Stadium at the University of Texas. Founded in 1925, the Relays attract about 50,000 spectators and 5,000 of the best athletes in Texas (and from around the country) at the high school, collegiate, and professional levels. Advance-sale tickets are recommended (and cheaper), but walk-up admission is also available. ✉ *Mike A. Myers Stadium, 707 Clyde Littlefield Dr., University of Texas Area* ☎ *512/471–3434* 🌐 *texassports.com/sports/relays.*

Pecan Street Festival

Austin hosts several art-driven festivals throughout the year, including this biannual art, music, and food event held on downtown's famed Sixth Street, once known as Pecan Street. Twice a year—on the first weekend in May and late in September—the East Sixth Street Historic District between Brazos Street and I–35 transforms, filling up with hundreds of artists' booths displaying paintings, jewelry, crafts, and much more for the public to peruse—and hopefully buy. More than 50 live musical performances, dozens of local food and drink vendors, and family-friendly activities add to the fun. ✉ *501 Old Pecan St., Sixth Street District* ☎ *512/485–3190* 🌐 *www.pecanstreetfestival.org.*

Republic of Texas Motorcycle Rally

Every June, tens of thousands of bikers invade Austin for three days of partying, camping, talking shop, and browsing vendors' wares. Based at the Circuit of the Americas just east of the city, the event includes a huge Friday motorcycle parade from the rally grounds all the way downtown to Congress Avenue, with thousands of Austinites looking on. Much partying ensues (both during and afterward) among bikers and spectators alike on Sixth Street. There are also live musical performances, stunt shows, flat track racing, custom bike shows, and dozens of local food trucks on the festival grounds. ✉ *Circuit of the Americas, 9201 Circuit of the Americas Blvd.* 🌐 *www.republicoftexasmotorcyclerally.com.*

Rodeo Austin

This historic stock show–turned rodeo was founded in 1938, and today's modern event, held at the Travis County Expo

Center, continues to be a showstopper. Family-friendly festivities typically run for 20 days in the first half of March, including several thrilling ProRodeo events and competitions, stock shows, Texas-style cook-offs, auctions, and a sprawling carnival. Entertainment ranges from big name acts like Willie Nelson, Dwight Yoakam, and Styx to nearly 50 local bands. Proceeds benefit local scholarships and youth education programs. ✉ *Travis County Expo Center, 9100 Decker Lake Rd.* ☎ *512/919–3000* 🌐 *www.rodeoaustin.com.*

South by Southwest

Austin's annual music, film, and interactive-tech conference and festival takes the city by storm every spring. The 10-day onslaught of entertainment brings a flood of hip corporations, technology-savvy startups, and independent film, comedy, and music industry folks and fans from around the world. Since its start in 1987, SXSW has evolved into one of the country's largest arts and technology festivals fusing music, film, and cutting-edge interactive ideas with more than 2,000 acts performing in hundreds of official and unofficial venues literally all over the city. It's such a take-over-the-city event that many Austin families evacuate to some far-off destination for its entirety (it is spring break after all). Hotel rooms are scarce (and pricey), restaurants and bars are packed, and everyone from SXSW badge–wearing VIPs to plain, music-loving plebeians mixes and mingles in expectation of finding "the next big thing." It pays to be organized in terms of the bands you want to see since SXSW happens all over town. Research showtimes and venues to reserve tickets as far in advance as possible—prices increase and available tickets disappear the closer you get to the festival date. ✉ *Downtown* ☎ *512/467–7979* 🌐 *www.sxsw.com.*

Getting Here and Around

AIR

If you have to be stuck in an airport, it might as well be Austin-Bergstrom International Airport (ABIA). It's only 7½ miles from downtown Austin and generally regarded as one of the most pleasant airports in the United States. With a total of 34 gates after a major expansion in 2019, it's the second-fastest-growing, midsize airport in the country—and most important, it's modern and user-friendly. Live music has been a distinguishing feature since its Music in the Air program launched in June 1999, and today, travelers can catch more than 1,500 live performances a year in different venues throughout the airport.

The concourse's restaurants keep it local with a smattering of hometown foodie favorites, like The Salt Lick, Matt's El Rancho, Austin Java, JuiceLand, and Amy's Ice Creams. Free Wi-Fi is available (up to four hours) and PowerPort stations offer plugs for laptops and chargers. There are also the usual souvenir shops and newsstands, as well as laptop rentals and printing services.

ABIA offers roughly 350 daily flights with direct service to more than 70 destinations, including international flights to London, Mexico City, Cancun, and Toronto.

Airport shuttles and taxis are located on the ground level (same level as baggage claim). A shared shuttle from the airport to downtown Austin will cost approximately $18–$20 per person. Nonstop shuttle services and multiple rideshare options are also available.

AIRPORTS Austin–Bergstrom International Airport. ✉ *3600 Presidential Blvd.* ☎ *512/530–2242* 🌐 *www.austintexas.gov/airport.*

AIRPORT SHUTTLE SuperShuttle. ✉ *Austin-Bergstrom International Airport, 3600 Presidential Blvd., Lower Level/Ticket Counter* ☎ *512/258–3826* 🌐 *www.supershuttle.com/locations/austin-aus.*

TAXIS Austin zTrip. ✉ *Austin-Bergstrom International Airport, 3600 Presidential Blvd.* ☎ *512/452–9999* 🌐 *www.ztrip.com/austin.*

BUS

Greyhound's main Austin terminal is open 24 hours a day and is located in central north Austin near the intersection of FM 2222 and I–35. There are frequent departures to Houston (the trip takes approximately four hours), Dallas (averaging five hours), and other cities, large and small, throughout Texas.

Megabus also offers service from Austin to Dallas, Houston, and San Antonio. If you're looking to travel in style and luxury, check out Vonlane. A one-way fare (priced at approximately $100) will get you free food, drink, and Wi-Fi service.

Austin's public bus system has several local bus routes, including 6 flyer routes, 14 high-frequency routes, and 12 University of Texas shuttle routes. All express buses offer free wireless Internet service, and the entire fleet is clean and efficient. The CapMetro app is free to download.

CONTACTS Greyhound Bus Lines. ✉ *916 E. Koenig La., North Austin* ☎ *512/458–4463* 🌐 *www.greyhound.com/en-us/bus-station-680174.* **Megabus.** ☎ *877/462–6342* 🌐 *us.megabus.com.* **Capital Metro.** ✉ *2910 E. 5th St., East Austin* ☎ *512/474–1200* 🌐 *www.capmetro.org.* **Vonlane.** ✉ *Austin* ☎ *844/866–5263* 🌐 *www.vonlane.com.*

CAR

While Austin's public Capital Metro bus system does serve thousands of locals on a daily basis, visitors will likely rely on walking and driving to get around. If you plan to check out any towns in the nearby Hill Country, renting a car is a smart idea, but if you don't expect to travel outside of downtown, there's no need to have a car at all. Bike-share terminals and dockless e-bikes and scooters are plentiful, and lots of bus routes can take you from place to place with relative ease. The tech-friendly city has several rideshare apps available, too (including popular ones like Uber and Lyft), as well as more traditional taxis.

The major north–south thoroughfares through Austin are I–35 and Loop 1 (also known as MoPac). U.S. 183 runs at a slight north–south diagonal through Austin. Although it doesn't serve any other major cities, U.S. 183 does act as a major artery through town, eventually meandering northward to western Oklahoma and southward toward the Gulf. East–west Highway 71 and U.S. 290 connect Austin and Houston. A recently added toll road, SH 130, is a quick way to zip through town.

Although the highways are clearly marked, many of them have been granted other names as they pass through Austin (some joke that every road in town has at least two names). Keep in mind that U.S. 183 runs parallel to Research Boulevard for one stretch, Anderson Lane at another, and Ed Bluestein Boulevard at yet another, and Highway 71 is also known as Ben White Boulevard. Congress Avenue, South First, and Lamar all serve as other main north–south thoroughfares in the downtown area, but Congress is interrupted at the State Capitol.

Austin has more roads per capita than the other major cities in Texas, and it needs all of them—there are nearly 27 million annual visitors, more than 50,000 university students, and a large commuter population to accommodate. Austin is generally navigable and car-friendly, but it's best to avoid the roads at rush hour on weekdays from 7 to 9 am and 4 to 7 pm, with Friday afternoon's rush starting a bit earlier.

Austin's downtown core is bordered by the two major north–south thoroughfares: MoPac (Loop 1) to the west and I–35 to the east. Highway 183 snakes north from the airport, crossing I–35 and MoPac in north Austin and continuing to the northwest suburbs; and Loop 360 (Capital of Texas Highway) runs from the Arboretum area in the northwest, through the upscale West Lake area, crosses MoPac and becomes Highway 71 (aka Ben White Blvd.), and runs through south Austin to the airport.

Much of downtown is laid out in a conventional grid of numerical streets, and the majority of these are one-way. Even-numbered streets generally run one way to the west, and odd-numbered streets generally run one way to the east.

Main drags within Austin include Lamar Boulevard, which runs from Ben White in the south all the way up to Parmer Lane and I–35 in the far north. Many major roads run in an east–west direction: in general, you'll find a good horizontal artery every 5 to 10 blocks.

Speed limits in Austin are strictly enforced, and fines can be stiff. Depending on the area, speed limits range 20–25 mph in residential and downtown areas, 30–45 mph on larger streets and boulevards, and 70 mph on local highways. Texas State Highway 130 has become the nation's fastest highway, with an 85-mph speed limit.

Both street and garage parking are plentiful in downtown Austin (but fill up fast on weekends and during special events). Currently, metered parking costs $2 an hour (for the first two hours). Parking lots and garages will charge anywhere from $8 to $20 a day (prices drastically increase during special events).

TRAIN

Austin sits at roughly the midpoint of Amtrak's Texas Eagle line, which snakes in a great V from Chicago through Illinois, Missouri, Arkansas, Texas, southern New Mexico, and Arizona before ending up in Los Angeles. One train departs from Dallas daily and arrives in Austin at around 6:30 pm.

Austin's Amtrak station is located downtown near the intersection of 3rd and Lamar, on the north bank of Lady Bird Lake. Although there are many basic amenities within walking distance, there's little to the station itself other than a ticket counter and waiting room. The ticket office is open daily, 9 am to 7 pm.

Austin also has a MetroRail that services 32 miles of existing freight tracks between Leander and downtown Austin. The Red Line has nine stations, including a stop in front of the Austin Convention Center. It runs weekdays every 30 minutes during peak morning and evening rush hours, with expanded service times on weekends. MetroRail one-way fares are $2 for one zone and $3 for all zones.

Restaurants

Though Mexican, Tex-Mex, and barbecue are the default cuisines in Austin, everything from Brazilian to Pacific Rim fusion has made headway here, and there are strong vegetarian and natural-food followers.To find the best barbecue, local consensus tends to be that you've got to head out of town to Lockhart, Luling, or Llano in the Hill Country. Nevertheless, there are several award-winning, master-class options within the city limits, including Franklin Barbecue and La Barbecue. In some venues the music and food share nearly equal billing, like Stubb's Bar-B-Q, where holy rollers can enjoy a popular gospel brunch on Sunday or queue up any other night of the week, whether it's for a meal or a sold-out rock show. Austin is a casual city, and the dress code is almost always "come as you are"; a few restaurants require a jacket for men. Reservations are generally recommended if you can make them (especially on weekends), but some places have a first-come, first-served policy that means legendary long lines (as at the aforementioned Franklin Barbecue).

Around late September or early October, many of Austin's best restaurants participate in Restaurant Week, when prix-fixe menus are offered for a low price, with some of the proceeds earmarked for charity. But no matter the time of year, the most popular "meal" in town is happy hour, and almost every establishment in Austin will feature discounted dishes and drinks every afternoon.

Hotels

Almost all the major hotel chains can be found in downtown Austin, and like in most cities, they all vary in their quality of service and price. Perhaps the most historic hotel is The Driskill. More upscale hotels downtown include the Four Seasons Hotel Austin, the W Austin, and the Fairmont Austin. Boutique hotels have surged in Austin as well. Among the most popular are Hotel San José, Hotel Saint Cecilia, Austin Motel, and the Carpenter Hotel.There are plenty of properties citywide that average no more than 15 miles from the city center. Almost all of them are conveniently located near shopping and restaurants. If you're looking for quality pampering time, several resort spas, like Lake Austin Spa and Miraval Austin, are less than an hour away.Festivals, conventions, and university events can pack the city during peak months as well as during legislative sessions (held in odd-numbered years), so planning ahead is recommended.

■ TIP→ **Hotel and restaurant reviews have been shortened. For full information, visit Fodors.com. Restaurant prices are per person for a main course at dinner or if dinner is not served, at lunch. Hotel prices are for two people in a standard double room in high season.**

What It Costs

$	$$	$$$	$$$$
RESTAURANTS			
under $14	$14–$22	$23–$30	over $30
HOTELS			
under $125	$125–$225	$226–$325	over $325

Nightlife

Austin's official title of "Live Music Capitol of the World" is not self-appointed—it's earned. Long known as a playground for late-night revelers, the city brought Texas country music to the forefront years before the emergence of mega-venues and craft cocktail lounges. Dancehalls and honky-tonks once ruled the roost, and down-and-out drifters played for their wages.

The music scene now pulls a diverse array of crowds, while staying true to its roots. Music lovers will find a variety of options every night of the week that span genres, all with a unique and soulful edge. It's not surprising that the city plays host to several of the most significant music festivals in the country, like SXSW and the Austin City Limits Music Festival. New bars open almost daily in Texas's ever-evolving and always-hospitable capital city.

Performing Arts

Austin has roughly 250 live music venues and more than enough musicians to book every night. Night owls can find a performance of any type of musical genre on any given evening—most clubs are packed into the downtown area, especially along the Red River Cultural District, so it's easy to bounce between venues. Austin's entire arts scene is thriving as well. Enthusiasts can find countless galleries downtown and on the

Did You Know?

Austin was originally a tiny settlement called Waterloo. It was renamed in honor of Texan hero Stephen F. Austin after it replaced Houston as the capital of the Republic of Texas in 1839.

east side in addition to outdoor flea and vintage pop-up markets, citywide studio tours are held twice a year, and there are a handful of independent theaters around town, too.

Shopping

The city's true shopping identity lies in its plethora of independently owned, unique boutiques. To get a real feel for Austin, browse the funky stores along South Congress, the record shops on South First, or the vintage boutiques around North Loop. For something more upscale, visit the hip downtown storefronts of 2nd Street District, the high-end galleries, antiques, and home-furnishings emporia on West 6th Street, or the luxury Domain shopping district in north Austin. A little north of town in Round Rock, shopping malls and outlet stores are plentiful.

Tours

AO Tours Austin

This company's signature 90-minute, 30-mile tour provides an outstanding overview of Austin and the surrounding Hill Country, including downtown, the historic districts, the university, the east side, and various shopping and entertainment hubs. Other tours, including a Best of ATX and Offbeat & Hidden Austin, are offered daily and their sleek Mercedes-Benz Sprinter vans depart either from the Austin Visitor Center (*602 E. 4th St.*) or Wild About Music (*615 Congress Ave.*). ✉ *Austin* ☎ *512/659–9478* 🌐 *aotoursaustin.com* 🎫 *From $25.*

Austin City Limits Tours

The acclaimed longest-running music series in American television, Austin City Limits originally began airing in 1975 on PBS from Austin's local KLRU affiliate station on the University of Texas campus. In 2010, ACL tapings were moved to a new home and now broadcast live from Second Street at the Austin City Limits Live at The Moody Theater (ACL Live). The show has hosted legends like Johnny Cash, Willie Nelson, and Queen Ida. Learn about the historic series and see exclusive collections of concert photos as you tour the new studios. Tours are 90 minutes and begin weekdays at 11 am at the ACL Live box office. ✉ *310 Willie Nelson Blvd.* ☎ *512/225–7999* 🌐 *www.acl-live.com/tours* 🎫 *From $6.*

Austin Duck Adventures

This deservedly popular tour uses amphibious Hydra Terra vehicles, driven by highly entertaining guides who distribute duckbill-shape quacking whistles to all on board (the better to honk at unsuspecting pedestrians). The 75-minute tour departs from the Austin Visitor Center and includes sights like the Historic Sixth Street District, the Bullock Texas State History Museum, the State Capitol, and the Governor's Mansion. The "Duck" ends the tour by splashing into the waters of Lake Austin. ✉ *Austin Visitor Center, 602 E. 4th St.* ☎ *512/477–5274* 🌐 *austinducks.com* 🎫 *$35.*

Austin Eats Food Tours

These tours help you find out exactly why Austin has become one of the country's great foodie destinations. Each tour, led by an expert guide and native Austinite, is approximately 3–4 hours long and features six or seven local eateries, with food (and sometimes drinks) included in the price. Tour options change throughout the year, but include evergreen favorites like "Best of Austin Food Trucks" and "East Austin Happy Hours." Meet-up times and locations vary and can be confirmed online. ✉ *Downtown* ☎ *512/963–4545* 🌐 *www.austineatsfoodtours.com* 🎫 *From $95.*

Austin Ghost Tours

This spookily unique operator offers historic downtown walking tours led by costumed guides. Considered by many to be one of the top 10 best ghost tours in the country, the 90-minute stroll, covering about one mile, delves into the real-life history and paranormal hauntings of the Live Music Capital of the World. Tours run Thursday through Sunday. Meet-up locations, times, and tour routes differ, and options include spirited pub crawls and special Halloween and Christmas holiday excursions. Research and book tours in advance online. *Downtown* *512/203–5561* *austinghosttours.com* *$22.*

Double Decker Austin Tours
This popular hop-on, hop-off bus service allows you to see some of the city's most popular sites at a customized pace. Buses run Thursday through Sunday, every 90 minutes from 10 am to 5 pm, starting out from the Austin Visitor Center and making stops at the LBJ Presidential Library, the Bullock Museum, the Capitol, South Congress Avenue, and Sixth Street. Each bus has a tour guide onboard to let you know what you're looking at along the way, point out photo ops, and answer questions. Single-loop and unlimited all-day tickets can be purchased online, at the Austin Visitor Center or the Sixth Street Museum of the Weird (*412 E. 6th St.*), or on the bus (as long as there are seats available). *Austin Visitor Center, 602 E. 4th St.* *512/596–2925* *doubledeckeraustin.com* *From $29.*

Downtown Guided Walking Tours
The Austin Visitor Center offers three free guided walking tours, with two departing from the State Capitol and one from the visitor center itself. Choose between the Capitol grounds and Congress Avenue tour, for a rich overview of Austin's local, state, and national history; the architecture delights of the downtown (west of Congress Avenue) tour; or an "Old and New" highlight reel of downtown's historic and hippest new sites. Call or check online to make reservations in advance. *Downtown* *512/478–0098,* *www.austintexas.org/plan-a-trip/downtown-walking-tours* *Free.*

Visitor Information

CONTACTS Austin Convention & Visitors Bureau. *111 Congress Ave., Suite 700* *512/474–5171, 800/462–8784* *www.austintexas.org.* **Austin Visitor Center.** *602 E. 4th St.* *866/478–0098* *www.austintexas.org/plan-a-trip/visitor-center.*

Downtown with Sixth Street and Rainey Street

Downtown Austin is the natural starting point for seeing the city's sights and is home to many of the major ones, including the State Capitol. Its boundaries are generally regarded as being I–35 to the east, Clarksville to the west, UT to the north, and the Colorado River (known to locals as Lady Bird Lake) to the south. It's relatively compact and well served by buses. There are also plenty of bike-share stations if you prefer pedal power.

And tucked into the southeast corner of downtown, historic Rainey Street's renovated bungalows are home to some of the city's hippest watering holes. The half-mile hive of nightlife attractions features a diverse smattering of nearly two dozen bars, from swanky date-night destinations like Clive Bar and high-end mixology at Half Step to rowdy hang-outs like Lustre Pearl, with weekly live music and bar games.

Sights

Austin City Hall
GOVERNMENT BUILDING | The home of municipal government since 2004 and the anchor of the Second Street District, City Hall is a striking modern showcase of the New Austin, loaded with energy-saving features like solar panels and decorated with modern art. The People's Gallery, for instance, is a public art exhibit

Experience Austin's skyline via kayaking on Lady Bird Lake.

that showcases local artists year-round, free of charge (weekdays). The angular, four-story limestone-and-concrete building is clad in 66,000 square feet of copper. A cascading 40-foot waterfall flows inside and back to Lady Bird Lake just across the street, and bands play on the outdoor amphitheater and plaza during free Friday concerts in the spring and fall. Tours are available by appointment. ✉ *301 W. 2nd St.* ☎ *512/974–2000* 🌐 *www.austintexas.gov/government/city-hall* ⏲ *Closed weekends.*

Austin Fire Museum

OTHER MUSEUM | Next door to the O. Henry Museum and the Susanna Dickinson Museum, this hidden gem is housed in Central Fire Station No. 1, Austin's busiest firehouse. The small museum has a collection of items from the "horse-drawn era" of 19th-century firefighting—leather fire helmets, brass firefighting nozzles, and bugles—as well as various other pieces of equipment that date through today. Displays cover specific incidents, local firefighting companies, Austin fire stations, and historic photographs, and are available to view on weekend afternoons or weekdays by appointment. ✉ *401 E. 5th St.* ☎ *512/974–3835* 🌐 *www.austintexas.gov/department/austin-fire-museum* 🎟 *Free* ⏲ *Closed weekdays (except by appointment).*

Austin History Center

LIBRARY | Part of the Austin Public Library system (and located in the beautiful and historic Central Library building), this is the central repository of all historical documents relating to Austin and Travis County. It contains a host of items, including over a million photographic images, from a priceless collection of all things relating to Austin, with regular exhibitions showcasing aspects of local history. Reservations for research are strongly recommended. ✉ *810 Guadalupe St.* ☎ *512/974–7480* 🌐 *library.austintexas.gov/ahc/about-us* 🎟 *Free* ⏲ *Closed weekends.*

Bremond Block Historic District

HISTORIC DISTRICT | A number of high-style Victorian homes built between the 1850s and 1910 fill this area just a few blocks from the State Capitol. They were once owned by wealthy Austinites, including several members of the Bremond family of merchants and bankers. The homes are not open to the public but inquire at the Austin Visitor Center about self-guided walking tours. ✉ *Bounded by 7th and 8th Sts., and Guadalupe and San Antonio Sts.*

★ The Contemporary Austin–Jones Center

ART MUSEUM | Originally known as the Austin Museum of Art, the Contemporary Austin's Jones Center is a striking downtown presence that features a wide array of contemporary art exhibits and hosts various special events that are open to the public, including "rooftop sessions" featuring outdoor film screenings as well as live musical and artistic performances. Advance reservations are recommended. Their sister site Laguna Gloria, in nearby west Austin, is also worth visiting for the outdoor sculpture gardens and overall ambience. ✉ *700 Congress Ave., Downtown* ☎ *512/453–5312* 🌐 *www.thecontemporaryaustin.org* 🎫 *$10* 🕒 *Closed Mon.–Wed.*

The Driskill

HOTEL | If you make time to stroll through one Austin hotel even though you're not staying there, make it The Driskill. A monument to Romanesque style right in the middle of Sixth Street, this delightful—and many say haunted—grande dame is embellished with limestone busts of its original owner, cattle baron Jesse Driskill, and his sons. Check out its gorgeous two-story porches with Romanesque Revival columns surrounding the arched entrances and the Texas-size lobby and mezzanine, where a café, bakery, and bar are open to the public. Over the years, countless legislators, lobbyists, and social leaders have held court behind the hotel's limestone walls, and it seems a few of them never left: according to guests, lights turn on by themselves, pipes bang eerily, and elevators without passengers go up and down. But management is quick to point out that the ghosts seem friendly, so don't let them stop you from paying a visit. ✉ *604 Brazos St., Sixth Street District* ☎ *512/439–1234* 🌐 *www.driskillhotel.com.*

★ Emma S. Barrientos Mexican American Cultural Center

ART MUSEUM | This stunning architectural site and museum is just off of the Hike and Bike Trail, overlooking Lady Bird Lake. Dedicated to celebrating notable Latino artists and empowering a new generation of Mexican-Americans, the museum has a phenomenal education department and offers popular youth and family programs. While there is no permanent collection on display, you'll find traveling exhibits. Various live performances and community events, from flamenco recitals to *Día de los Muertos* celebrations, are also hosted here. ✉ *600 River St.* ☎ *512/974–3772* 🌐 *www.austintexas.gov/department/emma-s-barrientos-mexican-american-cultural-center* 🎫 *Free* 🕒 *Closed Sun.*

Governor's Mansion

HISTORIC HOME | Abner Cook, a leading architect of his day, designed this mansion, one of Austin's most elegant dwellings. Since 1865, this building has been the home of every Texas governor since the state's fifth, Elisha Marshall Pease. Constructed of bricks made in Austin and wood from nearby forests, the two-story National Historic Landmark bears the marks of those who have lived here, including James Hogg, the governor who, to keep his children from sliding down the banister on their rears, hammered tacks into the railing (the tack holes are still visible). Many fine furnishings, paintings, and antiques are on display, including Sam Houston's bed and Stephen F. Austin's desk. Free 20-minute tours are available if you

Downtown with Sixth Street and Rainey Street
A
B
C
D
E
F
1
2
3
4
5
6
7
8
9
West 22nd Street
West 21st Street
West 21st Street
San Antonio Street
Guadalupe Street
Speedway
W. Martin Luther King Jr. Blvd.
Pease District Park
Enfield Road
Marshall Ln.
West 13th Street
Lorrain Street
West 12th Street
West 18th Street
West 17th Street
West 16th Street
West 15th Street
West 14th Street
West 13th Street
West 12th Street
West 11th Street
West 10th Street
West 9th Street
West 8th Street
West 10th Street
West 9th Street
Colorado Street
E. 17th St.
E. 16th St.
E. 15th Street
San Jacinto Boulevard
Trinity Street
East 12th Street
East 11th Street
East 10th St.
East 9th Street
East 8th Street
East 7th Street
East 6th St.
East 5th Street
East 4th Street
East 3rd Street
East 2nd Street
Brazos Street
San Jacinto Blvd
Trinity Street
Neches Street
Red River Street
Duncan Park
Blanco Street
Baylor Street
North Lamar Boulevard
Henderson Street
West 6th Street
West 5th Street
Bowie St.
West Avenue
Rio Grande Street
Nueces Street
San Antonio Street
Guadalupe Street
Lavaca Street
Colorado Street
Congress Avenue
Lamar Beach Park
West 3rd St.
DOWNTOWN
West 4th Street
West 3rd Street
West 2nd Street
West Cesar Chavez Street
Shoal Beach Park
Shoal Beach
E. Cesar Chavez Street
South Lamar Boulevard
West Riverside Drive
South 1st Street
S. Congress Ave
Lady Bird Lake
Colorado River
Rainey Street
Barton Springs Road
Post Oak St.
E. Riverside Dr.
South 1st Street
S. Congress Avenue
SOUTH AUSTIN
35
KEY
Sights
Restaurants
Hotels

G H I

Robert Dedman Dr.
Clyde Littlefield Dr.
Red River St.
35
Leona Street
E. Martin Luther King Jr. Blvd.
E. Martin Luther King Jr. Blvd.
Comal Street
0 1.000 ft
0 200 m
Waterloo Park
Olander St.
Walter St.
Navasota Street
San Bernard St.
East 13th Street
East 12th Street
Catalpa St.
Olive St.
Cotton Street
Juniper St.
35
East 11th Street
Rosewood Avenue
East 10th Street
East 11th Street
San Marcos Street
East 9th Street
East 8th Street
Navasota Street
Comal Street
East 6th Street
East 5th Street
East 4th Street
San Marcos Street
Medina Street
Waller Street
Attayac Street
Navasota Street
EAST AUSTIN
East 3rd Street
East 2nd Street
Willow Street
East Cesar Chavez Street
Canterbury Street
Garden Street
Comal Street
Chalmers Avenue
Holly Street
Chicon Street
Lynn Street
Haskell Street

G H I

Sights

1 Austin City Hall.......... D6
2 Austin Fire Museum..... F6
3 Austin History Center........... D4
4 Bremond Block Historic District......... D5
5 The Contemporary Austin—Jones Center.. E5
6 The Driskill................ E5
7 Emma S. Barrientos Mexican American Cultural Center........... E8
8 Governor's Mansion..... E4
9 Lora Reynolds Gallery... C6
10 Mexic-Arte Museum.... E6
11 O. Henry Museum F6
12 Old Bakery and Emporium................. E4
13 Susanna Dickinson Museum F6
14 Texas Capitol Visitors Center E4
15 Texas State Capitol...... E4
16 Willie Nelson Statue ... D6

Restaurants

1 Arlo Grey................. D7
2 the backspace E6
3 Casino El Camino F6
4 Comedor.................. D5
5 Emmer & Rye............. F8
6 The Iron Works Barbecue................. F7
7 La Condesa............... C6
8 Lamberts.................. C6
9 Parkside E6
10 Pelóns..................... F5
11 Stubb's Bar-B-Q.......... F5
12 Texas Chili Parlor E3
13 Truluck's D6
14 Via 313 Pizza............. F7

Hotels

1 Austin Proper C6
2 DoubleTree Suites by Hilton Hotel Austin....... E3
3 The Driskill................ E5
4 Fairmont Austin F7
5 Four Seasons Hotel Austin E7
6 Hilton Austin.............. F6
7 Hotel ZaZa............... D6
8 JW Marriott Austin...... E6
9 Kimpton Hotel Van Zandt................. F7
10 The LINE Austin......... D7
11 Omni Austin Hotel Downtown................ E5
12 The Stephen F. Austin Royal Sonesta Hotel..... E5
13 W Hotel D6

reserve in advance. ✉ *1010 Colorado St.* ☎ *512/463–5518* 🌐 *www.governor.state.tx.us/Mansion.*

Lora Reynolds Gallery

ART GALLERY | Owned by art enthusiast and collector Lora Reynolds, this gallery encompasses a wide range of artistic media. Having worked in London and New York galleries, Reynolds was inspired to bring a vast diversity of contemporary art to Austin in the downtown area. The small, linear art space is a one-of-a-kind in the Austin art community, attracting international artists with a modern aesthetic who show original drawings, sculptures, photography, and painting exhibits in the main exhibition space and the "Project Room," where more than a dozen artists are featured throughout the year. ✉ *360 Nueces St., Suite 50* ☎ *512/215–4965* 🌐 *www.lorareynolds.com* ⏲ *Closed Sun.–Tues.*

Mexic-Arte Museum

ART MUSEUM | Founded in 1984, this museum is a beguiling, moderate-size showcase devoted to traditional and contemporary Mexican and Latin American art. The permanent collection includes lithographs, prints, silkscreens, etchings, and traditional ritual masks. If you're in town for their popular annual Day of the Dead celebration, the Viva la Vida Fest (late October or early November), you're in for a treat. Admission is free on Sunday. ✉ *419 Congress Ave., Downtown* ☎ *512/480–9373* 🌐 *www.mexic-artemuseum.org* 🎫 *$7.*

O. Henry Museum

OTHER MUSEUM | Writer William Sydney Porter, better known as O. Henry, rented this modest cottage from 1893 to 1895. Moved a few blocks from its original location, the home today contains O. Henry memorabilia, including original drawings, artifacts, and period furniture. It also hosts the extraordinarily popular O. Henry Pun-Off World Championships, held in its backyard every May since 1977. ✉ *409 E. 5th St., Downtown* ☎ *512/974–1398* 🌐 *austintexas.gov/department/o-henry-museum* 🎫 *Free; donations accepted* ⏲ *Closed Mon. and Tues.*

Old Bakery and Emporium

NOTABLE BUILDING | In 1876, Swedish baker Charles Lundberg built this charming building near the Capitol and operated it as a bakery for the next 60 years. Rescued from demolition after years of neglect, the bakery is now a registered National Historic Landmark, owned by the city, and remains a beautiful mainstay of Congress Avenue. The Old Bakery is a welcoming space that houses historical collections that display Austin's transformation since the pioneer days, plus an art gallery featuring handmade artisanal crafts made by citizens aged 50 and over. It makes for a nice stop before or after touring the Capitol. ✉ *1006 Congress Ave., Downtown* ☎ *512/974–1300* 🌐 *austintexas.gov/department/old-bakery-and-emporium* ⏲ *Closed Sun.–Tues.*

Susanna Dickinson Museum

HISTORIC HOME | As war stories go, the most defining for Texas is, of course, the Alamo, and although Davy Crockett and James Bowie are often names you'll hear in association with that infamous 1836 battle, Susanna Dickinson, who lost her husband there, was the person who carried the news of its demise to Sam Houston. She became a renowned Texas figure and was dubbed the "Messenger of the Alamo." Today, her home is open to the public, showcasing belongings and artifacts from her life and that of her second husband, Joseph Hannig, in the permanent exhibit, with occasional traveling exhibits. The museum is one of three Brushy Square museums, including the O. Henry Museum and the Austin Fire Museum, all located on the same block. Advance reservations are required to visit. ✉ *411 E. 5th St., Downtown* ☎ *512/974–3830* 🌐 *www.austintexas.gov/department/susanna-dickinson-museum* 🎫 *Free* ⏲ *Closed Mon. and Tues.*

The Texas State Capitol building is even bigger than the U.S. Capitol in Washington, D.C.

Texas Capitol Visitors Center

VISITOR CENTER | Located on the southeast corner of the Capitol grounds in the only surviving government building from Austin's first 30 years, the Texas Capitol Visitors Center owes its Gothic style to its German-born architect, Conrad Stremme. This 2½-story structure of stuccoed stone and brick was opened for business in 1858 as the first home of the Texas General Land Office. Writer O. Henry worked as a draftsman here and used the building as the setting for two of his short stories. In 1989, the legislature approved a $4.5-million renovation project to restore the building to its original 1890s appearance. It now houses permanent and traveling exhibits, the visitor center, and a gift shop. ✉ *112 E. 11th St.* ☎ *800/305–8400* 🌐 *tspb.texas.gov/prop/tcvc/cvc/cvc.html* 🎫 *Free.*

★ **Texas State Capitol**

GOVERNMENT BUILDING | Built in 1888 of Texas pink granite, this impressive structure is even taller than the U.S. Capitol (yes, everything *is* bigger in Texas). The building dominates downtown Austin, and the surrounding grounds are nearly as striking. Stand in the center of the star on the ground floor under the rotunda and look up, up, up into the dome—it's a Texas rite of passage. Catch one of the free historical tours, offered 9:30–4 on weekdays and 12:30–4 on weekends. *You can also go on a self-guided tour of the building and its grounds.* ✉ *1100 Congress Ave., Downtown* ☎ *512/305–8400* 🌐 *tspb.texas.gov/prop/tc/tc/capitol.html.*

Willie Nelson Statue

PUBLIC ART | Back in the 1970s, when the mainstream country music scene was based in Nashville, Willie Nelson kept his feet firmly planted in Texas. Playing around Austin at old haunts like the Armadillo World Headquarters, Nelson developed a name for himself strumming his beloved tunes, like the classic "Blue Eyes Crying in the Rain" and his own "On the Road Again." Today, he's a living legend here in town, and in 2012 on, when else, 4/20, he was immortalized with his very own 8-foot-tall bronze statue, complete with his signature braids and his famed guitar Trigger, standing proudly right in front of ACL Live at the Moody Theater. ✉ *310 W. 2nd St., Downtown* 🌐 *www.capitalareastatues.com* 🎫 *Free.*

Restaurants

Arlo Grey

$$$$ | **AMERICAN** | Lady Bird Lake views stun at this flagship endeavor by *Top Chef 10* winner Kristen Kish within the LINE Hotel. The elegant presentations of French- and Italian-inspired dishes, made with seasonal Central Texas–sourced ingredients, are impressive but pricey. **Known for:** patio seating next to the small outdoor pool; international spotlight thanks to Top Chef winner; constantly rotating crowd of locals and guests at the LINE Hotel. $ *Average main: 36* ✉ *The LINE Hotel, 111 E. César Chávez St., Downtown* ☎ *512/478–2991* 🌐 *www.thelinehotel.com/austin/bars-restaurants* ⏲ *Closed Mon. and Tues. No lunch.*

the backspace

$$ | **PIZZA** | This stylish pizzeria, another hit from chef/restaurateur Shawn Cirkiel, is one of Austin's best bets for classic Neapolitan pizza and authentic Italian antipasti. Tables are hard to come by in this intimate downtown space, but the service and menu are laid-back and approachable. Antipasto selections, like baked ricotta and eggplant caponata, rival the main attraction: thin-crust, wood-fired pizzas, from margherita to the popular fennel sausage. **Known for:** cozy date-night ambience; seasonal antipasto selections; classic Neapolitan pizzas fired in an Italian brick oven. $ *Average main: $15* ✉ *507 San Jacinto Blvd., Downtown* ☎ *512/474–9899* 🌐 *www.backspacepizza.com* ⏲ *Closed Sun. and Mon.*

★ **Casino El Camino**

$ | **BURGER** | Most definitely the best place on the notorious "Dirty Sixth Street" strip of downtown to chow down is Casino El Camino, a longtime favorite of Austin burger lovers. Locals arrive in hungover droves around midday on the weekends, when wait times for signatures like the Amarillo and Buffalo burgers can stretch upward of an hour. **Known for:** trademark Bloody Marys with wild ingredients like taquitos and meatballs; Texas-size portions; punk rock jukebox and a gritty vibe to match. $ *Average main: $9* ✉ *517 E. 6th St., Sixth Street District* ☎ *512/469–9330* 🌐 *www.casinoelcamino.net.*

Comedor

$$$ | **MEXICAN** | This contemporary Mexican restaurant (from acclaimed chef Philip Speer) has people arriving in droves for the bone-marrow tacos with pecan gremolata. Servers will encourage you to mix and match inventive plates for the table. **Known for:** striking architecture and interior design; signature bone-marrow tacos; hot Sunday brunch that requires reservations. $ *Average main: 26* ✉ *501 Colorado St., Downtown* ☎ *512/499–0977* 🌐 *www.comedortx.com* ⏲ *No lunch Mon.–Sat.*

★ **Emmer & Rye**

$$$ | **MODERN AMERICAN** | The standard for Rainey District fine dining since 2015, eating at Emmer & Rye is an immersive experience that's best enjoyed when the expert servers take the reins. Prix-fixe dinner menus of their signature rustic American cuisine are available, but this exclusive dining delight comes with the option to partake in creative dim sum offerings from a circulating fleet of carts that crisscross the sleek interiors. **Known for:** dim sum service that creates memorable culinary experience; savory stand-outs, like dry-aged Wagyu tartare and Blue Beard Durum spaghetti; popular with preshow Moody Theater crowds. $ *Average main: 29* ✉ *SkyHouse Austin, 51 Rainey St., Unit 110, Downtown* ☎ *512/366–5530* 🌐 *www.emmerandrye.com* ⏲ *Closed Mon. No lunch.*

The Iron Works Barbecue

$$ | **BARBECUE** | From its creekside perch in the shadow of the Austin Convention Center, this spot caters to name-tagged conference attendees, construction workers, and thoroughly starched office workers alike. Dependable house specialties include pepper-crusted smoked pork loin, tender brisket, and Flintstones-size beef ribs (the junior rib plate will satisfy all but the hugest of appetites). **Known for:** historic site complete with outdoor patio; no-frills counter service; unbeatable downtown location. *Average main: $14 ✉ 100 Red River St., Downtown ☎ 512/478–4855 🌐 www.ironworksbbq.com ⏲ Closed Sun.*

La Condesa

$$ | **MEXICAN** | After an award-winning start in 2013, this sophisticated spot for modern Mexican cuisine has remained solid. Diners can still expect reliable mainstays, such as crispy pork shoulder *carnitas tacos* with black beans and tangy tomatillo-avocado salsa, and don't miss the the house ceviches (try the Acapulco) or the guacamole sampler, with varying seasonal combinations like watermelon with *queso fresco* or toasted almonds and chipotle puree. **Known for:** staggering tequila and mezcal selection; weekend crowds from surrounding Second Street shops; slightly steep price tag. *Average main: $20 ✉ 400A W. 2nd St., Downtown ☎ 512/499–0300 🌐 lacondesa.com ⏲ Closed Mon. and Tues.*

Lamberts

$$$ | **BARBECUE** | Smack in the middle of Second Street, Lamberts draws a broad range of downtown business crowds, local foodies, and tourists, all for its stylish take on Texas barbecue. You know this isn't your father's barbecue joint when you hear Belle & Sebastian coming from the speakers instead of Willie or Waylon; for further evidence, there's Chimay beer on tap and a $23 "breakfast Frito pie" on the Sunday brunch menu. **Known for:** mouthwatering Sunday brunch that's worth a reservation; all-night happy hour on Monday; hip atmosphere with weekly live music performances. *Average main: $29 ✉ 401 W. 2nd St., Downtown ☎ 512/494–1500 🌐 lambertsaustin.com.*

★ **Parkside**

$$$$ | **AMERICAN** | A gem in the midst of Dirty Sixth, Parkside's austere interior features exposed brick walls, a shotgun bar, and bare light bulbs suspended by black cables. Celebrated chef Shawn Cirkiel has created an equally simple menu, but delivers on taste with fresh oysters and ceviche-style offerings from the raw bar, in addition to a meat-centric array of bone marrow appetizers, savory grilled lamb, and shareable portions of steak and (perfectly crisped) fries. **Known for:** extensive raw bar; lively downtown location that makes dinner reservations a must; happy hour specials. *Average main: $31 ✉ 301 E. 6th St., Sixth Street District ☎ 512/474–9898 🌐 parkside-austin.com ⏲ Closed Sun. and Mon. No lunch.*

Pelóns

$ | **MEXICAN** | Situated between some of the city's best music venues, this lively joint has reasonably priced Tex-Mex standards you can enjoy on the oak tree-shaded patio. Or just indulge in the drink menu full of house margaritas, specialty cocktails, and premium tequila flights. **Known for:** ultimate pregaming spot for music shows; excellent margaritas; great happy hour specials. *Average main: 12 ✉ 802 Red River St., Downtown ☎ 512/243–7874 🌐 www.pelonstexmex.com.*

Stubb's Bar-B-Q

$ | **BARBECUE** | This Red River staple, which traces its roots to a legendary Lubbock barbecue joint founded in 1968, is known as much for music as food. The casual venue, an old stone building with wooden floors and tables, suits the fare, which many local barbecue aficionados rate as average; the hickory-smoked choices—beef brisket, pork ribs,

Amid the partying of raucous Sixth Street, you'll find the historic and stately Driskill Hotel.

sausage, chicken, and turkey breast—are tasty enough, but sides, like spicy serrano creamed spinach, are definite crowd-pleasers. **Known for:** gospel brunch for saints and sinners alike; tasty brisket before (or after) a live show; swift service with a smile. *Average main: $13 801 Red River St., Downtown 512/480–8341 www.stubbsaustin.com.*

★ Texas Chili Parlor

$ | AMERICAN | Don't miss out on the state dish of Texas at this downtown icon. Just a stroll away from the Capitol, the Chili Parlor has been a favorite of legislators, lobbyists, and local hellraisers alike for a midday meal (or late-night beer) since 1976. Get a gut-sticking bowl of bean-less chili (marked X, XX, and XXX for spice), an ice-cold Lone Star beer, or a fully loaded Bloody Mary, and soak up some Old Austin history. **Known for:** one of the best living legends of old-school Austin dive bars; low-key reputation for celeb sightings; daily lunch crowd of state and Capitol employees. *Average main: 8 1409 Lavaca St., Downtown and the Capitol Area (Second Street and Warehouse District) 512/472–2828.*

Truluck's

$$$$ | SEAFOOD | Pricey-but-excellent fish, shellfish, and steak are served in handsome surroundings that suggest a businesspeople's yacht club here at Truluck's, part of an upscale chain with restaurants in Texas and Florida. Every Monday is all-you-can-eat crab claw night, but you can get Truluck's signature stone crab any day of the week at the downtown and northwest locations. **Known for:** signature crab cakes; show-stopping desserts; special-occasion dining. *Average main: $55 400 Colorado St., Downtown 512/482–9000 trulucks.com No lunch.*

★ Via 313 Pizza

$$ | PIZZA | Detroit lives in Austin at the capital city's delicious purveyor of deep-dish pies. Its original location, a tiny trailer at the back of an east-austin dive bar, is still slinging pizzas for late-night crowds, but they have recently expanded with another trailer and brick-and-mortar locations popping up all over town, including here on Rainey Street. **Known for:** simple favorites like the Detroiter (a pepperoni deep-dish topped with pepperoni casing); the city's heavyweight champion of Detroit-style deep dish; long wait times. *Average main: 16 96 Rainey St., Downtown 5122/609–9405 www.via313.com.*

Hotels

★ Austin Proper

$$$ | HOTEL | This Second Street hotel is the perfect luxury counterpart to the surrounding chichi retail district. **Pros:** plush in-room amenities; free bike rentals available; fifth-floor pool deck. **Cons:** small rooms; pricey valet parking fees; atmosphere can come across as stuffy. *Rooms from: 315 600 W. 2nd St., Downtown 512/628–1500 www.properhotel.com/austin No Meals 244 rooms.*

DoubleTree Suites by Hilton Hotel Austin

$$ | HOTEL | One of the best-managed hotels in the city, the all-suites DoubleTree has a staff that anticipates your every need. **Pros:** each room has full kitchen; superbly run; free on-demand downtown shuttle. **Cons:** fees for parking and in-room Wi-Fi; café food receives lackluster reviews; can be crowded. *Rooms from: $127 303 W. 15th St., Downtown 512/478–7000 www.hilton.com/en/doubletree 188 rooms Free Breakfast.*

★ The Driskill

$$ | HOTEL | Built in 1886 and impeccably restored, The Driskill represents a time when people mingled in grandiose settings and continues to epitomize old-world Texas luxury. **Pros:** attentive, personal staff; historic ambience; lots of personality and Old Austin grandeur. **Cons:** thin walls and loud weekend crowds; sits on an unattractive city block; no pool. *Rooms from: $199 604 Brazos St., Sixth Street District 512/439–1234 driskillhotel.com 189 rooms No Meals.*

★ Fairmont Austin

$$$ | HOTEL | As more hotels have opened nearby, the sophistication and modern creature comforts of the Fairmont have kept this property at the top of the heap in terms of downtown accommodations. **Pros:** popular spa services and poolside bar; stunning city views from certain rooms; premium amenities, from toiletries and linens to 55" smart TVs. **Cons:** customer service can leave guests wanting; expensive parking fees; not all standard rooms include luxe add-ons like free breakfast and self-parking. *Rooms from: 320 101 Red River St., Downtown 512/600–2000 www.fairmont.com/austin No Meals 1048 rooms.*

★ Four Seasons Hotel Austin

$$$$ | HOTEL | FAMILY | You get what you pay for in superior service and amenities at this elegant hotel on beautifully manicured grounds overlooking Lady Bird Lake. **Pros:** luxurious, resort-like feel; prime downtown location; exceptional services and activities for kids. **Cons:** parking is just as pricey; not the largest or poshest outdoor pool; prohibitively expensive for most. *Rooms from: $800 98 San Jacinto Blvd., Downtown 512/478–4500 fourseasons.com/austin 294 rooms Free Breakfast.*

Hilton Austin

$$ | HOTEL | This 31-story hotel rises over one of downtown's quieter blocks, next to small Brush Square Park (home to the O. Henry House), but the Hilton is defined by its proximity to the Austin Convention Center. **Pros:** full-service Starbucks on first floor; prime downtown location; health club that takes over a whole floor and includes saltwater pool and gym. **Cons:** expensive parking; lots of convention attendees; huge size can make it feel rather impersonal. *Rooms from: $195 500 E. 4th St., Downtown 512/482–8000 www3.hilton.com 826 rooms No Meals.*

Hotel ZaZa

$$$ | **HOTEL** | This chic downtown destination sets the scene for being seen with its vibrant decor, au courant outdoor lounges, and a coveted rooftop pool that attracts hip, beautiful crowds of travelers and locals alike. **Pros:** central location; complimentary downtown shuttle service; rooftop pool with city views. **Cons:** frequent noise complaints about downtown revelers; extras, like pool cabanas and spa services, can book up fast; small pool can get cramped on weekends. *Rooms from: 290 400 Lavaca St., Downtown 512/542–9292 www.hotelzaza.com No Meals 159 rooms.*

JW Marriott Austin

$$ | **HOTEL** | Always a trusted brand, the JW Marriott is a one-stop-shop for modern business travelers. **Pros:** seven bars and three restaurants on-site; walking distance to most downtown attractions; rooftop pool and spa. **Cons:** very business-oriented; renovated in 2015, but some aspects already need updating; sprawling size can feel corporate and impersonal. *Rooms from: 219 110 E. 2nd St., Downtown 512/474–4777 www.marriott.com No Meals 1012 rooms.*

★ Kimpton Hotel Van Zandt

$$ | **HOTEL** | Popular with groups, from bachelorette parties to corporate weekenders, this Rainey Street hot spot has become a downtown mainstay since opening in 2015. **Pros:** sleek interiors and decor; lively downtown location; prides itself on customer service. **Cons:** corporate take on "local" music culture; not for anyone looking for a heavy dose of peace and quiet; expect crowds and traffic on any given weekend. *Rooms from: 200 605 Davis St., Downtown 512/542–5300 www.hotelvanzandt.com No Meals 319 rooms.*

The LINE Austin

$$ | **HOTEL** | Renovated from its run-down mid-century status into a newly reinstated player in downtown Austin's burgeoning hotel scene, the LINE's major appeal is its prime location overlooking Lady Bird Lake. **Pros:** direct access to Lady Bird Lake's hike-and-bike trail; free bikes for guests; walking distance to downtown's best attractions and restaurants. **Cons:** lakeview rooms will cost you; lackluster service and amenities; nightclub and poolside DJs on weekends don't appeal to all guests. *Rooms from: 185 111 E. César Chávez St., Downtown 512/478–9611 www.thelinehotel.com No Meals 424 rooms.*

Omni Austin Hotel Downtown

$$ | **HOTEL** | Your introduction to this bustling, business-oriented hotel is a soaring, granite-and-glass atrium lobby. **Pros:** everything for the business traveler; central location; heated rooftop pool. **Cons:** not an ideal romantic escape; loud street noise on weekends; can feel impersonal. *Rooms from: $200 700 San Jacinto St., Downtown 512/476–3700 www.omnihotels.com 393 rooms No Meals.*

The Stephen F. Austin Royal Sonesta Hotel

$$ | **HOTEL** | Locally known as the "Stephen F.," this 1924 hotel has modernized guest rooms while still retaining the landmark's historic charms. The location can't be beat: smack in the middle of Congress Avenue, next door to the Paramount Theater, one block from Sixth Street and four blocks from the Capitol. **Pros:** gym and indoor lap pool; downtown walkability; free Wi-Fi. **Cons:** pricey valet parking; service can be inconsistent; some rooms are small and stuffy. *Rooms from: $217 701 Congress Ave., Downtown 512/457–8800 www.sonesta.com/us/texas/austin/stephen-f-austin-royal-sonesta-hotel 190 rooms No Meals.*

W Hotel

$$$$ | **HOTEL** | Located next to Austin City Limits Live at the Moody Theater, Austin's W Hotel has fast become the see-and-be-seen spot in the city. **Pros:**

hip street-level lounges and weekly events; excellent service and "whatever/whenever" concierge; most rooms offer downtown views. **Cons:** gets noisy on the weekends; the pool is chic but small and fills up fast; bustling lobby can feel a bit hectic. *Rooms from: $425* ✉ *200 Lavaca St., Downtown* ☎ *512/542–3600* 🌐 *www.marriott.com* *251 rooms* *No Meals.*

Nightlife

BARS

Bar 508

COCKTAIL LOUNGES | It's three places all wrapped up in one—including Pelóns restaurant and Zorro bar—but this is where you'll find much of the action later in the evening. It's also a great spot to grab a preshow drink before heading over to Stubb's across the street or the Mohawk just two blocks down. The chic Mexican-inspired lounge has a mirrored ceiling, a cozy fireplace, and a classic bar menu of cocktails and beers, but you also have the luxury of ordering from the full dinner menu from Pelóns without having to leave your seat. Happy hour (5–7 pm) is one of the best in the city, featuring $2 Lone Stars/PBRs, $3 well drinks, $4 wine, and $5 house sangria and margaritas. ✉ *508 E. 8th St., Downtown* ☎ *512/243-7874* 🌐 *www.bar508austin.com.*

Cheer Up Charlies

DANCE CLUBS | This beloved LGBTQ-friendly dive bar and dance club on Red River offers a friendly pour (whether it's a Lone Star beer, biodynamic wine, or kombucha on tap) and serves as a great meetup point thanks to its open back patio and weekly live music and theme dance parties. With its location in the heart of SXSW madness, expect music showcases and music-lovers in droves during festival time. ✉ *900 Red River St., Downtown* ☎ *512/431–2133* 🌐 *www.cheerupcharlies.com.*

★ The Driskill Bar

BARS | The old-fashioned bar at the Driskill is where history is made, from heavy-hitter political and business deals made over a handshake to Austin Film elite sketching out their next big idea. (It's also the very spot where future president Lyndon Baines Johnson proposed to his wife, Lady Bird Johnson, in his early political career.) Rich fabrics, dark wood, and cowhide aplenty give this iconic bar a warm and cozy appeal. Patrons enjoy live piano music throughout the week on the classic Steinway, an amiable vibe, and stiff cocktails in true Texas fashion. This historic luxury hotel and hotel bar reside in the epicenter of downtown Austin, so a VIP SXSW scene is definitely on the agenda. ✉ *604 Brazos St., Sixth Street District* ☎ *512/391–7162* 🌐 *driskillhotel.com/dining/driskill-bar.*

Half Step

BARS | A prime spot for craft cocktail aficionados, Half Step is a swanky locale boasting first-rate bartenders who are serious about cocktails, but not too serious to keep away the fun. Right in the heart of the buzzing Rainey Street District, Half Step lets your tastebuds lead the way with expert guidance from the bar. The intimate tables out back are perfect for a relaxed evening with friends. ✉ *75½ Rainey St., Rainey Street District* ☎ *512/522–0083* 🌐 *halfstepbar.com.*

The Living Room—W Hotel

COCKTAIL LOUNGES | A swanky downtown bar during most of the year, this hotel bar brings Austin nightlife to the next level during big city events such as the Austin City Limits Music Festival, Pride Week, and, of course, SXSW. There are multiple lounge spaces and bars here, including the Records Room where DJs play weekly, and an air-conditioned Screen Porch hangout. ✉ *200 Lavaca St., Downtown* ☎ *512/542–3600* 🌐 *www.marriott.com.*

★ Lustre Pearl

BARS | This fun Rainey Street favorite within a charming Austin bungalow and attached courtyard is usually filled with patrons hula hooping or playing bar games. Lustre Pearl is one hot ticket during SXSW, always hosting some of the hottest free events and day parties of the festival (make sure to RSVP). ✉ *97 Rainey St., Rainey Street District* ☎ *512/469–0400* 🌐 *dunlapatx.com/lustre-pearl-rainey.*

Maggie Mae's

BARS | This is one of Sixth Street's longest-running establishments and features an Irish-style bar, New Orleans–style courtyard, three stages, and one of the largest rooftop bars in Austin's downtown historic district. This expansive venue hosts a variety of bands throughout SXSW. ✉ *323 E. 6th St., Sixth Street District* ☎ *512/478–8541* 🌐 *maggiemaesaustin.com/spaces.*

★ Midnight Cowboy

COCKTAIL LOUNGES | An evening reservation at this diminutive cocktail club is an absolute must for craft cocktail lovers. The premises formerly housed an Asian massage parlor busted by local law enforcement for running an in-house escort service, and the club perpetuates a measure of mystique with a reservation-only policy and a low-key speakeasy-style entrance. (You have to press the buzzer marked "Harry Craddock" to gain access.) But the tableside cocktails are the main attraction, and for an intimate occasion with a couple of friends this is the perfect place for a nightcap. Reservations are available in two-hour time blocks and each table has a two-drink minimum. ✉ *313 E. 6th St., Sixth Street District* ☎ *512/843–2715* 🌐 *www.midnightcowboymodeling.com.*

The Ranch

BARS | On Sixth Street's "grown-up" west side, this multilevel bar has a tendency to get a little rowdy on weekends but manages to keep a steady flow of young execs popping in throughout the week. Large-screen TVs, upbeat DJ tunes, and an outdoor patio with a great view of the city skyline make this a perfect place for large gatherings with friends. It's also near a few choice spots to grab a bite to eat. It's currently only open on weekends and during Longhorn and Patriots football games. ✉ *710A W. 6th St., Downtown* ☎ *512/694–2469* 🌐 *www.theranchaustin.com.*

Small Victory

COCKTAIL LOUNGES | Look closely or you'll miss the entrance to this little jewel box of a bar with plush blue banquettes, baroque wallpaper, and a wood-box back bar framed in blue and brown subway tiles. Classic cocktails are the specialty here—this is the perfect place to learn what a classic martini should really taste like—and there's cheese, charcuterie, and other light fare on offer. Reservations are currently required. ✉ *108 E. 7th St., Downtown* ☎ *512/903–9450* 🌐 *www.smallvictory.bar.*

Speakeasy

BARS | Although Austin is better known for hole-in-the-wall bars, live music venues, and couture cocktail emporiums, this club is one of the main spots in the city. It is almost too trendy for Austin, but visitors may enjoy the 1920s speakeasy feel and rooftop views. This downtown establishment always play hosts to a variety of SXSW acts, too. ✉ *412 Congress Ave., Downtown* ☎ *512/476–8017* 🌐 *www.speakeasyaustin.com.*

COMEDY CLUBS

★ Esther's Follies

COMEDY CLUBS | There's really only one place in downtown Austin known for its rip-roaring comedy shows. Esther's has kept Austin rolling with laughter for more than 25 years. Reservations for their popular, award-winning variety shows are required. ✉ *525 E. 6th St., Sixth Street District* ☎ *512/320–0198* 🌐 *www.esthersfollies.com.*

Live music is a staple of Austin, whether it's a local act at a dive bar or a major band playing Austin City Limits.

Fallout Theater

COMEDY CLUBS | Home to some of Austin's top comedy and improv performances, the Fallout Theater draws a broad audience who journey into the rather small venue for cheap, free-sketch, stand-up, and improv comedy on most days of the week, often with two performance time-slots a night. The theater also offers eight-week classes on improv or sketch writing. There is a full-service bar, but some shows are BYOB. ✉ *616 Lavaca St., Downtown* ☎ *512/676–7209* 🌐 *fall-outcomedy.com.*

LIVE MUSIC

The Belmont

LIVE MUSIC | The grand dame of the trendy West 6th Street District, this fashionable bar and club has a swanky appeal with a lovely courtyard and Hollywood-esque waitstaff. It offers an impressive lineup, from indie rock to electronic dance music, and tends to bring an interesting mix of showcases to Austin during SXSW, partnering with several hot indie record labels. ✉ *305 W. 6th St., Downtown* ☎ *512/476–2100* 🌐 *www.thebelmontaustin.com.*

Cedar Street Courtyard

LIVE MUSIC | This place serves up a good time every night of the week, with live music from national and local bands. People love to catch the Spazmatics—a local '80s cover band—on Wednesday night as the courtyard becomes a playground after dark for revelers. Cedar Street offers one of the top SXSW showcases every year. RSVP and pick up your wristband early to catch a great lineup throughout the festival. ✉ *208 W. 4th St., Suite C, Downtown* ☎ *512/913–3289* 🌐 *www.cedarstreetatx.com.*

★ **Elephant Room**

LIVE MUSIC | Jazz fanatics hold court at this basement locale, named one of the top 10 jazz venues in the United States by the famed trumpeter Wynton Marsalis. A long-standing Austin venue, it's one of the reasons the town lives up to its Live Music Capital status. Though the Elephant's not a festival hot spot, the jazz staple always hosts its share of

South By Southwest 101

The annual South by Southwest (SXSW) Conference & Festivals takes the city by storm every March for roughly 10 days. The event, which presents music, independent films, comedy, and emerging technologies from around the globe, transforms downtown Austin as its main vein of action. The days-long, city-wide party brings together thousands of music and film lovers, young entrepreneurs, trend-seeking corporations, and entertainment industry insiders.

Even for those who thrive in organized chaos, the jam-packed days of SXSW can be overwhelming if you don't prepare. With over 2,300 bands performing in over 100 venues all over the city—not to mention countless film screenings, keynote speakers, interactive panels, free parties, and VIP events—it's smart to know ahead of time what you're looking to accomplish.

Buy the Badge

If you are in the entertainment industry and looking to expand your knowledge and network, go with the official SXSW option, aka: Buy the Badge. The Platinum Badge is pricey but will grant you full access to all elements of the Music, Film, and Interactive Conference and Festivals. This means nine days of film screenings and premieres; music, film, and interactive programming; and presentations and mentor sessions. Not to mention all the performances during the SXSW Music Festival.

Badge-holders also gain access to the SXSW Trade Show as well as all official Film, Interactive, and Music openings, closings, and awards parties throughout the event. The fact that badge-holders also receive preferred access to all nonofficial events and parties is icing on the cake once you see the lines the rest of the festival-goers will be standing in.

Visit the SXSW website (🌐 www.sxsw.com) to buy your badge—the site is a fantastic guide for all things official, from booking your hotel to customizing your personal festival agenda with the most current lineup of musical acts.

Go Unofficial

If you are not in the industry and just want to enjoy Austin at its finest, SXSW is still your festival. Celebrate in the streets, ramble across a lifetime's array of live music, and drink as much free beer as possible, also known as: Go Unofficial. There will be live music streaming from every nook and cranny in Austin throughout the festival. Gas stations, churches, and private residences are fair game. Like it or not, you will hear music. However, with a little bit of planning, you can have access to a full spectrum of free parties and events with fantastic lineups.

Visit various local venue and party websites and RSVP ahead of time, and you'll receive an email confirmation with directions on picking up your wristband. Lines to pick up wristbands are notoriously long, so arrive early. It's worth it though—those with the most wristbands are rewarded with the most access to music. Oh yeah—drinks are generally complimentary thanks to the festival's generous sponsors.

South by Southwest sees an influx of artists and entrepreneurs in the city along with many interactive and thought-provoking art installations.

musicians during SXSW. ✉ *315 Congress Ave., Downtown* ☎ *512/473–2279* 🌐 *www.elephantroom.com.*

The Gibson Room at Maggie Mae's

LIVE MUSIC | One of the top spots for live music on the perpetually vibrant East Sixth Street since 1978, the Gibson Room is one of famed bar Maggie Mae's music spaces and has its own entrance on the other side of the building. Sponsored by Gibson Guitars, this exclusive music venue is an artful homage to some of the world's greatest rock artists, styled with Gibson guitars associated with legendary musicians like Jimmy Page and Jimi Hendrix. Regular shows are open to the public, especially during SXSW, but the venue also hosts private events. ✉ *323 E. 6th St., Sixth Street District* ☎ *512/478–8541* 🌐 *maggiemaesaustin.com/spaces.*

Lamberts

LIVE MUSIC | Lamberts offers a luxurious take on barbecue in its swanky Second Street historic district locale while offering live music almost every night of the week in their upstairs loft. They host a mix of popular local musicians as well as highly acclaimed acts in an intimate setting and offer a full spectrum of SXSW offerings, including an impressive music-infused brunch. ✉ *401 W. 2nd St., Downtown* ☎ *512/494–1500* 🌐 *lambertsaustin.com.*

★ Mohawk

LIVE MUSIC | By sheer force, this Red River District establishment is one of the best live music venues in Austin. With a cool, indoor indie-rock space complemented with a killer outdoor stage and the area's only rooftop deck and bar, these guys know how to throw a party. Expect serious jams and strong pours seven nights a week. "The Hawk" bleeds SXSW and hosts a festival within a festival. ✉ *912 Red River St., Downtown* ☎ *512/666–0877* 🌐 *www.mohawkaustin.com.*

The Parish

LIVE MUSIC | This split-level bar and music venue offers an impressive lineup of musicians, DJs, and bands year-round on both its upstairs stage and its smaller, downstairs lounge stage at the bar. Aside from the music, the main draws for this Sixth Street locale are cocktails and good eats from the grill. Expect great things during SXSW. Hours of operation vary daily depending on their show calendar, so be sure to check their website. ✉ *214 E. 6th St., Sixth Street District* ☎ *No phone* 🌐 *www.parishaustin.com.*

★ Stubb's

LIVE MUSIC | One of the city's most highly touted venues, Stubb's is owned by C3 Presents, which books many of the top shows in Austin (in addition to producing the annual ACL Fest) and also manages an impressive roster of nationally renowned musicians. This massive outdoor venue (and barbecue joint by day) hosts an impressive lineup in downtown's Red River District. It's one of the hottest SXSW tickets in town. ✉ *801 Red River St., Downtown* ☎ *512/480–8341* 🌐 *www.stubbsaustin.com.*

Performing Arts

★ ACL Live at the Moody Theater

CONCERTS | The iconic PBS music show *Austin City Limits*is one of the city's treasures, and anyone can see it live. In true ACL fashion, live tapings for each season are still announced to the public at a moment's notice, and general admission is still free for those who wait in line for tickets. The theater also hosts an additional lineup of amazing musical acts throughout the year, independent of the television show's taping schedule. The 2,750-seat auditorium manages to maintain an intimate feel where every seat is a good seat. ✉ *310 Willie Nelson Blvd., Downtown* ☎ *512/225–7999* 🌐 *www.acl-live.com.*

Ballet Austin

BALLET | **FAMILY** | Now in a state-of-the-art downtown center, Ballet Austin has risen in prominence over the years as the city's preeminent dance company. Part performance company and part dance academy (with classes available to the general public), Ballet Austin puts on a regular lineup of ballet productions, performed at the Long Center, throughout the year, including an annual rendition of the classic *The Nutcracker*each holiday season. The season runs from September through May, with season tickets options that offer better seating for frequent attendees. ✉ *501 W. 3rd St., Downtown* ☎ *512/476–9151* 🌐 *www.balletaustin.org.*

★ The Paramount Theatre

THEATER | **FAMILY** | In a restored downtown vaudeville house and movie palace, this gorgeous 1915 theater presents musicals and plays by touring theater companies and hosts concerts by well-known jazz, folk, and rock artists, along with the occasional stand-up comedian and speaker series. In April, it hosts the annual four-day Moontower Comedy Festival, and during the summer, movie lovers escape the heat for the Summer Classic Film Series, featuring time-honored films from *Gone with the Wind* to *The Wizard of Oz.* ✉ *713 Congress Ave., Downtown* ☎ *512/472–5470* 🌐 *www.austintheatre.org.*

Shopping

★ BookPeople

BOOKS | **FAMILY** | Texas's largest independent bookstore is a homegrown alternative to monster chain stores. It was established in 1970 and has been voted Austin's best bookstore for more than 20 years, stocking bestsellers along with books on topics such as women's studies, personal growth, and alternative home building; there's also a good children's section. Browse magazines; shop for quirky, hard-to-find gifts; and catch readings and signings by local authors, literati luminaries, and even former presidents who make stops here while on book tours. ✉ *603 N. Lamar Blvd., Clarksville* ☎ *512/472–5050* 🌐 *www.bookpeople.com.*

★ Toy Joy

TOYS | FAMILY | This fantastic place is so much the ultimate toy store of your childhood fantasies that it's too good to save for actual children—don't be embarrassed to come in even if you don't have little ones of your own. It's *the* place to get things like Edgar Allan Poe and Beethoven action figures, vinyl dinosaur figurines, reproductions of vintage toys you played with as a kid, and floor-to-ceiling diversions for all ages, including science toys, metal robots, stuffed animals, costumes, hard-to-find candy, baubles and bangles, and more. ✉ *403 W. 2nd St., Downtown* ☎ *512/320–0090* 🌐 *www.toyjoy.com.*

Whole Foods Market

MARKET | Right at the cusp of downtown, the 80,000-square-foot flagship store for the natural/organic supermarket chain's world headquarters is both a showcase for the company's philosophy and one of the most entertaining supermarkets you'll ever visit. It's been a major tourist attraction (seriously) since it opened in 2005. There are several places inside the massive store to enjoy a casual sit-down lunch, and the options are abundant, whether you're craving sushi, pizza, or seafood. The store also has one of Austin's largest wine selections and a walk-in beer cooler (to keep those six-packs cold). There's ample free garage parking available. ✉ *525 N. Lamar Blvd., Downtown* ☎ *512/542–2200* 🌐 *www.wholefoodsmarket.com.*

Central Austin and the University of Texas

Envisioning Austin without the University of Texas is like envisioning Washington, D.C., without the National Mall. The sprawling campus itself is both charming (winding pathways past austere stone university buildings) and inspiring (the landmark UT Tower, the Blanton Museum of Art, the LBJ Library and Museum) and sometimes even thrilling (Darrell K. Royal–Texas Memorial Stadium, home of the Longhorns).

Perhaps the best-known area around campus where students hang out is known as the Drag. This busy (and gritty) strip on Guadalupe Street borders the west side of the UT campus and is packed with trendy boutiques, vintage-clothing shops, and restaurants. Keep in mind that parking around campus can be a challenge, with the large student body and faculty getting priority.

Sights

★ Blanton Museum of Art

ART MUSEUM | FAMILY | One of the largest university art museums in the United States, with 200,000 square feet that includes two buildings and the adjacent Ellsworth Kelly *Austin*installation, the Blanton is the city's de facto art collection. There are more than 19,000 various works on display (from ancient Greek pottery to abstract expressionism) and a year-round schedule of incredible traveling exhibitions. As part of an ongoing "New Grounds" initiative, the Blanton campus (featuring outdoor and indoor event spaces, classrooms, a museum shop, and a café) will soon include additional public art installations, such as a massive mural by Cuban-American artist Carmen Herrera that will span both sides of the entrance. Admission is free on Thursday. ✉ *200 E. Martin Luther King Jr. Blvd., University of Texas Area* ☎ *512/471–5482* 🌐 *www.blantonmuseum.org* 🎟 *$12* ⏲ *Closed Mon. and Tues.*

Briscoe Center for American History

HISTORY MUSEUM | Named in honor of former governor Dolph Briscoe, the Briscoe Center at the University of Texas is a go-to scholarly resource for 750,000-plus photographs, thousands of archival documents, hundreds of handmade quilts, and over 50,000 music recordings.

The Blanton Museum of Art is a highlight of Austin's art scene.

The staff are expert researchers who sift through these artifacts to chronicle a fascinating stockpile of American and Texas history. While much of the center functions as a research facility (available by reservation only), frequently changing exhibits of items from the collections are open to the public on weekdays. ✉ *2300 Red River St., University of Texas Area* ☎ *512/495–4515* 🌐 *www.briscoecenter.org* 🕓 *Closed weekends* ☞ *Reservations essential.*

★ Bullock Texas State History Museum
HISTORY MUSEUM | FAMILY | The 38th lieutenant governor of Texas, Bob Bullock—a potent political force in his day—lobbied hard to establish a museum of state history during his years of public service. Bullock didn't live to see it happen—he died in 1999—but his dream came true in 2001 with the opening of this fascinating museum just a few blocks north of the Capitol. Now, over 9 million visitors from around the world have toured the museum's 34,000 square feet of exhibit space that showcases "The Story of Texas." See exhibitions of archaeological objects, historical documents, and touring shows from regional museums throughout the state. You can also check out educational and family-friendly programs, or get tickets to a show at the 400-seat IMAX theater. ✉ *1800 Congress Ave., Downtown* ☎ *512/936–8746* 🌐 *www.thestoryoftexas.com* 🎟 *$13* 🕓 *Closed Mon. and Tues.*

Darrell K. Royal—Texas Memorial Stadium
SPORTS VENUE | FAMILY | Longhorns bleed burnt orange and nowhere is that more evident than at a game at Darrell K. Royal—Texas Memorial Stadium. Originally constructed in 1924, the stadium was renamed after the famed football coach in 1996. Today, it stands as a large reminder of his legacy. Catch a game or tailgate party, and make sure to look ahead: sometimes there are special exhibits in the end zone. The stadium does offer tours, but you'll have to check the website to see when the next one will be held. ✉ *2139 San Jacinto Blvd.,*

University of Texas Area ☎ *512/471–3333* 🌐 *www.texassports.com.*

Harry Ransom Center

COLLEGE | Part of the University of Texas, the Ransom Center is one of the world's greatest collectors and exhibitors of important literary papers and other artifacts related to the arts and humanities. Among its fantastic riches are the papers of Norman Mailer, Isaac Bashevis Singer, and Arthur Miller; Woodward and Bernstein's Watergate research materials; more than 10,000 film, television, and radio scripts; more than 10,000 film posters; and one million rare books, including an original Gutenberg Bible. Traveling exhibitions bring artifacts from classic masterpieces like *Gone With the Wind* and artist Frida Kahlo's "Self-Portrait with Thorn Necklace and Hummingbird" to the space. ■ **TIP→ Many documents can only be seen with advance notice, so call ahead if you have a specific item in mind.** ✉ *300 W. 21st St., University of Texas Area* ☎ *512/471–8944* 🌐 *www.hrc.utexas.edu* 🎫 *Free* ⏲ *Closed Mon.*

LBJ Presidential Library

HISTORY MUSEUM | The artifacts and documents on exhibit here provide some insight into the 36th president's mind and motivations, and though his foibles are downplayed, a clear sense of the man—earthy, conniving, sensitive, and wry—emerges. In an age when the average car is loaded with digital gadgets and 12-year-olds with cell phones are commonplace, Johnson's black Lincoln limousine and clunky, command-central telephone seem quaintly archaic, though they were state-of-the-art during his presidency. If you schedule your visit to the reading room in advance of your arrival, you can listen to recordings of conversations Johnson had using that telephone. The 30-plus hours of tape recordings include ruminations on Vietnam, economic inflation, and a New York City transit strike. Gordon Bunshaft designed the monolithic travertine building that houses the library; like the limo and the phone, it's a bit of a period piece. There are rotating temporary exhibits on the ground floor. ■ **TIP→ Be sure to check out the second floor, where a life-size audio-animatronic figure of LBJ spins humorous anecdotes; it's a hoot.** ✉ *2313 Red River St., University of Texas Area* ☎ *512/721–0200* 🌐 *www.lbjlibrary.org* 🎫 *$13.*

Texas Memorial Museum

HISTORY MUSEUM | French architect Paul Cret's 1936 plans for Texas Memorial Museum called for north and south wings to extend from a central building, a tailored limestone box with subtle art deco flourishes. The wings were scuttled because of funding difficulties, leaving only Cret's alabaster midsection. But the chic interior, with brass doors, glass embellishments, and blood-red marble walls, floors, and ceilings, mitigates any sense of abridgement. Among the popular draws at the museum are the dinosaur models (including a 30-foot-long mosasaur and a 40-foot-long pterosaur) and the life-size dioramas, which depict buffalo, roadrunners, cougars, mountain lions, and flying squirrels. ✉ *2400 Trinity St., University of Texas Area* ☎ *512/471–1604* 🌐 *www.tmm.utexas.edu* 🎫 *$7* ⏲ *Closed Sun. and Mon.*

The University of Texas at Austin

COLLEGE | The nearly 450-acre campus breeds Texas Longhorns, as passionate about football (and other sports) as they are about academics (UT has one of the country's top research libraries). The university is the largest employer in Austin (even more than the state government), employing more than 80,000 people. The number of students here is staggering, too: 39,500 undergraduates and more than 51,000 university-wide. Come to the grounds any time to stroll on your own, visit one of the museums or libraries (the Harry Ransom Center, for example, is the repository for the Watergate papers), or attend a fun annual event like Explore UT, Gone to Texas, or commencement,

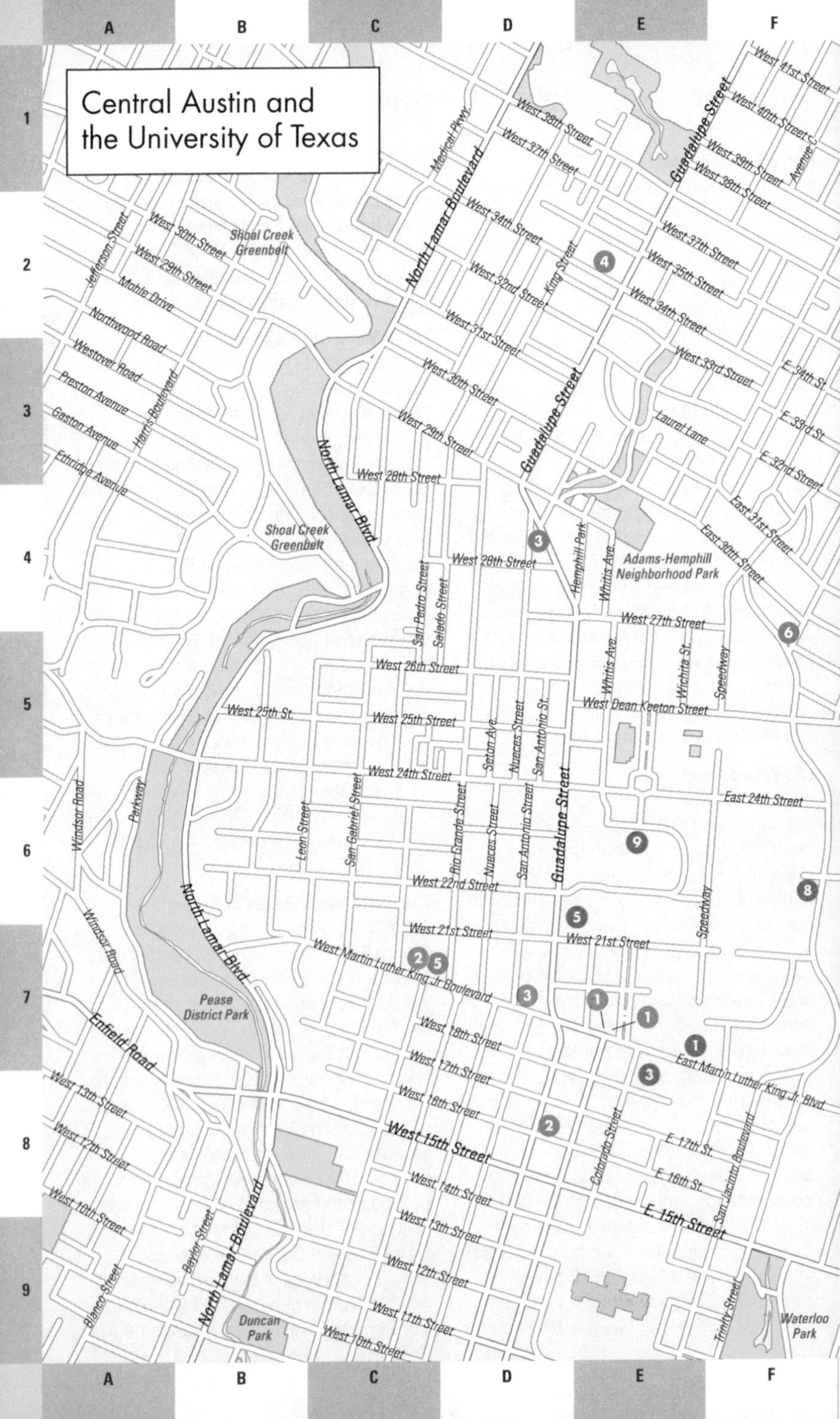
Central Austin and the University of Texas
A
B
C
D
E
F
1
2
3
4
5
6
7
8
9
West 41st Street
West 40th Street
West 39th Street
West 38th Street
Avenue C
Guadalupe Street
West 38th Street
West 37th Street
Medical Pkwy.
North Lamar Boulevard
West 34th Street
West 37th Street
West 35th Street
West 34th Street
West 32nd Street
King Street
West 31st Street
West 33rd Street
E. 34th St.
West 30th Street
Guadalupe Street
Laurel Lane
E. 33rd St.
West 29th Street
E. 32nd Street
East 31st Street
East 30th Street
West 28th Street
North Lamar Blvd.
Shoal Creek Greenbelt
Jefferson Street
West 30th Street
West 29th Street
Mohle Drive
Northwood Road
Westover Road
Harris Boulevard
Preston Avenue
Gaston Avenue
Ethridge Avenue
Shoal Creek Greenbelt
West 28th Street
Hemphill Park
Whitis Ave.
Adams-Hemphill Neighborhood Park
San Pedro Street
Salado Street
West 27th Street
West 26th Street
Whitis Ave.
Wichita St.
Speedway
West 25th St.
West 25th Street
Seton Ave.
Nueces Street
San Antonio St.
West Dean Keeton Street
West 24th Street
East 24th Street
Windsor Road
Parkway
Leon Street
San Gabriel Street
Rio Grande Street
Nueces Street
San Antonio Street
Guadalupe Street
West 22nd Street
Speedway
North Lamar Blvd.
West 21st Street
West 21st Street
Windsor Road
West Martin Luther King Jr Boulevard
Pease District Park
West 18th Street
Enfield Road
West 17th Street
East Martin Luther King Jr. Blvd.
West 13th Street
West 16th Street
West 12th Street
West 15th Street
Colorado Street
E. 17th St.
E. 16th St.
San Jacinto Boulevard
West 14th Street
West 10th Street
Baylor Street
North Lamar Boulevard
West 13th Street
E. 15th Street
West 12th Street
Blanco Street
Duncan Park
West 11th Street
West 10th Street
Trinity Street
Waterloo Park
1
1
1
2
2
3
3
3
4
5
5
6
8
9

Sights

1 Blanton Museum of Art............E7
2 Briscoe Center for American History.................H6
3 Bullock Texas State History Museum...................E8
4 Darrell K Royal—Texas Memorial Stadium.........G7
5 Harry Ransom Center..............E6
6 LBJ Presidential Library..........G6
7 Texas Memorial Museum.........G6
8 The University of Texas at Austin.....................F6
9 UT Tower............................E6

Restaurants

1 The Carillon..........................E7
2 Clay Pit.............................D8
3 Dirty Martin's Place...............D4
4 FoodHeads..........................E2
5 Goodall's.............................C7
6 Posse East...........................F5

Hotels

1 AT&T Hotel and Conference Center.................E7
2 Hotel Ella.............................C7
3 The Otis Hotel......................D7

which includes fireworks. ✉ *1 University Station, University of Texas Area* ☎ *512/471–3434* 🌐 *www.utexas.edu* 🎫 *Free.*

★ **UT Tower**

VIEWPOINT | The centerpiece of the University of Texas campus is a living piece of Austin history. Still functioning as a university administration office, the 27-floor tower (which shines with bright-white and burnt-orange lights on special occasions and game days) houses rich regional and national experience from the 1930s on. Self-guided tours (complete with 360-degree views of the campus and city from the observation deck) are available, but advance reservations are required. ✉ *110 Inner Campus Dr., University of Texas* ☎ *512/475–6633* 🌐 *www.tower.utexas.edu* 🎫 *$6.*

Restaurants

The Carillon

$$$$ | AMERICAN | In 2014, executive Chef Josh Watkins left the Carillon—a stylish New American concept he helped launch in 2008—but the highly regarded fine-dining destination in the heart of the UT campus has retained its dedicated team of in-house chefs and fleet of exceptional servers. The four-course tasting selection ($50) is an artfully presented, well-proportioned sampling of any four dishes on the menu, diner's choice. **Known for:** expertly prepared prix-fixe menus; impeccable service; Wednesday happy hour specials. 💲 *Average main: $32* ✉ *AT&T Executive Center, 1900 University Ave., University of Texas Area* ☎ *512/404–3655* 🌐 *www.thecarillonrestaurant.com.*

★ **Clay Pit**

$$ | INDIAN | A tried-and-true destination for homemade Indian cuisine, Clay Pit has developed a devoted following in Austin since 1998. Wash down some of their signature curried mussels with garlic and red wine sauce with one of their sweet lassi drinks. **Known for:** incredible quality without any hype; popular lunch service; amazing vegan options. 💲 *Average main: 15* ✉ *1601 Guadalupe St., Central Austin/Downtown/Capitol Area* ☎ *512/322–5131* 🌐 *www.claypit.com.*

★ **Dirty Martin's Place**

$ | BURGER | This greasy spoon just north of the UT campus has been satisfying the guilty pleasures of students (and those from all walks of life) since 1926. There might not be dirt floors and open-flame grills anymore, but the burgers and sides are still classically unpretentious (with no grass-fed menu descriptions) but with plenty of flavor (and grease). **Known for:** best stick-to-your-gut burger in town; raucous game-day crowds; classic campus vibe complete with cheap prices. 💲 *Average main: $6* ✉ *2808 Guadalupe St., University of Texas Area* ☎ *512/477–3173* 🌐 *www.dirtymartins.com.*

FoodHeads

$ | SANDWICHES | This Austin classic is a refreshing change of pace from the trendy hot spots and long lines downtown and on the east side. The relaxed counter service and down-home decor at the charming cottage-turned-café matches the classic handmade offerings of sandwiches, soups, and salads. **Known for:** no-frills counter service with long lines during peak hours; funky, chill vibes in an "at home" setting; organic, locally sourced vegetarian options with a dedicated lunch following. 💲 *Average main: 12* ✉ *616 W. 34th St., University of Texas Area* ☎ *512/420–8400* 🌐 *www.foodheads.com* 🕓 *Closed Sun. No dinner.*

Goodall's

$$$ | AMERICAN | Now Hotel Ella, the historic Goodall Wooten mansion still retains its stately, old-world charm, and Goodall's occupies the main floor. The romantic setting screams special occasion, with a concise (and pricey) menu. **Known for:** wonderful on-site luxury for hotel guests; exclusive, special occasion atmosphere; popular brunch service. 💲 *Average main:*

Head to the top of UT Tower for an excellent view of the University of Texas campus.

$26 ✉ Hotel Ella, 1900 Rio Grande St., University of Texas Area ☎ 512/495–1800 🌐 www.hotelella.com/goodalls.

Posse East

$ | **AMERICAN** | This campus-adjacent hangout has been the preeminent destination to meet with friends and fellow sports lovers, knock back brews, and eat burgers on game day since 1971. The patio can be packed to the gills on weekends or just dotted with casual groups of friends on slow weeknights, but the kitchen is always serving its pub-grub menu of sandwiches, burgers, and wings—and the flat-screen–covered walls are always flickering. **Known for:** famed game day and tailgating outpost; walking distance to UT stadium; shareable pub grub that won't break the bank. *[$] Average main: 8 ✉ 2900 Duval St., University of Texas Area ☎ 512/477–2111 🌐 www.posseeast.com.*

Hotels

AT&T Hotel and Conference Center

$$ | **HOTEL** | Business travelers, conference attendees, and a host of visiting relatives in town for UT graduations and other special events frequent this campus-area hotel. **Pros:** great location to explore UT by foot; wonderful on-site dining; very business-friendly. **Cons:** crowds during UT games and other citywide events; downtown and other major neighborhoods are a short drive away; vibe can be corporate/stuffy. *[$] Rooms from: $195 ✉ 1900 University Ave., University of Texas Area ☎ 512/404–1900 🌐 www.meetattexas.com 297 rooms No Meals.*

Hotel Ella

$$$ | **HOTEL** | Historical elegance and modern amenities converge in this 47-room boutique hotel, located in the Goodall Wooten mansion on the south edge of the UT campus, a Texas Historic Landmark completed in 1900 that still shines in all its Classical Revival glory.

Eat Like a Local

Austin is defined by an inventive, fusion-inspired food scene that goes way beyond the city's breakfast-taco obsession and its long-standing love of all things barbecue. As the influx of thousands of international transplants and adventurous foodies continues, the culinary scene is thriving and changing on an almost daily basis. Here's what you need to know in order to eat like an Austin local.

Breakfast Tacos

Greasy Tex-Mex and Texas-size portions of Mexican food aren't for everybody, but the indulgence of breakfast tacos is a daily sacrament for Austinites. They come in all shapes and sizes, from the massive signatures at Juan in a Million and the hidden gems of El Primo to the popular creations at Veracruz All Natural. It doesn't matter what time of day or how fancy the establishment—odds are, breakfast tacos are on the menu.

Food Trucks

Austin was an early pioneer in the food-truck movement, and visitors can still find almost anything—from doughnuts to lobster rolls—at a humble trailer. Some food trucks find permanent homes at hip local bars. Others, such as The Mighty Cone and Habibi ATX, congregate together at popular open-air food courts that have popped up all over town, like The Picnic food-truck lot on Barton Springs Road.

BBQ

Barbecue is a hallowed Texas institution, but it's currently having a big revival in Austin, with everyone from cowboys to bearded hipsters waiting in long lines for a succulent slab of fatty brisket. Presentation now runs the gamut, so it's become the type of food that's perfect for a casual lunch (think picnic-style at la Barbecue trailer), a bucket-list day in line at Franklin Barbecue, or a fancy night out at Lamberts on Second Street.

Healthy Food

Austin is no Los Angeles and its penchant for fried and barbecued fare is a testament to its culinary grit. But the city is also known for being extremely fit, and a host of health-conscious options, from Daily Juice Cafe and JuiceLand (two popular juice and smoothie purveyors) to all-vegetarian eateries like Bouldin Creek Cafe and Counter Culture are definite hot spots.

Locavore

A bevy of new and diverse destinations, from New American to Asian fusion, have arrived on the scene within the past few years, but their binding similarity is their commitment to locally sourced cuisine. Certain hip eateries can sway into an almost *Portlandia*-realm of locavore status, with some chefs personally foraging their own ingredients from the surrounding Hill Country. But the perceived trendiness shouldn't put visitors off. The culinary community's dedication to local farms and food purveyors is a very serious, enduring commitment, from food trucks to fine dining.

Pros: attentive staff; beautifully restored; perfect for romantic getaways. **Cons:** noise can be an issue; standard rooms are cramped, with no views; pricey. *Rooms from: $250 1900 Rio Grande St., University of Texas Area 512/495–1800, 800/311–1619 www.hotelella.com 47 rooms No Meals.*

The Otis Hotel

$$ | **HOTEL** | The first Autograph Collection property in Austin, the Otis features clean, chic, and modern rooms and on-site dining options that are unmatched for the area. **Pros:** exceptional service and personal amenities, like customized vinyl selections on demand; great views from the rooftop pool and bar; amazing location for visiting UT or attending Longhorn games. **Cons:** connected to the AC Hotel, so busy weekends can be congested and noisy; short drive to downtown and other hubs; rooms are comfortable but have a corporate feel. *Rooms from: 169 1901 San Antonio St., University of Texas Area 512/473–8900 www.otishotel.com No Meals 191 rooms.*

Nightlife

BARS

Cain & Abel's

BARS | Things are always distinctly "fratty" at this wildly popular local haunt for college students and alumni alike right in the heart of the University of Texas campus. The crowds here on game day aren't for the faint of heart. *2313 Rio Grande St., University of Texas Area 512/476–3201 www.abels.com.*

Scholz Garten

BEER GARDENS | When they're not tailgating for the University of Texas Longhorns, sports fans can be found living it up at this historic hall. In continuous operation since 1866, the "little beer joint that could" is the oldest operating business not only in Austin but also in the entire state. Although it's not in the downtown entertainment district, this Austin classic hosts live music and other events and always welcomes performers during SXSW. *1607 San Jacinto Blvd., Central Austin/Downtown/Capitol Area 512/474–1958 www.scholzgarten.com.*

LIVE MUSIC

★ Cactus Cafe

LIVE MUSIC | For an intimate live music experience unmatched by any other venue in Austin, head to this café on the UT campus and get in line for tickets. Texas singer-songwriter legends such as Lyle Lovett, Robert Earl Keen, Patty Griffin, and Austin-renowned Bob Schneider have graced this tiny stage since the 1970s. It doesn't get much better than this. *Texas Union, UT Campus, 24th and Guadalupe St., University of Texas Area 512/475–6515 www.cactuscafe.org.*

★ Spider House Ballroom

LIVE MUSIC | For over 25 years, this near-campus joint established itself as the perfect coffee shop escape for studying sessions or catching up with friends. Recently, the full-service bar and café has consolidated and changed up its array of offerings with its adjacent Ballroom space and transformed more exclusively into a live music and event operation, with weekly lineups of local music, theme parties, movie screenings, and stand-up comedy. Their bar still serves hip crowds of locals who can also dine at the on-site food trucks. *2906 Fruth St., University of Texas Area No phone www.spiderhouseatx.com.*

Performing Arts

PERFORMING ARTS VENUES

Bass Concert Hall

MUSIC | The flagship theater of the Texas Performing Arts is the largest of its kind in Austin and attracts visitors from near and far for special symphony, orchestra, choral, ensemble, and concert band performances. The 2,900-seat auditorium is world-class in every way. Also inside, the smaller, more intimate Bates Recital Hall features performances by both students and faculty of the University of Texas as well as professional visiting musicians. ✉ *2350 Robert Dedman Dr., University of Texas Area* ☎ *512/471–2787* 🌐 *www.texasperformingarts.org/visit/venues/bass-concert-hall.*

McCullough Theatre

CONCERTS | Not only the performance space for the University of Texas at Austin's excellent orchestra, dance, drama, and lyric opera productions, this intimate, modern 400-seat proscenium theater also brings a wide range of professional musicians to the stage, including chamber music and solo recitals. In addition to classical music, you might catch a show, such as *Jersey Boys* or *Annie*, or recording artists, such as Stewart Copeland or John Mellencamp. The theater is located in the same building as Bass Concert Hall. ✉ *2375 Robert Dedman Dr., University of Texas Area* ☎ *512/471–1444* 🌐 *texasperformingarts.org/visit/venues/mccullough-theatre.*

Moody Center

CONCERTS | A multipurpose arena and venue currently under construction, Moody Center is set to replace downtown's existing (42-year-old) Frank Erwin Center in April 2022. The state-of-the-art stadium will feature a staggering 530,000 square feet that will welcome performers from around the world, as well as athletes from the University of Texas's men's and women's basketball teams. ✉ *2001 Robert Dedman Dr., University of Texas Area* ☎ *512/975–2222* 🌐 *www.moodycenteratx.com.*

Shopping

GIFTS AND SOUVENIRS

★ University Co-Op

SOUVENIRS | **FAMILY** | The beating burnt-orange heart of Longhorn Nation is on display at the ultimate showcase of UT sports paraphernalia, located right smack in the middle of the Drag on campus. You can find burnt-orange-and-Longhorn-logoed everything at this three-level emporium, from Crocs and dress shirts to bath mats, a full set of luggage, and even a $350 pair of Lucchese cowboy boots and a $600 acoustic guitar. An entire room is devoted to children's wear, from the nursery on up. Founded in 1896 and modeled after a similar co-op at Harvard, UT's Co-op (which offers discounts to faculty, students, and staff) claims to be the largest seller of used textbooks in the country. Even if you have no direct (or indirect) connection to UT, do stop in if you're in the neighborhood; it's gawk-inducing and unforgettable. ✉ *2246 Guadalupe St., University of Texas Area* ☎ *512/476–7211* 🌐 *www.universitycoop.com.*

HOUSEHOLD GOODS

Breed & Co.

GENERAL STORE | The classiest hardware store in Austin doesn't just stock a prism of paints and garden gadgets. It's dedicated to home improvement in all regards. Browse the Waterford china, Simon Pearce dinnerware, and aisles upon aisles of kitchen tools. It's the go-to place for popular local cookbooks from the Tipsy Texan, Uchi, and Fonda San Miguel and a variety of other locally made art and gifts, like sweetly scented soaps and candles and swoon-worthy leather goods. ✉ *718 W. 29th St., University of Texas Area* ☎ *512/474–6679* 🌐 *shop.breedandco.com.*

MARKETS

★ 23rd Street Artists' Market

MARKET | This year-round, open-air market with roots stretching back to the early 1970s is the soul of the Drag. The unreconstructed hippie ambience is at least as much of a draw as the actual merchandise crafted and sold by various local artisans. The wares include jewelry, leatherwork, candles, photographs, paintings, sculpture, textiles, and the inevitable tie-dyed T-shirts. Note that the market is firmly regulated by the city, and all vendors must be licensed by a commission. Days and hours of operation have been changed and scaled down since COVID; current status updates can be found on their website and social media pages. ✉ *23rd at Guadalupe St., University of Texas Area* ☎ *512/974–4000* 🌐 *www.austinartistsmarket.com/directory/entry/23rd-street-artists-market/*.

MUSIC

Antone's Record Shop
RECORDS | In the self-proclaimed Live Music Capital of the World, nothing is as sweet as finding a record store like this one. With an emphasis on local Texas players and blues music, the shop opened as a hangout for showgoers back when Antone's Nightclub was across the street. Over the years, performers like Memphis Slim, James Cotton, Pinetop Perkins, and Doug Sahm played the club and recorded for the Antone's label. Today, you'll find bins of vinyl as well as new releases and various posters and gifts. An expert staff can help serious music lovers with any and all inquiries. ✉ *2928 Guadalupe St., Suite 101, University of Texas Area* ☎ *512/322–0660* 🌐 *www.antonesrecordshop.com*.

West Austin and Zilker Park

West Austin generally refers to the area just west of Lamar Boulevard (not to be confused with West Lake, the area west of Lake Austin). It's a laid-back, pleasant part of town with great outdoor activities, some of Austin's largest music festivals, and wonderful local eateries. The gem of the neighborhood is undoubtedly Zilker Park, Austin's backyard—and playground—where people go swimming and jogging or just hang out for hours with food, drinks, and friends.

Sights

Austin Nature & Science Center
SCIENCE MUSEUM | **FAMILY** | Adjacent to Zilker Botanical Garden on the western edge of Zilker Park, this complex has an 80-acre preserve trail, interactive exhibits in the Discovery Lab that teach about the ecology of the Austin area, and animal exhibits focusing on subjects such as bees, birds of prey, and native wildlife. Parking is available under the Mopac Bridge. ✉ *2389 Stratford Dr., Zilker Park* ☎ *512/974–3888* 🌐 *www.austintexas.gov/department/austin-nature-science-center* 🎟 *Free.*

★ Barton Creek Greenbelt
TRAIL | **FAMILY** | This 12-mile series of hike-and-bike trails follows the contour of Barton Creek and the canyon it created west along an 8-mile-long area from Zilker Park to west of Loop 360. The popular Greenbelt features even more sought-after swimming holes when the creek is full (very rain-dependent, it's usually in spring and fall). Several access points will get you on the riverside trails, including at Zilker Park, Loop 360, Twin Falls, Scottish Woods Trail Falls (near the intersection of MoPac and Loop 360), and Scottish Woods Trail (at the trail's northern border, off Loop 360). ✉ *3755 S. Capital of Texas Hwy. B, West Austin/Zilker Park* ☎ *512/974–6700* 🌐 *www.austinparks.org/barton-creek-greenbelt/* 🎟 *Free.*

★ Barton Springs Pool
POOL | **FAMILY** | No visit to Austin is complete without a ceremonial dip in the sacred waters of Barton Springs. The hallowed crown jewel of the Zilker Park area, this historic spring-fed pool maintains a constant 68° temperature year-round, and the chilly waters attract hordes of people from all walks of life. It's an idyllic paradise for free-spirited people-watching and unique experiences, like the nightly and full-moon (when revelers howl at the moon in unison) free swims and the annual Polar Bear

Locals flock to Barton Springs Pool on hot days for a swim in its always-temperate waters.

Plunge held on New Year's Day. Weather can affect operating hours throughout the season, so be sure to check their website in advance. ✉ *Zilker Park, 2201 Barton Springs Rd., West Austin/Zilker Park* ☎ *512/974–6300* 🌐 *www.austintexas.gov/department/barton-springs-pool* 🎟 *From $2* ⏲ *Closed Thurs.*

★ The Contemporary Austin–Laguna Gloria
ART MUSEUM | FAMILY | Set on a lush Lake Austin peninsula, this 1915 Mediterranean-style villa was once home to Clara Driscoll, who led the fight to save the Alamo from demolition in the early 20th century. In this lovely environment, the villa is surrounded by impressively kept grounds (which include lakeside walking trails) and a stunning collection of outdoor sculptures and rotating exhibits of world-renowned artists. An art school shares the idyllic setting of this building, which is listed on the National Register of Historic Places, and there's now a gift shop and on-site café, Spread & Co., that help elongate an afternoon visit to this scenic spot. Advance ticket reservations are currently required in advance. ✉ *3809 W. 35th St., West Austin* ☎ *512/458–8191* 🌐 *www.thecontemporaryaustin.org/lagunagloria* 🎟 *$10* ⏲ *Closed Mon. and Tues.*

Deep Eddy Pool
POOL | FAMILY | The oldest swimming pool in Texas (1915), this man-made, spring-fed swimming hole just off Lake Austin Boulevard was the centerpiece of an early-20th-century resort and was purchased and restored by the Works Progress Administration in the mid-1930s. In recent years, Friends of Deep Eddy, a volunteer community group, led a successful effort to fully restore the long-closed 1936 bathhouse. Today it remains a beloved local institution for all ages and walks of life. ✉ *401 Deep Eddy Dr., West Austin* ☎ *512/472–8546* 🌐 *www.deepeddy.org* 🎟 *Free.*

★ Mount Bonnell
MOUNTAIN | Rising to a height of 785 feet, Mount Bonnell offers the best views of Austin from its location several miles northwest of the Barton Creek

Greenbelt. Stop by during the day for a glimpse of the sweeping panorama of rolling hills, the Colorado River and the 360 Bridge, and the downtown skyline in the distance. It's a short but steep climb up from a parking area near the road (more of a diversion than a serious hike); at the top, you'll find first dates, nature photographers, families, picnickers, and just plain old tourists here. ✉ *Mount Bonnell Rd., off E. 35th St., West Austin* 🌐 *www.mountbonnell.com* 🎫 *Free.*

Texas Military Forces Museum

HISTORY MUSEUM | Here you'll find exhibits dedicated to preserving the history of the military in Texas, from the inception of the Texas Militia to the modern war on terror. Artillery, a half-track, and tanks are on permanent display in the 45,000-square-foot museum. They also host living history events, including World War II reenactments, on certain weekends throughout the year. **■ TIP→ Remember to bring your valid photo ID—you'll need it to get on the Camp Mabry grounds.** ✉ *Camp Mabry, Bldg. 6, 2200 W. 35th St., West Austin* ☎ *512/782–5659* 🌐 *www.texasmilitaryforcesmuseum.org* 🎫 *Free* 🕑 *Closed Mon.*

★ Treaty Oak

NATURE SIGHT | Many local legends attach themselves to Austin's most famous tree. At least 500 years old, the live oak tree on Baylor Street (between 5th and 6th Streets) is the last survivor of a sacred group of trees known as the Council Oaks, used in ceremonies and meetings by Native American tribes. The tree's name derives from a legend that Stephen F. Austin negotiated the first boundary agreement between local tribes and settlers underneath its branches. In 1989, a disturbed individual attempted to poison the tree with a powerful herbicide and was later apprehended. Intensive efforts to save the tree were successful, although nearly two-thirds of the Treaty Oak died and it is now a shadow of its former self. Still, it's well worth a visit to pay your respects to this venerable survivor. ✉ *Treaty Oak Sq., 507 Baylor St., Downtown* ☎ *512/974-6700* 🌐 *www.austinparks.org* 🎫 *Free.*

UMLAUF Sculpture Garden + Museum

GARDEN | **FAMILY** | This pleasant space at the south end of Zilker Park houses 53 of Charles Umlauf's sculptures in the house where he lived and worked. Umlauf, who taught at the University of Texas Art Department from 1941 to 1981, created an incredibly diverse body of work that ranged in style from realistic to abstract, using such materials as granite, marble, bronze, wood, and terra-cotta. His subjects were equally wide-ranging, from religious figures and nudes to whimsical animals and family groupings. Visitors can admire the works in the verdant beauty of the surrounding gardens, which also hosts special events and community happenings, like food festivals, live music, outdoor yoga classes, and free family days, in addition to a coveted register of weddings. ✉ *605 Azie Morton Rd., Zilker Park* ☎ *512/445–5582* 🌐 *www.umlaufsculpture.org* 🎫 *$5* 🕑 *Closed Mon.*

West Chelsea Contemporary

ART GALLERY | With a collection more akin to a first-class art museum than a commercial gallery, Lisa Russell's showcase, recently rebranded as West Chelsea Contemporary, has a long-standing reputation for being the go-to place in Austin for serious art collectors. The permanent collection has more than 100 original works, some dating back to the 1600s, including pieces by Rembrandt, Renoir, Picasso, Toulouse-Lautrec, Matisse, and more displayed year-round. Contemporary artists are also a main attraction, with work from the likes of Cody Hooper, Michael Kessler, and Daniel Maltzman. Check the website for special exhibits and events hosted throughout the year. ✉ *1009 W. 6th St., Suite 120, Downtown* ☎ *512/478–4440* 🌐 *wcc.art* 🎫 *Free* 🕑 *Closed Sun.*

A
B
C
D
E
F
1
2
3
4
5
6
7
8
9
Lake Austin
Tom Miller Dam
Lake Austin Boulevard
Rockmoor Ave.
Raleigh Ave.
Robinhood Trail
Clearview Drive
Cherry Lane
Bridle Path
Bonnie Road
Enfield Road
Dillman Street
Hopi Trail
Mountain View Rd.
Meadowbrook Drive
Exposition Boulevard
Bowman Avenue
Indian Trail
Windsor Road
Elton Lane
Vista Lane
Sharon Lane
Woodmont Avenue
Bridle Path
Redbud Trail
Enfield Road
Elton Lane
Kent Lane
Quarry Road
Meriden Ln.
West 12th Street
West 11th Street
Lake Austin Boulevard
Exposition Boulevard
Wayside Drive
West 9th Street
West 8th Street
Pruett Street
West 7th Street
Winsted Lane
North Mopac Expressway
West 10th Street
Colorado River
Lady Bird Lake
Stratford Drive
Hearn Street
Deep Eddy Ave.
Upson Street
Atlanta Street
Eilers Park
West 6th Street
Park Hills Drive
Hatley Drive
Wallis Drive
BLUFFINGTON
Rollingwood Park
Riley Road
Vale Street
Rollingwood Drive
Bee Caves Road
WESTPARK
South Mopac Expressway
Stratford Dr.
Barton Springs Road
Town Lake Metropolitan Park
Barton Springs Road
Azie Morton Road
KEY
Exploring Sights
Restaurants
Hotels
0
1,000 ft
0
200 m

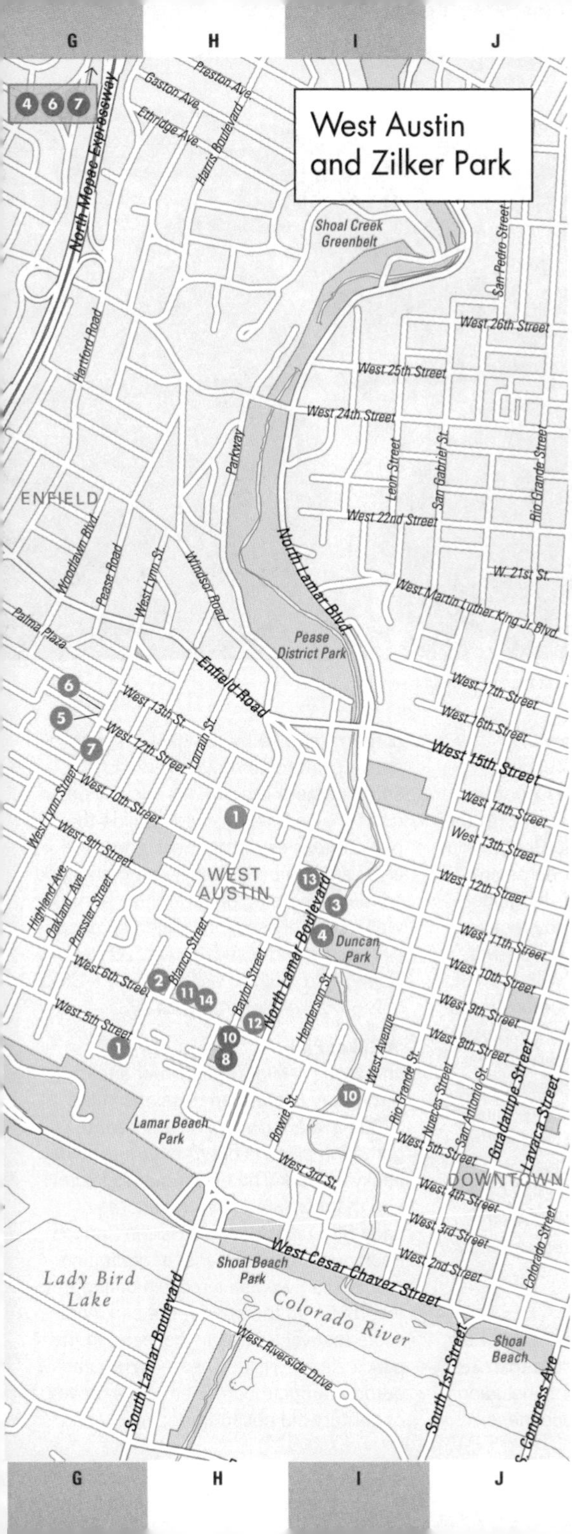

West Austin and Zilker Park

Sights

1 Austin Nature & Science Center D7
2 Barton Creek Greenbelt........... B8
3 Barton Springs Pool................ E9
4 The Contemporary Austin–Laguna Gloria G1
5 Deep Eddy Pool.................... D6
6 Mount Bonnell....................... G1
7 Texas Military Forces Museum G1
8 Treaty Oak.......................... H7
9 UMLAUF Sculpture Garden + Museum.................. F9
10 West Chelsea Contemporary..... H7
11 Wild Basin Wilderness Preserve.............. A7
12 Zilker Botanical Garden........... D7
13 Zilker Park........................... E8

Restaurants

1 Better Half.......................... G7
2 Clark's Oyster Bar................. H6
3 40 North.............................. I6
4 Fresa's I6
5 Jeffrey's G5
6 Josephine House.................. G5
7 Medici Roasting G5
8 Mozart's Coffee Roasters......... B1
9 Pool Burger.......................... D5
10 Sammie's Italian I7
11 Swedish Hill........................ H7
12 24 Diner H7
13 Wink Restaurant & Wine Bar I6
14 Z'Tejas H7

Hotels

1 Brava House H5

One of the nicest views in Austin is at the top of Mount Bonnell.

Wild Basin Wilderness Preserve
NATURE PRESERVE | FAMILY | Stunning contrasting views of the Hill Country and the Austin skyline make it worth the trip to this area near the 360 Bridge. You can wander among the 227 acres on walking trails or take one of the guided tours offered on weekends (by reservation only). The cool folks at the on-site research center (partnered with local St. Edward's University) offer numerous outdoor-oriented classes, nighttime stargazing sessions, and even concerts by well-known touring musicians. Reservations to hike the basin trails are not required on weekdays but highly recommended on weekends. Staff closes the gates whenever the parking area is full. ✉ *805 N. Capitol of Texas Hwy., West Austin* ☎ *512/327–7622* 🌐 *www.stedwards.edu/wild-basin/visit* 🎫 *Free.*

★ Zilker Botanical Garden
GARDEN | FAMILY | Across from Zilker Park, this botanical garden has more than 28 acres of horticultural delights, including butterfly trails, bonsai and Japanese gardens, and xeriscape gardens with native plants that thrive in an arid southwestern climate. It's a lovely urban oasis that is best enjoyed outside the peak of Texas summer heat. There are also various family-friendly programs and hands-on learning opportunities here, as well as a lively seasonal calendar of special events and festivals. ✉ *2220 Barton Springs Rd., Zilker Park* ☎ *512/477–8672* 🌐 *www.zilkergarden.org* 🎫 *$8.*

★ Zilker Park
CITY PARK | FAMILY | The former site of temporary Franciscan missions in the 1700s and a former Native American gathering place is now Austin's everyday backyard park. The enormous 351-acre site that sprawls along the shores of Lady Bird Lake includes Barton Springs Pool, numerous gardens, a meditation trail, and a Swedish log cabin dating from the 1840s. In the spring, the park hosts a kite festival as well as concerts in the park's Zilker Hillside Theater, a natural outdoor amphitheater beneath a grove of century-old pecan trees; in July and

August, musicals and plays take over. And, of course, the annual Austin City Limits Music Festival rules here every year in October. ✉ *2100 Barton Springs Rd., Zilker Park* ☎ *512/974–6700* 🌐 *www.austintexas.gov/department/zilker-metropolitan-park* 🎟 *Free.*

Restaurants

★ Better Half

$$ | **AMERICAN** | Local critics consistently rank this Clarksville newcomer as one of the city's best restaurants, and the sprawling patio is almost always packed. It's a lovely downtown-adjacent atmosphere to enjoy upscale, indulgent takes on juicy burgers and pastrami (as a sandwich or a queso topping), and with great coffee and cocktails to boot. **Known for:** all-day menus; pet-friendly patio seating; decadent hair-of-the-dog destination. $ *Average main: 15* ✉ *406 Walsh St., West Austin* ☎ *512/645–0786* 🌐 *www.betterhalfbar.com.*

★ Clark's Oyster Bar

$$$ | **SEAFOOD** | One of local restaurateur Larry McGuire's white-hot eateries, Clark's has occupied a top seat in the Austin repertoire of hot spots since its 2012 debut. The hip, and decidedly cozy, oyster bar tucked into a modest corner lot of West 6th has all the appeal of a sophisticated seafood restaurant, with the comfort of a neighborhood bistro. **Known for:** impeccably twee setting and decor; decadent happy hour deals; reputation for the freshest oysters in town. $ *Average main: $30* ✉ *1200 W. 6th St., Clarksville* ☎ *512/297–2525* 🌐 *clarksaustin.com.*

40 North

$$ | **PIZZA** | Situated in a charming cottage just northwest of downtown, 40 North is a standard for classic Neapolitan pizza and light Italian fare. It's a lovely neighborhood setting with cozy patio seating and bright white interiors. **Known for:** original food truck still outside, along with more seating; signature pizzas like the Hot Honey and Dandelion; minimalist interior. $ *Average main: 17* ✉ *900 W. 10th St., West Austin* ☎ *512/660–5779* 🌐 *www.40northpizza.com* ⏲ *Closed Mon.*

Fresa's

$ | **MEXICAN** | **FAMILY** | It's hard to think a drive-through could have such high-quality fare, but Fresa's has built a name for its charcoal-grilled chicken *al carbon*, which is slow-roasted over post oak and served with homemade tortillas and sides like Mexican street corn and crispy brussels sprouts out of this trendy Clarksville take on fast food. Breakfast tacos, aguas frescas, and Stumptown coffee service the early morning crowd, but the family-style lunch and dinner menu is the real signature, with whole- or half-chicken orders (choose from achiote and citrus or Yucatán spice), accompanied by house-made salsas, corn tortillas, charro beans, and rice. **Known for:** heaping family-style sides to mix and match; fast and friendly service; healthy and vegan options on-the-go. $ *Average main: $12* ✉ *915 N. Lamar Blvd., Clarksville* ☎ *512/428–5077* 🌐 *www.fresaschicken.com.*

Jeffrey's

$$$$ | **FRENCH** | Homegrown restaurateur Larry McGuire has revitalized Clarksville's beloved Jeffrey's steak house, with rave reviews for the French American haunt that haven't stopped rolling in. The chichi vibe starts curbside, with pink seersucker-clad valets, and extends to the lavish interior and menu, with accoutrements like martini carts and Petrossian caviar service. **Known for:** unmissable crispy Gulf oysters; ultra-glam setting that's ideal for special occasions; pre-Prohibition cocktails with a whimsical flair. $ *Average main: $56* ✉ *1204 W. Lynn St., Clarksville* ☎ *512/477–5584* 🌐 *www.jeffreysofaustin.com* ⏲ *No lunch.*

Josephine House

$$$ | **AMERICAN** | The adorable little sister of Jeffrey's occupies a beautifully restored, light-filled bungalow next door to the Clarksville fine-dining institution, offering a slightly more approachable, but still sophisticated, option for cocktails and modern American cuisine. Locals love to sit at the patio or front-lawn tables during the daily happy hour, and reservations are recommended for the popular Monday Steak Frites Night (4–10 pm), when a three-course meal (featuring a choice of steak, from rib eye to tartare) costs less than $50. **Known for:** picture-perfect outdoor patio ideal for sipping cocktails and lounging in style; quaint Clarksville location with a neighborhood feel; afternoon snack menu and daily happy hour. *Average main: $30* *1601 Waterston Ave., Clarksville* *512/477–5584* *www.josephineofaustin.com.*

★ **Medici Roasting**

$ | **CAFÉ** | For quite possibly the best coffee in Austin, visit this little Clarksville coffee house that draws quite a crowd for quick business meetings and weekend socializing. Here, baristas pull exquisite shots for espresso drinks and even leave creative designs in latte and cappuccino foam. **Known for:** homey neighborhood feel; exceptional house roasts popular with coffee aficionados; family-friendly outdoor seating. *Average main: 5* *1101 W. Lynn St., Clarksville* *512/524–5049* *mediciroasting.com.*

★ **Mozart's Coffee Roasters**

$ | **CAFÉ** | **FAMILY** | On any given sunny day, Austinites flock to Mozart's spacious lakeside patio to enjoy great coffee and indulgent baked goods. The expansive, multitiered deck overlooking Lake Austin can get crowded with weekend patrons, and weekdays are equally popular times for locals to post up and work remotely. **Known for:** Lake Austin views; sprawling patio seating open until midnight; top winter destination thanks to signature hot cocoa and award-winning Christmas light display. *Average main: 5* *3825 Lake Austin Blvd., West Austin* *512/477–2900* *mozartscoffee.com.*

Pool Burger

$ | **BURGER** | Tucked between Deep Eddy Cabaret and Deep Eddy Pool, this burger joint/tiki bar is the ultimate island-inspired hideaway for sun-drenched Austinites. Take an afternoon off to enjoy yourself at the popular west Austin walk-up hut, where Wagyu beef burgers are on the grill every day, along with cult favorites like the Dazed and Confused veggie burger. **Known for:** slap-happy cocktails like frozen Hurricanes and rum shrubs; cool-kid crowd of local regulars; perfect afternoon destination after a dip at Deep Eddy. *Average main: 13* *2315 Lake Austin Blvd., West Austin* *512/334–9747* *www.poolburger.com.*

Sammie's Italian

$$$$ | **ITALIAN** | Located in the former home of historic burger joint Hut's Hamburgers, on the western edge of downtown, Sammie's specializes in classic Italian cuisine in a lively setting. The cozy digs (restored to preserve the original art deco design) get loud during peak hours, but this homage to the great "red sauce institutions" of New York City is still a wonderful option for a modernized "Taste of Old Italy" date night. **Known for:** noisy atmosphere; signature arrabiata sauce featured in most dishes; long wait-list for reservations. *Average main: 36* *807 W. 6th St., West Austin* *512/474–2054* *www.sammiesitalian.com* *No lunch Sat.–Thurs.*

Swedish Hill

$$ | **BAKERY** | This longtime Clarksville institution (formerly known as Sweetish Hill) got a facelift and overhaul in 2019, and the bougie bakery and café came back in full force with updated interiors, more inside seating, and an expanded all-day menu. The stunning pastry case–lined counter is still filled

with homemade pastry, bread, and bagel selections, but now there's more room to enjoy standout classics from their housemade coffee and breakfast buns to a deli case of hot and cold bites and a rotisserie-chicken menu. **Known for:** caviar and charcuterie menus; weekend-only bakery specials that sell out fast; frustrating on-site parking situation. *Average main: 16 ✉ 1120 W. 6th St., West Austin ☎ 512/472–1347 🌐 www.swedishhillaustin.com.*

24 Diner

$$ | **AMERICAN** | The upscale breakfast fare and comfort food of this Clarksville favorite might carry an unconventional price tag for a diner, but the quality of dishes (from Belgian waffles to meat-loaf sandwiches) has earned a loyal fan base. The always bustling interior is an efficient mix of mid-century retro and contemporary efficiency, with booths and barstool seating at high tables. **Known for:** savory sweet signatures like fried chicken and waffles; long wait times on weekends; specialty milk shakes. *Average main: $16 ✉ 600 N. Lamar Blvd., Clarksville ☎ 512/472–5400 🌐 www.24diner.com.*

Wink Restaurant & Wine Bar

$$$ | **AMERICAN** | Tucked in a small strip mall off Lamar Boulevard, this sleek, petite restaurant is as dedicated to excellence in service and artful dishes as it is to fresh, quality ingredients from local purveyors. Put your trust in chef Eric Poltzer's tasting menu (vegetarian options available), which changes daily. **Known for:** daily seasonal tasting menus; intimate date-night vibes; elevated but unpretentious atmosphere. *Average main: $25 ✉ 1014 N. Lamar Blvd., Suite E, Clarksville ☎ 512/482–8868 🌐 www.winkrestaurant.com ⏲ Closed Sun.–Tues. No lunch.*

Z'Tejas

$$ | **SOUTHWESTERN** | **FAMILY** | This stylish Southwestern fusion outpost is popular for its upscale yet unpretentious vibe and attractively presented Southwestern dishes at fair prices. Try the jerk-chicken *Diablo* pasta or Tex-Mex plates like the smoked-chicken poblano chile relleno. **Known for:** long wait during peak weekend hours; sprawling menu options for all ages and appetites; limited on-site parking. *Average main: $20 ✉ 1110 W. 6th St., Clarksville ☎ 512/478–5355 🌐 www.ztejas.com.*

Hotels

Brava House

$$ | **B&B/INN** | One of Austin's most impressive 1880s Victorian homes provides an excellent base for travelers in the heart of Clarksville, just west of downtown. **Pros:** free parking; charming Clarksville location; pedestrian-friendly and close to bus stop. **Cons:** no pool or fitness center; not all rooms are pet-friendly; no hot breakfast dishes on weekdays. *Rooms from: $217 ✉ 1108 Blanco St., Clarksville ☎ 512/478–5034 🌐 www.bravahouse.com 5 Rooms Free Breakfast.*

Nightlife

★ Deep Eddy Cabaret

BARS | Touted as Austin's neighborhood beer joint, this place has a true dive-bar atmosphere, complete with ice-cold brews, pool tables, and a killer jukebox. While not directly in the downtown scene, this music-heavy bar usually hosts a mix of bands during SXSW. *✉ 2315 Lake Austin Blvd., West Austin ☎ 512/472–0961 🌐 deepeddycabaret.com.*

★ Donn's Depot

BARS | A hole-in-the-wall heaven, Donn's dance floor has attracted fans of Texas two-step, waltz, polka, honky-tonk, and swing since 1972. Tucked in an old train car just west of downtown, the Christmas decor–laden interior of this aging Old Austin beauty is as charming as its weekly lineup of local musicians. Don't feel like dancing? Belly up to the bar for some cheap drinks and complimentary popcorn while you watch everyone else groove. ✉ *1600 W. 5th St., West Austin* ☎ *512/478–0336* 🌐 *www.donnsdepot.com.*

Mean Eyed Cat

BARS | Now overshadowed by a towering condo project, this little shack of a bar owes its name to the Man in Black. The dive is an Austin cult favorite, with worn barnwood walls covered with tattered Johnny Cash memorabilia, a shabby-chic patio with a random assortment of tables and chairs where patrons can enjoy a wide selection of beers, and freshly smoked Metcalf barbecue. This legendary dive bar also showcases a variety of Austin-esque acts during SXSW. ✉ *1621 W. 5th St., West Austin* ☎ *512/920–6645* 🌐 *www.themeaneyedcat.com.*

Performing Arts

THEATER

Zilker Theatre Productions

THEATER | **FAMILY** | Bring a blanket and picnic basket and enjoy a Broadway-inspired musical under the warm Texas sky. Right in the heart of the Zilker Park complex, this locally run outdoor theater has been performing on the hillsides just across from Barton Springs for 61 years and counting. The shows run through summers only and charge a pay-as-you-wish admission. ✉ *2206 William Barton Dr., Zilker Park* ☎ *512/479–9491* 🌐 *www.zilker.org.*

Shopping

Artworks

ART GALLERIES | Look no further than this ultra-modern shop when you're on the hunt for unique pieces like hand-carved onyx sculptures from Mexico. The large establishment also offers contemporary art, custom framing, and art restoration, but it's the extensive selection of knockout contemporary art glass of the highest quality (including huge pieces of Murano glass) that really sets this space apart. Founded in 1985, it also carries exceptional crafts from throughout the world, plus small bronzes and exquisite stemware. ✉ *1214 W. 6th St., Suite 105, Clarksville* ☎ *512/472–1550* 🌐 *www.artworksaustin.com.*

Outdoor Voices

OTHER SPECIALTY STORE | Calling all sports fans: this Austin lifestyle brand is reinventing workout gear. Somewhere between Nike's high-performing, sweat-wicking staples and your favorite broken-in cotton T-shirt or bottoms, the Outdoor Voices gear is wearable and fashionable without being overly sporty. You'll find sweats, hoodies, and tanks that have movement and are perfect for a hike on the Greenbelt, an afternoon spent at Zilker Park, or an evening perched around a fire. ✉ *606 Blanco St., Clarksville* ☎ *512/356–9136* 🌐 *www.outdoorvoices.com.*

Rogue Running

SPORTING GOODS | Austin runners frequent this shop as much for its selection of everything from Asics to Adidas shoes as for the expert advice on which pair to pick. Starting out as a training program back in 2004, Rogue opened a storefront after rousing success and today has two other Austin training centers and another in Cedar Park. Runners can join clubs to train for anything from a 5K to a full marathon, or just join a free community-run with other local runners. The store has a full fuel bar serving smoothies and even beer and wine, along with the hydration and energy snacks you'll need to hit the happy trails. ✉ *410 Pressler St.* ☎ *512/373–8704* 🌐 *www.roguerunning.com.*

★ **Waterloo Records**

MUSIC | This large independent shop is an Austin institution that's been an integral part of the local music scene since 1982. With an outstanding selection, superb customer service, and free in-store concerts (including some pretty impressive names during SXSW), it may be the only Austin record store you'll ever need. ✉ *600A N. Lamar Blvd., West Austin* ☎ *512/474–2500* 🌐 *www.waterloorecords.com.*

Whole Earth Provision Co.

SPORTING GOODS | FAMILY | South Congress gets more attention from tourists, but stores like this huge, sun-filled and fun-filled outdoor/travel outfitter are why Austinites prize North Lamar as a shopping destination. The local branch of a Texas chain, it carries a lot of the same things you'd find at any REI—backpacks, tents, sleeping bags, running shoes, rugged clothing—but it's much more entertaining. Jazz is on the speakers, the front space is filled with kids' toys (and a few for adults), and there's a good variety of books for all ages. The staff is laid-back, but friendly and ever-willing to help. There is another branch at the Westgate Mall (4477 South Lamar) in south Austin. ✉ *1014 N. Lamar Blvd., West Austin* ☎ *512/476–1414* 🌐 *www.wholeearthprovision.com.*

South Austin and South Congress District

Known to most Austinites as the area that still keeps Austin weird, this funky neighborhood is home to some of the city's oldest live music venues. Cute little houses, boutique hotels, storied restaurants, and bustling new eateries by some of the city's top up-and-comers populate this lively part of town.

Just south of Lady Bird Lake, South Congress Street—or "SoCo"—is a vibrant and walkable stretch that's packed with eclectic boutiques, dining, and music joints. Pick up a pair of boots at Allen's, or check out live music almost every night of the week at The Continental Club or C-Boy's Heart & Soul.

Sights

Auditorium Shores at Town Lake Metropolitan Park

CITY PARK | Depending on when you visit this lush green park, you'll have a totally different experience. If you manage to make it here for a concert, the venue has one of the finest views of the city skyline as a stage backdrop—during a festival like SXSW, it's easy to see why Austin's the Live Music Capital of the World. Free concerts can get packed, so if you're there for the music, make sure to arrive early. On any random day of the week, however, you'll find that the open green space is the perfect place to stretch out and read a book, catch a pick-up game of frisbee, or snap a photo of the Stevie Ray Vaughan Memorial statue along the hike-and-bike trail. ✉ *800 W. Riverside Dr., South Austin* ☎ *512/974–6700* 🌐 *www.austintexas.org/listings/auditorium-shores/8371.*

★ The Bats at Congress Avenue Bridge

BRIDGE | FAMILY | Austin is home to the largest urban bat population in the world, with as many as 1.5 million of them taking up residence in the capital city every year. Every night starting in late March and continuing through fall, locals and visitors congregate all along (and underneath) Congress Avenue to watch the Mexican free-tailed bats take flight from under the Ann Richards Congress Avenue Bridge into the air for their nightly feeding ritual. While you're waiting for the bats, make sure not to miss the view to the west as the sun drops below the jagged skyline. Paid parking is available on-site at the Austin American-Statesman parking lot. ✉ *305 S. Congress Ave., South Congress District* ☎ *512/474–5171 Austin CVB* 🌐 *www.austintexas.org* 🎫 *Free.*

I Love You So Much Mural

PUBLIC ART | The story goes that Austin musician Amy Cook took a can of red spray paint to write her then-partner, Liz

Austin's Bat Colony

The world's largest urban bat colony—estimated at around 1.5 million Mexican free-tailed bats—hangs out beneath Austin's Ann Richards Congress Avenue Bridge from around March through October. Visitors and locals alike come downtown to claim a spot before dusk and watch the tiny winged critters make their dramatic appearance against the setting sun for feeding.

Some of the best viewing spots are from the hike-and-bike trail by the bridge or patio spaces at the lakefront hotels, especially the Four Seasons. Viewing the bats from the lake, aboard a pleasure boat, kayak, canoe, or paddleboard, is also a wonderful experience. But most visitors (whether they're on a budget) should stand on top of the bridge itself and face eastward as that's the direction of the bats' mass exodus. Be sure to arrive early (as much as an hour ahead) in peak season; the bridge and adjacent parking lot get crowded.

Lambert, a love letter on the side of Jo's Coffee (one of Lambert's businesses). The mural has since become a photo op for locals and visitors alike, and on any given day, you could see a couple getting engagement photos snapped or best friends hamming it up for Instagram against the now-famous mint-green backdrop. Lines for a quick photo op can stretch around the block on weekends. ✉ *Jo's Coffee, 1300 S. Congress Ave., South Congress District* ☎ *512/444–3800* 🌐 *www.joscoffee.com* 🎟 *Free.*

The Long Center for the Performing Arts
PERFORMANCE VENUE | FAMILY | You'll want to visit the Long Center as much for what's happening inside as for the ultra-modern exterior. The lakefront community gathering place and performance venue space is home to a range of live performances, including lyric opera, ballets, rock concerts, and many of Austin's prime foodie events, including the Austin Food + Wine Festival. Food trucks and pop-up art installations and special events are also featured on the City Terrace, which offers up one of the best views of downtown and Lady Bird Lake. ✉ *701 W. Riverside Dr., South Austin* ☎ *512/474–5664* 🌐 *www.thelongcenter.org.*

Restaurants

Aba
$$$ | MEDITERRANEAN | This sophisticated outpost of the Chicago-based Mediterranean restaurant opened to high acclaim in the Music Lane mixed-use development on South Congress Avenue. Specializing in Israeli, Turkish, Greek, and Lebanese cuisine, the extensive menu would be overwhelming without the helpful direction of the servers, but you can't really go wrong with the variety of hummus, mouthwatering homemade pita bread, and delicious mains, like *shawarma*-spiced skirt steak and black-garlic shrimp scampi. **Known for:** multiple-level terrace and patio seating; reputation as a celeb-sighting destination; excellent cocktails. 💲 *Average main: 25* ✉ *1011 S. Congress Ave., Bldg. 2, Suite 180, South Congress District* ☎ *737/273–0199* 🌐 *www.abarestaurants.com.*

Bouldin Creek Cafe
$ | VEGETARIAN | A vegetarian-only restaurant might sound like a bland option at first, but even devoted carnivores frequent this hip South First neighborhood café, home to some of the best

From March through October, crowds gather at the Congress Avenue Bridge each evening to watch its bat colony take flight.

meat-free dishes in the city. Friendly servers help newcomers navigate their vegan and gluten-free options, whether it's a maple latte and plate of zucchini *migas*, a tofu and broccoli salad, or a draft beer to pair with the Fajitas *Italianas*, made with roasted portabello and zucchini strips and chipotle pecan pesto. **Known for:** hip but casually unpretentious atmosphere; large crowds of beautiful people waiting for tables on weekends; super-affordable. *$ Average main: $8 ✉ 1900 S. 1st St., South Austin ☎ 512/416–1601 🌐 www.bouldincreekcafe.com.*

Curra's Grill

$$ | **MEXICAN** | **FAMILY** | If you're looking for authentic Mexican food at an affordable price (read: cheaper than Fonda San Miguel), then head to Curra's. The *cochinita pibil* (marinated slow-roasted pork) is moist, tender, and flavorful; the shrimp and fajitas are a cut above most local establishments. **Known for:** signature avocado margaritas; popular brunch destination for families; specialty enchiladas menu. *$ Average main: $14 ✉ 614 E. Oltorf St., South Austin ☎ 512/444–0012 🌐 www.currasgrill.com.*

Eberly

$$$$ | **AMERICAN** | Austin is known as a laid-back capital of style, whether it's food or fashion, but this swanky spot injects a lot of glamour into the South Lamar scene. Honoring Angelina Eberly, a storied local innkeeper who helped preserve Austin as the capital in 1842, the contemporary restaurant takes inspiration from its courageous namesake with an ambitious slew of snazzy dining areas, like a beautiful interior "atrium" room and an inviting rooftop terrace. **Known for:** various private dining options in intimate settings; glitzy decor and elevated level of service; historic Cedar Tavern bar centerpiece, deconstructed and restored from its original home in Greenwich Village. *$ Average main: 38 ✉ 615 S. Lamar Blvd., South Austin ☎ 512/916–9000 🌐 eberlyaustin.com ⏲ Closed Mon. No lunch weekdays and no dinner Sun.*

South Austin and South Congress District
A
B
C
D
E
F
1
2
3
4
5
6
7
8
9
Toomey Road
South Lamar Blvd.
West Riverside
Barton Springs Road
Barton
Spring Creek Dr.
Barton Hills Drive
Treadwell St.
Kerr St.
Dexter St.
Margaret St.
Post Oak St.
Dywer Ave.
West Bouldin Creek Greenbelt
Bouldin Ave.
Ashby Avenue
BOULDIN
Peach Tree St.
Anita Dr.
ZILKER
Kinney Avenue
Barton Pkwy.
Rabb Road
South 5th Street
Nash Ave.
Bouldin Ave.
South 3rd Street
Paramount Ave.
Ann Arbor Ave.
Bluebonnet Lane
Hether Street
Bauerle Ave.
Jewell Street
West Monroe Street
Rabb Glen Street
Arpdale St.
Garner Avenue
South 6th Street
Paramount Ave.
Ann Arbor Ave.
South Lamar Boulevard
West Annie Street
La Casa Drive
South 5th Street
Bouldin Avenue
South 3rd Street
South 2nd Street
South 1st Street
W. Mary St.
West Live Oak Street
W. Johanna St.
Thornton Rd.
Del Curto Road
West Oltorf Street
SOUTH AUSTIN
South Austin Park
S. 4th Street
Lightsey Road
Cumberland Road
Wilson Street
Valleyridge Dr.
South 5th Street
Oak Crest Ave.
El Paso Street
SOUTH LAMAR
GALINDO
Clawson Road
Southridge Drive
Cardinal Lane
DAWSON
Havana Street
South Congress Avenue
Garden Villa Lane
South Center Street
South 1st Street
Lightsey Road
West Alpine Road
S. 2nd St.
Moody Drive
Woodward Street
Post Road Dr.
Krebs Lane
Fort McGruder Ln.
290
KEY
Exploring Sights
Restaurants
Hotels

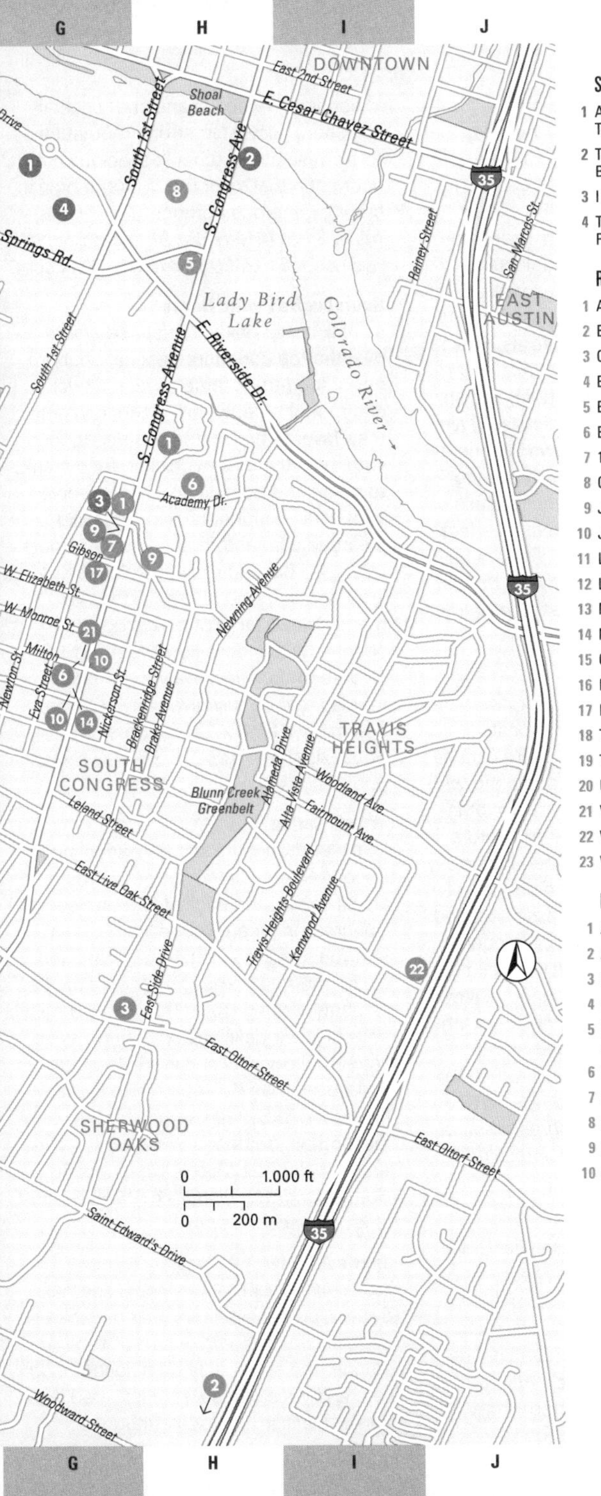

Sights

1 Auditorium Shores at Town Lake Metropolitan Park.... G1
2 The Bats at Congress Avenue Bridge.............................. H1
3 I Love You So Much Mural G4
4 The Long Center for the Performing Arts.................... G2

Restaurants

1 Aba.................................. H3
2 Bouldin Creek Cafe................. F5
3 Curra's Grill......................... G7
4 Eberly E2
5 Elizabeth Street Café............... F4
6 Enoteca Vespaio.................. G4
7 1417.................................... F4
8 Gourdough's Public House A5
9 Jo's Coffee G4
10 June's All-Day...................... G5
11 Lenoir F5
12 Loro.................................... C4
13 Matt's El Rancho.................. A5
14 Neighborhood Sushi G5
15 Odd Duck E3
16 P. Terry's............................. E1
17 Perla's................................ G4
18 Terry Black's BBQ F2
19 Thai Fresh E4
20 Uchi E2
21 Vespaio G4
22 Whip in................................ I6
23 Winebelly............................ E6

Hotels

1 Austin Motel......................... G3
2 Austin Southpark Hotel H9
3 Carpenter Hotel..................... E1
4 Colton House Hotel................. F7
5 Embassy Suites by Hilton Austin—Downtown H2
6 Hotel Saint Cecilia H3
7 Hotel San José..................... G4
8 Hyatt Regency Austin H1
9 Kimber Modern H4
10 South Congress Hotel............ G4

★ Elizabeth Street Café

$$ | **VIETNAMESE** | This clever nouveau Vietnamese-French concept from chef-restaurateur Larry McGuire—of Lamberts and Clark's fame—sits on the corner of South First and Elizabeth Streets as a cozy little café serving a delectable menu of banh mi and pho as well as a fantastic array of French pastries, including daily macaron specials. Fresh shrimp spring rolls, pork meatball banh mi (served on fresh baguettes), and spicy beef and pork buns with thick, soft, airy noodles are safe bets. **Known for:** bright and cheery wait staff; mouthwatering macaron display cases at the hostess stand; cozy outdoor patio that's perfect for a weekday happy hour. *Average main: $17* ✉ *1501 S. 1st St., South Austin* ☎ *512/291–2881* 🌐 *www.elizabethstreetcafe.com.*

Enoteca Vespaio

$$ | **ITALIAN** | **FAMILY** | Known for its tantalizing deli counter of antipasti, charcuterie, and pâté, this bistro café has an authentic trattoria feel, complete with cheerful Italian countryside tablecloths and patio seating. Sink your fork into a bowl of plump gnocchi bathed in garlicky tomato- *arrabiata* sauce or nibble on a slice of classic margherita pizza studded with garden-fresh basil. Juicy hanger steak and crispy fries leave you wanting more, but don't fill up on dinner. **Known for:** lively atmosphere that can get a little overwhelming at peak hours; homemade Italian desserts; pasta made from scratch. *Average main: $17* ✉ *1610 S. Congress Ave., South Congress District* ☎ *512/441–7672* 🌐 *www.enotecaatx.com.*

1417

$$$$ | **FRENCH** | This casual Bouldin Creek neighborhood bistro with a breezy back patio is a refreshing respite for a leisurely happy hour or a midday meal during a day of shopping around nearby South Congress. The French-inspired cuisine is light and straightforward, with a wonderful wine list and craft cocktail selection. **Known for:** strong reputation as a "from-scratch kitchen"; spacious outdoor patio that's popular with the brunch crowd; generous portions. *Average main: 34* ✉ *1417 S. 1st St., South Austin* ☎ *51212/551–2430* 🌐 *www.1417atx.com.*

Gourdough's Public House

$ | **AMERICAN** | **FAMILY** | Austin's favorite over-the-top doughnut destination, born out of food-truck fame, is now a brick-and-mortar café, where diners can get their favorite perforated pastries topped with everything from chicken-fried steak to beer-battered oysters. Salads (served with garlic doughnuts) and sides like creamed corn and fried brussels sprouts, plus a full bar and rotating selection of local beers, round out the extensive menu. **Known for:** gluttonous doughnut options for any occasion; weekend favorite for families; lively, celebratory atmosphere on any given day. *Average main: $10* ✉ *2700 S. Lamar Blvd., South Austin* ☎ *512/912–9070* 🌐 *www.gourdoughs.com.*

★ Jo's Coffee

$ | **CAFÉ** | Though its sister location in the Second Street District attracts a more chichi crowd, the original Jo's on South Congress is where you're likely to run into your neighbor, catch the latest gossip on the Austin music scene, or spot a celebrity visiting town. The morning rush hour for their delicious coffee is intense, yet somehow cool and lively; local beers and frozen rosé (frosé) are also available. **Known for:** SXSW hot spot; excellent coffee; limited, outdoor-only seating. *Average main: 7* ✉ *1300 S. Congress Ave., South Congress District* ☎ *512/444–3800* 🌐 *www.joscoffee.com.*

June's All Day

$$$ | **MODERN AMERICAN** | This is another South Congress standby that matches its impeccable style with a heft of substance. The sunny-side-up neighborhood café and wine bar is a sophisticated injection of Parisian, alfresco attitude on the

pedestrian-heavy strip of south Austin. **Known for:** bright and cheery interiors; dual strengths for grab-and-go pastries and leisurely bistro lunches; patio seating with primo SoCo people-watching. $ *Average main: 25* ✉ *1722 S. Congress Ave., South Austin* ☎ *512/416–1722* 🌐 *www.junesallday.com.*

★ Lenoir

$$$$ | AMERICAN | Bouldin Creek's best date-night destination might have limited dining space, but the seasonal prix fixe selections and shabby-chic decor is worth the hype. In addition to the nightly menu offerings, diners can indulge in a chef's choice menu ($64) with five courses that could be creations like striped-bass crudo and bowfin caviar, green curry *fumé*, seared antelope heart, or jerk quail with pecan butter and watermelon radish. **Known for:** exceptional service; romantic atmosphere with delicate interiors and decor; inspiring prix-fixe menus and wine pairings. $ *Average main: $40* ✉ *1807 S. 1st St., South Austin* ☎ *512/215–9778* 🌐 *www.lenoirrestaurant.com* ⊙ *Closed Mon. and Tues. No lunch.*

Loro

$$ | ASIAN FUSION | No one knows meat better than the James Beard award–winning team (namely, chefs Tyson Cole and Aaron Franklin) behind this Asian-Texan fusion smokehouse. The carnivore-centric menu features smoked meats, like Malaysian chicken *bossam* and incredible smoked baby back duroc-pork ribs, paired with Southeast Asian and Japanese sides and sauces that are all best enjoyed when shared. **Known for:** innovative spirit on the food and drink menus; sprawling patio; barbecue fusion from two of Austin's most famous chefs. $ *Average main: 20* ✉ *2115 S. Lamar Blvd., South Austin* ☎ *512/916–4858* 🌐 *www.loroeats.com.*

Matt's El Rancho

$$ | MEXICAN | FAMILY | This south Austin landmark has been slinging classic Tex-Mex cuisine since 1952, and while the latest Austin food trends have overlooked the establishment as a bland flyover, you'll hear few complaints from the steady crowd of happy diners. Combination dinners are many and varied, with all the usual standbys: tamales, crispy tacos, and more. **Known for:** bustling family-friendly atmosphere; patio happy hour done right; signature "Bob" starter queso dip. $ *Average main: $22* ✉ *2613 S. Lamar Blvd., South Austin* ☎ *512/462–9333* 🌐 *www.mattselrancho.com* ⊙ *Closed Tues.*

Neighborhood Sushi

$$$ | SUSHI | If you're looking for Austin's best sushi, you might just find it here. The tatami-lined interiors are sleek and sophisticated, and chefs achieve unparalleled quality in every dish, whether it's *nigiri* or hand rolls, Wagyu short ribs or snow crab. *Omakase* is available for connoisseurs, and don't sleep on their sake pairings and delicious desserts like lychee jellies and milk chocolate *semifreddo*. **Known for:** daily-changing menu with seasonal favorites; coveted bar seating for front-row viewing of the chefs at work; outdoor sake garden with small drink and bar-food menu. $ *Average main: 28* ✉ *1716 S. Congress Ave., South Austin* ☎ *512/579–0939* 🌐 *www.neighborhoodsushi.com.*

★ Odd Duck

$$$$ | AMERICAN | This food truck turned brick-and-mortar was an early trailblazer of the city's farm-to-table movement, thanks to chef Bryce Gilmore's inventive take on locally sourced, modern American cuisine. Gilmore and his team's artistic approach to Southern seasonal fare comes in tapas-size portions, so servers recommend a few dishes per patron. **Known for:** rotating menu of highly inventive, bite-size creations; heavy emphasis on locally sourced ingredients; popular daily happy hour. $ *Average main: $34* ✉ *1201 S. Lamar Blvd., South Austin* ☎ *512/433–6521* 🌐 *www.oddduck-austin.com.*

Perla's

$$$$ | **SEAFOOD** | Seafood, service, and panache are pretty as a pearl at this homage to yacht clubs in the Northeast. One of Austin's original high-end patio destinations still delivers the city's best fish, punched up with Texas style and zing. **Known for:** best patio to see and be seen; exceptionally fresh seafood; Wes Anderson–level attention to detail and decor. *Average main: $34* *1400 S. Congress Ave., South Congress District* *512/291–7300* *www.perlasaustin.com.*

★ P. Terry's

$ | **FAST FOOD** | **FAMILY** | This local drive-through and fast-food chain turned burger empire is an Austin favorite for a reason. What started as a humble mom-and-pop operation on the corner of South Lamar and Barton Springs Road has evolved into a sprawling web of locations all over Austin and beyond, but the original location is still the ideal spot to experience the simple pleasures of a fresh patty of hormone-free Black Angus beef (or black-bean veggie), hand-cut fries, and hand-spun shakes that make eating bad feel good. **Known for:** best bet for a post–Barton Springs refresh; impeccable service and attention to detail; cult local following. *Average main: 7* *404 S. Lamar Blvd., South Austin* *512/473–2217* *www.pterrys.com.*

Terry Black's BBQ

$$ | **BARBECUE** | **FAMILY** | A relatively recent addition to Austin's barbecue scene, its newcomer status is bolstered by generations of pitmasters hailing from the famed BBQ epicenter of nearby Lockhart. The laid-back Barton Springs location and cafeteria-style service keep things casual, with diners picking out their sides (all the classics, from mac 'n' cheese to potato salad) before selecting their cut of meat. **Known for:** classic cafeteria-style counter service; brisket above all; pitmasters with pedigrees. *Average main: $14* *1003 Barton Springs Rd., South Austin* *512/394–5899* *www.terryblacksbbq.com.*

★ Thai Fresh

$$ | **THAI** | **FAMILY** | Relaxed and locally sourced, this Bouldin Creek café is a staple for lovers of high-quality Thai food in a casual neighborhood setting. Part grab-and-go market and coffee bar, part café, and part cooking-class destination, Thai Fresh is a popular lunch and dinner spot, with a diverse range of curries, stir-fries, and noodle and fried-rice dishes. **Known for:** terrific vegan offerings; homemade breakfast tacos with a Thai twist; hidden-gem quality tucked in the Bouldin Creek neighborhood. *Average main: $14* *909 W. Mary St., South Austin* *512/494–6436* *www.thai-fresh.com.*

★ Uchi

$$$ | **JAPANESE** | Respectful of traditional sushi and sashimi methods—but not limited by them—this standout sushi bar (and consistently ranked top restaurant in Austin) starts with super-fresh ingredients. After that, anything goes, including touches of the South or south-of-the-border: yellowtail with ponzu sauce and sliced chilies, tempura-style fried green tomatoes, or seared monkfish cheeks with Vietnamese caramel, Belgian endive, roasted red grapes, and cilantro. **Known for:** one of the most sought-after happy hour seats in town; high-octane interiors to match the food, both of which can be loud; raw bar that doesn't miss. *Average main: $25* *801 S. Lamar Blvd., South Austin* *512/916–4808* *www.uchiaustin.com* *No lunch.*

Vespaio

$$$ | **ITALIAN** | This buzzing Italian bistro consistently attracts hordes of South Congress Avenue's heavy foot traffic, with patrons crowding the narrow, warmly lit bar while waiting for a table in the small, tawny-hued dining room. Noshing on the gratis white-bean puree with basil-infused olive oil makes perusing the menu of delicate handmade pastas, thin wood-fired pizzas, and robust northern

Italian–inspired entrées an even greater treat. **Known for:** traditional, straight-forward Italian staples; usually bustling throughout the evening thanks to SoCo foot traffic; cozy ambience. *Average main: $28* *1610 S. Congress Ave., South Congress District* *512/441–6100* *www.vespaioristorante.com* *No lunch.*

Whip In

$ | **INDIAN** | This convenience store, café, and neighborhood pub has been a Travis Heights hallmark since the 1980s. A long shotgun bar, boasting 72 taps of local and imported beers, greets diners upon entrance, with a range of daily chalk-board specials advertised above. **Known for:** all-in-one pit stop for discerning beer lovers; live in-store music; no-frills counter service for Indian curries. *Average main: $13* *1950 S. I–35, South Austin* *512/442–5337* *www.facebook.com/whipin.*

Winebelly

$$ | **WINE BAR** | This South First Street spot sits alongside a gas station on an unattractive corner lot at Oltorf, but the trendy wine bar and Mediterranean-style tapas eatery boasts all the appeal of a cozy local hangout. Tapas are slightly larger (and pricier) than a traditional Spanish outpost, but the savory small plates deliver, from customary selections like cured anchovies and *bravas* fries (with pimento and chili peppers) to more unconventional, locally sourced dishes like short-rib bruschetta and pan-seared Gulf shrimp with smoked pork jowl and polenta. **Known for:** international wine list and specialty cocktails; expansive patio seating; sharing-friendly signatures. *Average main: $15* *519 W. Oltorf St., South Austin* *512/487–1569* *www.austinwinebelly.com* *Closed Mon. No lunch.*

Hotels

★ Austin Motel

$$ | **HOTEL** | What used to be a fading 1938 motor court is now a beloved, quintessentially Austin motel that sits pretty in the heart of South Congress's famed stretch of trendy restaurants, clubs, and shops. **Pros:** retro pool complete with full bar service; prime location in a hip neighborhood; chill chic. **Cons:** not for fussy luxury travelers; pricey; throw-back style could read as outdated to some. *Rooms from: $190* *1220 S. Congress Ave., South Congress District* *512/441–1157* *austinmotel.com* *41 rooms* *No Meals.*

Austin Southpark Hotel

$$ | **HOTEL** | This elegant 14-story hotel, near the tangled intersection of I–35 and US 290, earns high marks for value but can feel removed from the city, despite being only 3 miles from downtown. **Pros:** customer-oriented staff; better value than comparable hotels downtown; indoor-outdoor heated pool. **Cons:** immediate neighborhood is a major highway intersection; in need of a renovation; noisy highway-facing rooms. *Rooms from: $200* *4140 Governors Row, South Austin* *512/448–2222* *www.austinsouthparkhotel.com* *312 rooms* *No Meals.*

Carpenter Hotel

$$ | **HOTEL** | Tucked away just south of downtown and Lady Bird Lake, this addition to the local Bunkhouse Hospitality group comes with a hip look that attracts some of the city's chicest travelers. **Pros:** charming outdoor terrace in each room; high marks for housekeeping and hospitality; great location to explore south Austin. **Cons:** guest rooms are spartan and basic; neighboring dog-boarding business causes noise complaints; on-site café is pricey. *Rooms from: 215* *400 Josephine St., South Austin* *512/682–5300* *www.carpenterhotel.com* *No Meals* *93 rooms.*

Colton House Hotel

$$$ | **HOTEL** | Although not technically on the main drag of South Congress, this boutique hotel has all the modern accoutrements, trendy interior design, and up-to-the-minute amenities you could want without an ambience of overhype. **Pros:** all rooms are suites with well-stocked kitchenettes; heated outdoor pool; thoughtful amenities like lounge games and pool toys. **Cons:** pool area isn't exactly scenic; breakfast not included; removed from SoCo's main drag. *Rooms from: 229 ✉ 2510 S. Congress Ave., South Austin ☎ 512/220–1795 🌐 www.coltonhousehotel.com 🍽 No Meals 🛏 80 rooms.*

Embassy Suites by Hilton Austin—Downtown

$$ | **HOTEL** | Location is everything at this central hotel, just south of Lady Bird Lake and the surrounding hike-and-bike trail, four blocks from the Convention Center, and within walking distance of most South Congress restaurants and attractions. **Pros:** great location for events like ACL or SXSW; clean and attractive; free breakfast and evening happy hour. **Cons:** surcharges for parking and in-room Wi-Fi; parking garage is in a separate building; chain-hotel feel. *Rooms from: $140 ✉ 300 S. Congress Ave., South Congress District ☎ 512/469–9000 🌐 www.hilton.com 🛏 259 rooms 🍽 Free Breakfast.*

★ Hotel Saint Cecilia

$$$$ | **HOTEL** | The Saint Cecilia goes beyond anything you'd expect in eclectic, decidedly Austin accommodations, from its art deco–style bar to the neon lights that read "S-O-U-L" shining above the heated outdoor pool. **Pros:** exclusive vibe with grounds closed to the general public; secluded yet central SoCo location; luxuriously spacious rooms. **Cons:** exquisite yet expensive breakfasts; staff can be a bit too cool; very pricey. *Rooms from: $550 ✉ 112 Academy Dr., South Austin ☎ 512/852–2400 🌐 hotelsaintcecilia.com 🛏 14 rooms 🍽 No Meals.*

★ Hotel San José

$$ | **HOTEL** | This uber-hip, bungalow-style boutique hotel, located in the midst of the South Congress Avenue action, features a modern, minimalist style, adorned with balconies, patios, and tropical vegetation. **Pros:** antidote to antiseptic hotels everywhere; epitome of south Austin cool; high-end amenities. **Cons:** not ideal for business or more conservative travelers; upscale vibes means upscale prices; the hopping lounge can mean late-night noise for courtyard-facing rooms. *Rooms from: $195 ✉ 1316 S. Congress Ave., South Congress District ☎ 512/444–7322 🌐 www.sanjosehotel.com 🛏 40 rooms 🍽 No Meals.*

Hyatt Regency Austin

$$ | **HOTEL** | On the shores of Lady Bird Lake in between the Congress and South First Street Bridges, this hotel provides great views and convenient downtown access. **Pros:** well-equipped and-staffed for meetings; attractive and comfortable rooms; excellent views of downtown from some rooms. **Cons:** a bit far from the South Congress Street action; noisy on lower levels; some find it too corporate. *Rooms from: $185 ✉ 208 Barton Springs Rd., South Austin ☎ 512/477–1234 🌐 www.hyatt.com 🛏 466 rooms 🍽 Free Breakfast.*

Kimber Modern

$$$ | **B&B/INN** | A stunning, design-lover's dream, this boutique hotel is tucked one block off South Congress Avenue and boasts the dual appeal of an exclusive, private escape and direct access to an urban neighborhood. **Pros:** Zen vibes and high-tech amenities; daily happy hour and organic self-service breakfast; 24/7 access to full kitchen, beverage bar, and lounge. **Cons:** limited off-street parking; virtual concierge and spartan design not suited for everyone; no pool. *Rooms from: $300 ✉ 110 The Circle, South Austin ☎ 512/985–9990 🌐 kimbermodern.com 🛏 7 rooms 🍽 Free Breakfast.*

South Congress Hotel
$$$ | HOTEL | Not only does this boutique hotel boast swanky accommodations, a rooftop pool, three on-site restaurants, and street-level retail shops, but guests are also mere steps away from everything South Congress Avenue has to offer. **Pros:** three on-site restaurants; great option for travelers without a car; unbeatable SoCo access and location. **Cons:** communal spaces can be closed for frequent special events; maintenance and service woes reported by many guests; noisy on weekends and holidays. *Rooms from: 265 ✉ 1603 S. Congress Ave., South Austin ☎ 512/920–6405 🌐 www.southcongresshotel.com 🍽 No Meals 🛏 83 rooms.*

Nightlife

BARS

Austin Beer Garden Brewing Company
BEER GARDENS | A community beer garden of sorts—locals call it The ABGB—this collaboration of five friends operates as both a full-scale brewery and a beer grub restaurant and music venue. Throughout the year, they offer a rotating selection of craft beers in a wide variety of styles, including lagers, ales, IPAs, and pilsners. The outdoor backyard is shaded by oak and elm trees and is a perfect backdrop for evening rockabilly gigs featuring local artists. Enjoy crisp pizzas, an assortment of super-stuffed sandwiches, and salads while you sip a few suds. *✉ 1305 W. Oltorf St., South Austin ☎ 512/298–2242 🌐 www.theabgb.com.*

Aviary Wine & Kitchen
WINE BARS | Once a delightful home-style shop by day and wine bar by night, the former Aviary Lounge's multipurpose design concept now focuses exclusively on wining and dining. The contemporary decor is still a lovely backdrop here, but the main star is the international wine list. There's rooftop space, too, for when the weather is nice, especially during the weekday happy hour. *✉ 2110 S. Lamar Blvd., Suite C, South Austin ☎ 512/916–4445 🌐 www.aviarywinekitchen.com.*

Bouldin Acres
GATHERING PLACES | This happy haven of food and fun, a "restaurant and drinkery" as it calls itself, has kept up a steady buzz since opening in 2020. There's a fun but fratty vibe here, complete with full-size pickleball courts and lawn games, an area for kids and dogs, a rotating selection of food trucks, and a full bar. Guests can order from the picnic tables on the outdoor Astroturf courtyard via a QR code. Gam-day watch parties attract crowds during UT football season. *✉ 2027 S. Lamar Blvd., South Austin ☎ 512/536–0132 🌐 www.bouldinacres.com.*

★ Hotel San José Courtyard Lounge
COCKTAIL LOUNGES | It may be the hippest hotel in town, and the San José is also home to one of the best outdoor bars in the city. On nice days, grab a poolside patio seat and order a reasonably priced bottle of wine and the city-renowned cheese plate. Happy hour is all day on Tuesday. Year-round special events feature local bands, while weekly sets by a varied lineup of DJs can be enjoyed in the lounges. South By San José is one of SXSW's premier yearly events. The hotel, combined with Jo's Coffee, joins forces to showcase a huge variety of music in an outdoor setting throughout SXSW in the heart of South Congress. The event is free for passersby and open throughout the festival. *✉ 1316 S. Congress Ave., South Congress District ☎ 5122/444–7322 🌐 www.sanjosehotel.com/hotel/lounge.*

★ Tiki Tatsu-Ya
COCKTAIL LOUNGES | This immersive tiki bar is a melting pot of Asian, Hawaiian, and Polynesian influences that come together to create an adult Disneyland of delights. The drinks don't disappoint, but it's the theater and presentation that steal the show. Order fish-bowl–size drinks that serve four- to six people, try out an exciting cocktail that cues special

Live music is everywhere in Austin, including streets like Congress Avenue.

lights and music when served, or take selfies behind the dry ice of your drink in your own theme booth. ✉ *1300 S. Lamar Blvd., South Austin* ☎ *512/772–3700* 🌐 *www.tiki-tatsuya.com.*

DANCE CLUBS

★ Broken Spoke

DANCE CLUBS | This legendary honky-tonk is touted as the last of the true Texas dance halls. If live country music and dancing are your thing, then two-step down to this venerable venue, where Old Austin lives (and dances) on. The classic haunt boasts live music (with world-famous celebrities like Dolly Parton and beloved locals like Dale Watson) and lively crowds almost every night, with or without SXSW. ✉ *3201 S. Lamar Blvd., South Austin* ☎ *512/442–6189* 🌐 *www.brokenspokeaustintx.net.*

LIVE MUSIC

★ The Continental Club

LIVE MUSIC | This is an authentic Austin original—and one of the city's signature live music hubs, drawing a hard-drinking, music-loving crowd every night of the week. The club hosts a variety of live acts but specializes in country-fused rock, like local favorite James McMurtry. The upstairs gallery maintains an exclusive jazz club vibe. A full spectrum of acts is always hosted here during SXSW. ✉ *1315 S. Congress Ave., South Congress District* ☎ *512/441–2444* 🌐 *continentalclub.com.*

Emo's

LIVE MUSIC | Once a classic Red River haunt in the middle of downtown, this indie rock and punk venue is now on East Riverside, where a much larger main stage hosts internationally acclaimed names in the music industry, including the likes of Blues Traveler and Lauryn Hill. A long-time player in the Austin music scene, expect plenty of SXSW showcases. ✉ *2015 E. Riverside Dr., South Austin* ☎ *888/512–7469* 🌐 *www.emosaustin.com.*

Saxon Pub

LIVE MUSIC | If you can get past the Saxon's low ceilings and sticky, beer-stained floors, then you'll find a phenomenal music experience. Bands play every night, usually from the local rock and blues scene. This is a small Austin classic with Shiner Bock on tap and a well-worn pool table that draws regulars from all over the city. The legendary venue always packs bands in back-to-back throughout SXSW. ✉ *1320 S. Lamar Blvd., South Austin* ☎ *512/448–2552* 🌐 *www.thesaxonpub.com.*

Performing Arts

FILM

Alamo Drafthouse

FILM | The original Drafthouse location in downtown Austin may have permanently closed, but the locally grown cult movie theater-turned-national-chain still operates other locations around town that remain must-visits for movie lovers. A Drafthouse movie is always an experience, whether you pregame with some karaoke at the attached Highball bar and lounge or attend a theme sing-a-long screening in full costume with friends. Expect new releases, cult classics, and loads of seasonal and special event screenings, all paired with a full food and drink menu served in-theater. ✉ *1120 S. Lamar Blvd., South Austin* ☎ *512/861–7040* 🌐 *www.drafthouse.com/austin/theater/south-lamar.*

THEATER

Austin Opera

OPERA | Austin's first professional opera company has been putting on multiple mainstage productions a year for 35 seasons and counting. Voted "Opera Company of the Year" for 2020 in a national *BroadwayWorld.com* poll, the company combines international stars with extraordinary local talents. Performances are hosted at the Long Center. ✉ *Long Center, 701 W. Riverside Dr., South Austin* ☎ *512/472–5992* 🌐 *www.austinopera.org.*

Austin Symphony Orchestra

MUSIC | **FAMILY** | Eight classical concerts, four pops concerts, a holiday-favorite performance, a children's Halloween presentation, and many free events are performed by the Austin Symphony, Austin's oldest performing arts organization, throughout the year. Performances are held at the Long Center. ✉ *Long Center, 701 Riverside Dr., Austin* ☎ *512/476–6064* 🌐 *austinsymphony.org.*

ZACH Theatre

THEATER | **FAMILY** | One of the city's most vibrant and innovative theaters, this nonprofit now has an expansive multistage complex that hosts a number of theatrical performances, intimate celebrity talks, and special events year-round. An integral part of the Austin community for nearly 90 years, ZACH also serves the local arts community with a year-round season of shows, theater camps, and educational activities. ✉ *202 S. Lamar Blvd., South Austin* ☎ *512/476–0541* 🌐 *www.zachtheatre.org.*

Shopping

ACCESSORIES

Kendra Scott

JEWELRY & WATCHES | What started more than a decade ago as a small Austin jewelry outfit has grown to be one of the capital city's most successful businesses, with stores nationwide. Though owner and designer Kendra Scott does design ready-to-wear pieces, the genius behind her work is a paint-by-numbers approach to jewelry making: she's fixed the templates, and you get to be the designer. At the Color Bar, select from a rainbow of stones to make endless combinations of custom earrings, bracelets, and necklaces. The flagship store on SoCo is retail therapy and art therapy in one. ✉ *1701 S. Congress Ave., South Congress District* ☎ *512/792–4581* 🌐 *www.kendrascott.com.*

ANTIQUES

★ Uncommon Objects

ANTIQUES & COLLECTIBLES | This eclectic purveyor was a staple of South Congress Avenue for decades but has moved its treasure trove of antiques and collectibles to a different location off South Lamar. If you're looking for something out of the ordinary or want to browse the King of Austin vintage, this is the place. Stocked with antique items that have been procured from dozens of vendors, Uncommon Objects has an ever-changing stock that at varying times has included mourning jewelry made of human hair, tribal masks, anatomical charts from the turn of the 20th century, and plenty of taxidermy. ✉ *1602 Fortview Rd., Austin* ☎ *512/442–4000* 🌐 *www.uncommonobjects.com.*

CANDY

★ Big Top Candy Shop

CANDY | **FAMILY** | South Congress is filled with shops that pack a nostalgia factor, from vintage goods to home cooking, but none is quite as sweet as this place, where bins upon bins of colorful sour candies, chocolates, and lollipops line the oh-so-colorful walls. There's Shakespearean Insult Gum, Texas-made Chick-O-Sticks, and gobs of themed candy. And if you slide up to the bar, you can order milkshakes, shaved ice, or old-fashioned sodas. ✉ *1706 S. Congress Ave., South Congress District* ☎ *512/462–2220* 🌐 *www.bigtopcandyshop.com.*

CLOTHING

ByGeorge

WOMEN'S CLOTHING | This is not your average Austin clothing boutique. While you may find up-and-coming independent designers when perusing other store's racks, ByGeorge's inventory looks like a compilation of the season's greatest high-fashion runway hits. At its two Austin locations, you'll be smitten with extravagances like SUNO frocks, Givenchy dresses, and Helmut Lang and Derek Lam tailored trousers. Austin's all about keeping things weird, but in this shop, chic wins every time. ✉ *1400 S. Congress Ave., South Congress District* ☎ *512/441–8600* 🌐 *www.bygeorgeaustin.com.*

Service Menswear

MEN'S CLOTHING | Sharp dressers take note: some of the coolest guys' clothes and grooming products around are on display within the industrial-chic walls of Service. The open space has been designed to fit racks of tailored blue blazers, graphic tees, selvedge denim, and designer footwear and cases of rock-star Ray-Ban and Super sunglasses. If you find yourself without the right thing to wear on your travels to Austin, this is the place to fix that. ✉ *1400 S. Congress Ave., South Congress District* ☎ *512/447–7600* 🌐 *www.servicemenswear.com.*

STAG Provisions for Men

MEN'S CLOTHING | For guys who like that American-made look, search no further than this upscale boutique. Start with a pair of good-fitting denim—STAG stocks brands like imogene + willie and RRL—then move on to a flannel shirt, which come in endless color combinations here. Finish with a cool pair of Red Wing boots and accessorize from a selection of watches, wallets, and belts galore. Best yet? Once you're dressed, Home Slice is next door, so you can grab some pizza on your way out. They really did think of everything. ✉ *1423 S. Congress Ave., South Congress District* ☎ *512/373–7824* 🌐 *www.stagprovisions.com.*

GIFTS AND SOUVENIRS

Parts & Labour

CRAFTS | On South Congress Avenue, in the epicenter of Austin's weird culture, this nondiscreet store offers tokens of the city from local designers. Yes, you'll find typical souvenirs like Texas-branded tees and tote bags, but then you'll discover the rest of the store. Local artists design everything from the huge collection of screen-printed gig posters to the fabulous leather goods; the variety is incredible. Whatever the type of souvenir or handcrafted artisan creation you're looking to take from the capital city, this is the place to get it. ✉ *1704 S. Congress Ave., South Congress District* ☎ *512/326–1648* 🌐 *partsandlabourstore.myshopify.com.*

IMPORTS

Mi Casa Gallery

ANTIQUES & COLLECTIBLES | **FAMILY** | Perhaps Austin's top outlet for quality and unusual Mexican art and crafts, Mi Casa goes far beyond your usual Mexican-imports souvenir shop. You'll find contemporary paintings and sculptures, painted furniture, religious art, ceramics, and much more. It's a great place to go for gifts for folks back home. ✉ *1700 S. Congress Ave., South Congress District* ☎ *512/707–9797* 🌐 *www.micasagallery.com.*

★ Tesoros Trading Company

ANTIQUES & COLLECTIBLES | **FAMILY** | The buyers for this large, independently owned world-market store comb the planet for colorful and unusual examples of folk art from more than 40 countries. African trade beads and baskets, Nepalese jewelry, Turkish textiles, and lots of Mexican items (including *milagros,* postcards, and cheap souvenirs and gifts) are just a few of the goodies stashed away in this delightful place. ✉ *1500 S. Congress Ave., South Congress District* ☎ *512/447–7500* 🌐 *www.tesoros.com.*

SHOES

★ Allens Boots

SHOES | A South Congress landmark for decades, this place is impossible to miss—just look for the huge red boot above the door. Set amid trendy, touristy SoCo, Allens is anything but. More than a dozen brands of cowboy boots (including Frye, Justin, Lucchese, Liberty Black, and Tony Lama) are displayed on rows upon rows of shelves, along with other Western wear. If you're a newcomer to the boot world, study the store's website before your visit for some basics on proper fit. Staff members are exceptionally helpful. ✉ *1522 S. Congress Ave., South Congress District* ☎ *512/447–1413* 🌐 *www.allensboots.com.*

SPORTING GOODS

Trek Bicycle Lamar

SPORTING GOODS | With ample trails and roads with generous bike lanes, Austin is home to many serious bicyclists, and this homegrown shop has been outfitting them for more than three decades. Seasoned athletes use Trek as a resource. Not only is the store stocked with clothing and accessories from brands like Pearl, Bontranger, and Endura, it also hosts mountain, road, cyclo-cross, and triathlon clubs so that bicyclists can ride with others in the community. Newer riders will find a helpful staff of bike pros, who are ready and willing to answer questions about their wide selection of bicycles. ✉ *517 S. Lamar Blvd., South Austin* ☎ *512/477–3472* 🌐 *www.trekbikes.com/retail/lamar.*

East Austin

Head to east Austin to explore one of the funkiest and fastest-growing areas in town—there are hundreds of artist studios, community gathering places, and an always-bustling stretch of East Sixth Street that's home to countless quirky bars, food trucks, and public artwork. Other hubs include East César Chávez and 11th Street, where you can find everything from vegan bakeries to jazz clubs.

Sights

MASS Gallery

ART GALLERY | Decidedly un-artsy in its former incarnation as an auto-body shop, this space now hosts an exciting, artist-managed gallery that has launched many a contemporary artist onto the scene. In addition to the 1,500 square feet of gallery space, there are several project studios where local and national artists create new works in a variety of media, making for a singularly unique gallery experience for visitors. MASS also has a lively program of seasonal film screenings, musical performances, artist talks, and community outreach activities. ✉ *705 Gunter St., East Austin* ☎ *512/535–4946* 🌐 *www.massgallery.org* 🎫 *Free* 🕒 *Closed Mon.–Thurs.*

★ Modern Rocks Gallery

ART GALLERY | This sleek modern-day art gallery celebrates everything that rocks—both in terms of beautiful geologic finds and of some of the world's most iconic rock and roll performers, who are featured in the gallery of fine art photography. The marriage of the two is truly a sight to behold. While walking the whitewashed halls of this contemporary domain, you'll see beautiful displays of geodes, crystals, minerals, and other forms of natural history as well as never-before-seen images of the likes of Miles Davis, David Bowie, Paul Simon, and Austin's own son, Stevie Ray Vaughan. ✉ *Canopy Studios, 916 Springdale Rd., East Austin* ☎ *512/524–1488* 🌐 *www.modernrocksgallery.com* 🎫 *Free* 🕒 *Closed Sun. and Mon.*

Texas State Cemetery

CEMETERY | In 1851, the general Edward Burleson was the first person to be buried in the Texas State Cemetery. Today it's the final resting place of some of the state's most important figures, including Stephen F. Austin, John Connally, Darrell K Royal, Ann Richards, and Bob Bullock. Inside the cemetery, you'll find monuments dedicated to September 11th, the Vietnam War, and the War of 1812; you'll also find special headstones for the mothers who have lost sons and daughters in wars and a Purple Heart monument. ✉ *909 Navasota St., East Austin* ☎ *512/463–0605* 🌐 *cemetery.tspb.texas.gov* 🎫 *Free.*

Thinkery

CHILDREN'S MUSEUM | **FAMILY** | In 2013, the former Austin Children's Museum moved into a new state-of-the-art building and evolved into Thinkery, where kids (and kids at heart) can find fun exhibits brimming with opportunities to learn something new. *Light Lab* lets you play architect and build light structures; the *Let's Grow* exhibit aims to get kids moving and teach them the benefits of eating locally grown foods; and an *Innovators' Workshop* puts inquiring minds to work on creative problem-solving. All the exhibits blend education and recreation with ease; to utilize physical energy, there's a superb climbing and water play-area out in the backyard. ✉ *1830 Simond Ave., East Austin* ☎ *512/469–6200* 🌐 *www.thinkeryaustin.org* 🎫 *$14* 🕒 *Closed Mon.*

Yard Dog Art Gallery

ART GALLERY | After nearly 25 years on South Congress Avenue, this contemporary folk art, fine art, and pop art gallery moved its wares to the Canopy artist studios on the city's east side. Founded in 1995, the local gallery features works by artists from the great American South, in addition to Canada and Europe. The modest space is open afternoons (Thursday–Saturday) as well as by appointment. ✉ *916 Springdale Rd., Bldg. 3, #104, South Congress District* ☎ *512/912–1613* 🌐 *www.yarddog.com* 🎫 *Free* 🕒 *Closed Sun.–Wed.*

Restaurants

Canje

$$$ | **CARIBBEAN** | The Guyanese roots of chef Tavel Bristol-Joseph take hold in this Caribbean concept eatery on the east side. In addition to Guyana, the house specialties feature influences from Jamaica to Puerto Rico, with standouts like jerk chicken and wild-boar pepper pot. **Known for:** established pedigree from the team behind Emmer & Rye; reservations essential; melt-in-your-mouth savory "trytating" specials like Guyana-style roti. *$ Average main: 28 ✉ 1914 E. 6th St., East Austin ☎ 512/706–9119 ⊕ www.canjeatx.com ⏲ No lunch.*

Cisco's

$ | MEXICAN | FAMILY | The interior of this family-owned east-side bakery and restaurant might be shabby, with worn linoleum floors and various Texas-theme memorabilia and fading newspaper articles hanging on the walls, but the hole-in-the-wall's classic Mexican fare still attracts a loyal breakfast and lunch crowd seven days a week. They are drawn by straightforward trademarks like *migas* (generously covered in melted cheese) and huevos rancheros that aren't accompanied by the typical Austin-brunch price tag. **Known for:** local east-side landmark; frequented by UT fans and a "who's who" of alumni; weekend crowds. *$ Average main: $10 ✉ 1511 E. 6th St., East Austin ☎ 512/478–2420 ⊕ www.ciscosaustin.com.*

★ Contigo

$$ | AMERICAN | FAMILY | The predominantly outdoor layout of Texas ranch–inspired Contigo consistently draws a steady evening crowd—even when summer temps are well over 100 degrees. With a chef-driven stable of cocktails and a creative Southern-comfort-meets-contemporary-American menu, it's easy to understand why: ox tongue sliders, house-made pigs in a blanket, a gooey cheddar-filled grilled cheese sandwich on brioche, and the cast-iron sautéed okra with jalapeño and walnuts are among the top menu picks. **Known for:** expansive outdoor seating that's ideal for all ages; dog-friendly policy; locally sourced comfort food. *$ Average main: $16 ✉ 2027 Anchor La., East Austin ☎ 512/614–2260 ⊕ www.contigotexas.com ⏲ Closed Mon. and Tues. No lunch.*

Counter Cafe

$ | AMERICAN | Austin's iconic Counter Cafe closed its original (beloved, but tragically tiny) diner on North Lamar, but this east-side location doubles the square footage and offers an extended menu with signatures like polenta-fried oysters. The mid-century–styled interior looks almost identical, from the wooden countertops and blackboard of daily specials to the line of expert short-order chefs knocking out the familiar menu of classic breakfast and lunch dishes. **Known for:** hypnotic views of speedy short-order chefs; very loud during peak weekend hours; heaping portions. *$ Average main: $12 ✉ 1914 E. 6th St., East Austin ☎ 512/351–9961 ⊕ www.countercafe.com ⏲ No dinner.*

Cuantos Tacos

$ | MEXICAN | A popular anchor at the east side's Arbor Food Park, this cheery yellow truck has become Austin's go-to for Mexico City–style street tacos. A helpful diagram at the walk-up window showing the actual size of the *pequeño* tacos (100% nixtamal) is as straightforward as the service and menu here. **Known for:** great value; authentic Mexico City–style tacos worthy of a connoisseur; tiny tacos that pack a punch. *$ Average main: 6 ✉ Arbor Food Park, 1108 E. 12th St., East Austin ☎ 512/903–3918 ⊕ www.cuantostacosaustin.com ⏲ Closed Sun. and Mon.*

★ Dai Due

$$$$ | AMERICAN | This Manor Road hot spot hangs their hat on seasonal local cuisine, with an emphasis on farmers' markets, Texas beer and wines, and even ingredients foraged by the chefs themselves. A butcher-shop display-case greets patrons upon entering, showcasing various charcuterie and house-made canned and pantry goods. **Known for:** hyper-local offerings focusing on meat; outstanding cocktail program; servers with encyclopedic knowledge of the menu. *$ Average main: $41 ✉ 2406 Manor Rd., East Austin ☎ 512/524–0688 ⊕ www.daidue.com ⏲ Closed Mon. No lunch weekdays.*

East Austin
A
B
C
D
E
F
1
2
3
4
5
6
7
8
9
35
BLACKLAND
FOSTER HEIGHTS
EAST AUSTIN
Waterloo Park
Rosewood Park
Parque Zaragoza Park
Longhorn Dam
East 32nd St.
Dancy Street
Lafayette Ave.
French Place
Cherrywood Road
Larry Lane
Manor Road
Alexander Ave.
East 22nd Street
Red River St.
Comal Street
Leona Street
East 21st Street
East 20th Street
East Martin Luther King Jr Boulevard
East Martin Luther King Jr. Blvd
E. Martin Luther King Jr Blvd.
San Jacinto Blvd.
Chestnut Avenue
Cedar Avenue
Walnut Avenue
Ulit Avenue
Miriam Avenue
East 18th St.
East 17th St.
East 16th Street
Salina Street
Poquito Street
Singleton Ave.
Alamo St.
Coleto Street
East 14th Street
East 13th Street
E. 15th Street
Trinity Street
Navasota Street
Waller St.
Olander St.
San Bernard St.
East 12th Street
New York Avenue
East 12th Street
Catalpa St.
Olive St.
Juniper St.
Cotton Street
East 11th Street
East 10th Street
East 9th Street
Pleasant Valley Road
Rosewood Avenue
San Marcos Street
East 8th Street
Northwestern Ave.
Chicon Street
Lincoln St.
Swenson Ave.
Comal St.
Concho St.
Chalmers Avenue
Chicon St.
East 9th St.
Prospect Ave.
East 10th St.
East 8th St.
Webberville Rd.
East 7th Street
East 6th Street
East 5th Street
East 4th Street
Medina Street
Attayac Street
East 3rd Street
East 2nd Street
Willow Street
Canterbury Street
Garden Street
Holly Street
East Cesar Chavez Street
Calles Street
Santa Rosa Street
Santa Maria Street
Santa Rita Street
Pedernales Street
San Saba Street
Robert T Martinez Junior Street
Anthony Street
Lynn Street
Chicon Street
Mildred Street
Broadway St.
Canterbury St.
Haskell Street
Riverview St.
KEY
Exploring Sights
Restaurants
Hotels

Sights

1	MASS Gallery	H8
2	Modern Rocks Gallery	I7
3	Texas State Cemetery	C6
4	Thinkery	G1
5	Yard Dog Art Gallery	I7

Restaurants

1	Canje	D7
2	Cisco's	C7
3	Contigo	H1
4	Counter Cafe	D7
5	Cuantos Tacos	B4
6	Dai Due	E1
7	Easy Tiger	C6
8	Franklin Barbecue	B5
9	Hoover's Cooking	D1
10	Jacoby's Restaurant & Mercantile	G9
11	Juan in a Million	E8
12	Justine's Brasserie	I9
13	Kerlin BBQ	D8
14	la Barbecue	E9
15	L'Oca d'Oro	G1
16	Lou's	C8
17	Oseyo	C8
18	Salt & Time	D7
19	Salty Sow	D2
20	Sawyer & Co.	H9
21	Sour Duck Market	D2
22	Suerte	D7
23	Veracruz All Natural	F7
24	Wright Bros. Brew & Brew	A6

Hotels

1	ARRIVE Austin	D7
2	East Austin Hotel	B6
3	Heywood Hotel	C8
4	Super 8 by Wyndham Austin Downtown	B4

★ Easy Tiger

$$ | **GERMAN** | The newest location of this beloved German-style bakery and beer garden features 15,000 square feet of outdoor space, plus a spacious interior, for beer and sausage lovers. The sprawling outdoor patio attracts lively lunch, happy hour, and late-night crowds with a full menu of artisan sandwiches, house-made sausages, and "big as your face" pretzels, as well as one of the best beer selections in the city. **Known for:** dog-friendly outdoor patio and weekend crowds; wholesale bakeshop with excellent early-morning special; charcuterie-fueled happy hours. *Average main: $15* *1501 E. 7th St., East Austin* *512/839–8523* *www.easytigerusa.com.*

★ Franklin Barbecue

$$ | **BARBECUE** | If Central Texas is the hub of the state's best barbecue, then this place has become its favorite darling. The former food truck become full-fledged, world-renowned restaurant, owned by pit master Aaron Franklin, attracts a daily throng of fans who wait in line upward of three hours in hopes of devouring a paper-lined tray of brisket, sausage, and pork ribs pulled straight from the smoker. **Known for:** infamous lines if you don't pre-order; mouthwatering brisket that lives up to the hype (and usually sells out by 2 pm); crowds of fellow, cheerful barbecue lovers. *Average main: $14* *900 E. 11th St., East Austin* *512/653–1187* *www.franklinbbq.com* *Closed Mon. No dinner.*

★ Hoover's Cooking

$ | **SOUTHERN** | **FAMILY** | Local chef and native east Austinite Hoover Alexander has created one of the city's best comfort-food oases, blending Mama's home cooking, diner short-order specials, Tex-Mex favorites, and Cajun influences in one Southern comfort mecca. The self-styled "Smoke, Fire & Ice House" is known for its large portions and flavorful recipes, like a Jamaican jerk chicken and a chicken-fried steak that puts most others to shame. "Side mates" like mac 'n' cheese, fried okra, and creamed jalapeño spinach round out any home-style cravings. **Known for:** fast and casual service; portions that will have diners leaving with leftovers; finger-licking-good pies. *Average main: $12* *2002 Manor Rd., East Austin* *512/479–5006* *www.hooverscooking.com* *Closed Mon.*

Jacoby's Restaurant & Mercantile

$$ | **SOUTHERN** | The "ranch-to-table" cuisine of this east-side hot spot speaks to the Southern comfort cravings of Austinites, with savory classics like stuffed Salisbury steak, pickled fried green tomatoes, and shrimp-and-grits. The interiors, boasting natural hardwoods and salvaged materials from the Jacoby family ranch, provide an ideally casual place to kick back and relax with cocktails like mezcal margaritas and West Texas shandys; the scenic back patio overlooks the Colorado River. **Known for:** impressive signature house burger; shabby-chic decor; scenic patio views. *Average main: $22* *3235 E. César Chávez St., East Austin* *512/366–5808* *www.jacobysaustin.com* *Closed Mon. and Tues. No lunch weekdays.*

★ Juan in a Million

$ | **MEXICAN** | **FAMILY** | The not-so-secret weapon of this classic east Austin breakfast spot is its owner and namesake, local legend Juan Meza, who has run his modest eatery since 1981 and still greets every diner with a bone-crushing handshake and a smile. Juan's strong community spirit is infectious, but the simple, filling, and reliably good fare will start your day off right on its own. The Don Juan taco (a massive mound of eggs, potato, bacon, and cheese) is the true east Austin breakfast of champions; the *machacado con huevo* (shredded dried beef scrambled with eggs), *migas* (eggs scrambled with torn corn tortillas, onions, chile peppers, cheese, and spices), and huevos rancheros are also

Franklin Barbecue in East Austin is famous for its long lines and delicious barbecue.

above average. **Known for:** hangover cure for the ages; weekend crowds of sunglasses-wearing hipsters; extra tortillas to help finish the signature Don Juan breakfast taco. *Average main: $8* *2300 E. César Chávez St., East Austin* *512/472–3872* *www.juaninamillion.com* *No dinner.*

Justine's Brasserie

$$$ | BRASSERIE | On a distinctly unromantic stretch of far East 5th Street, this intimate French brasserie is a romantic oasis, perfect for any first date or special occasion celebration. You can't go wrong with the steak frites (featuring a Texas-size rib eye), while the escargots and ratatouille are reliably exceptional. **Known for:** ultra-chic date-night destination; romantic atmosphere that stays open late; French-centric special events, especially around Bastille Day. *Average main: $23* *4710 E. 5th St., East Austin* *512/385–2900* *www.justines1937.com* *Closed Tues. No lunch.*

Kerlin BBQ

$$ | BARBECUE | The long lines, rain or shine, at this east-side food truck make no secret of its epic Texas barbecue. The cheesy brisket kolaches wrapped in mouthwatering sweet dough (only sold on Sunday) have been lauded by everyone, including the barbecue editor at *Texas Monthly,* who samples the fiercest and finest BBQ all across the state. **Known for:** classic Texas barbecue done right; signature brisket kolaches that live up to the hype; reputation for selling out fast. *Average main: 18* *2207 E. César Chávez St., East Austin* *512/412–5588* *www.kerlinbbq.com* *Closed Mon.–Thurs. No dinner.*

★ la Barbecue

$ | BARBECUE | This lovely east-side spot has moved from its original trailer location into a shared space within Quickie Pickie, the quaint local neighborhood grocery and bodega, and remains another top spot for Texas barbecue. Portions of their prizewinning BBQ are Texas-size, including their popular El

Sancho brisket sandwich with "Bobby Sauce." Lines are to be expected, but service is friendly and swift. **Known for:** free taste of brisket at the counter while you order; a line that's worth the wait; equally fine backup if Franklin BBQ sells out. *Average main: 10 2401 E. César Chávez St., East Austin 512/605–9696 www.labarbecue.com Closed Mon. and Tues. No dinner.*

L'Oca d'Oro

$$ | **ITALIAN** | **FAMILY** | The Mueller development has welcomed several eateries over the last few years, and this top-notch neighborhood Italian restaurant, which means "the Golden Goose," might be its most delicious addition. Whether it's date night or a quick happy hour with friends, dishes like Texas Wagyu tartare and from-scratch *cavatelli al pomodoro* will dazzle. **Known for:** Italian classics made from scratch; frequently ranked as one of the best restaurants in Texas; great for groups and celebratory dinners. *Average main: 22 1900 Simond Ave., East Austin 512/212–1876 www.locadoroaustin.com Closed Mon. and Tues. No lunch.*

Lou's

$ | **AMERICAN** | **FAMILY** | Housed in an old east Austin tire shop, this counter-service outdoor café is a favorite of families and on-the-go locals. Local hospitality juggernauts Larry McGuire and Liz Lambert kept the Aztec iconography, walk-up service, and sparse layout of the preexisting spot, and the new back patio is ideal for lazy lunches, family outings, and weekend day-drinking. **Known for:** weekly live music, trivia nights, and community events; lively outdoor setting that's great for pets and kids; popular rotisserie chicken to-go. *Average main: 9 1900 E. César Chávez St., East Austin 512/660–5171 www.lousaustin.com.*

Oseyo

$$ | **KOREAN** | Korean for "please come in," this Korean restaurant on César Chávez has a chic, organic atmosphere complete with an inviting garden courtyard. Dinner menus include traditional and nontraditional dishes "inspired by mom's recipes," from bibimbap (rice with seasonal veggies) to the comforting kimchi *bokkeumbap* (fried rice), alongside wood-grilled bulgogi (thinly sliced marinated meat) and *japchae* (stir-fried noodles) with *banchan* (condiments). **Known for:** share-size portions; soju specials and rotating kimchi cocktails; tasty bibimbap served in hot stone bowls. *Average main: 22 1628 E. César Chávez St., East Austin 512/368–5700 www.oseyoaustin.com Closed Mon. and Tues. No lunch.*

Salt & Time

$$ | **AMERICAN** | Sure, it's become a hipster-certified option for locally sourced charcuterie, meatball subs, and an intimate (and meat-heavy) dinner service, but many Austinites still frequent Salt & Time solely for their expert butcher selections and services. Traditional salumi, tartare, and daily offal specials aren't always for the faint of heart, but the lunch and dinner menus are extremely satisfying, with entrées like a popular "butcher's burger" and a braciole stuffed with Parmesan, garlic, smoked tomatoes, and okra. **Known for:** decidedly not vegan-friendly; expert butchers; adventurous specials. *Average main: $16 1912 E. 7th St., East Austin 512/524–1383 www.saltandtime.com Closed Mon.*

Salty Sow

$$ | **AMERICAN** | This porcine-theme gastropub in the midst of Manor Road's burgeoning food scene might sport a range of pig illustrations and artwork on their walls, but their contemporary farmhouse cuisine extends far beyond pork. Diverse options include bacon and gruyere–roasted bone marrow, slow-cooked beef shoulder, and chicken liver mousse. **Known for:** "cheeky" pig-theme decor; expertly prepared beef and pork dishes; popular happy hour that fills up

the spacious seating area fast. $ *Average main: $20* ✉ *1917 Manor Rd., East Austin* ☎ *512/391–2337* 🌐 *www.saltysow.com* ⏲ *No lunch.*

Sawyer & Co.

$ | **CAJUN** | This Cajun diner attracted attention for its stylish, retro interior, complete with vintage booths and an Astroturf rear patio, before Austinites even had the chance to sample its New Orleans–style comfort food. But the mid-century motif has only bolstered the growing reputation of its all-day breakfast, lunch, and dinner menus. **Known for:** deviled eggs with praline bacon to start any meal; bright and fun-loving mid-century decor; casual atmosphere and excellent service. $ *Average main: $13* ✉ *4827 E. César Chávez St., East Austin* ☎ *512/531–9033* 🌐 *www.sawyerand.co.*

Sour Duck Market

$$ | **AMERICAN** | The award-winning team behind local restaurants Odd Duck and Barley Swine opened their "everyday" restaurant in east Austin in 2018 to rave reviews from critics and locals alike. The bustling gathering spot consists of two buildings (the main front entry, with counter service for pastries, snacks, and drinks, plus the back bar) that are connected by an outdoor patio that serves as a beer and wine garden. **Known for:** baked goods at the counter that go fast on weekends; hopping crowds at any time of day; great people-watching in the back courtyard. $ *Average main: 15* ✉ *1814 E. MLK Jr. Blvd., East Austin* ☎ *512/394–5776* 🌐 *www.sourduckmarket.com* ⏲ *Closed Mon. and Tues.*

Suerte

$$ | **MEXICAN** | This contemporary take on Mexican fare makes for a fun dining experience on the east side. Interiors are spacious and bright (if a bit impersonal and loud during peak hours), and the menu is playful (with categories like "snackcidents," "frio and raw," and "masa y mas"), as is the food, like goat-rib Barbacoa and huarache duck carnitas. **Known for:** fun, bubbly atmosphere with great service; popular items like bite-size brisket tacos; daily "Lucky Hour" with $5 "snackcident" plates. $ *Average main: 16* ✉ *1800 E. 6th St., East Austin* ☎ *512/953–0092* 🌐 *www.suerteatx.com* ⏲ *No lunch weekdays.*

★ **Veracruz All Natural**

$ | **MEXICAN** | Veracruz wears a taco tiara in the Austin food scene and for good reason. The *migas*lives up to the local lore, and this always-hopping original location has a convivial patio where its best to enjoy tasty quesadillas, *barbacoa,* vegetarian and fish tacos on homemade tortillas, and fresh aguas frescas alfresco. **Known for:** original spot for chain with growing number of local locations; signature migas taco and diverse vegan options; homemade tortillas and chips. $ *Average main: 7* ✉ *2505 Webberville Rd., East Austin* ☎ *512/981–1760* 🌐 *www.veracruzallnatural.com* ⏲ *No dinner Mon.–Thurs.*

★ **Wright Bros. Brew & Brew**

$ | **CAFÉ** | What started as a streamlined coffee and craft beer purveyor with sparse hours has evolved into an all-day east Austin mainstay. The industrial garage vibe blends in well with its I–35-adjacent neighbors and attracts a hip clientele from morning to night, who flock here for cold brews and stacked breakfast sandwiches and then like to stick around for their local lineup of draft brews. **Known for:** popular hangout for locals working remotely; skyline views from the side patio; in-house specialty sub shop with expanded lunch menu. $ *Average main: 9* ✉ *500 San Marcos St., Suite 105, East Austin* ☎ *512/655–3442* 🌐 *www.thebrewandbrew.com.*

Hotels

ARRIVE Austin

$$ | **HOTEL** | The hipster mecca of East Sixth Street is a great place for this appropriately hipster boutique hotel. **Pros:**

on-site restaurant with Goan-inspired cuisine; chic rooms and decor; walking distance to East Sixth shops, bars, and restaurants. **Cons:** pricey valet only parking option available; sparse amenities; gritty up-and-coming immediate surroundings. *$ Rooms from: 165 ✉ 1813 E. 6th St., East Austin ☎ 737/242–8080 🌐 www.arrivehotels.com/austin 🍴 No Meals 🛏 83 rooms.*

★ East Austin Hotel

$$ | **HOTEL** | More hotels are slowly arriving in the otherwise rapidly developing hub of east Austin, and a highlight is the East Austin Hotel, which provides unbeatable access to the East Sixth Street District, which is swarming with delicious local restaurants, hip boutiques, and live music venues. **Pros:** hip, walkable location on the cheap; luxe comfort for a great value; outdoor pool and bar. **Cons:** Scandinavian-inspired decor translates to spartan accommodations; not for travelers who value privacy; immediate street scene isn't picturesque. *$ Rooms from: 125 ✉ 1108 E. 6th St., East Austin ☎ 512/205–8888 🌐 www.eastaustinhotel.com 🍴 No Meals 🛏 75 rooms.*

Heywood Hotel

$$$ | **B&B/INN** | This boutique hotel debuted amidst the rapidly gentrifying strip of East Cesar Chavez, and the hip hood has continued to flourish around the restored 1920s bungalow, elevating its desirable indie locale. **Pros:** luxury amenities and attention to detail by the staff; free off-street parking and complimentary bikes; chic but approachable design. **Cons:** pricier than conventional downtown chain hotels; noise can be an issue; construction in the rapidly gentrifying surrounding area can cause adjacent street closures. *$ Rooms from: $230 ✉ 1609 E. César Chávez St., East Austin ☎ 512/271–5522 🌐 www.heywoodhotel.com 🛏 7 rooms 🍴 No Meals.*

Super 8 by Wyndham Austin Downtown

$ | **HOTEL** | For no-frills, reasonably priced lodging close to downtown, you could do worse than this basic two-story brick motel located just east of the northbound I–35 access road. **Pros:** proximity to downtown; unbeatable price point; free Wi-Fi and parking. **Cons:** guests tend to be partiers; pool is not inviting; not scenic. *$ Rooms from: $65 ✉ 1201 N. I–35, East Austin ☎ 512/472–8331 🌐 www.wyndhamhotels.com/super-8 🛏 65 rooms 🍴 Free Breakfast.*

Nightlife

BARS

★ The Liberty

BARS | This East Sixth Street dive bar has a huge back-patio space filled with picnic tables. The on-site food truck, the original location of East Side King, is one of the most famous trailers in town. Grab a beer before hitting the town, or end up here for a late-night bite. The Liberty also provides a great place to socialize during SXSW with its hip east-side address. *✉ 1618 E. 6th St., East Austin ☎ 512/514–0502 🌐 www.facebook.com/thelibertyaustin.*

LoLo

WINE BARS | This natural wine bar and shop has popped up amidst the dive bars and music venues of East Sixth, offering an incredible respite for respectable wine lovers. Friendly staff help navigate the selection of biodynamic and natural wines of various varietals at the shop's front counter, and the shady back patio has communal seating and live music some nights. Stop in for a bottle to-go or enjoy their happy hour with an artisanal cheese board. *✉ 1504 E. 6th St., East Austin ☎ 512/906–0053 🌐 www.lolo.wine.*

Nickel City

BARS | Named one of the best bars in America by *GQ* magazine, Nickel City holds court amidst one of the most bustling stretches of east Austin. With an arsenal of heavy pours, classic cocktails, and a "damn good" whiskey selection,

Austin After Dark

Austin is known for being the Live Music Capital of the World, but its after-hours scene stretches far beyond its multitude of live music venues. The capital city is a bustling hive of nocturnal offerings, from downtown theaters and hallowed honky-tonks to citywide festivals and nighttime swimming holes.

Bars

Austin is an international destination with a small-town feel, and its myriad cocktail bars, dives, hipster haunts, and high-end speakeasies speak to the city's diversity. Downtown is an obvious hub, from the seedy, college-aged clubs of Dirty Sixth Street (from around Neches St. to Brazos St.) to the more posh (but still rowdy) bars of West Sixth. The Warehouse district is home to the best gay bars and dance clubs in the city, and the east-side entertainment district (centered on East Sixth just east of I–35) has a variety of emerging bars and special event venues.

Festivals

Hundreds of thousands of visitors descend upon Austin every year for its astounding array of annual festivals. There's the citywide monoliths, most notably SXSW and the Austin City Limits Music Festival, the underground darlings like Moontower Comedy Festival, and cultural convergences such as the Austin Film Festival. A growing international attraction are the races at Austin's premier Formula One facility, Circuit of the Americas.

Dancing

With so much music, it's easy to see why the city has a variety of dance clubs and venues. Two-stepping and Western swing is still hip at historic honky-tonks—the Broken Spoke and Donn's Depot are favorites. DJ sets and dance parties stretch into the wee hours throughout the Warehouse District, and east-side venues like Scoot Inn and The White Horse showcase frequent cumbia, salsa, and hip-hop nights.

Theater

International acts grace the stages of downtown's Paramount Theatre and the Long Center for the Performing Arts just south of Lady Bird Lake, but neighborhood venues like the Hyde Park and Zilker theaters are just as popular for local productions. Formal venues and casual stages host weekly poetry readings, spoken-word performances, improv, and open-mike nights. There's also a range of theme movie nights at the various Alamo Drafthouse locations; expect anything from quote-a-longs and costume contests to after-parties at the adjacent Highball lounge.

Exercising After Dark

Austinites are always on the go, even after dark, and visitors can tap into the local vitality with popular nocturnal activities. There are nightly free swims at Barton Springs, after-dinner strolls on the South Lamar Pedestrian Bridge, and weekly social-cycling rides that attract hundreds of bicyclists who trace various routes throughout the east side, ending, of course, at a local bar.

bartenders serve loyal customers without gimmicks or frills. Food trucks are on-site, and weekly specials are promoted for the pedestrian-heavy street. ✉ *1133 E. 11th St., East Austin* ☎ *512/987–4294* 🌐 *www.nickelcitybar.com.*

Scoot Inn

LIVE MUSIC | This historic outdoor music venue, established in 1871, is tucked away on the east side and offers a funky and fresh mix of music and theme parties in a dive-bar–esque setting with an impressive outdoor stage. On-site parking can be tough to find, so ridesharing is encouraged. Be sure to check out their lineup during SXSW. ✉ *1308 E. 4th St., East Austin* ☎ *No phone* 🌐 *www.scootinnaustin.com.*

Whisler's

COCKTAIL LOUNGES | A top spot for craft cocktails in an intimate atmosphere along East 6th Street, Whisler's consistently draws a see-and-be-seen crowd who not only expect the best cocktail of their choice, but are also willing to pay top-dollar for it. If you take craft cocktails seriously, you won't regret an evening here. You'll find an inviting array of seasonal drinks on the menu, but be sure to ask your server about off-the-menu options, too. And their "back bar," a Oaxacan-inspired mezcal bar, Mezcalería Tobalá (open Friday and Saturday), is not to be missed. ✉ *1816 E. 6th St., East Austin* ☎ *512/480–0781* 🌐 *www.whislersatx.com.*

DANCE CLUBS

Hotel Vegas & The Volstead

DANCE CLUBS | If the sun has set, midnight is approaching, and you're ready to not only hear but feel some beats, then hit up these side-by-side sister bars for killer DJ sets and dance parties in the heart of East Sixth Street. Expect a throwdown of sound during SXSW. ✉ *1500 E. 6th St., East Austin* ☎ *No phone* 🌐 *www.texashotelvegas.com.*

LIVE MUSIC

★ The White Horse

DANCE CLUBS | Cowboys, hipsters, and dancing queens mix and mingle with surprising ease at this honky-tonk for the modern age. The on-site food truck, Bomb Tacos, is open every day, live music is onstage every night, and newcomers can take free two-step classes before the main dance floor fills up. ✉ *500 Comal St., East Austin* ☎ *512/553–6756* 🌐 *www.thewhitehorseaustin.com.*

Shopping

take heart

SOUVENIRS | It's not that you'll find anything out of the ordinary at this east Austin boutique, it's just that everything you find will be extraordinary. Take the kitchen wares, for instance, like porcelain mugs from Japan beside the shop's artisanal wooden serving tools. Knickknacks from across the country, such as wooden toys and mobiles, blend impossibly well with vintage items, almost as though they were curated to live in the gallery-worthy space. The store has a beautiful assortment of hand-pressed cards by artists if you'd like to write home. ✉ *1111 E. 11th St., Suite 100, East Austin* ☎ *512/366–5667* 🌐 *www.takeheartshop.com.*

North Austin

Located just 10 minutes north of downtown, North Austin neighborhoods like Hyde Park, Rosedale, and North Loop are home to some of Austin's best local eateries and shops. Cruise along North Loop Boulevard and Burnet Road to discover dozens of cafés, bars, and vintage/thrift stores tucked comfortably between quaint blocks of historic homes and Old Austin charms.

Sights

Elisabet Ney Museum

HISTORIC HOME | FAMILY | The 19th century lives on at this delightfully eccentric museum, where German Romanticism meets the Texas frontier. The historic home and studio of sculptor Elisabet Ney is a lovely gem in the Hyde Park neighborhood that showcases Ney's life and work, with more than 70 sculptures on display. Ney's studio, where she produced sculptures of historic figures, like Stephen F. Austin and Sam Houston, is set up as she knew it, with sculpting tools, hat, teacup, and other items all in their proper places. The castle-like home is surrounded by native prairie grasses and more outdoor sculptures. Family-friendly art classes and special events are also hosted throughout the year. *✉ 304 E. 44th St., Hyde Park ☎ 512/974–1625 🌐 www.theney.org 🎫 Free ⏲ Closed Mon. and Tues.*

Q2 Stadium

SPORTS VENUE | The home of the Austin Football Club (the city's first major professional sports team) is a state-of-the-art stadium located just north of downtown off Burnet Road. There are clear-bag restrictions at the gate, but staff is helpful and informative when it comes to navigating the facility, which includes a great selection of local food stalls, like Tacodeli and Bao'd Up. You'll see fans decked out in green throughout the city on game days as they head to the stadium. A bevy of local restaurants, bars, and breweries are nearby for pre- or postgame parties. *✉ 10414 McKalla Pl., North Austin ☎ 512/572–8932 🌐 www.austinfc.com/stadium.*

Restaurants

★ Barley Swine

$$$$ | AMERICAN | Reservations are essential at this intimate eatery (and can be made a month in advance), but there are also a limited number of communal tables available for walk-in patrons. The strictly seasonal, locally sourced daily specials blend the artistic style of Japanese sushi with the familiarity of Southern comfort food. **Known for:** bougie vibe for an elevated date night; fixed menu of chef-selected small plates that gives serious street cred for adventurous foodies; a beer list for the true aficionado. *$ Average main: $105 ✉ 6555 Burnet Rd., Suite 400, North Austin ☎ 512/394–8150 🌐 www.barleyswine.com ⏲ Closed Mon.–Wed. No lunch.*

DipDipDip Tatsu-Ya

$$ | JAPANESE | Another rave-worthy hit from the team behind Ramen Tatsu-Ya, this modern take on traditional Japanese hot pot is Austin's long-awaited answer to a new-school shabu-shabu–style destination. The required meal here is in the name: thinly sliced meats and veggies designed for dipping shabu-style in various house-made broths and dips. **Known for:** intimate interior that makes seating limited and reservations essential; a to-die-for "Baller Omakase" menu; sleek shabu shabu–style hot pot creations. *$ Average main: 22 ✉ 7301 Burnet Rd., North Austin ☎ 512/701–6767 🌐 www.dipdipdip-tatsuya.com ⏲ No lunch.*

★ Fonda San Miguel

$$$ | MEXICAN | FAMILY | This beloved villa-style North Loop spot combines sophisticated ambience with a solid menu of authentic Mexican classics. Start with the ceviche Veracruzano (with chiles, onion, tomato, and spices), and continue with a multilayered dish like the ancho relleno San Miguel—a roasted pepper stuffed with chicken, capers, raisins, and cilantro cream—or try the *pollo pibil*, chicken baked in a banana leaf. **Known for:** from-scratch ingredients, most notably their homemade tortillas; signature ancho relleno; striking interiors that transport patrons to interior Mexico. *$ Average main: $30 ✉ 2330 W. North Loop Blvd., North Austin ☎ 512/459–4121*

North Austin
A
B
C
D
E
F
1
2
3
4
5
6
7
8
9
ALLANDALE
BRENTWOOD
ROSEDALE
ALTA VISTA
HYDE PARK
HERITAGE
Shoal Creek Greenbelt
North Mopac Expressway
White Horse Trail
Shoal Creek Blvd.
Nasco Drive
Bull Creek Rd.
Shoalwood Avenue
Wynona Ave.
Burnet Road
Burnet Ln
Laird Drive
Burbank St.
Brentwood St.
Karen Avenue
Payne Avenue
Pequeno Street
Alegria Road
Romeria Drive
Alguno Road
Palo Duro Road
Goodnight Lane
Arroyo Seco
Cullen Avenue
Justin Lane
Dwyce Drive
Choquette Drive
Ruth Avenue
Brentwood Street
Arcadia Avenue
Grover Ave.
West Koenig Lane
Northland Drive
Woodview Avenue
Montview Street
Lawnmont Avenue
Clay Avenue
William Holland Ave.
Jim Hogg Avenue
Joe Sayers Avenue
Woodrow Avenue
Roosevelt Ave.
Aurora Dr.
Houston Street
West North Loop Boulevard
North Lamar Boulevard
Guadalupe Street
Hancock Drive
Westfield Drive
West Frances Place
West Park Drive
Placid Place
West 50th St.
Shoal Creek Boulevard
Bull Creek Road
West 45th St.
Sinclair Ave.
Ramsey Ave.
West 46th St.
Shoalwood Avenue
W. 44th St.
W. 43rd St.
Rosedale Ave.
W. 42nd St.
Burnet Rd.
Marie Ave.
Bellvue Avenue
West 41st Street
West 40th Street
West 39th Street
Lewis Lane
Marathon Boulevard
W. 40th St.
W. 39th St.
West 38th St.
West 37th St.
West 36th St.
West 35th Street
Avenue A
Avenue B
Avenue C
Avenue D
West 46th Street
West 45th Street
West 44th Street
West 43rd Street
West 42nd Street
West 41st St.
West 40th St.
West 39th Street
West 38th Street
Speedway
Avenue F
Avenue G
Avenue H
Duval Street
Peck Avenue
Oakmont Blvd.
Beverly Road
Bryker Drive
Jefferson Street
West 30th Street
West 29th Street
Mohle Drive
West 34th Street
West 38th Street
West 32nd Street
W. 31st Street
W. 37th St.
W. 35th St.
West 34th Street
1
2
3
5
9
10
11
12
13
16

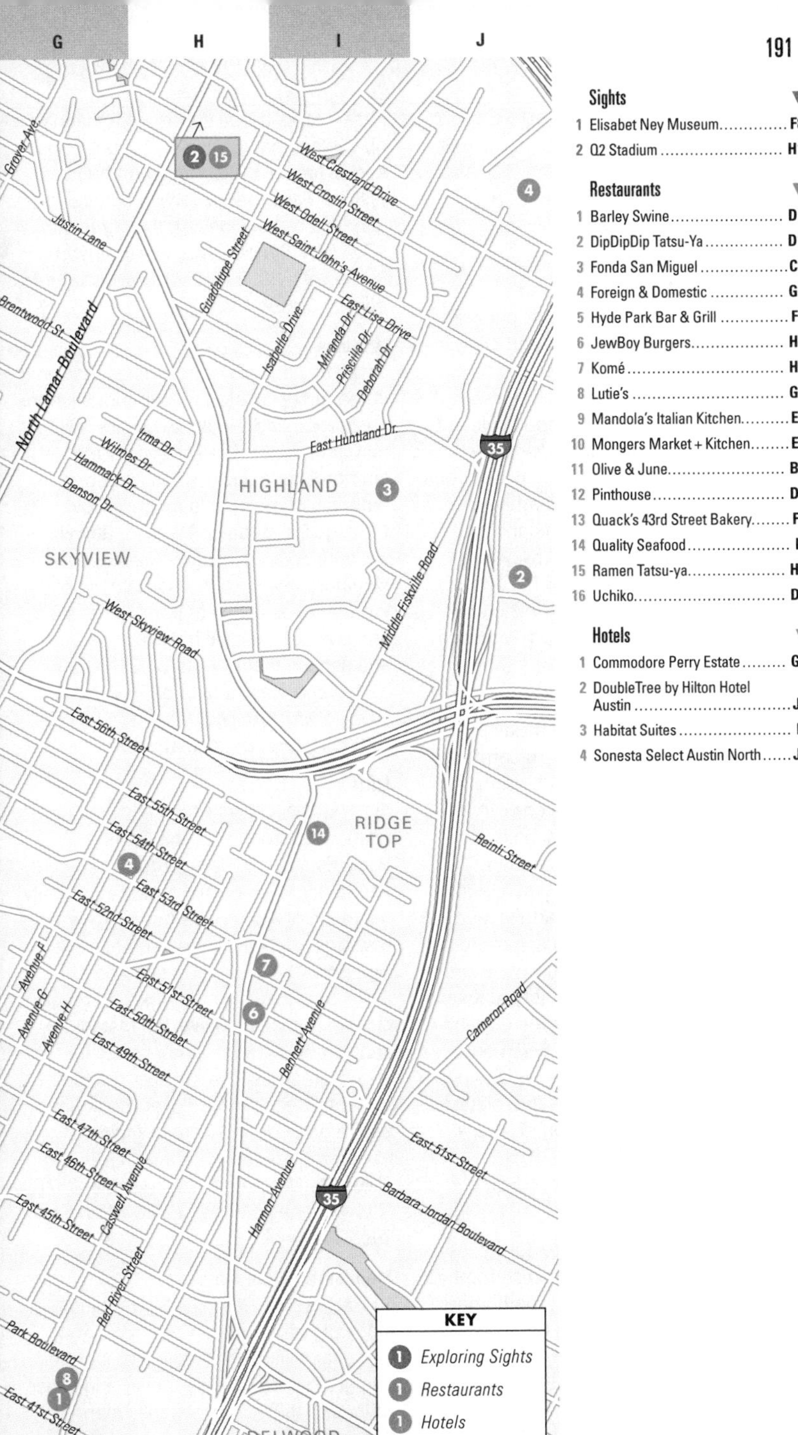

Sights

1 Elisabet Ney Museum.............. F8
2 Q2 Stadium H1

Restaurants

1 Barley Swine....................... D1
2 DipDipDip Tatsu-Ya D1
3 Fonda San Miguel C4
4 Foreign & Domestic G6
5 Hyde Park Bar & Grill F8
6 JewBoy Burgers.................... H7
7 Komé H6
8 Lutie's G9
9 Mandola's Italian Kitchen.......... E6
10 Mongers Market + Kitchen........ E8
11 Olive & June........................ B8
12 Pinthouse D5
13 Quack's 43rd Street Bakery........ F8
14 Quality Seafood I5
15 Ramen Tatsu-ya..................... H1
16 Uchiko............................... D7

Hotels

1 Commodore Perry Estate G9
2 DoubleTree by Hilton Hotel Austin J4
3 Habitat Suites I3
4 Sonesta Select Austin North...... J1

🌐 *www.fondasanmiguel.com* 🕓 *Closed Sun. No lunch.*

Foreign & Domestic

$$$ | **AMERICAN** | This upscale, 47-seat North Loop gastropub was a trailblazer in the city's locavore and "nose-to-tail" movements. And it's remained a reliably inventive spot that keeps loyal patrons on their toes with seasonal (and daily rotating) creations, from fried pig ears and shishito peppers to fresh market fish artfully accented with squid ink and foamed butter. **Known for:** addictive cheddar biscuit starters; menu of adventurous dishes that an exceptional staff helps navigate and explain; cozy neighborhood vibe with a loyal local following. 💲 *Average main: $25* ✉ *306 E. 53rd St., North Austin* ☎ *512/459–1010* 🌐 *www.fndaustin.com* 🕓 *Closed Mon. No lunch Tues.–Sat.*

Hyde Park Bar & Grill

$$ | **AMERICAN** | **FAMILY** | With a classic but eclectic menu focusing on comfort foods, this welcoming neighborhood hangout has kept the locals coming in since 1982. Both the original on Duval Street and the newer south Austin location decorate with pleasant, colorful paintings (for sale) by local artists, and maintain an easygoing atmosphere for both the shorts-and-T-shirt crowd and the dressier, special-occasion fraction. **Known for:** giant fork towering over the entrance, decorated with seasonal impalements on holidays; buttermilk-battered and peppered fries, served on shareable platters; lovely neighborhood location. 💲 *Average main: $17* ✉ *4206 Duval St., Hyde Park* ☎ *512/458–3168* 🌐 *www.hpbng.com.*

JewBoy Burgers

$ | **BURGER** | This local favorite combines the founder's El Paso and Jewish roots to create some of the best flat-top burgers, "border-style" burritos, and homemade potato latkes in town. Highlights include "the Goyim" burger (a JewBoy patty with grilled pastrami, bacon, Swiss, pickles, and mustard) and the "Que Pasa" *carne asada* burrito with marinated rib eye and grilled onions and poblanos. **Known for:** unique burgers and burritos; tasty El Paso-meets-Jewish cultural creations; tater-tot sides. 💲 *Average main: 10* ✉ *5111 Airport Blvd., North Austin* ☎ *512/291–3358* 🌐 *www.jewboyburgers.com* 🕓 *Closed Mon.*

★ Komé

$ | **JAPANESE** | This North Austin sushi joint is the best place to find superior sashimi, sushi rolls, and Japanese cuisine without daunting prices. The *izakaya*-style menu (an homage to Japan's casual pub-style eateries) offers a wide range of cold, fried, grilled, and rice dishes. **Known for:** outstanding sushi and Japanese signatures without the upscale prices; wonderful selection of beer, wine, sake, and cocktails; casual izakaya-style dishes and service that's great for lunch dates. 💲 *Average main: $13* ✉ *5301 Airport Blvd., Suite 100, Hyde Park* ☎ *512/712–5700* 🌐 *www.kome-austin.com.*

Lutie's

$$$$ | **MODERN EUROPEAN** | On the glamorous grounds of the Commodore Perry Estate, this chic garden restaurant seems far removed from the casual daily aesthetic of Austin. The hotel's Italianate mansion lends to the restaurant's Jazz Age vibes, with opulent, floral decor and a decadent menu of Texas heritage cuisine to match. **Known for:** Instagram- and swoon-worthy bathroom; exclusive, glamorous location and interiors; romantic sunset views over the country estate grounds. 💲 *Average main: 36* ✉ *Commodore Perry Estate, 4100 Red River St., North Austin* ☎ *512/675–2517* 🌐 *www.luties.com* 🕓 *Closed Mon. and Tues. No lunch.*

Mandola's Italian Kitchen

$ | **ITALIAN** | **FAMILY** | Houston restaurateur (and cofounder of the Carrabba's restaurant chain) Damian Mandola brought his "neighborhood grocery store" and Italian *ristorante* to The Triangle apartment and retail complex, just north of the UT

The Elizabet Ney Museum displays the work of famous local sculptor Elizabet Ney.

campus, and the cafeteria-style café has become a favorite for families and hungry college students looking to carbo-load on a budget. Hearty portions of southern Italian specialties, from pizza to daily-rotating raviolis, hit the spot at the right price. **Known for:** family-style takeout and package meals; leaving stuffed college students with leftovers; feeding everyone on a budget. *Average main: $13 4700 W. Guadalupe St., Suite 12, North Austin 512/419–9700 www.mandolas.com.*

Mongers Market + Kitchen

$$$$ | **SEAFOOD** | Hyde Park's best date-night destination might just be this neighborhood seafood restaurant and raw bar. Chef Shane Stark opened Mongers in 2015 (in the former home of wine bar Vino Vino), and it's developed a reputation for some of the freshest and best seafood in a town that doesn't necessarily have a coastal reputation. **Known for:** fully loaded lobster roll; great daily happy hour that includes bar food; limited lunch menu. *Average main: 34 4119 Guadalupe St., North Austin 512/215–8972 www.mongersaustin.com Closed Sun. and Mon.*

Olive & June

$$$$ | **ITALIAN** | Whether you're grabbing a cocktail at the bar, sharing a few appetizers with friends on the treehouse-like outdoor patio, or settling in to one of the elegant-yet-cozy booths for a romantic dinner with your honey, this Bryker Woods locale in northwest Austin serves up a satisfying lineup of fresh, Italian-inspired fare. Top picks from the popular *picolo piatti* (small plates) menu include scallop crudo with butternut squash and thinly sliced zucchini involtini wrapped around a decadent mushroom filling. **Known for:** very limited on-site parking; popular daily happy hour, especially on the shady patio; homemade gelato. *Average main: $36 3411 Glenview Ave., North Austin 512/467–9898 www.oliveandjune-austin.com Closed Sun. and Mon. No lunch.*

★ Pinthouse

$$ | **PIZZA** | This approachable pizza place and brew pub is a great addition to the burgeoning Burnet Road food scene. The parking lot can fill up fast on weekends, but an award-winning selection of beers makes it easy to wait for signature house-made pies, like the Armadillo, with artisan sausage and poblano peppers, or the Shroomin' Goat, with local goat cheese and roasted mushrooms. **Known for:** popular lunch special of a pizza roll, salad, and drink; long waits and crowds on weekends; staggering selection of draft beer. *Average main: 17 4729 Burnet Rd., North Austin 512/436–9605 www.pinthouse.com.*

★ Quack's 43rd Street Bakery

$ | **BAKERYBAKERY** | **FAMILY** | Hyde Park's iconic neighborhood bakery has been a local staple for over 40 years, serving scratch-made breakfast pastries, cupcakes, cookies, and various seasonal and custom creations. The friendly vibe of the bustling coffee shop attracts a loyal tribe of locals, usually seen hanging out on the outdoor patio tables throughout the day, as well as streams of UT students, families, and fans of the house-made chai. **Known for:** mouthwatering cinnamon rolls, carrot cake cupcakes, and theme sugar cookies that sell out quickly; long-standing local favorite for coffee and sweets; adorable neighborhood setting on the corner of Duval Street. *Average main: 6 411 E. 43rd St., North Austin/Hyde Park 512/453–3399 quacksbakery160953351.wpcomstaging.com.*

Quality Seafood

$$ | **SEAFOOD** | **FAMILY** | Serving the landlocked city's freshest seafood (fresh off the plane, if not the boat), this combination seafood market and casual eatery traces its history back to 1938 and has been at its Airport Boulevard address—amidst one of Austin's major commercial arteries—since 1970. Prices are low, preparation is straightforward, and blackboard specials include regional and Cajun favorites like gumbo and bacon-wrapped scallops. **Known for:** oysters on the half shell that won't put a dent in your wallet; no-frills atmosphere complete with basic counter service; classic Gulf Coast cuisine. *Average main: $14 5621 Airport Blvd., North Austin 512/452–3820 www.qualityseafoodmarket.com Closed Sun. and Mon.*

★ Ramen Tatsu-Ya

$$ | **JAPANESE** | Austin's ramen craze went into full swing a few years ago, and this happening spot was one of the city's first (and favorite) establishments. Try the "Ol' Skool," a chicken-based shoyu ramen with a traditional array of toppings, like *aijitama* (marinated soft-boiled egg), and optional "flavor bombs" from creamed corn and butter to Thai chili and habanero pepper paste. **Known for:** menu's helpful "how to enjoy" instruction section for ramen rookies; friendly counter service; small plates of Japanese comfort food. *Average main: $14 8557 Research Blvd., Suite 126, North Austin 512/893–5561 www.ramen-tatsuya.com.*

Uchiko

$$ | **JAPANESE** | This spot might have started out as the "little brother" of chef Tyson Cole's now famed Uchi restaurant, but the contemporary Japanese fusion eatery has become a standard in its own right. Led by the James Beard Award–winning Cole, Uchiko impresses with dishes like Jar Jar Duck, served in a mason jar and opened tableside to release a rosemary-smoke fog that reveals confit and smoked duck amid cracklings, kumquats, and pickled endives. **Known for:** swanky ambience, starting curbside with complimentary valet; signature brussels sprouts with sweet Thai chili sauce; daily happy hour with selected plates, sakes, and beer for cheap. *Average main: $22 4200 N. Lamar Blvd., North Austin 512/916–4808 www.uchikoaustin.com No lunch.*

★ Commodore Perry Estate

$$$$ | **HOTEL** | Tucked on the edge of the quaint Hyde Park neighborhood, just north of campus and downtown, the 1928 Commodore Perry mansion has been renovated to Italianate-style perfection and is now this upscale boutique hotel in the Auberge Resorts Collection. **Pros:** on-site Lutie's restaurant is one of the hottest tickets in town; complimentary car shuttle service; Instagram-friendly outdoor pool and lounge spaces. **Cons:** café service is spotty; luxurious atmosphere can attract a certain level of snootiness in clientele; immediate area outside of hotel lacks charm. *Rooms from: 599 ✉ 4100 Red River St., North Austin ☎ 512/817–5200 🌐 www.aubergeresorts.com/commodoreperry 🍽 No Meals 🛏 42 rooms.*

DoubleTree by Hilton Hotel Austin

$ | **HOTEL** | This vintage hotel turns its back on the rat race of nearby I–35 and transports guests to a surprisingly convincing Spanish colonial world. **Pros:** close (but not too close) to highway; proximity to downtown and UT; charming, pseudo-grand-hotel atmosphere. **Cons:** rooms starting to show wear-and-tear; fee for parking, unusual for this area; not a walkable area. *Rooms from: $124 ✉ 6505 N. I–35, North Austin ☎ 512/454–3737 🌐 www.hilton.com 🛏 350 rooms 🍽 No Meals.*

Habitat Suites

$ | **HOTEL** | Native plants and old-growth trees surround this environmentally friendly lodging that feels more like an apartment complex than a budget hotel. **Pros:** eco-friendly ethos; free breakfast and evening cocktail receptions; peaceful location. **Cons:** not a pedestrian-friendly location; outdated interiors and appliances; low-quality furniture. *Rooms from: $109 ✉ 500 E. Highland Mall Blvd., North Austin ☎ 512/467–6000 🌐 habitatsuites.austinhotelsweb.com/en 🛏 96 rooms 🍽 Free Breakfast.*

Sonesta Select Austin North

$ | **HOTEL** | Set back from the roar of I–35, this handsome five-floor hotel (formerly a Hyatt Hotel) is a step up from your usual off-ramp inn. **Pros:**; great value; free breakfast; outdoor pool. **Cons:** hard to access during rush hour; not much great dining nearby; removed from downtown. *Rooms from: $100 ✉ 7522 N. IH–35, North Austin ☎ 512/323–2121 🌐 www.sonesta.com 🛏 120 rooms 🍽 Free Breakfast.*

BARS

Carousel Lounge

BARS | Opened in 1963, this north Austin haunt is one of the most adored, longest-running bars in the city. The unassuming dive looks like a gritty hole-in-the-wall from the parking lot, but it's a surreal circus inside. You'll find no-frills service amidst all the frills of the decor straight out of a *Twin Peaks* episode, from pink elephants and clowns to circus tents and fire-breathers. The decor is wild, the drinks are cheap, and the live music is classic honky-tonk. *✉ 1110 E. 52nd St., North Austin ☎ 512/452–6790 🌐 www.carousellounge.net.*

Drink.Well.

COCKTAIL LOUNGES | A North Austin neighborhood hot spot, Drink.Well. has all the comforts of a local community pub with all the sophistication of a sleek downtown bar. Creative cocktails and local beers dominate the beverage menu, while a tasty spread of snacks and savory bar food keeps guests pulled up to the cozy bar for a couple of hours. *✉ 207 E. 53rd St., North Austin ☎ 512/614–6683 🌐 www.drinkwellaustin.com.*

Emerald Tavern Games & Cafe

BARS | **FAMILY** | For good food, great drinks and, yes, board games, Emerald

Tavern is the place to go. The front retail portion resembles a simple old-school book shop, but with a variety of games lining the shelves. In the back, the tavern offers a unique selection of beers on tap, a sizable wine list, a few café-style bites, and fresh coffee from local roaster Cuvée Coffee. Both indoors and out on the patio, you can sip and savor while passing the time playing a selection of classic, European, and role-playing games, as well as tabletop miniature games that involve tiny figurines. ✉ *9012 Research Blvd., Suite C-1, North Austin* ☎ *512/994–4649* 🌐 *www.emeraldtaverngames.com.*

★ The Little Longhorn Saloon

BARS | Looking for an authentic honky-tonk dive-bar experience? This Burnet Road haunt is an Old Austin favorite, though from the looks of the rather shabby exterior, you may not believe it at first. It's not glamorous, but the beer is cold and the service is friendly. Local music legend Dale Watson often takes the tiny stage here (there's live music every night), and the cast of regulars at this honored saloon is too good to miss. The claim to fame here is the riotous goodtimes had at the weekly Chicken Sh*t Bingo played every Sunday. ✉ *5434 Burnet Rd., North Austin* ☎ *512/524–1291* 🌐 *www.thelittlelonghornsaloon.com.*

Yard Bar

BARS | You don't have to bring a dog to be a patron at Austin's first hybrid restaurant, bar, and dog-park, off Burnet Road. The shaded outdoor patio is a great place to people- and puppy-watch while you chow down on sliders and fries served at the on-site Fat City walk-up window. Find several local beers on draft here, too, plus seasonal cocktails and cheap tall boys. ✉ *6700 Burnet Rd., North Austin* ☎ *512/900–3773* 🌐 *www.yardbar.com.*

COMEDY CLUBS

★ Cap City Comedy Club

COMEDY CLUBS | If you find yourself in North Austin, Cap City packs quite a punch with its stand-up comedian lineup. It's been the city's premier spot for stand-up comedy for over 35 years and regularly attracts world-class headliners and sold-out crowds, in addition to heaps of local talent showcased at weekly open-mic nights and at the club's annual "Funniest Person in Austin" contest. ✉ *8120 Research Blvd., Suite 100, North Austin* ☎ *512/467–2333* 🌐 *www.capcitycomedy.com.*

Shopping

GROCERY STORES

Central Market

MARKET | **FAMILY** | This upscale, foodie-friendly offshoot of the giant Texas-based H-E-B supermarket chain is a few years older than its competitor, Whole Foods, down Lamar Boulevard but no less popular (expect big weekend crowds). It's equally serious about the cheeses, wine, beer, meat, and deli products it purveys, but compared to Whole Foods it seems more like a place real people go to shop (rather than gawk). It's a great spot to grab prepared foods on the run or join the weekday lunch crowds at the in-house café, where an outdoor patio pleases kids and where bands play on Friday and Saturday evening. The market is in a shopping center that also houses some chic boutiques and gift shops. ✉ *4001 N. Lamar Blvd., North Austin* ☎ *512/206–1000* 🌐 *www.centralmarket.com.*

MALLS AND DEPARTMENT STORES

The Chinatown Center

MARKET | **FAMILY** | This modern, 750,000-square-foot open-air mall is almost completely occupied by Asian businesses (mainly Chinese and Vietnamese), including restaurants, a travel agency, and retail outlets selling clothing, jewelry, and videos. The mall's cornerstone is the 55,000-square-foot MT (My Thanh) Supermarket, which stocks all manner of Asian foods and related items. Dining standouts include First Chinese BBQ and Pho Saigon; though a bit short on atmosphere, both eateries deliver well-prepared, simply presented lunch plates and noodle-based soups at easy-to-digest prices. The center is open daily, but some stores close one day a week. ✉ *10901 N. Lamar Blvd., North Austin* ☎ *512/502–8887* 🌐 *www.chinatownaustin.com.*

THRIFT STORES

Top Drawer Thrift

SECOND-HAND | Run by Project Transitions (an organization providing hospice, housing, and support for HIV/AIDS patients) as a funding source, this large store is fun and funky as all thrift shops should be. Go for posters, vintage costume jewelry, bric-a-brac, and even used computer and stereo components. The selection is in a state of constant flux, and, as you'd expect, everything is dirt-cheap. ✉ *4902 Burnet Rd., North Austin* ☎ *512/454–5161* 🌐 *www.projecttransitions.org.*

TOYS

Terra Toys

TOYS | **FAMILY** | Make-believe has never seemed as real as it does in this hometown toy store. Imaginations ignite amid shelves of dump trucks and rainbow-bright kites, pretty pink castles and music sets, and an unreal amount of children's books. Nostalgic adults will love the selection of novelty candy: Razzles, Smarties, and Pop Rocks instantly bring to mind sunny summer childhood days. The staff is full of kids at heart, who are helpful and knowledgeable about the store's inventory and who are always ready to make suggestions or, if you twist their arm, play for a while. ✉ *2438 W. Anderson La., North Austin* ☎ *512/445–4489* 🌐 *www.terratoys.com.*

Greater Austin

The sights and sounds of Austin are by no means confined to the center of the city. Those willing to venture outside its most visited neighborhoods will find trendy boutiques, hip bars and clubs, and attractive green spaces—all with a fraction of the downtown crowds.

The fifth in the series of Highland Lakes fed by the Colorado River, Lake Travis is a refreshing playscape for the Austin and Lago Vista areas, with dramatic Hill Country slopes. When the sun sets on the lake, some of the most brilliant views are enjoyed from the decks of hillside restaurants, where spectators applaud the visual pyrotechnics.

Along the southwest shores of the lake, the town of Lakeway is home to some of Austin's most celebrated golf courses, tennis centers, and boating operations. In the 1970s, Lakeway was little more than a quiet retreat for retired Austinites, but today the area is a thriving extension of the Austin-metro area.

Sights

Circuit of The Americas

SPORTS VENUE | Most of Austin moves at a relaxed pace, but here, just a few miles outside the city limits, things speed up considerably. Circuit of The Americas was primarily built for Formula One Grand Prix racing—currently the only such facility in the United States—and when the F1 Grand Prix stops in the Lone Star State as part of a 19-country worldwide tour, 500 million pairs of eyes are on Austin. A wide range of other motor-racing events also take place here, and the grounds have hosted ESPN's X-Games. The on-site 14,000-capacity amphitheater is a venue for countless big-name music acts, from Taylor Swift to the Rolling Stones. ✉ *9201 Circuit of The Americas Blvd.* ☎ *512/301–6600* 🌐 *www.circuitoftheamericas.com.*

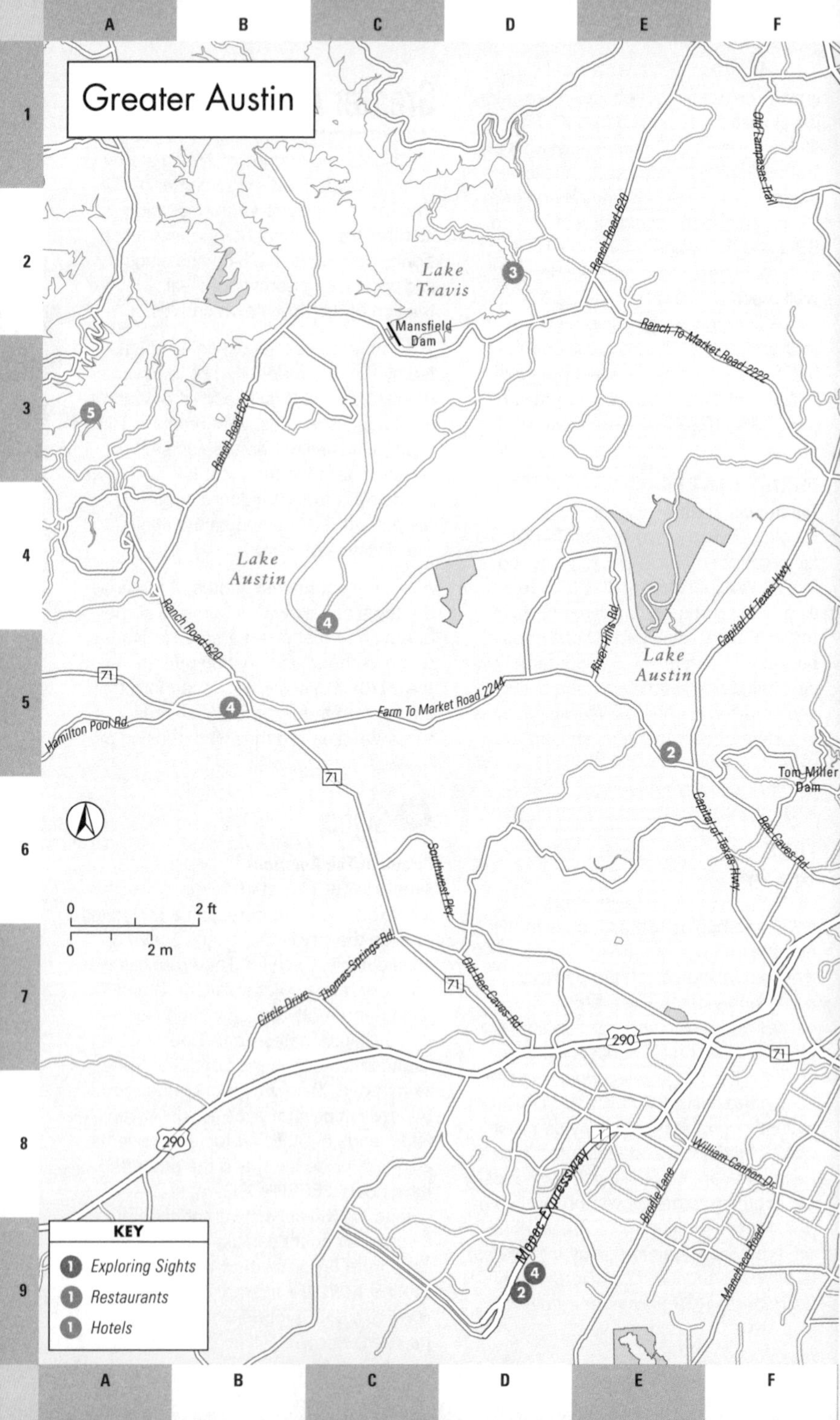

Greater Austin
A
B
C
D
E
F
1
2
3
4
5
6
7
8
9
Lake Travis
Mansfield Dam
Ranch Road 620
Ranch To Market Road 2222
Old Lampasas Trail
Lake Austin
Lake Austin
Capital Of Texas Hwy
River Hills Rd
71
Hamilton Pool Rd.
Farm To Market Road 2244
Tom Miller Dam
Bee Caves Rd.
Capital of Texas Hwy.
Southwest Pky.
0
2 ft
0
2 m
Thomas Springs Rd.
Circle Drive
Old Bee Caves Rd.
290
1
Mopac Expressway
William Cannon Dr.
Brodie Lane
Manchaca Road
KEY
Exploring Sights
Restaurants
Hotels

Sights

1 Circuit of the Americas............ I9

2 Lady Bird Johnson Wildflower Center................. D9

3 McKinney Falls State Park H9

4 The Veloway D9

Restaurants

1 Asia Cafe G1

2 The County Line..................... E5

3 The Oasis on Lake Travis D2

4 Rosie's Tamale House............ B5

5 Rudy's Bar-B-Q..................... H2

6 Whataburger......................... J8

Hotels

1 Aloft Austin at the Domain........ H2

2 Hilton Austin Airport................ J8

3 Hilton Garden Inn Austin NW/Arboretum H2

4 Lake Austin Spa Resort............ C4

5 Lakeway Resort and Spa A3

6 Lone Star Court H2

7 Renaissance Austin Hotel H2

8 The Westin Austin at The Domain......................... H2

Lady Bird Johnson Wildflower Center
GARDEN | **FAMILY** | This 43-acre complex, founded in 1982 by Lady Bird Johnson and actress Helen Hayes, has extensive plantings of native Texas wildflowers that bloom year-round (although spring is an especially attractive time). The grounds include a visitor's center, nature trails, an observation tower, elaborate stone terraces, and flower-filled meadows. Seasonal calendars include various family-friendly and educational events that are free and open to the public. ✉ *4801 La Crosse Ave.* ☎ *512/232–0100* 🌐 *www.wildflower.org* 🎫 *$12.*

★ **McKinney Falls State Park**
STATE/PROVINCIAL PARK | **FAMILY** | This 744-acre state park is 13 miles southeast of downtown Austin. Per the name, the park has two waterfalls (visitors should exercise extreme caution near the water, as people have drowned here). You can hike or bike nearly 9 miles of trails, including the Onion Creek Hike and Bike Trail (2.8 miles), with its paved, hard surface that's good for strollers and road bikes. The Rock Shelter Trail (only for hikers) leads to where early visitors camped. Other popular activities in the park are fishing, picnicking, camping, and wildlife-viewing (including bird-watching and sightings of white-tailed deer, raccoons, squirrels, and armadillos). ✉ *5808 McKinney Falls Pkwy., off U.S. 183* ☎ *512/243–1643* 🌐 *tpwd.texas.gov/state-parks/mckinney-falls* 🎫 *$6.*

The Veloway
TRAIL | This paved asphalt loop winds for a little more than 3 miles through Slaughter Creek Metropolitan Park and is reserved exclusively for bicyclists and rollerbladers. Riders always travel in a one-way clockwise direction. It's a bit off-the-beaten path, but not far from the Lady Bird Johnson Wildflower Center. There are no facilities other than a water fountain that sometimes doesn't work. The loop track is open every day, from dawn to dusk. No dogs are allowed. ✉ *4900 La Crosse Ave., Greater Austin* ☎ *512/974–6700* 🌐 *austintexas.gov/department/veloway* 🎫 *Free.*

 Restaurants

Asia Cafe
$ | **CHINESE** | This no-frills favorite of off-duty chefs keeps its diehard Sichuan fans satisfied. The unassuming strip mall location in far northwest Austin might look rundown, but the order-at-the-counter joint serves up reliably authentic specialties, like the palate-tingling Asia Eggplant and the Chicken Delight (*kou shui ji*, bone-in, chilled chicken slices in a spicy sauce). **Known for:** best Spicy Fish (and they mean spicy) in town; authentic Sichuan standards at cheap prices; gluten-free options. 💲 *Average main: $11* ✉ *8650 Spicewood Springs Rd., Suite 114A, Greater Austin* ☎ *512/331–5788* 🌐 *www.asiacafetx.com.*

The County Line
$$ | **BARBECUE** | **FAMILY** | Part of a local chain, The County Line has a few too many amenities to be considered a classic Central Texas barbecue joint. Chairs instead of bargain-basement picnic setups, little loaves of multigrain bread on tables, and functional air-conditioning make things downright civilized, but anyone seeking a traditional BBQ meal in bucolic surroundings can find solace in the slow-smoked ribs—huge slabs of beef and tender pork—that can be ordered in family-style options, replete with generous sides of coleslaw, potato salad, and beans. **Known for:** Texas-size portions; scenic views; family-style sharing makes it a favorite for celebratory gatherings. 💲 *Average main: $20* ✉ *6500 W. Bee Cave Rd., West Lake* ☎ *512/327–1742* 🌐 *www.countyline.com.*

★ **The Oasis on Lake Travis**
$$ | **AMERICAN** | **FAMILY** | This scenic Austin institution, on a 450-foot cliff above Lake Travis, is famed for its sunsets and special-occasion atmosphere, popular with

tourists, birthday revelers, and anniversary lovebirds. If you can, arrive early to get a table directly overlooking the lake, but most seats in the multitiered eatery have decent views. **Known for:** rather unremarkable Tex-Mex cuisine outshone by the views; surrounding Oasis Complex, including the Lakeview Winery, that's good for after-dinner browsing; ultimately romantic date spot. *$ Average main: $20 ✉ 6550 Comanche Trail, Lake Travis ☎ 512/266–2442 🌐 www.oasis-austin.com.*

Rosie's Tamale House

$ | **MEXICAN** | This little nondescript shack usually has a swarm of locals each morning clamoring for their favorite breakfast tacos. But for a sit-down meal, head across the street to the official restaurant in a big, red building where you can order Rosie's signature tamales or enchiladas. **Known for:** authentic tamales; BYO-alcohol policy; delicious breakfast tacos. *$ Average main: 10 ✉ 13436 State Hwy. 71, Greater Austin ☎ 512/263–5245 ⏲ No lunch Tues.*

Rudy's Bar-B-Q

$ | **BARBECUE** | **FAMILY** | Many local barbecue snobs turn up their noses at Rudy's because it's a chain (albeit Texas-based) with hokey interiors, but plenty of Austinites count this as their "go-to" choice for a laid-back BBQ lunch. Three kinds of brisket—regular, extra moist, and extra lean—are cooked with dry spices over oak wood (not mesquite). **Known for:** speedy counter service perfect for a quick bite; house-made peppery "sause" (available bottled); exceptional creamed corn side. *$ Average main: $6 ✉ 11570 Research Blvd., North Austin ☎ 512/418–9898 🌐 www.rudysbbq.com.*

Whataburger

$ | **BURGER** | **FAMILY** | Another kind of orange mascot now greets visitors at the Austin airport: Texas fast-food favorite Whataburger, a statewide chain that any true Texan will tell you is a must-try on any visit. Situated at the cell-phone waiting lot, the 24/7 drive-through and 72-seat casual eatery offers a last-chance opportunity to satisfy any preflight cravings for patty melts and onion rings. **Known for:** fast and tasty burgers for all ages, with a kids' menu; ultimate last-minute snack before takeoff; silver lining for delayed travelers. *$ Average main: 7 ✉ Austin-Bergstrom Airport, 2901 Spirit of Texas Dr., #100, Near the Airport ☎ 737/228–1311 🌐 locations.whataburger.com.*

Hotels

Aloft Austin at the Domain

$$ | **HOTEL** | This Domain outpost provides basic, Euro-chic accommodations that placate the sensibility of the hotel's up-and-coming urban guests, especially within this retail-obsessed district. **Pros:** business-friendly location in the Domain; free Wi-Fi; 24-hour grab-and-go snack bar. **Cons:** good value, but not exactly luxurious; functional, but no real local flavor here; far drive from downtown and the airport. *$ Rooms from: $180 ✉ 11601 Domain Dr. ☎ 512/491–0777 🌐 www.aloftaustinatthedomain.com 140 rooms No Meals.*

Hilton Austin Airport

$$ | **HOTEL** | Convenience is the specialty of the only hotel on the grounds of Austin–Bergstrom International Airport. **Pros:** unbeatable airport access; good business facilities; nice pool and 24-hour fitness center. **Cons:** slightly rundown rooms in need of updating; not a very diverse food selection on-site; isolated from any notable areas of interest. *$ Rooms from: $148 ✉ 9515 Hotel Dr. ☎ 512/385–6767 🌐 www.hilton.com 262 rooms No Meals.*

Hilton Garden Inn Austin NW/Arboretum

$$ | **HOTEL** | Business and some short-term leisure travelers patronize this five-story hotel in suburban, shopaholic northwest Austin. **Pros:** free Wi-Fi; clean and up-to-date interiors; rooms

Did You Know?

A hike in McKinney Falls State Park will take you to two gorgeous waterfalls.

have flat-screen TVs and Sleep Number mattresses. **Cons:** not scenic or pedestrian-friendly; very small indoor pool; far from downtown. *Rooms from: $133 11617 Research Blvd. 512/241–1600 www.hilton.com 138 rooms Free Breakfast.*

★ Lake Austin Spa Resort

$$$$ | RESORT | One of Austin's most exclusive escapes, this Hill Country resort and spa is located 30 minutes from town, on a prime stretch of Lake Austin shoreline. **Pros:** all-inclusive and intimate, with only 40 rooms; superb service; indoor and outdoor pools. **Cons:** three-night minimum rates are expectedly pricey; prohibitively expensive; far from any local Austin sights. *Rooms from: $1300 1705 S. Quinlan Park Rd. 512/372–7300 www.lakeaustin.com 40 rooms All-Inclusive.*

Lakeway Resort and Spa

$$$ | RESORT | FAMILY | This lakeside resort getaway is centered on water in every way: nestled right on the shores of Lake Travis (about a 45-minute drive west of downtown), it boasts lake views, three pools, a swim-up bar, Jacuzzis, waterslides, and a terrific spa that features water-centric signature treatments like the Texas River Rock massage. **Pros:** amazing lake views from the pool; great for families, with luxuries for all ages; fun activity options like sailing and fishing. **Cons:** mixed reviews about staff and service; there is an adults-only oasis area, but not all areas lend themselves to privacy; far from downtown and airport. *Rooms from: $290 101 Lakeway Dr., Lake Travis 512/261–6600 www.lakewayresortandspa.com 168 rooms No Meals.*

★ Lone Star Court

$$$ | HOTEL | The expansive Domain shopping district is known for its high-end retail and upscale dining, so it's refreshing that the area has this boutique hotel, inspired by retro motor courts, that's more affordable and approachable than its competitors. **Pros:** good food at on-site food truck; located within the Domain, in walking distance of numerous shops and restaurants; free bike rentals. **Cons:** thin walls and loud overflow from late-night bar hours; warm breakfast options, like tasty breakfast tacos, are extra; quite a drive to downtown or the airport. *Rooms from: $230 10901 Domain Dr., Greater Austin 512/814–2625 www.lonestarcourt.com 123 rooms Free Breakfast.*

Renaissance Austin Hotel

$$ | HOTEL | The enormous, skylighted lobby and atrium of this hotel—connected to the Arboretum shopping center—is a cavernous gathering place, befit for the conventioneer clientele. **Pros:** great for business or retail-driven travelers; luxurious, contemporary rooms; Peloton room and fitness center. **Cons:** lower-level atrium-view rooms can be noisy; atmosphere can be corporate and stuffy; removed from downtown. *Rooms from: $155 9721 Arboretum Blvd. 512/343–2626 www.marriott.com 521 rooms No Meals.*

The Westin Austin at The Domain

$$$ | HOTEL | Another chain hotel in the Domain shopping district, the Westin offers the dependability of an established brand with a slightly more sophisticated sheen. **Pros:** business-friendly; lively location amid the Domain's shops and restaurants; nice outdoor pool. **Cons:**; in-room Wi-Fi and breakfast not included; significant drive to downtown or the airport; better values in the area. *Rooms from: $229 11301 Domain Dr. 512/832–4197 www.marriott.com 341 rooms No Meals.*

Nightlife

Moontower Saloon

BARS | Tucked away in south Austin, this mainly outdoor venue is the quintessential escape for a classic Texan live music and special event experience. The neighborhood gathering place attracts a wide range of patrons for listening, lounging, or playing a few backyard games in the expansive patio area, shaded by native live oak trees. Regular live music from local artists, an affordable beer, wine and cocktail menu, and a couple of food trailers keep things buzzing. ✉ *10212 Manchaca Rd.* ☎ *512/712–5661* 🌐 *www.moontowersaloon.com.*

Performing Arts

MUSIC VENUES

Germania Insurance Amphitheater

CONCERTS | The Circuit of the Americas racetrack doesn't just showcase a regular season of Formula One motor-racing—it's also home to this state-of-the-art live music amphitheater hosting a diverse range of big-name artists and bands as well as various festivals and special events throughout the year. Previously known as the Austin 360 Amphitheater, the Germania Insurance Amphitheater offers assigned seating with great stage views from any vantage point. The green parkland behind the assigned seating lets you bring your own picnic blanket to listen under the stars. There's a regular lineup of food trucks and plenty of full-service bars on-site. ✉ *9201 Circuit of the Americas Blvd.* ☎ *512/301–6600* 🌐 *www.germaniaamp.com.*

Shopping

The Domain

MALL | A postmodern vision of an affluent downtown district, the Domain is home to Gucci, Neiman Marcus, Tiffany & Co., the Apple Store, and other name-brand shops that cater to the platinum-card set. Those on more modest budgets should check out kitchenware emporium Sur La Table, Macy's, and the large, cheerful Anthropologie. Some complain that there's very little Austin-specific about the open-air Domain, but more local flavor is showing up in the growing shopping district, such as popular food truck Little Lucy's Mini Donuts and the new location of the Cap City Comedy Club. It's a pleasant place to spend a few hours (if only to gawk at the pricey goods in the windows). You'll find it along North MoPac (Loop 1) between Braker Lane and Burnet Road, near the North Austin IBM campus. ✉ *11410 Century Oaks Terr.* ☎ *512/795–4230* 🌐 *www.simon.com/mall/the-domain.*

Activities

Pace Bend Park

HIKING & WALKING | **FAMILY** | Explore some of Lake Travis's narrow coves and great limestone cliffs at Pace Bend Park. Here you'll experience spectacular sunsets over the lake. Visitors can hike and bike the rustic trails that lead to different lake and Hill Country views. Pace Bend Park is a favorite of college students who like to jump off the high cliff walls (up to 30 feet) into the water below. Be warned: the only way back up is to climb and varying lake levels make this a risky activity. ✉ *2805 Pace Bend Rd. N, Spicewood* ☎ *512/264–1482* 🌐 *parks.traviscountytx.gov/parks/pace-bend* 🎟 *$5.*

Chapter 5

THE TEXAS HILL COUNTRY

Updated by
Veronica Meewes

Sights ★★★★☆ | Restaurants ★★★☆☆ | Hotels ★★★★☆ | Shopping ★★★☆☆ | Nightlife ★★☆☆☆

WELCOME TO THE TEXAS HILL COUNTRY

TOP REASONS TO GO

★ **Fredericksburg:** An afternoon on this favorite town's Main Street means plenty of shopping, a hearty German meal, and a few samplings of German beer and Texas wine.

★ **Scenic Drives:** Some of the most spectacular views can be experienced from the seat of a car, or the back of a Harley, if you prefer. Though most of the land along the roadside is private, you will not be hampered from enjoying many a breathtaking vista from the endless roads traversing the region.

★ **Enchanted Rock State Natural Area:** Who wouldn't be curious about scaling the face of a massive pink rock protruding to an elevation of 1,825 feet? Camping, hiking, and rock climbing are also popular attractions at this spectacular state reserve.

★ **Wine:** Set out on a journey down the Texas Wine Trail and taste for yourself why some wine critics see a robust and full-bodied future for Hill Country wine.

The Hill Country encompasses the region west and southwest of Austin and north of San Antonio. The distance between these two gateway cities is 60 miles, with Interstate 35 marking the eastern border and San Antonio's State Loop 1604 the southern limit. The northern border is ambiguous but generally includes everything south of Lake Buchanan and along Highway 29. The western border is also open to interpretation but is roughly U.S. 83 from Junction to Uvalde.

1 **Fredericksburg.** The German gateway to the Texas Hill Country.

2 **Luckenbach.** A ghost town turned country music mecca.

3 **Johnson City.** The birthplace of Lyndon B. Johnson and home of the juiciest peaches in Texas.

4 **Kerrville.** The cultural center of the Texas Hill Country.

5 **Comfort.** A quaint little town filled with historic buildings.

6 **Bandera.** The cowboy capital of the world.

7 **Boerne.** A Hill Country town where every route is the scenic route.

8 **New Braunfels.** A German-influenced town with lots of outdoor activities.

9 **Gruene.** A German-Texas gem along the Guadalupe River.

10 **San Marcos.** A lively college town where the San Marcos River rules.

11 **Lockhart.** The barbecue capital of Texas, with some bohemian flair.

12 **Wimberley.** A charming hamlet where Cypress Creek meets the Blanco River.

13 **Dripping Springs.** A small town that keeps getting cooler thanks to its wineries and outdoor activities.

14 **Marble Falls.** A cute Texas town surrounded by natural wonders.

15 **Burnet.** The best place in Texas to see bluebonnet wildflowers.

16 **Llano.** A little Texas town filled with enchanted rocks.

17 **Mason.** An underrated Hill Country small town.

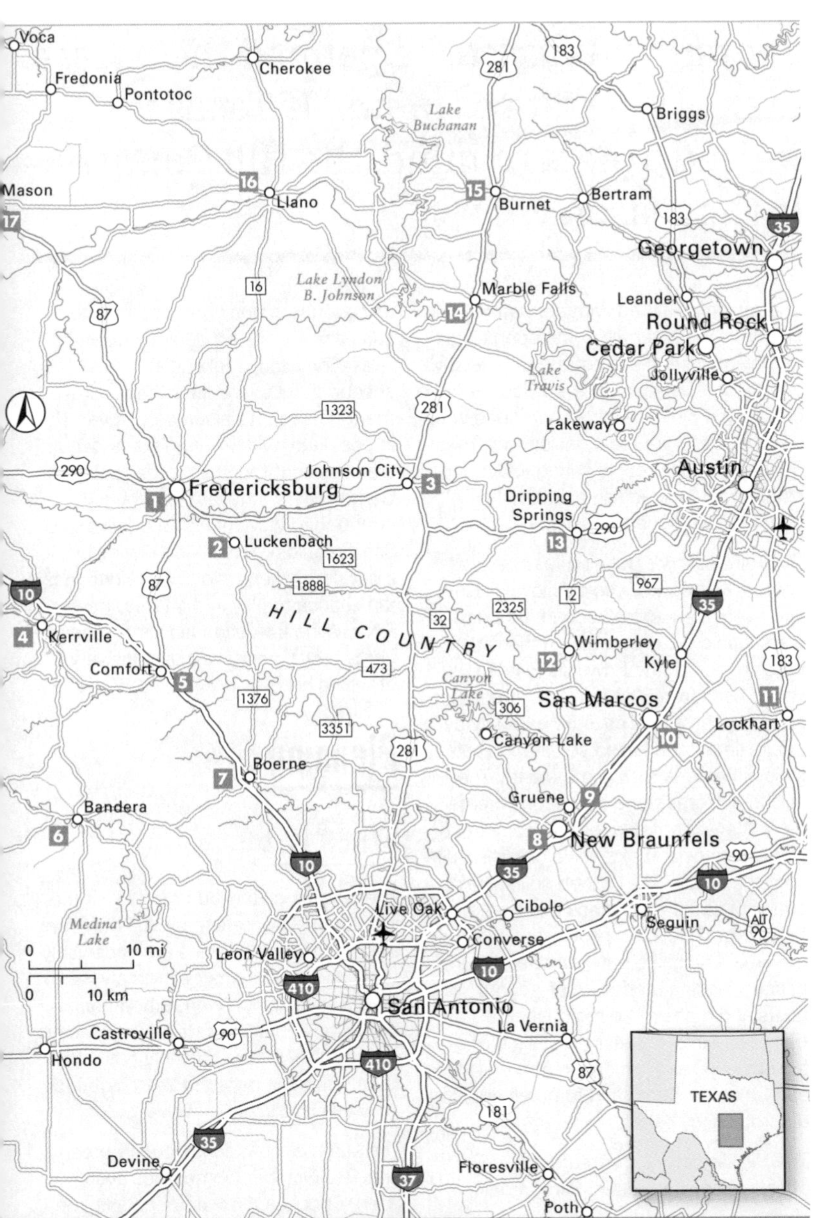
Voca
Fredonia
Pontotoc
Cherokee
Lake Buchanan
Briggs
Mason
Llano
Burnet
Bertram
Georgetown
Lake Lyndon B. Johnson
Marble Falls
Leander
Round Rock
Cedar Park
Lake Travis
Jollyville
Lakeway
Johnson City
Fredericksburg
Austin
Dripping Springs
Luckenbach
HILL COUNTRY
Kerrville
Comfort
Wimberley
Kyle
Canyon Lake
San Marcos
Lockhart
Canyon Lake
Boerne
Gruene
Bandera
New Braunfels
Medina Lake
Live Oak
Cibolo
Seguin
Converse
Leon Valley
San Antonio
La Vernia
Castroville
Hondo
Devine
Floresville
Poth
0 10 mi
0 10 km
TEXAS

When the writer John Steinbeck explored the United States for his 1962 travelogue, *Travels with Charley: In Search of America*, he penned the phrase "Texas is a state of mind." If Texas is indeed a state of mind, the Hill Country is the reason why.

The region is etched with dramatic slopes of rocky terrain, wide-open vistas displaying an endless horizon of blue sky, and roads that go on forever. Countless creeks and old cedar posts wrapped in rusty barbed wire meander through mesquite-filled pastures; in spring, blooming bluebonnets and Indian paintbrushes brighten the rugged landscape.

The Hill Country's defining feature is, of course, its hills (the region's lovely lakes and rivers are a close second, though). Geographically, the area comprises the lower region of the Edwards Plateau, which rises from 750 feet to 2,700 feet in some places and is covered primarily by a thin, limestone-based soil that reveals solid, limestone rock just beneath. The calcite-rich limestone formations create perfect environments for the many freshwater springs and extensive caverns that spot the region. The rugged soil sustains grass for cattle and weeds and tree foliage for sheep and goats, thus making the area a ranching hub and one of the nation's leading producers of Angora goats and mohair. The region is also home to the Llano Basin, a stretch of land that lies at the junction of the Llano and Colorado Rivers and features granite outcroppings.

The Hill Country is a retreat for businesspeople from Austin, San Antonio, and even Houston, who trade in their suits and city life for denim and ranch relaxation each weekend at their second homes (and later their retirement homes). It's also been growing in popularity with Winter Texans, who are passing through en route to the Rio Grande Valley at Texas's tip. Tourists make up the third wave of visitors, flying into San Antonio or Austin and driving out for a day or weekend trip. They're drawn by the chance to play in the lakes, travel the Texas Wine Trail, sample fruit at roadside farm stands, and take in expansive views of rolling hills.

Planning

When to Go

There really isn't a bad time to visit the Hill Country. Winters are mild, with days averaging 50°. Summers are undeniably the high season, albeit extremely warm in July and August, with temperatures averaging about 85°–90° (but many days above 100°). Sunny, stiflingly hot days keep visitors in constant search of cool activities that usually involve water.

The summer heat doesn't really break until late October (sometimes even later). But once the weather cools, the

Hill Country comes alive with food and wine festivals, such as New Braunfels's Wurstfest and Fredericksburg's Oktoberfest, both of which deliver plenty of beer, German sausage, and good times. October is also Texas Wine Month, with many of the Hill Country wineries offering tastings and special events.

Though late winter can be cold and seemingly desolate, the festive holiday season transforms the small towns into Dickens-like portraits of Christmas carolers, building facades with flickering lights, and Main Street parades. Fly-fishers usually find fantastic winter action in any of the hundred or so stocked lakes and rivers for trophy rainbow trout.

By early March, outdoor enthusiasts are ready to head into the wild for cool, fresh mornings at a campsite, hiking Enchanted Rock, and cycling the back roads. It's also the season for wildflowers. Brilliant red Indian paintbrushes, yellow brown-eyed Susan's, and the state's famed bluebonnets flourish in fields along the road. It's a sight to behold, and one deeply cherished by Texans statewide.

Getting Here and Around

AIR

The most direct and economical way to reach the Hill Country by air is to fly into either San Antonio or Austin, though there is also a small airport at Del Rio. From San Antonio International Airport, take Highway 281 north for about 90 miles to go through Blanco, Johnson City, Marble Falls, and Burnet, or cut across on State Loop 1604 heading west to I–10 West and you'll go through Boerne, Comfort, and Kerrville, and can then easily make your way to Bandera and Medina, or Fredericksburg and Mason. From Austin–Bergstrom International Airport, take Highway 290 west to Highway 281 to get to most of the Hill Country towns.

CONTACTS San Antonio International Airport. ✉ *9800 Airport Blvd., San Antonio* ☎ *210/207–3411* 🌐 *flysanantonio.com.* **Austin-Bergstrom International Airport.** ✉ *3600 Presidential Blvd., Austin* ☎ *512/530–2242* 🌐 *austintexas.gov/airport.*

CAR

The Hill Country is the land of the open road. The best and really the *only* way to travel here is by car.

You can access the region from I–35 or I–10, coming from the north and south or east and west, respectively. The gateway cities are Austin and San Antonio. (Austin is technically even part of the Hill Country.) These two cities are about 60 miles from each other on I–35. Between these two hubs on the interstate lie New Braunfels, Gruene, and San Marcos. Running north and south through the Hill Country is Highway 281, which intersects with I–10 West and San Antonio and can be reached from Austin via Highway 71 or Highway 290, the latter traversing the region from east to west.

You can rent a car from any of the major national chains at Austin-Bergstrom International Airport and San Antonio International Airport.

Restaurants

As the Texas Hill Country continues to develop, so does its dining options. German cuisine has long been prevalent in the region, thanks to the immigrants who settled here in the 1800s. Both German and Czech settlers also brought meat preservation traditions with them and popularized the low-and-slow method of meat-smoking that became Texas barbecue, which you'll find plenty of throughout the region, especially in towns like Lockhart. Though the term "Tex-Mex" wasn't coined until the 1960s (by food historian and chef Diana Kennedy), Tejanos living on the border began combining Mexican and American cooking styles at the end of the 19th century, a trend that quickly began making its way through Central Texas.

But these days, the Hill Country is so much more than barbecue, Tex-Mex, and German cuisine. You'll find globally inspired tasting menus and state-of-the-art fine dining experiences as well as food trucks, tapas bars, gastropubs, and wood-fired pizza.

Hotels

Most of the accommodations you'll encounter in the Texas Hill Country come in the form of quaint, independently owned bed-and-breakfasts. As the region continues to evolve, and as both destination weddings and Texas wine country become more of a draw for visitors from all over the country, more historic hotels and houses are being renovated into high-end lodging.

■ TIP→ Hotel and restaurant reviews have been shortened. For full information, visit Fodors.com. Restaurant prices are per person for a main course at dinner or if dinner is not served, at lunch. Hotel prices are for two people in a standard double room in high season.

What It Costs

$	$$	$$$	$$$$
RESTAURANTS			
under $14	$14–$22	$23–$30	over $30
HOTELS			
under $125	$125–$225	$226–$325	over $325

Fredericksburg

78 miles west of Austin, 70 miles north of San Antonio.

Once a secret weekend getaway for Texans in the know, Fredericksburg has bloomed in popularity in recent years, thanks to a distinct Bavarian culture that has attracted visitors from all over Texas and beyond.

Indeed, Fredericksburg is a heavily German-influenced town. The city square is called Marktplatz, there's a "Wilkommen" sign hanging from every shop door, and the main bed-and-breakfast booking organization is called Gästehaus Schmidt. It's really Oktoberfest year-round in this quaint little town, and luckily everyone's invited.

Named for Prince Friedrich of Prussia, Friedrichburg (now Fredericksburg) was established in 1846 by Baron Ottfried Hans von Meusebach (better known as John O. Meusebach in Texas). It was the second main settlement, after New Braunfels, by the Society for the Protection of German Immigrants in Texas, or Adelsverein. This organization of German nobles brokered land in Texas to increase German emigration. Meusebach also managed to broker a peace treaty with the Comanche tribe that prevented raids and helped promote trade in the area (to this day, it is the only unbroken Native American treaty in the state). Cattle and agriculture eventually became the primary sustainable commerce in the city as it grew through the Civil War and moved into the 20th century.

In addition to the town's German roots, there's something else to keep in mind: Fredericksburg is primarily a weekend destination. Locals enjoy the influx of visitors, but they also say their favorite days are Sunday and Monday because people pack up and leave, meaning that, for a short while, it feels like a small town again. If you want that experience, visit during the week, particularly in fall or winter.

VISITOR INFORMATION

CONTACT Fredericksburg Convention & Visitors Bureau. ✉ *302 E. Austin St., Fredericksburg* ☎ *830/997–6523* 🌐 *visitfredericksburgtx.com.*

Sights

★ Enchanted Rock State Natural Area
NATURE SIGHT | Protruding from the earth in the form of a large pink dome, Enchanted Rock looks like something from another planet. This granite formation rises 1,825 feet—the second-largest in the nation, after Georgia's Stone Mountain—and its bald vastness can be seen from miles away. Today the massive batholith is part of the 624-acre Enchanted Rock State Natural Area and one of the most popular destinations in the Hill Country region. Once considered to have spiritual powers by the Tonkawa tribe, Enchanted Rock is traversed day in and day out by those curious about its mysterious occurrence. The park is perfect for day hikers, most of whom can't wait to scale the summit. The rock also yields a number of faces to test the skills of technical rock climbers, plus there are caves for spelunkers to explore. And even if you're not into rock climbing, the area is a perfect spot for camping, picnicking, and hiking. Arrive early; once parking lots reach capacity, the area is closed to more visitors to protect the resources. Amenities include restrooms, an interpretative center, and campgrounds. ✉ *16710 RR 965, Fredericksburg* ☎ *830/685–3636* 🌐 *tpwd.texas.gov/state-parks/enchanted-rock* 🎫 *$8.*

Fredericksburg Herb Farm
FARM/RANCH | Just a short jaunt from downtown Fredericksburg is this magical little herb farm churning out an endless variety of fresh herbs and serving guests culinary creations inspired by an edible garden. Fredericksburg Herb Farm offers blissful relaxation in its cozy B&B and spa and has created a vast array of heavenly scented candles, toiletries, cooking oils, and herbal rubs and marinades for cooking. One of the gardens is artfully designed in the shape of a star with an old windmill in the center. Each arm of the star represents herbs for specific purposes—medicinal, cosmetic, culinary, crafting, or ornamental. ✉ *405 Whitney St., Fredericksburg* ☎ *830/997–8615* 🌐 *www.hillcountryherbgarden.com.*

Kalasi Cellars
WINERY | Nikhila Narra Davis co-founded Narra Vineyards in the Texas High Plains with her family, and together they sustainably farm 140 acres of grapes for some of the best winemakers in the state. Davis began experimenting making her own wine using lesser-known varieties like Teroldego, a red Italian varietal typically grown in northeastern Italy, and has now launched her own brand of wine under the label Kalasi Cellars. At the spacious, modern tasting room in northeast Fredericksburg, sheep keep the grounds free from weeds and a refurbished tuk-tuk promises rides down to the production facility. Wines like Malvasia Bianca and Muscat of Alexandria perfectly complement the Indian-inspired snack menu with offerings like samosas, tikka masala pizza, and a chaat sampler plate. ✉ *414 Goehmann La., Fredericksburg* ☎ *830/992–3037* 🌐 *www.kalasicellars.com* 🎫 *From $20* ⏲ *Closed Tues. and Wed.*

Lady Bird Johnson Municipal Park
CITY PARK | This city park just 3 miles south of downtown features 330 acres of rolling hills, five outdoor pavilions with large barbecue pits, baseball and softball fields, basketball and sand volleyball courts, and a golf course—plus

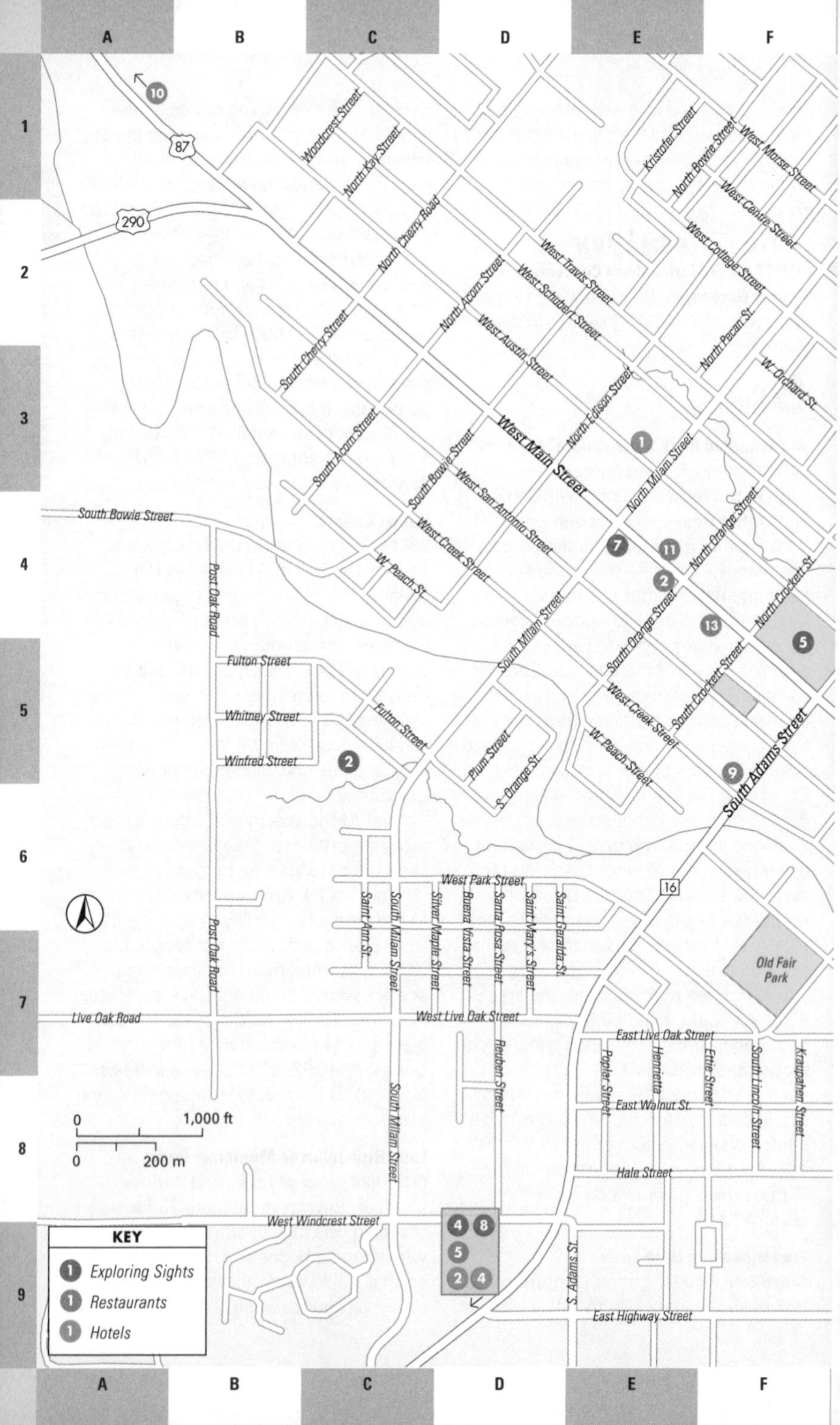

A
B
C
D
E
F
1
2
3
4
5
6
7
8
9
87
290
Woodcrest Street
North Kay Street
North Cherry Road
South Cherry Street
North Acorn Street
West Travis Street
West Schubert Street
West Austin Street
Kristofer Street
North Bowie Street
West Morse Street
West Centre Street
West College Street
North Pecan St.
W. Orchard St.
North Edison Street
West Main Street
North Milam Street
North Orange Street
North Crockett St.
South Acorn Street
South Bowie Street
West San Antonio Street
West Creek Street
W. Peach St.
South Bowie Street
Post Oak Road
Fulton Street
Whitney Street
Winfred Street
Fulton Street
South Milam Street
South Orange Street
South Crockett Street
West Creek Street
W. Peach Street
South Adams Street
Plum Street
S. Orange St.
West Park Street
16
Saint Ann St.
South Milam Street
Silver Maple Street
Buena Vista Street
Santa Rosa Street
Saint Mary's Street
Saint Geralda St.
Old Fair Park
Live Oak Road
West Live Oak Street
East Live Oak Street
Post Oak Road
Reuben Street
Poplar Street
Henrietta
Ettie Street
South Lincoln Street
Kraupaher Street
East Walnut St.
Hale Street
South Milam Street
0
1,000 ft
0
200 m
West Windcrest Street
S. Adams St.
East Highway Street
KEY
Exploring Sights
Restaurants
Hotels

Sights

1 Enchanted Rock State Natural Area G1
2 Fredericksburg Herb Farm C5
3 Kalasi Cellars J8
4 Lady Bird Johnson Municipal Park D9
5 Marktplatz von Fredericksburg F5
6 National Museum of the Pacific War H5
7 Pioneer Museum Complex E4
8 Slate Mill Wine Collective D9
9 Southold Farm + Cellar J7
10 Wildseed Farms J8

Restaurants

1 Alamo Springs Café J8
2 Altdorf Biergarten E4
3 August E's G6
4 The Ausländer Restaurant and Biergarten H6
5 Cabernet Grill D9
6 Der Lindenbaum H6
7 Emma + Ollie G8
8 Fredericksburg Brewing Company G6
9 Hill & Vine F5
10 Hill Top Café A1
11 Hondo's On Main E4
12 La Bergerie H6
13 Old German Bakery & Restaurant F4
14 Otto's German Bistro H6
15 Silver Creek Beer Garden and Grill H6
16 Vaudeville G5

Hotels

1 Austin Street Retreat E3
2 Cotton Gin Village D9
3 Fredericksburg Inn & Suites G7
4 Hangar Hotel D9
5 Hoffman Haus I7
6 Inn on Barons Creek G7
7 The Roadrunner Inn H6

a pool and a creek. ✉ *432 Ladbird Dr., Fredericksburg* ☎ *830/997–4202* 🌐 *www.fbgtx.org/236/Lady-Bird-Johnson-Municipal-Park* 🎫 *Free.*

Marktplatz von Fredericksburg

CITY PARK | Located right in the center of the city, Marktplatz is a park that wraps around the Vereins Kirche Museum, an octagonal building that was the site of the first church and the first school in Fredericksburg. It boasts picnic areas, play spaces, and a winter ice skating rink and also hosts various events and festivals throughout the year. ✉ *126 W. Main St., Fredericksburg* ☎ *830/997–7521* 🌐 *www.fbgtx.org/237/Marktplatz-Market-Square.*

★ National Museum of the Pacific War

HISTORY MUSEUM | Dedicated solely to telling the story of the Pacific battles of World War II, this museum is the only one of its kind in the nation, making it a popular attraction for history buffs and veterans alike. Opened in 1967, the museum was originally named the Fleet Admiral Chester W. Nimitz Memorial Naval Museum, after the admiral famous for successfully halting the Japanese advances following the attack on Pearl Harbor. Today, the museum has been expanded to include an Admiral Nimitz Gallery and a George H. W. Bush Gallery in addition to a number of memorials, and it also houses the Center for Pacific War Studies. In its more than 45,000 square feet of exhibit space, the museum exhibits both Allied and Japanese airplanes, tanks, and guns among its numerous displays. ✉ *340 E. Main St., Fredericksburg* ☎ *830/997–8600* 🌐 *www.pacificwarmuseum.org* 🎫 *$18* 🕓 *Closed Tues.*

★ Pioneer Museum Complex

HISTORY MUSEUM | Those looking to dig a little deeper into the history of this area may find some answers at the Pioneer Museum Complex, which also encompasses the Vereins Kirche Museum. Both museums offer permanent exhibits with collections of woodworking tools, textile pieces, furniture, paintings, and a number of domestic artifacts from the area. Other historic buildings in the complex include a pioneer log cabin, an old First Methodist Church, and a smokehouse. Also on the premises stands a typical 19th-century "Sunday house" that catered to farmers and their families who traveled long distances to attend church services and had to stay the night. ✉ *325 W. Main St., Fredericksburg* ☎ *830/990–8441* 🌐 *www.pioneermuseum.net* 🎫 *$8* 🕓 *Closed Sun.*

Slate Mill Wine Collective

WINERY | Located just south of downtown Fredericksburg, this collaborative concept evolved from a family-operated boutique winery called 1851 Vineyards before restructuring as Slate Mill Collective. The collective expanded the vineyard, winery, and tasting room to include 35 planted acres and a state-of-the-art wine-making facility. It's also a great place for visitors to come for a production tour (with plenty of samples along the way) to learn more about the Texas wine industry. Afterward, head to the tasting room to enjoy labels from multiple local producers, like Wine for the People, Tatum Cellars, and C.L. Butaud. ✉ *4222 S. State Hwy. 16, Fredericksburg* ☎ *830/998–8930* 🌐 *slatemillwinecollective.com* 🎫 *$30* 🕓 *Closed Tues. and Wed.*

★ Southold Farm + Cellar

WINERY | Reagan Meador began making wine in Long Island but decided to return to his native Texas to put down roots (literally). At Southold Farm + Cellar, he crafts unique, limited-release wines using very little intervention with the Texas grapes he currently sources as he waits for his estate-grown grapes to be ready for production. Visits to the tasting room are by reservation only, and guests can choose from several different options: an "Introduction" tasting of four wines, a "Prologue" featuring four wines plus a spread of dishes made

Enchanted Rock is the most popular hiking destination in the Hill Country.

with local ingredients, or an eight-course "Sunset Supper" set in the gorgeous, western-facing restaurant overlooking the vineyard. No matter which tasting you choose, be sure to get in some time on their cozy wooden porch swings that look out across the rolling hills. ✉ *330 Minor Threat La., Fredericksburg* ☎ *512/829–1650* 🌐 *www.southoldfarmandcellar.com* 🎫 *From $25* ⏲ *Closed Tues. and Wed.*

★ Wildseed Farms

FARM/RANCH | If you're heading west on Highway 290 to Fredericksburg from Johnson City in the warmer months, you'll inevitably note a large, expansive spread of land flush with vibrant colors. (You may see less of this color in late fall and winter, but the sweeping fields are still hard to miss.) You're looking at the largest working wildflower farm in the country. Owner John Thomas created Wildseed Farms in 1983 in an effort to share the Hill Country's bounty with all who visited. The farm has more than 200 acres under cultivation and produces 88 varieties of wildflower seeds. You can walk the meadows, step into the live butterfly house, and purchase packets of wildflower seeds. ✉ *100 Legacy Dr., Fredericksburg* ☎ *830/990–1393* 🌐 *wildseedfarms.com* 🎫 *Free.*

Restaurants

Alamo Springs Café

$ | **AMERICAN** | You can dig into one of the best burgers in the region here. The more adventuresome eaters order theirs with the jalepeño-cheese bun—it's really not as spicy as it sounds. **Known for:** excellent burgers; homemade peach crisp for dessert; laid-back atmosphere. $ *Average main: $9* ✉ *107 Alamo Rd., Fredericksburg* ☎ *830/990–8004* 🌐 *www.alamospringscafetx.com* ⏲ *Closed Mon.–Wed. No dinner Thurs. and Sun.*

★ Altdorf Biergarten

$$ | **GERMAN** | This biergarten on Main Street is always buzzing, and for good reason. Choose from a wide array of craft German beer while enjoying the live

Learn more about World War II at the National Museum of the Pacific War in Fredericksburg.

music that happens nearly nightly. **Known for:** traditional beer garden vibes; live music; hearty German cuisine. *Average main: $15* *301 W. Main St., Fredericksburg* *830/997–7865* *www.altdorfs.com* *Closed Mon. and Tues. No dinner Sun.*

★ August E's

$$$$ | **AMERICAN** | In the heart of downtown Fredericksburg, August E's features a sleek Zen-like atmosphere thanks to its contemporary Asian decor. Chef-owner Leu Savanh adds a subtle hint of his Thai background to such dishes as the New Zealand lamb with balsamic honey-glaze and a cloudlike fillet of Hawaiian escolar pan-seared and served with a tempura-fried lobster tail, baby bok choy, and mascarpone whipped potatoes. **Known for:** Asian fusion; unique seafood creations; extensive sake offerings. *Average main: $38* *203 E. San Antonio St., Fredericksburg* *830/997–1585* *www.facebook.com/augustesfbg* *Closed Sun. No lunch.*

★ The Ausländer Restaurant and Biergarten

$$ | **GERMAN** | With its authentic German architecture, the Ausländer draws quite a crowd for lunch and dinner. For more than 20 years, it has been one of the town's most popular beer gardens, and you're bound to find a few things to your liking—perhaps the Spicy Texas Schnitzel, a bold concoction featuring a hand-breaded pork loin cutlet smothered with Tex-Mex ranchero sauce and melted Monterey Jack cheese. **Known for:** Munich biergarten atmosphere; huge beer selection; Tex-Mex and German fusion dishes. *Average main: $17* *323 E. Main St., Fredericksburg* *830/997–7714* *theauslanderfredericksburg.com* *Closed Wed.*

★ Cabernet Grill

$$$$ | **AMERICAN** | If you want a Texas-size meal in the heart of the Hill Country, the Cabernet Grill has just what you're looking for. Chef-owner Ross Burtwell uses a smattering of local ingredients to inspire a menu that reflects the bold flavors of the Lone Star State. **Known**

for: wine menu with exclusively Texas wines; steak and seafood; homey interior and spacious patio. *Average main: $31 2805 S. State Hwy. 16, Fredericksburg 830/990–5734 www.cabernetgrill.com Closed Sun. and Mon. No lunch.*

Der Lindenbaum

$$ | **GERMAN** | Set in a historic limestone building at the end of Main Street, Der Lindenbaum started as a bakery for chef Ingrid Hohmann to showcase traditional German desserts like apple strudel and Black Forest cake, but customers quickly latched onto her savory lunch specials, and it organically grew into a full-fledged restaurant. The menu features dishes directly from the Rhineland (especially the Alsace-Lorraine region between Germany and France). **Known for:** historic setting; excellent German pastries; regional Rhineland offerings. *Average main: $18 312 E. Main St., Fredericksburg 830/997–9126 www.derlindenbaum.com Closed Mon. and Tues.*

Emma + Ollie

$$ | **BAKERY** | Local baker Rebecca Rather, well-known for her now-shuttered Rather Sweet Bakery, opened this sweet breakfast and lunch spot and bakery to much acclaim. Breakfast items span from a build-your-own biscuit bar to a croissant egg sandwich, while the lunch menu exudes farm-to-table Southern comfort, with offerings like fried oyster nachos and a pimiento cheese BLT. **Known for:** farm-to-table Southern breakfast; homemade baked goods; adorable rustic-chic setting. *Average main: 20 607 S. Washington St., Fredericksburg 830/383–1013 emmaolliefbg.com Closed Sun. and Mon. No dinner.*

Fredericksburg Brewing Company

$ | **GERMAN** | Serving a variety of homemade German-style brews from the large copper beer tanks accenting the far wall, the brewery is a popular nightspot for both locals and visitors. The German food is all well prepared, but the Texas-size chicken-fried steak is no slouch either. **Known for:** oldest operating brewpub in Texas; German-style beer; cozy interior with copper tanks. *Average main: $13 245 E. Main St., Fredericksburg 844/997–1646 www.yourbrewery.com.*

Hill & Vine

$$$ | **AMERICAN** | There's a reason you'll likely have to wait for a table at this spacious, modern farm-to-table restaurant in the heart of town. The chef-driven menu is casual but uses top ingredients and perfected techniques. **Known for:** farm-to-table dining; great cocktails; spacious patio. *Average main: 25 210 S. Adams St., Fredericksburg 830/307–3401 www.hillandvinetx.com No dinner Sun.*

Hill Top Café

$$$ | **AMERICAN** | **FAMILY** | Ten miles north of town, this hilltop dive set in a 1930s gas station truly feels like it's in the middle of nowhere, but it's luckily a beautiful trip to nowhere. All menu conventions are thrown out the window to create the Athens-meets–New Orleans dishes. **Known for:** live blues music; historic vibes; unique Greek and Cajun menu. *Average main: $26 10661 U.S. Hwy. 87, Fredericksburg 830/997–8922 www.hilltopcafe.com Closed Mon.*

Hondo's on Main

$ | **AMERICAN** | Named for John Russell "Hondo" Crouch, self-proclaimed mayor of Luckenbach, this local dive is somewhat of a legend of its own. If the live music and Texas country decor aren't entertaining enough, the menu certainly is: from the "What's David Smokin' Plate" of finger-lickin' fabulous barbecue to the "Supa Chalupa Salad," everything about this place radiates good old-fashioned fun. **Known for:** massive burgers; rustic Texas decor; live music. *Average main: $10 312 W. Main St., Fredericksburg 830/997–1633 www.hondosonmain.com Closed Mon. and Tues.*

La Bergerie

$$ | **AMERICAN** | If you've had your fill of German food in Fredericksburg, opt for a beautiful cheese and charcuterie board from La Bergerie, an adorable European-style wine bar and market located just off the town's main strip. Relax on the patio or choose from the well-curated selection of meats, cheeses, and small-production wines to-go if you prefer to picnic somewhere in the Hill Country. **Known for:** well-curated wine selection; cheese and charcuterie boards; picnic fare to-go. *Average main: 18 ✉ 312 E. Austin St., Fredericksburg ☎ 830/992–3036 🌐 www.labergeriemarket.com.*

★ Old German Bakery & Restaurant

$$ | **GERMAN** | Though it's also open for lunch, most locals flock to this family-owned restaurant for a delicious and hearty breakfast. Lacy German pancakes come with butter pats, orange slices, and powdered sugar for sprinkling. **Known for:** indulgent breakfast plates; homemade German baked goods; family-friendly atmosphere. *Average main: $14 ✉ 225 W. Main St., Fredericksburg ☎ 830/997–9084 🌐 www.oldgermanbakeryandrestaurant.com ⏲ Closed Wed. and Thurs. No dinner.*

★ Otto's German Bistro

$$ | **GERMAN** | At his sleek but cozy bistro, chef Henry Gutkin focuses on some of Germany's lesser-known dishes, reimagined with creative, refreshing twists. Bavarian *Frittatensuppe* (crepe soup) is brightened with herbs and rainbow carrots, while the *Düsseldorfer Senfrostbraten* (Dusseldorf mustard roast) is elevated with Akaushi steak and an onion-mustard-cheese crust. **Known for:** lesser-known German dishes; farm-to-table dining; German and Austrian wine selections. *Average main: 18 ✉ 316 E. Austin St., Fredericksburg ☎ 830/307–3336 🌐 ottosfbg.com ⏲ No lunch Mon.–Sat.*

Silver Creek Beer Garden and Grill

$ | **GERMAN** | It may not boast a German name, but don't overlook Silver Creek if you're seeking cuisine from the motherland. With an abundance of outdoor dining, regular live music, and an extensive beer selection, this place is a spring and summer favorite. **Known for:** huge beer selection; plenty of outdoor seating; regular live music. *Average main: $11 ✉ 310 E. Main St., Fredericksburg ☎ 803/990–4949 🌐 www.silvercreekfbg.com ⏲ Closed Tues.–Thurs.*

★ Vaudeville

$$ | **BISTRO** | This hip, modern interpretation of a European bistro also includes a retail showroom, art gallery, supper club, and wine club. The restaurant features rotating specials, such as lump crab curry, duck confit, and herb-roasted chicken, plus a daily menu with gourmet sandwiches (try the French dip, made with Angus prime beef), soups, salads, cheese, charcuterie, and wood-fired pizzas. **Known for:** gourmet sandwiches; Monday night supper club; on-site art gallery and retail showroom. *Average main: 18 ✉ 230 E. Main St., Fredericksburg ☎ 830/992–3234 🌐 www.vaudeville-living.com ⏲ No dinner Sun.–Thurs. except supper club.*

Hotels

Austin Street Retreat

$$ | **B&B/INN** | One of the most popular downtown guesthouses, the Austin Street Retreat offers five elegantly appointed private suites, each featuring the original fachwerk log-cabin and limestone architecture used by the first Fredericksburg settlers. **Pros:** bathrooms are all spacious and welcoming, with oversize tubs; very authentic historical decor; large and comfortable beds. **Cons:** Victorian accents are tasteful but may be a little too historic for some; spotty Wi-Fi; two-night minimum can be inconvenient. *Rooms from: $200 ✉ 408 W. Austin St., Fredericksburg ☎ 830/997–5612*

austinstreetretreat.com 5 suites Free Breakfast.

★ Cotton Gin Village

$$$ | **B&B/INN** | Stepping back in time is as simple as turning the key to your own private cottage at the Cotton Gin Village, just outside Fredericksburg. **Pros:** delicious breakfast included; charming and relaxing rustic atmosphere; excellent on-site restaurant. **Cons:** layout of each cabin is different; spotty Wi-Fi; location is removed from the charm of the town. *Rooms from: $229 2805 S. State Hwy. 16, Fredericksburg 830/990–8381 www.cottonginvillage.com 15 cabins Free Breakfast.*

Fredericksburg Inn & Suites

$$ | **B&B/INN** | Just a couple of blocks off Main Street and nestled on the banks of Barons Creek, this no-frills, straightforward inn offers comfortable rooms, refreshing pools, and a quiet respite from the hustle and bustle of the main thoroughfare. **Pros:** close to Main Street; huge pool; pleasant view of Barons Creek. **Cons:** staff can be somewhat cold and unhelpful; water pressure is weak for showers and toilets; some rooms cleaner than others. *Rooms from: $180 201 S. Washington St., Fredericksburg 830/997–0202 www.fredericksburg-inn.com 104 rooms Free Breakfast.*

Hangar Hotel

$$ | **HOTEL** | Literally located along the landing strip of Fredericksburg's local airport, the Hangar Hotel is an homage to the town's famed National Museum of the Pacific War, designed and outfitted with just about every relic and detail you can imagine in a World War II–era hotel. **Pros:** good on-site bar; unique theme and design; quiet rooms despite proximity to airport. **Cons:** not an easy location to find; theme not for everyone; not many activity options on-site or nearby. *Rooms from: $179 155 Airport Rd., Fredericksburg 830/997–9990 www.hangarhotel.com 50 rooms Free Breakfast.*

★ Hoffman Haus

$$ | **B&B/INN** | Stepping onto this beautiful property spotted with historic cabins and private courtyards with glowing firepits, you won't believe Main Street is just a stone's throw away. **Pros:** close to Main Street yet private and peaceful; excellent, comfortable beds; breakfasts are hot, filling, and delicious—and delivered right to your room. **Cons:** not ideal for children; outdated televisions; difficult to relax if a big event, such as a wedding, is going on in the main lodge. *Rooms from: $165 608 E. Creek St., Fredericksburg 830/997–6739 www.hoffmanhaus.com 12 rooms, 1 cabin Free Breakfast.*

Inn on Barons Creek

$$ | **B&B/INN** | If you're looking for a more traditional hotel atmosphere and want to stay close in, this locally owned operation fits the bill. **Pros:** spacious rooms; centrally located; friendly, helpful staff. **Cons:** not the quaint experience you'd find in guesthouses or B&Bs; food could be better; some residual noise when bands play at the nearby Ausländer restaurant. *Rooms from: $145 308 S. Washington St., Fredericksburg 830/990–9202 www.innonbaronscreek.com 90 suites Free Breakfast.*

★ The Roadrunner Inn

$$ | **B&B/INN** | Not all B&Bs are stuffed with Victorian decor and period pieces, and this is one of Fredericksburg's best urban-minded accommodations offering a more contemporary environment. **Pros:** unique retro decor; clean rooms and beautiful bathrooms; proximity to Main Street is hard to beat. **Cons:** Main Street–facing rooms get street noise; only three rooms, so books up fast; might be too trendy for some. *Rooms from: $150 306 E. Main St., Fredericksburg 830/997–0153 www.theroadrunnerinn.com 3 rooms Free Breakfast.*

While bluebonnets get all the attention, wildflowers of all colors make an appearance in the Hill Country.

Nightlife

★ Chase's Place Cocktails + Kitchen

COCKTAIL LOUNGES | Craft cocktails are the focus at this stylish lounge set in a renovated house tucked off Fredericksburg's main strip. Go stiff and classic with a barrel-aged Boulevardier, get lifted with a riff on a classic with the Woodstock Mule (Houston's own Highway hemp-seed vodka infused with indica CBD flower, with ginger beer, fresh ginger, and lime), or go out on a limb with one of the bar's unique seasonal creations, like the Phuket Island (Thai iced tea, Monkey Shoulder Scotch, and Grand Marnier). Don't overlook the small but mighty food menu, which features bites like oysters and lamb lollipops, plus a short list of specials that rotates weekly. ✉ *313 E. San Antonio St., Fredericksburg* ☎ *830/320–9020* 🌐 *www.chasesplacecocktails.com.*

Pioneer

BARS | Fredericksburg might not be known for its nightlife, but you wouldn't know that from the inside of Pioneer. This local dive serves decent, well-priced cocktails and local wine and features live music on most nights. It's even open until 2 am on Friday and weekends. ✉ *212 E. Main St., Fredericksburg* ☎ *830/992–3733* 🌐 *www.pioneerfbg.com.*

The Stable Cocktail Bar and Lobster House

COCKTAIL LOUNGES | Step into this equestrian-theme cocktail bar, with its exposed brick walls and black-and-white photos, and you'll feel worlds away from downtown Fredericksburg. The Stable is known for their well-crafted signature and classic cocktails, plus an entire menu of martinis and several options for spirit-based flights. This is also the place in town for lobster, in either mac 'n' cheese or roll form. Best of all, they're open daily, with later hours on Friday and Saturday. ✉ *102 E. Ufer St., Fredericksburg* ☎ *830/307–9204* 🌐 *www.thestablefbg.com.*

Fredericksburg's Peaches

When driving in and even near Fredericksburg in the summer, you can almost smell the fresh, sweet aroma of peaches all around. The Fredericksburg–Stonewall area is actually known as the Peach Capital of Texas. More than one-third of the peach production in the state happens in this area. The sandy soils and cool (but not too cold) winter climate merge to create ideal conditions for peach production.

The process of pruning the orchards, managing the ripening process, and harvesting is a year-round affair, and one that is well worth the work when peach season comes around. (Depending on the weather, the season can begin as early as the beginning of May and end as late as August.) Some farms will even let you grab a crate and pick your own peaches off the trees.

Shopping

CLOTHING

Fredericksburg Natural Baby + Kids
CHILDREN'S CLOTHING | This family-owned retail shop features a curated collection of natural and organic clothes, toys, and products for babies and children. ✉ *203 E. Main St., Fredericksburg* ☎ *830/992–3601* 🌐 *fbgnaturalbaby.com.*

Haberdashery
WOMEN'S CLOTHING | Country-chic fashion is defined at the Haberdashery, where women with a flair for sassy style with unmistakable Western inspiration will find a clothing treasure trove. ✉ *221 E. Main St., Fredericksburg* ☎ *830/990–2462* 🌐 *www.haberdasheryboutique.com.*

Hill Country Outfitters
MIXED CLOTHING | This family-owned store specializes in American-made men's and women's casual outdoor clothing and accessories. ✉ *115 E. Main St., Fredericksburg* ☎ *830/997–3761* 🌐 *hillcountry-outfitters.net.*

Parts Unknown
MIXED CLOTHING | Just like its Austin flagship, the Fredericksburg location of this shop showcases hip men's and women's clothing, shoes, and accessories. ✉ *146 E. Main St., Fredericksburg* ☎ *830/997–2055* 🌐 *www.partsunknown.com.*

★ **Texas Jack Wild West Outfitter**
OTHER SPECIALTY STORE | A one-stop shop for all things Western, here you can find anything from fringed suede jackets and scalloped leather belts to roper boots, spurs, saddles, and even a replica firearm. ✉ *117 N. Adams St., Fredericksburg* ☎ *830/997–3213* 🌐 *www.texasjacks.com.*

FOOD

Burg's Corner
FOOD | Since 1948, Burg's Corner has been peddling peaches from Jimmy Duecker Orchards, alongside a wide range of other fruits, vegetables, and products from local vendors. Stop by for a bowl of homemade peach ice cream topped with fresh peach compote, and snap a photo in front of the "Life Is Peachy" mural. Off-season, there is plenty of other beautiful produce to purchase, as well as a plethora of preserved peach products. ✉ *15194 U.S. 290 E, Stonewall* ☎ *830/644–2604* 🌐 *www.burgscorner.com.*

★ Fisher & Weiser's Das Peach Haus

FOOD | A phenomenal stop for specialty jellies and preserves, Fisher & Weiser's is located in an early-1900s brewery and the property features more than 1,000 peach trees surrounded by pines. Fresh peaches are available June through August, but it is also home to a cooking school, and wine tastings occur year-round. ✉ *1406 S. U.S. 87, Fredericksburg* ☎ *866/997–8969* 🌐 *www.jelly.com.*

The Peach Basket General Store

FOOD | Family-owned since 1977, the Peach Basket General Store offers much more than just peaches. The natural shop on Main Street also features a wide array of essential oils, supplements, CBD products, African baskets, juices, and coffee. ✉ *334 W. Main St., Fredericksburg* ☎ *830/997–4533* 🌐 *peachbasketonline.com.*

Studebaker Farms

FOOD | This small roadside peach stand is continually working with state and national horticulturists and scientists to improve production. They carry more than 30 peach varietals throughout the year, including their own. It's cash-only, so be sure to bring some along. ✉ *9405 Hwy. 290 E, Fredericksburg* ☎ *830/990–1109* 🌐 *studebakerfarms.com.*

Vogel Orchard

FOOD | This family orchard, established in 1953 by George and Nelda Vogel, offers a variety of homemade products, including delicious peach butters, peach preserves, and other fruit jellies. Try a scoop of homemade blackberry or peach butter ice cream before hitting the road with a box or two of Vogel peaches in tow. ✉ *12862 US-290, Fredericksburg* ☎ *830/644–2404* 🌐 *vogelorchard.wixsite.com/vogelorchard.*

HOME ACCESSORIES

Amish Market

HOUSEWARES | This family-owned showroom sells unique, solid wood furniture handmade by Amish craftsmen. ✉ *408 W. Main St., Fredericksburg* ☎ *830/992–3546* 🌐 *www.amishtexas.com.*

★ The Christmas Store

OTHER SPECIALTY STORE | No matter what time of year you're visiting Fredericksburg, don't miss a chance to get into the holiday spirit at this huge shop that sells everything Christmas-theme you could possibly imagine. From holiday villages and Nativity scenes to ornaments and stockings, you're guaranteed to find something to add to your decoration collection here. ✉ *155 E. Main St., Fredericksburg* ☎ *830/997–5259* 🌐 *fredericksburgchristmasstore.com.*

Home Simple Goods + Design

HOUSEWARES | Create a stylish, upscale farmhouse look in your own house by shopping the beautifully curated home goods at this aptly named shop, where earth tones and natural materials abound. ✉ *109 N. Adams St., Fredericksburg* ☎ *830/307–9798* 🌐 *simplegoodsshop.com.*

Jabberwocky

OTHER ACCESSORIES | Tucked away from Main Street, Jabberwocky offers unique gifts, trendy clothes, and a wide array of linens. ✉ *105 N. Llano St., Fredericksburg* ☎ *830/997–7071.*

Pottery Ranch

CERAMICS | If it's made of ceramic, you'll find it here—whether it's a *calavera* (skull), a chili pepper, an armadillo, or a pot of just about any size. You'll also find fountains, benches, and plenty of whimsical metal yard art. ✉ *614 W. Main St., Fredericksburg* ☎ *830/990–2622* 🌐 *www.facebook.com/potteryranchfredericksburg.*

Activities

Cross Mountain Park

HIKING & WALKING | This historic mountain—made of granite and marl—was used as a Native American lookout before the arrival of German settlers.

Now it features a single trail leading to an expansive view of Frederickberg and the surrounding region, plus a small hillside grotto (where the eponymous cross can be found). The park is open dawn to dusk. ✉ *Fredericksburg* ☎ *830/997–4202* 🌐 *www.fbgtx.org/415/Cross-Mountain-Park.*

Old Tunnel State Park

WILDLIFE-WATCHING | This small piece of land (just 16 acres) managed by Texas Parks & Wildlife has one particular draw: its bats. From April to October, this old abandoned railroad tunnel is home to more than 3 million Mexican free-tailed bats. If you want to view them, arrive at the tunnel just before sunset, when the bats begin emerging in fleets of thousands for their evening hunt. You can view the bats seven nights a week, but may want to opt for an evening Thursday through Sunday, when interesting educational presentations are given on-site. ✉ *102 E. San Antonio Rd., Fredericksburg* ☎ *866/978–2287* 🌐 *tpwd.texas.gov/state-parks/old-tunnel* 🎫 *Free.*

Luckenbach

10 miles southeast of Fredericksburg.

Luckenbach isn't just some fabled Texas town romanticized by classic country singers Willie Nelson and Waylon Jennings. In fact it's hardly a town at all, but more a cul-de-sac at the end of a country road. Luckenbach is an attitude. It's a place to which Texas songwriters and music lovers from Nacogdoches to El Paso dream of traveling to pay homage to Texas music legends. Of course, if you blink while driving south on Ranch Road 1376 from Highway 290 West, you just might miss it. Aside from the general store, post office, rows of picnic tables, and ample parking for the many daily visitors, there's not much else here.

Though officially established in 1849 by German immigrants, it wasn't until 1970 that it became famous, when John Russell "Hondo" Crouch purchased the town—with a population of just three at the time—and created what soon became a legendary dance hall. The legend began when Texas singer-songwriter Jerry Jeff Walker recorded his album "Viva Terlingua!" at the dance hall in 1973. Four years later the town was memorialized by Willie Nelson and Waylon Jennings in the famed song "Luckenbach, Texas (Back to the Basics of Love)."

During Crouch's reign as the self-proclaimed town mayor, he coined the famous phrase "Everybody's somebody in Luckenbach," a motto still heard today.

Whether you're a fan of country music or not, you haven't officially been to Luckenbach without grabbing an ice-cold brew, listening to whoever may be strumming the guitar on stage, and picking up a souvenir bumper sticker for the road.

 Nightlife

★ Luckenbach Texas

LIVE MUSIC | This saloon and dance hall, made famous by the song crooned by Waylon Jennings and Willie Nelson, was originally built by German settlers as a town hall, eventually growing into a post office, general store, blacksmith shop, and dance hall. In 1970, it was sold to a local humorist (and self-proclaimed "mayor of Luckenbach") who turned the entire space into a music venue. Within a decade, the site was attracting musicians from all over to play against its rustic walls plastered with historic signs and relics. These days, Luckenbach features three stages for live music performances, a beer garden, a kitchen serving barbecue and burgers, and a food truck specializing in loaded baked potatoes. Photo opportunities abound, and there's even a general store stocked with a wide variety of souvenirs. It's an essential stop for any fan of country music, and Texas

The small town of Luckenbach's claim to fame is its dance hall (confusingly also named "Luckenbach Texas").

history. ✉ *412 Luckenbach Town Loop, Luckenbach* ☎ *830/997–3224* 🌐 *www.luckenbachtexas.com.*

Johnson City

30 miles east of Fredericksburg; 30 miles west of Austin; 60 miles north of San Antonio.

Aside from its proximity to some of the Hill Country's main towns, Johnson City is probably most famous as the home of Lyndon Baines Johnson—though the president is not the town's namesake.

Johnson City was actually founded in the late 1870s by James Polk Johnson, a second cousin to the former U.S. president. It was established as the county seat for Blanco County, but the town experienced little growth economically in the early 20th century. LBJ may have first brought notoriety to the area in the 1930s, when he was a junior congressman from Texas. He was the first to lobby for full electric power to the area, and in a 1959 letter wrote, "I think of all the things I have ever done, nothing has ever given me as much satisfaction as bringing power to the Hill Country of Texas."

Following his presidency, LBJ offered his family ranch to the United States as a National Historical Park. It is preserved as a peaceful spot about 14 miles west of Johnson City, near Stonewall.

Sights

Crowson Wines

WINERY | Johnson City is becoming a small but mighty natural wine destination thanks in big part to this small mom-and-pop operation in the center of the town. Book an appointment for a tasting with animated winemaker Henry Crowson to experience his unique natural fermentations made without sulfites or filtration. Crowson and his dad craft about 2,500 cases of minimal-intervention wine each year in the adjacent production space, using the best Texas-grown fruit he can find and letting it spontaneously ferment using ambient yeast. Stand-outs include the lively Malvasia Bianca, the complex barrel-aged Sangiovese rosé, and the earthy, juicy Mourvedre fermented in concrete tanks. ✉ *102 N. Ave. G, Johnson City* ☎ *830/225–8880* 🌐 *crowsonwines.com* 🎫 *$18.*

Exotic Resort Zoo

ZOO | Wild animals—from goats, deer, and kangaroos to buffalo, zebras, and oryx—eat right out of your hand when you take a safari tour of this 137-acre wildlife park. When you purchase your ticket, be sure to buy the pellets so you have something to give the animals. ✉ *235 Zoo Trail, Johnson City* ☎ *830/868–4357* 🌐 *www.zooexotics.com* 🎫 *$18.*

★ Lyndon B. Johnson National Historical Park

HISTORIC SIGHT | History buffs will enjoy wandering through the rooms of Lyndon Baines Johnson's boyhood home in Johnson City, where every effort has been made to restore the home to its 1920s appearance. LBJ lived here from the age of five until his 1924 high school graduation, and the house gives an insightful look into the 36th president's childhood and how he grew into the man he became. ✉ *100 Ladybird La., Johnson City* ☎ *830/868–7128* 🌐 *www.nps.gov/lyjo* 🎫 *Free.*

Lyndon B. Johnson State Park & Historic Site

HISTORIC SIGHT | It's easy to feel confused, but the state park and the national park that honor LBJ are technically separate entities that operate in conjunction with each other. The national park includes Johnson's boyhood home in Johnson City proper, while the state park is confined to this property 14 miles west of town. This historic site encompasses the World War I–era Sauer-Beckmann Living History Farm, historic cabins and trails, and the LBJ Ranch, which includes the family cemetery where the 36th president is buried and the Texas White House, the home where LBJ and his wife, Lady Bird, lived before and after his presidency and often returned to during his time as the nation's leader. A self-guided tour of the ranch begins at the visitor center, and afterward you can hike the many park trails, fish the Pedernales River, picnic, and even take a dip in the pool during the summer. ✉ *199 Park Rd. 52, Stonewall* ☎ *830/644–2252* 🌐 *tpwd.texas.gov/state-parks/lyndon-b-johnson* 🎫 *Free.*

Flash Floods

Flash floods are a common phenomenon among the rivers in the Texas Hill Country. If while visiting any of the region's rivers, you notice the water levels beginning to rise, leave the area immediately. Visitors to state rivers are advised to remain aware of weather conditions and any potential for flash flooding.

Pedernales Falls State Park

STATE/PROVINCIAL PARK | With cool aquamarine pools created from the picturesque Pedernales River shaded by towering cypress trees, this park brings a respite from the glaring sun on hot summer days, especially if you're here to partake of its water-based activities, like swimming or tubing. If you're here to burn calories with a long trek, you've also come to the right place. Hikers and mountain bikers can embark on 19.8 miles of trails, with an additional 14 miles of backpacking trails (hiking only). Fishing, bird-watching, picnicking, and camping are also popular here. Park facilities include picnic sites, restrooms (some with showers), a trailer dump station, and campsites (some with water and electricity, others that are primitive and must be hiked to, with a 2-mile or longer hike). No pets are allowed within the park. ✉ *2585 Park Rd. 6026, Johnson City* ☎ *830/868–7304* 🌐 *tpwd.texas.gov/state-parks/pedernales-falls* 🎫 *$6.*

At Lyndon B. Johnson State Park & Historic Site, you can visit the World War I–era Sauer-Beckmann Living History Farm.

Restaurants

Bryan's on 290

$$$ | **AMERICAN** | Chef Bryan Gillenwater serves well-executed New American cuisine in a laid-back environment at this spot that has become a mainstay in the area. Cooking with live fire is Gillenwater's specialty, so you can't go wrong ordering flame-kissed dishes like grilled shrimp with Hopi blue-corn grits and andouille Creole sauce or prime Angus rib eye with buttermilk whipped potatoes. **Known for:** elevated live-fire cooking; well-curated wine selection; Tuesday night tasting menu. *Average main: 28 300 E. Main St., Johnson City 830/868–2424 www.bryanson290.com Closed Sun. and Mon. No lunch Tues. and Wed.*

Hye Thai

$$ | **THAI** | This popular Thai trailer opened a physical restaurant in Johnson City, where the staff serves a short but stellar menu of dishes like the Crying Tiger, featuring char-grilled steak and served with Thai dipping sauce, rice, and salad greens. Other options include gluten-free Alaskan cod fish-and-chips served with house-made Thai basil tartar sauce; there are also daily specials, like banh mi on Thursday and fried chicken sandwiches on Sunday. **Known for:** fresh ingredients; sizable portions; spicy options. *Average main: 15 502 W. Main St., Johnson City 830/225–0001 www.hyethai.com Closed Mon.–Wed.*

★ Pecan Street Brewing

$$ | **AMERICAN** | Locals will tell you Pecan Street Brewing is one of the area's best-kept secrets—not only for the house brews, but for the food, too. Try their refreshingly light-bodied No Conviction Stout (poured through a nitro tap) alongside the crispy-crusted *flammkuchen* topped with crème fraîche, house-smoked bacon, mushrooms, and Swiss cheese. **Known for:** wood-fired pizzas; nitro stouts; Texas craft spirits. *Average main: 18 106 E. Pecan Dr., Johnson City 830/868–2500 www.*

pecanstreetbrewing.com ⏲ *Closed Tues.–Thurs.*

 Nightlife

The Parlour

WINE BARS | This sunlit, white-tiled bar from the folks behind Southold Farm + Cellar pours low-intervention wine from its own winery plus bottles from other winemakers that co-owner Regan Meador admires. While a tasting at Southold—located just down the road in Fredericksburg—is always a good idea, a visit to this wine bar is another great way to try some of the maker's available vintages in a fun setting while also sampling other area producers. Just be sure to stop by on the early side, since the bar is only open until 9 pm on Friday and Saturday and 6 pm on Sunday. ✉ *109 N. Nugent Ave., Johnson City* ☎ *No phone* 🌐 *www.theparlourjctx.com.*

Kerrville

24 miles southwest of Fredericksburg.

Years ago, Kerrville had the small-town appeal that draws thousands to Fredericksburg and Boerne today. With the arrival of the railroad in the late 1800s, this settlement of primarily shingle-makers became a center for trade and commerce, bringing droves of urban refugees from all walks of life. Now it's one of the biggest little cities in the region.

With a population of more than 20,000, Kerrville has become the source for necessities that can't be found in the smaller towns in the area. Happily situated among some of the most dramatic bluffs and valleys in the Hill Country, with the Guadalupe River running through it, the town also has some of the more picturesque views in Texas.

VISITOR INFORMATION

Kerrville Convention & Visitors Bureau
✉ *2108 Sidney Baker St., Kerrville* ☎ *830/792–3535* 🌐 *www.kerrvilletexas-cvb.com.*

FESTIVALS

Kerrville Folk Festival

Founded in 1972, the Kerrville Folk Festival is the oldest continuously running music festival of its kind in the country. It usually begins the Thursday before Memorial Day and continues 24/7 for 18 days straight, with performances by more than a hundred singer-songwriters and their bands. Approximately 30,000 music lovers come from all over the world to see both longtime and emerging bluegrass, folk, and Americana artists give intimate performances. ✉ *3876 Medina Hwy., Kerrville* ☎ *830/257–3600* 🌐 *www.kerrvillefolkfestival.com.*

 Sights

Kerrville Hill Winery

WINERY | Sitting at the highest point in Kerr County and overlooking the beautiful Texas Hill Country, Kerrville Hills Winery was the first winery established in Kerrville in 2008. Built on the footprint of a Kerrville homestead, the tasting room features the building's original double-sided fireplace, winery-facing windows, and unique rustic warehouse decor. Award-winning winemaker John Rivenburgh has a passion for growing high-quality, sustainable Texas grapes, and has gained acclaim for his full-bodied reds like Tannat, Tempranillo, and the Sagrantino. After a wine tasting, grab a glass of your favorite selection as you watch the sun set behind the hills. ✉ *3600 Fredericksburg Rd., Kerrville* ☎ *830/895–4233* 🌐 *www.kerrvillehills-winery.com* ⏲ *Closed Mon.–Wed.*

The Museum of Western Art

HISTORY MUSEUM | **FAMILY** | Dedicated to preserving the authenticity of America's Western heritage, this museum not only

Holiday Events in Comfort

A magnetic warmth glows through the streets of Comfort, an energy that is palpable during the annual July 4 parade as well as the Christmas in Comfort parade the first Saturday after Thanksgiving, the latter of which draws quite a crowd from miles around. The main streets of town become pedestrian-only for this event so that shoppers can peruse the art, collectibles, knickknacks, and more set up in tents during the day. When evening falls, the streets are cleared, the Christmas lights are lit, and the sidewalks are lined with chairs of visitors wrapped in blankets and sipping hot chocolate to watch the Christmas floats parading by them.

showcases Western art from past and present artists, but also shares the rich and complex history of Native Americans, settlers, mountain men, cowboys, and tradesmen in the West through educational programs. Interactive seminars give youngsters a chance to build their own "home on the range" and see how difficult life was on the open frontier. ✉ *1550 Bandera Hwy., Kerrville* ☎ *830/896–2553* 🌐 *www.museumofwesternart.com* 🎟 *$7* ⏲ *Closed Sun. and Mon.*

Restaurants

The Cowboy Steak House

$$ | **AMERICAN** | With a name like the Cowboy Steak House, you pretty much know what to expect. Western paintings and the smoke-stained limestone hearth of the wood-burning fire create a homey life-on-the-ranch feel. **Known for:** serious ranch vibes; live-fire cooking; excellent steaks. $ *Average main: $17* ✉ *416 Main St., Kerrville* ☎ *830/896–5688* 🌐 *www.cowboysteakhouse.com* ⏲ *No lunch. Closed Sun.*

Mamacita's

$$ | **MEXICAN** | In Kerrville, Mamacita's is as much a tradition as Frito pie at high-school football games. Though billed as "authentic" Mexican food, it's more along the lines of standard Tex-Mex fare and about as straightforward as you can get. **Known for:** great Tex-Mex dishes; good for groups; family-friendly atmosphere. $ *Average main: $15* ✉ *215 Junction Hwy., Kerrville* ☎ *830/895–2441* 🌐 *www.mamacitas.com.*

Rails

$$ | **AMERICAN** | Just off the railroad tracks in Kerrville is a cheery café with cream timber siding and red trim. Built in 1915, the house once served as a train depot but has been transformed into a fantastic little restaurant offering a variety of homemade soups, salads, and hearty entrées. **Known for:** historic setting; daily specials; venison burger. $ *Average main: $18* ✉ *615 E. Schreiner St., Kerrville* ☎ *830/257–3877* 🌐 *www.railscafe.com* ⏲ *Closed Sun.*

Hotels

Y.O. Ranch Hotel & Conference Center

$$ | **HOTEL** | Even though you're on one of the bustling main streets of Kerrville, a stay at the Y.O. Ranch Hotel is a little like a retreat to a star 1950s dude ranch. **Pros:** friendly and helpful staff; good for "old-fashioned" Texas feel; large and affordable rooms. **Cons:** entire property could use some updating and remodeling; limited restaurant hours; room decor is sparse and drab. $ *Rooms from: $195* ✉ *2033 Sidney Baker St., Kerrville* ☎ *830/257–4440* 🌐 *www.yoranchhotel.com* 🛏 *200 rooms* 🍽 *No Meals.*

Nightlife

Grape Juice

BARS | This cozy, art-filled spot beckons you to tuck away into its curtained-off private dining areas or sit and stay awhile on the tree-lined patio. Choose a bottle of wine from the well-curated selection, to enjoy on-site or take home, or choose from the array of craft beer. But definitely don't sleep on the food, which features crave-worthy dishes done right, like the Boom Boom Burger (a brisket burger with cream cheese and candied jalapeño and onions) and "crack-eroni" mac 'n' cheese topped with antelope chili. ✉ *623 Water St., Kerrville* ☎ *830/792–9463* 🌐 *grapejuiceonline.com.*

Pint & Plow Brewing Company

BARS | This community-focused coffeeshop and beer bar boasts a small but mighty menu of house-made craft beer served inside a warm, wood-paneled space and on a spacious, breezy patio. The simple food menu is made up of sandwiches, salads, pizzas, and snacks. Note that they do keep small-town hours, closing by 9 pm each night. ✉ *332 Clay St., Kerrville* ☎ *830/315–7468* 🌐 *pintandplow.com.*

Comfort

18 miles southeast of Kerrville.

At first glance, Comfort resembles a lot of quiet Hill Country towns. It has the standard Dairy Queen and a small downtown with historic buildings and antiques shops. But Comfort, known to many as the start of the Texas Hill Country, seems to have a magic effect on the people who visit. You don't find the crowded sidewalks of Fredericksburg, Boerne, and Kerrville. Here time slows to a crawl, and the friendly faces of locals on High Street, the town's main thoroughfare, make you want to pull up a chair and stay a while.

The laid-back mentality mirrors the mindset of those who settled here in 1852 along the banks of Cypress Creek. Unlike the austere German settlers of Fredericksburg, New Braunfels, and Boerne, Comfort was settled by Ernst Hermann Altgelt and a community of Germans known as the Freethinkers, who fled political and religious oppression and lived a far less conservative life than traditional Germans.

The community prospered in this new way of thinking until the outbreak of the Civil War. While most Texans were pledging their oath to the Confederacy, the Freethinkers swore loyalty to the Union army. Fearful of threats from Confederate loyalists, much of the community fled toward the Mexican border for protection. Those who didn't, or didn't make it, met their doom: on August 10, 1862, 36 men were slaughtered in the Battle of the Nueces. Today, Comfort is home to one of only six flags across the country that fly at half-mast year-round in remembrance of the Union patriots.

Restaurants

Comfort Pizza

$ | **PIZZA** | Townies and visitors alike love this pizza joint housed in a former gas station, for both its wood-fired sourdough pies and its good selection of American and Belgian craft beer. Kick back in the colorful patio furniture and enjoy one of their signature creations, like the California Club pie, which is loaded up with mozzarella, bacon, roasted chicken, avocado, greens, and tomatoes. **Known for:** wood-fired sourdough pizzas; American and Belgian craft beer; family-friendly atmosphere. 💲 *Average main: 14* ✉ *802 High St., Comfort* ☎ *830/995–5959* 🌐 *www.comfortpizza.com* 🕒 *Closed Mon. and Tues.*

Food for the Soul Bistro

$$ | **BISTRO** | True to its name, this family-owned bistro makes food that is simultaneously simple and satisfying, from sandwiches to salads to burgers. Friday night is reserved for their famous buttery steaks, served alongside baked potatoes with the works. **Known for:** homestyle fare; Friday night steaks; delicious bread pudding. *Average main: 18 ✉ 702 High St., Comfort ☎ 210/355–3745 🌐 www.facebook.com/foodforthesoulbistro ⏲ Closed Sun. and Mon. No dinner Tues.–Thurs. and Sat.*

★ High's Cafe & Store

$ | **AMERICAN** | This is the gathering spot in the morning for locals looking to savor a rich cup of coffee or a fully cooked breakfast. But lunch is just as popular, with a daily menu of flavorful soups, salads, and sandwiches, including the "salad trio," which is a scoop of homemade chicken salad and a scoop of homemade tuna salad on a fresh field-greens salad. **Known for:** great coffee; amazing sandwiches; freshly baked goodies. *Average main: $9 ✉ 726 High St., Comfort ☎ 830/995–4995 🌐 highscafeandstore.com ⏲ Closed Mon. and Tues. No dinner.*

The Wander'n Calf

$ | **CAFÉ** | This coffeeshop set in a renovated bungalow invites you to settle in and stay a while. And with its cozy vibe, cute decor, great coffee (pour-over, French press, Chemex, espresso, or just plain drip), homemade baked goods, and tasty sandwiches, there's really no reason to say no. **Known for:** wide variety of coffee options; homemade baked goods; tasty sandwiches. *Average main: 12 ✉ 817 Front St., Comfort ☎ 830/428–2710 🌐 www.wanderncalf.com ⏲ Closed Sun. and Mon. No dinner.*

Hotels

★ Camp Comfort

$$$ | **B&B/INN** | It's like summer camp for adults at this boutique bed-and-breakfast built in a former bowling alley and situated on the banks of Cypress Creek. **Pros:** spacious, serene place to get away from it all; incredible hospitality; luxurious details like down pillows, duvets, and jetted tubs. **Cons:** not a lot to do in the immediate area; limited on-site food and drink options; high prices for the area. *Rooms from: 300 ✉ 601 Water St., Comfort ☎ 877/836–1748 🌐 www.camp-comfort.com No Meals 7 rooms, 3 cabins, 1 airstream.*

Meyer Inn on Cypress Creek

$$ | **B&B/INN** | Originally a stage stop for travelers preparing to cross the Guadalupe River for the Old Spanish Trail, Meyer Inn is beautifully situated on 27 wooded acres along the banks of Cypress Creek and is also just a few blocks' walk from town shopping. **Pros:** excellent proximity to shops; delicious breakfast included; riverfront location is serene and inviting. **Cons:** some of the newer rooms aren't as atmospheric as historic rooms; must often book far in advance; pretty pricey for what you get. *Rooms from: $155 ✉ 845 High St., Comfort ☎ 830/995–2304 🌐 www.meyerbedandbreakfast.com 27 rooms Free Breakfast.*

★ Riven Rock Ranch

$$$$ | **B&B/INN** | It's a bit off the beaten path, but if you can bear with a bend or two in the road, you'll find this Hill Country treasure. **Pros:** immaculate property with beautifully designed accommodations; gorgeous views; afternoon refreshments are a nice bonus. **Cons:** remote location makes visiting area towns a longer journey; very event-focused; fairly expensive compared to other Hill Country accommodations. *Rooms from: $425 ✉ 390 Hermann Sons Rd., Comfort ☎ 830/995–4045 🌐 www.rivenrockranch.com 9 rooms Free Breakfast.*

Nightlife

The Cocky Rooster Bar

BARS | Experience Comfort like a local at this relaxed, open-air bar with garage-door entrances. Most nights feature entertainment of some sort, whether that's a booked band or an open mic, and you'll usually find a food truck here as well. Be sure to try out the swings in the backyard. ✉ *1014 Front St., Comfort* ☎ *830/256–7491*.

Comfort Meet Market
BARS | After a day of antiquing, pop into this local watering hole, with its Beatles poster–wrapped walls, for live music and a cold beer. ✉ *714 High St., Comfort* ☎ *210/367–7087*.

Just Chillin in Comfort
BARS | This family-owned bar features wine by the glass or bottle, rotating snack offerings (think pizza, smoked salmon, hummus, and more), and near-nightly live music. ✉ *702 High St., Comfort* ☎ *210/355–3745* 🌐 *chillinincomfort.com*.

Shopping

ANTIQUES AND HOME DECOR

★ Comfort Antique Mall
ANTIQUES & COLLECTIBLES | Set aside at least a few hours or more to navigate this sprawling antique mall, filled with furniture, jewelry, housewares, and innumerable other relics from the past. ✉ *734 High St., Comfort* ☎ *830/995–4678* 🌐 *www.visitcomfortantiquemall.com*.

The 8th Street Market
ANTIQUES & COLLECTIBLES | This former 1940s Ford dealership is filled with a mix of architectural, industrial, repurposed, and vintage art and collectibles, and there's even a coffeeshop with drinks and snacks so you can make a whole day of treasure hunting. The main building, filled with unique and well-curated antiques, is only the beginning at the 8th Street Market—there are also little houses in the back packed with still more. ✉ *523 8th St., Comfort* ☎ *830/201–0214* 🌐 *www.facebook.com/8thStreetMarketComfortTexas*.

Bandera

28 miles southwest of Comfort, 52 miles northwest of San Antonio.

Dust off your chaps, loosen your saddle cinch, and stay a while. In Bandera, the mythic tales of rodeos, ranches, and the "cowboy way" are all true. Not only will you see beat-up boots, worn Wrangler jeans, and more than a few cowboy hats, you may even catch a glimpse of one of the local ranch hands riding his horse to the general store on Main Street. After all, this isn't considered the "Cowboy Capital of Texas" for nothing. Open rodeos take place twice weekly from Memorial Day through Labor Day, and you can't drive any direction outside of town without passing a dude ranch.

This tiny ink spot on the Texas map was originally established in 1853 as a sawmill town based solely on the cypress trees along the Medina River. Throughout much of the late 1800s, both German and Polish settlers made their home here. After the Civil War the town boomed with cattle drives to the Great Western Cattle Trail. But the rugged terrain slowed things down, as railroads couldn't find passages through the hills and most roads weren't even paved until the 1950s.

VISITOR INFORMATION

Bandera Convention & Visitors Bureau
✉ *126 Hwy. 16 S, Bandera* ☎ *830/796–3045* 🌐 *www.banderacowboycapital.com*.

Sights

Frontier Times Museum
OTHER MUSEUM | Hand-built in 1933 by Hough LeStourgeon's company from stones gathered from the region, this popular tourist stop teems with oddities and relics—take, for instance, the two-headed goat or the mummified cow fetus. The collection here is truly eclectic.

The Dude Ranch Experience

Bandera's "Cowboy Capital" title stems not only from the long-standing cattle ranches in the area, but also from all the visitors who pony up the cash for a bit of the cowboy life for themselves, albeit a bit cushier than the real thing in some cases.

The dude ranch experience allows people to catch a glimpse of what it means to live and work on the open range. Most ranches pride themselves on combining a rustic, outdoorsy, and sometimes primitive environment with today's modern amenities. Depending on the ranch, guests may be able to take daily horseback rides, learn about the area's natural history, watch wranglers barrel race and rope cattle (and sometimes participate), take evening hayrides, and sit around the campfire roasting marshmallows and listening to cowboys sing old trail songs. You don't have to worry about throwing a lasso your first time out, and horseback-riding instruction is available for all levels of experience.

Ranch activities tend to die down in the late fall through the winter. Although accommodations are often still available in the off-season, some high-season activities, such as horseback riding, are discontinued or only available with special reservations.

These *City Slickers*–type adventures began with one enterprising couple back in 1920. Kate and Ebenezer Ross had come into ownership of the Buck Ranch in 1901 and decided to open their property on San Julian Creek, just outside Bandera, to guests from Houston who were looking for a change of pace. Before long, other established ranches began opening their gates to those curious about a Western style of living. With the influx of these seasonal wannabe cowhands, Bandera became famous for its resort-like camps, rodeos, cowboy bars, and restaurants to compliment these newly appointed guest ranches. (Before this, through much of the early 1900s, small rodeos and livestock shows took place in a lot of the different areas in the Hill Country, but centered primarily on trade, not as much for show as they are today.)

Many of these dude ranches have changed in appearance since the old days. While early ranches were bare-bones, offering room for only a few families and usually serving not-so-gourmet cuisine, many have added such amenities as rustic cabins or high-end guest accommodations, dining lodges serving old-fashioned Southern dishes with modern twists, cable TV, Wi-Fi, an on-site spa, and golf courses.

Most ranches operate their guest programs from the early spring to the late fall, providing all-inclusive packages with meals and daily horseback rides included.

✉ 510 13th St., Bandera ☎ 830/796–3864 🌐 www.frontiertimesmuseum.org 🎟 $6 ⏲ Closed Sun.

Hill Country State Natural Area

STATE/PROVINCIAL PARK | With more than 5,300 acres of rolling hills, spring-fed creeks, and thick patches of live oaks, this natural park is a slice of backcountry paradise. Adventurers seeking an avenue for primitive camping, mountain biking, backpacking, limited fishing, and even horseback riding will find happiness here. The park is undeveloped, so you'll need to bring your own water, and you'll need to pack out what you bring in. *✉ 10600 Bandera Creek Rd., Bandera ☎ 830/796–4413 🌐 tpwd.texas.gov/state-parks/hill-country 🎟 $6.*

Restaurants

★ Brick's River Cafe

$$ | **AMERICAN** | Locals and visitors alike flock to Brick's for country cooking with a view. The restaurant itself has a humble interior, but it's the patio overlooking the river that wins everyone's heart. **Known for:** beautiful river views; weekend breakfast buffet; homestyle fare. *Ⓢ Average main: 17 ✉ 1205 N. Main St., Bandera ☎ 830/796–9900 🌐 www.bricksrivercafe.com.*

The Dough Joe

$$ | **PIZZA** | Once you've had your fill of Tex-Mex and chicken-fried steak, turn to the locally beloved The Dough Joe, a pizzeria and coffeeshop in the heart of Bandera. Morning brings an entire menu of breakfast pizza to accompany your latte, while lunch and dinner offerings include an array of specialty pies, with the option to build your own creation (even with a cauliflower crust). **Known for:** excellent coffee; unique breakfast pizza; build-your-own pies. *Ⓢ Average main: 15 ✉ 702B Main St., Bandera ☎ 830/796–7437 🌐 www.doughjoebtx.com ⏲ No dinner Sun.*

The Hen's Nest

$ | **DINER** | If a hearty, comforting plate of cheesy eggs, crispy bacon, and buttered waffles is what you're looking for, head to The Hen's Nest. The digs are humble (in fact, the day's featured dishes are written on postcards in lieu of a menu), but this tiny little café packs a big breakfast punch. **Known for:** homestyle breakfasts; farmhouse vibes; always changing daily specials. *Ⓢ Average main: 10 ✉ 1134C Main St., Bandera ☎ 210/912–0311 🌐 www.facebook.com/thehensnestbandera ⏲ Closed Mon.–Thurs. No dinner.*

The O.S.T. Restaurant

$$ | **AMERICAN** | This is John Wayne country, and the patrons of The O.S.T. (Old Spanish Trail) don't let you forget it, thanks to an entire wall covered with photos and memorabilia of the Duke. Authentic Tex-Mex and hearty American plates are served, including a Texas-size chicken-fried steak that covers the whole plate. **Known for:** BYO-alcohol policy; classic Americana decor; family-style meals. *Ⓢ Average main: 15 ✉ 311 Main St., Bandera ☎ 830/796–3836 🌐 www.ostbandera.com.*

Hotels

Dixie Dude Ranch

$$ | **RESORT** | **FAMILY** | One of Bandera's oldest dude ranches, the Dixie opened its doors to guests in 1937. **Pros:** two horseback rides a day included; overnight trail-ride package; on-site masseuse. **Cons:** two-night minimum; can go overboard on the Western kitsch decor; some of the modern amenities are somewhat dated. *Ⓢ Rooms from: $195 ✉ 833 Dixie Dude Ranch Rd., Bandera ☎ 830/796–7771 🌐 www.dixieduderanch.com 🛏 20 rooms 🍽 All-Inclusive.*

★ Flying L Ranch Resort

$$$$ | **HOTEL** | **FAMILY** | Though it's been around since 1946, the Flying L is anything but stuck in the past: guests can horseback ride, go on hayrides, and enjoy roasting nightly s'mores, as is the case with most dude ranches, but this expansive 772-acre property also has an 18-hole golf course, a water park and lounging pool, and an entire kids' activity program. **Pros:** variety of activities to choose from; well-appointed condos that include washer/dryer; excellent hospitality. **Cons:** expensive; bar and restaurant have limited hours; thin walls make things audible between condos. *Rooms from: $400* *675 Flying L Dr., Bandera* *830/796–7745* *www.flyingl.com* *59 rooms* *All-Inclusive.*

Mayan Dude Ranch

$$ | **HOTEL** | Each morning here begins with orange juice and coffee delivered to your split-timber and river-stone cabin. **Pros:** fun staff; very family-friendly; access to the Medina River. **Cons:** some rooms not as well maintained as others; strict meal times; no liquor on premises, only beer and wine. *Rooms from: $170* *350 Mayan RR, Bandera* *830/796–3312* *www.mayanranch.com* *36 rooms, 21 cabins* *All-Inclusive.*

Nightlife

Arkey Blue's Silver Dollar

Originally known as The Fox Hole, Arkey Blue's is the oldest continually operating honky-tonk in Texas. And like any historic, divey honky-tonk, there are pieces of history hanging all over the walls. An excellent jukebox provides the soundtrack for pool tables, pinball machines, and ice-cold beer—and even ice and mixers, if you'd rather bring your own bottle of whiskey. *308 Main St., Bandera* *830/796–8826.*

11th Street Cowboy Bar

BARS | The truly honky-tonk 11th Street Cowboy Bar, with its outdoor patio and music stage, is always crammed with locals. Be ready to look the part in some Wranglers and boots, and perhaps be prepared to get pulled onto the dance floor for a little boot scootin'. *307 11th St., Bandera* *830/796–4849* *www.11thstreetcowboybar.com.*

Boerne

25 miles east of Bandera, 31 miles northwest of San Antonio.

A decade ago, Boerne was a quiet spot with a smattering of shops and small-town restaurants. Even though it had easy access to San Antonio (just a 30-minute drive), Boerne flew under the radar while Fredericksburg boomed. But in recent years a whole slew of big-city Texans seeking a slower-paced lifestyle have descended upon the place, buying ranches in the hills or retiring to the many high-end developments that have popped up along Highways 16 and 46. The result is a revitalized downtown district with a number of restaurants—though still few accommodations—and a passel of shops along Main Street. Even so, you won't find the shopping hordes that you might in Fredericksburg.

Weekends in December here are particularly festive. From the lighting of the town tree to an evening of Charles Dickens–inspired carolers, Boerne knows how to get people in the holiday spirit.

Originally settled in the 1840s by the same group of German Freethinkers that set up communities in nearby Comfort and its surrounding areas, Boerne (pronounced *burr*-knee) grew steadily along the banks of Cibolo Creek. The town bears remnants of its German heritage around every corner, including the bilingual German-style street signs along the *Hauptstraße* (Main Street).

VISITOR INFORMATION

Boerne Convention & Visitors Bureau

Boerne Convention & Visitors Bureau. *282 N. Main St., Boerne* *830/249–7277* *www.ci.boerne.tx.us/1197/Convention-Visitors-Bureau.*

Guadalupe River State Park is your best chance to experience the beauty of the Guadalupe River.

Sights

Cascade Caverns

CAVE | Take a half-mile tour here past awe-inspiring limestone formations, deep caverns, stalactites, and stalagmites; you may even catch a glimpse of the endangered Cascade Caverns salamander. Watch for the impressive 100-foot waterfall spilling into a black pool at the end of the tour. ✉ *226 Cascade Caverns Rd., (I–10 W, Exit 543), Boerne* ☎ *No phone* 🌐 *www.cascadecaverns.com* 🎫 *$20.*

★ Cave Without a Name

CAVE | That's not a typo; this cave officially has no name—or rather, not having a name is part of its name. The story goes that in 1939, the owner of the cave, James Horne, held a public contest to name the cave. A young boy commented that the geological site was too beautiful to name and won the contest with the suggestion that it be called Cave Without a Name. Similar to the other living limestone caverns in the region, the cave has magnificent stalactite and stalagmite formations and calcite deposits. Be sure to make reservations in advance. ✉ *325 Kreutzberg Rd., Boerne* ☎ *830/537–4212* 🌐 *www.cavewithoutaname.com* 🎫 *$20.*

Cibolo Center for Conservation

NATURE PRESERVE | **FAMILY** | Nature lovers will enjoy strolling the trails through a 100-acre nature center set aside for the conservation of natural grasslands, marshlands, and riverbeds. Educational outdoor workshops and camps are available for kids. At Herff Farm, you can explore community gardens and trails as well as learn about land stewardship. ✉ *140 City Park Rd., Boerne* ☎ *830/249–4616* 🌐 *www.cibolo.org* 🎫 *Free.*

★ Guadalupe River State Park

STATE/PROVINCIAL PARK | This park gives some of the best public access to the shady cypress tree–lined Guadalupe River, a wonderful spot for kayaking, swimming, and fishing. And in the winter, fly-fishing fanatics have a top opportunity to land rainbow trout stocked here by the state each year. ✉ *3350 Park Rd. 31, Spring Branch* ☎ *830/438–2656* 🌐 *tpwd.texas.gov/state-parks/guadalupe-river* 🎫 *$7.*

Restaurants

Bear Moon

$$ | **CAFÉ** | On weekends you may find a line out the door at this town favorite known for its extensive breakfast buffet with eggs, fruit, and fresh-baked muffins, pastries, and breads. Most patrons brave the long counter line for cinnamon rolls, which are as big as a Frisbee. **Known for:** popular breakfast buffet; homemade baked goods; massive cinnamon rolls. 💲 *Average main: $15* ✉ *401 S. Main St., Boerne* ☎ *830/816–2327* 🌐 *www.bearmoonbakery.com* 🕒 *Closed Mon. No dinner.*

Compadre's Hill Country Cocina

$$ | **MEXICAN** | This veteran-owned and -operated Tex-Mex barbecue kitchen is a favorite among locals for its heaping trays of mesquite-smoked chicken, beef fajitas, and pulled pork served in tacos or by the pound. Also not to be missed are the generous loaded nachos, massive enchiladas, and succulent birria tacos. **Known for:** Tex-Mex/barbecue fuision; great group dining; lively atmosphere. 💲 *Average main: 20* ✉ *209 Lohmann St., Boerne* ☎ *830/331–2198* 🌐 *www.facebook.com/compadreshillcountrycocina* 🕒 *Closed Sun. No dinner Mon.–Thurs. and Sat.*

★ **The Creek Restaurant**

$$$$ | **AMERICAN** | Dining alongside Cibolo Creek in this historic house while listening to the rhythmic turn of a water mill is a treat. The upscale restaurant offers a nice array of steaks, fresh seafood, and wild game. **Known for:** creekside dining; blue-crab fingers; top-notch service. 💲 *Average main: $35* ✉ *119 Staffel St., Boerne* ☎ *830/816–2005* 🌐 *www.thecreekrestaurant.com* 🕒 *Closed Sun. and Mon.*

Cypress Grille

$$$ | **AMERICAN** | Come for the inventive, delicious food and stay for the extensive wine menu at the Cypress Grille on Main Street. From the small bistro tables in the front of the narrow wine bar, you can sip a glass of wine and nibble on crisp crab cakes while watching the passersby. **Known for:** extensive wine list; wood-fired entrées; inventive dishes. 💲 *Average main: $30* ✉ *170 S. Main St., Boerne* ☎ *830/248–1353* 🌐 *cypressgrille.com* 🕒 *Closed Mon. No dinner Sun.*

The Dienger Trading Co.

$ | **BISTRO** | This quirky bistro and coffeeshop serves breakfast, brunch, and lunch in a 19th-century building, with a connected retail shop selling clothing, housewares, and gift items. Choose from a classic breakfast plate or croissant sandwich, or step up your morning with French toast sliders or chicken-fried steak Benedict. **Known for:** great coffee; delicious breakfast; picnic fare to-go. 💲 *Average main: 13* ✉ *210 N. Main St., Boerne* ☎ *830/331–2225* 🌐 *thediengertradingco.com* 🕒 *No dinner.*

Little Gretel Restaurant

$$ | **GERMAN** | At this cozy café tucked in a historic home near Cibolo Creek, chef-owner Denise Mazal specializes in central European cuisine, with selections from Hungary, Austria, and the Czech Republic and a particular focus on German fare. Try the *kasseler rippchen*, a smoked-in-house center-cut pork chop served with fresh horseradish sauce and toasted almonds, or the Bavarian meat loaf (half lamb, half beef) with mashed potatoes and mushroom sauce. **Known for:** European cuisine with a German focus; perfect potato pancakes; amazing house-made desserts. 💲 *Average main: 17* ✉ *518 River Rd., Boerne* ☎ *830/331–1368* 🌐 *littlegretel.com* 🕒 *Closed Mon. and Tues. No dinner Fri.*

★ Peggy's on the Green

$$$ | **AMERICAN** | Set in a restored 19th-century dining room, this charming spot showcases elevated Southern cuisine created by chef Mark Bohanan (of San Antonio's Bohanan's steak house fame). Decadent dishes like eggnog-battered sweet-roll French toast and a bourbon-battered ham Monte Cristo with huckleberry jam make this a perfect special-occasion brunch spot, and the creamy-but-light milk punch shouldn't be missed either. **Known for:** historic space; incredible cocktails; decadent brunch. *Average main: 28 The Kendall, 128 W. Blanco St., Boerne 830/572–5000 www.peggysonthegreen.com Closed Mon. and Tues.*

PO PO Family Restaurant

$$ | **AMERICAN** | You might rub your eyes when you first walk into this landmark country café, which boasts over 21,000 collector plates lining the walls and ceiling. When it first opened in 1929, Prohibition was still in full swing and countless bootleggers would sell moonshine in the parking lot, but now people come for the perfect fried chicken, chicken-fried steak, and onion rings. **Known for:** historic setting; eclectic decor; fried frogs' legs. *Average main: $22 829 FM 289, via the Welfare exit (#533) off I–10 W, Boerne 830/537–4194 www.poporestaurant.com Closed Mon. and Tues.*

Richter Tavern

$$ | **AMERICAN** | Natural light floods the brick-laden interior of this renovated 1920s industrial space, setting the scene for thoughtful and elevated casual cuisine. Start with an order of pulled pork poutine for the table before moving on to one of their many diverse offerings: towering sandwiches served with house-made chips, wood-fired pizza (try the spinach, bacon, and Brie with balsamic), or entrées like Akaushi New York strip and Shrimp creole. **Known for:** pretty decent sushi; wood-fired pizzas; giant cocktails. *Average main: 18 153 S. Main St., Boerne 830/331–2675 richterboerne.com/home/ Closed Sun. and Mon.*

Hotels

★ The Kendall

$$$ | **B&B/INN** | Built in 1859 as Boerne's stagecoach stop, this inn is now a recognized state and national historic landmark. **Pros:** lovely pool; excellent location on river and near Main Street; nice spa and gym. **Cons:** no overnight front-desk staff; breakfast is not included; some rooms have a slightly musty smell. *Rooms from: $229 128 W. Blanco Rd., Boerne 830/249–2138 www.yekendallinn.com 36 rooms No Meals.*

Paniolo Ranch

$$$ | **B&B/INN** | You'll have to drive down a winding back road to reach this Hawaiian-named retreat, but once you see the beautiful rolling valley below its hilltop perch, you'll be glad you made the trip. **Pros:** beautiful remote property; on-site spa; luxurious decor. **Cons:** slightly difficult to find; prices are fairly high in comparison to other Hill Country accommodations; lots of weddings on the property. *Rooms from: $295 1510 FM 473, Boerne 830/324–6666 www.panioloranch.com 4 cottages Free Breakfast.*

★ The William

$$$ | **HOTEL** | This 11-room boutique hotel is the only one located right on Boerne's Main Street, and the private New Orleans–style balconies make the experience even more special. **Pros:** great hospitality and customer service; extremely comfortable beds; excellent central location. **Cons:** breakfast not included; steep prices; very thin walls between rooms. *Rooms from: 295 170 S. Main St., Boerne 361/420–1270 thewilliamboerne.com No Meals 11 rooms.*

Nightlife

Botero Tapas + Wine Bar

WINE BARS | Enjoy wine by the bottle or glass and a variety of authentic Spanish tapas and paella at this adorable wine bar with a cozy patio. Do mind the hours, as it closes at 9 pm most nights (and 10 pm on Friday and Saturday). ✉ *161 S. Main St., Boerne* ☎ *830/446–3035* 🌐 *www.botero161.com.*

Cork and Keg

WINE BARS | From the owners of Richter Tavern comes Cork and Keg, an intimate speakeasy-style wine bar tucked below the tavern. Choose from an extensive menu of wine by the glass or bottle (you can take retail bottles home as well if you wish). Richter's full menu is available Tuesday through Saturday, and snack specials are offered on Sunday and Monday. ✉ *153 S. Main St., Boerne* ☎ *830/331–2675* 🌐 *richtercorkandkeg.com.*

The Dodging Duck Brewhaus

BREWPUBS | This appropriately named brewpub serves house beers and global comfort food and features a spacious covered patio overlooking a duck-filled pond. The menu includes customizable burgers, Hill Country sausages, and plenty of beer-friendly snack plates, like giant pretzels, fried green tomatoes, and hot artichoke dip. ✉ *402 River Rd., Boerne* ☎ *830/248–3825* 🌐 *www.dodgingduck.com.*

Shopping

ANTIQUES AND ART

Flashback Funtiques

ANTIQUES & COLLECTIBLES | Find an impressive collection of fun, unique items at this Main Street vintage emporium, from gumball machines and Coca-Cola coolers to jukeboxes and pinball machines. Plan to spend some time here, discovering hidden treasures and restored gems. ✉ *248 S. Main St., Boerne* ☎ *830/331–9911* 🌐 *www.facebook.com/flashbackfuntiquesboerne.*

The Red Rooster

HOUSEWARES | This Main Street shop boasts a nice combination of antiques, home goods, and accessories, making it the perfect stop for a host or housewarming gift—or just a new item for your own abode. ✉ *225 S. Main St., Boerne* ☎ *830/816–5466* 🌐 *www.facebook.com/redroosterboerne.*

CLOTHING AND ACCESSORIES

Bechants Men's

MEN'S CLOTHING | This men's shop has it all, from three-piece suits, jeans, and button-downs to athletic clothing and accessories. You'll also find a nicely curated selection of shoes, handmade leather wallets and billfolds, shave products, and dopp kits—there's even a humidor filled with cigars to choose from. ✉ *305 S. Main St., Boerne* ☎ *830/249–9879* 🌐 *bechantsmens.com/.*

celeste

WOMEN'S CLOTHING | Check out this boutique for casual, contemporary women's clothing that also happens to be reasonably priced. ✉ *140 S. Main St., Boerne* ☎ *830/249–9660* 🌐 *www.shopcelestetx.com.*

Chloe Rose

WOMEN'S CLOTHING | This boutique specializes in cute, stylish pieces for women, in various high-quality fabrics across a spectrum of mainly neutral earth tones. ✉ *136 S. Main St., Boerne* ☎ *830/331–9410* 🌐 *www.boutiquechloerose.com.*

HOME FURNISHINGS

Boerne Farmhouse

HOUSEWARES | You'll be inspired to create the farmhouse of your dreams after visiting this architectural salvage and home goods store, where you'll find a treasure trove of unique furnishings, decorative pieces, and vintage building materials, including corbels, gables, awnings, windows, and doors. ✉ *1488 S. Main St.,*

Boerne ☎ *830/331–1391* 🌐 *boernefarmhouse.com.*

Calamity Jane's Trading Company
FURNITURE | Ordering custom-designed furniture is a pleasurable experience here at Calamity Jane's, where owner Shawn Beach meticulously conjures up Texas Hill Country decor. ✉ *404 S. Main St., Boerne* ☎ *830/249–0081* 🌐 *www.calamityjanestradingco.com.*

Jac's
HOUSEWARES | Find a well-curated selection of home goods and accessories at this Main Street shop, from kitchenware and place settings to serving pieces and glassware. ✉ *170 S. Main St., Boerne* ☎ *830/249–3003.*

New Braunfels

41 miles east of Boerne; 30 miles north of San Antonio; 45 miles southwest of Austin.

With a name like New Braunfels, it's a safe bet that Germans had a great deal of influence in this town. And in fact, they did. New Braunfels was the first of the *Adelsverein*-movement settlements in the 1840s to create secure land in Texas under the German flag. The town was founded by Prince Carl of Solms-Braunfels, the Commissioner General of the organized mass emigration. In 1845 Prince Carl led hundreds of sea-lagged German settlers from Galveston to a plot of land north of San Antonio on the banks of the Comal River. The settlement would later be named for his hometown in Germany, Braunfels (pronounced *brawn*-fells).

The settlement endured a shaky beginning with the outbreak of the Mexican-American War in 1846, rainy seasons that produced great floods in the Comal and Guadalupe Rivers, and an outbreak of cholera. But by 1850, the town was a thriving community boasting the title of the fourth largest city in Texas.

It lies along the Balcones Fault, where the Hill Country meets rolling prairie land to the east, putting New Braunfels barely inside the realms of the Hill Country region. The fault line produced a string of artesian springs, known as Comal Springs, that create the Comal River. Stretching a mere 3 miles before flowing into the Gaudalupe River, the Comal is considered the shortest river in the world.

Whereas many Hill Country towns are frequented for their shopping, wine, romantic getaways, or pure beautiful scenery, New Braunfels is considered more of an activity town. People come to tube down the Guadalupe River and splash around at Schlitterbahn Waterpark, or to get a taste (literally) of the annual Wurstfest in late October and early November celebrating the town's German heritage.

Sights

Cruz de Comal
WINERY | This spot may be located a short jaunt from the rest of the traditional Texas Wine Trail, but it's absolutely worth a visit to experience a winery that's always done things a little differently. Inspired by his friend and fellow winemaker Tony Coturri, Lewis Dickson began planting grapes and producing natural wine back in 2000. Since 2011, all Dickson's wines have been made using only estate-grown Blac du Bois and Black Spanish grapes. The winery is named after the old Mexican graveyard cross in the vineyard (ask Dickson for the full story behind it), and the eclectic tasting room is set in a historic house filled with plenty of art, photographs, and relics to marvel at while you sample the wines. Be sure to buy bottles to go because you won't find them anywhere else but here. ✉ *7405 FM 2722, New Braunfels*

The Texas Hill Country has some of the most underrated wineries in the world.

713/725–4260 www.lacruzdecomalwines.com $20 Closed weekdays.

Schlitterbahn Waterpark & Resort
WATER PARK | FAMILY | Thousands of sun-beaten travelers seek refuge from the Texas heat each year at this 65-acre waterpark with more than 40 rides and family activities spread over six areas. *400 N. Liberty Ave., New Braunfels 830/625–2351 www.schlitterbahn.com $40 Closed mid-Sept.–mid-Apr.*

Restaurants

The Alpine Haus
$$ | GERMAN | Set in a 164-year-old home in downtown New Braunfels, this restaurant specializes in food from the Alps, with a focus on Germany. Schnitzel offerings reach beyond basics to include *Rahm*schnitzel (pork or chicken schnitzel topped with sour-cream gravy) and *Zigeuner* schnitzel, which is a pork or chicken version topped with spicy paprika, bell pepper, and onion gravy. **Known for:** elevated Alpine cuisine; lesser-known German dishes; great German wine selections. *Average main: 18 251 S. Seguin Ave., New Braunfels 830/214–0205 www.alpine-haus.com.*

Huisache Grille
$$ | AMERICAN | Hidden near the train tracks off San Antonio Street, the Huisache (pronounced wee- *satch*) is a must-stop. Consistently delivering fantastic soups, salads, sandwiches, and main dishes, there's a lot to love about this place, and the beautiful 1920s building only adds to the experience. **Known for:** historic setting; delicious grilled meats; chicken tortilla soup. *Average main: $15 303 W. San Antonio St., New Braunfels 830/620–9001 www.huisache.com Closed Mon. No dinner.*

Krause's Cafe
$$ | GERMAN | At Krause's, you can even have schnitzel for breakfast: the *Bauern*schnitzel comes topped with two eggs and hollandaise sauce plus home fries, hash browns, and grits. Texas-German mashups can be found throughout the rest of the menu, too. **Known for:**

Hill Country Wines 101

You don't have to go to Napa or Burgundy to sample good wine. Vintners across Texas are abuzz with hearty blends that have started turning heads from wine spectators worldwide. Some of the most talked about wines originate in the Hill Country, straight from the region's arid limestone earth—the same type of soil you'd find in northwestern Italy, southern Spain, and Provence.

The best time to come is in the fall, when wine-related festivals are underway. These include the Fredericksburg Food & Wine Fest held at the end of October, the Gruene Music & Wine Fest held in the beginning of October, and the San Antonio New World Wine & Food Festival at the beginning of November. If you come in the spring, you'll be treated to the splash of wildflowers (including the vibrant bluebonnets) along the roads as well as Austin's Texas Hill Country Wine and Food Festival in mid-March.

The highest concentration of wineries is in the Fredericksburg area, in Fredericksburg itself as well as the townships of Sisterdale, Comfort, and Stonewall. Most are open daily year-round, providing tours and tastings (some are free, some are not). This is a great place for a wine-tasting road trip—but remember, those sips add up. Limit your tastes and drink water if you're driving.

Local visitor bureaus and gift shops stock the "Hill Country Wine Trail" pamphlet, with a handy map inside (🌐 *texaswinetrail.com*).

Munich-style beer hall; some of the best schnitzel in Texas; house-made sausage. *$ Average main: 18 ✉ 148 S. Castell Ave., New Braunfels ☎ 830/625–2807 🌐 www.krausescafe.com.*

McAdoo's Seafood Company

$$$ | SEAFOOD | Even if the food here wasn't so good, McAdoo's would be worth a visit for the beautiful interior alone. Set inside a converted post office from 1915, the restaurant features upscale Southern and Cajun-style plates, with a focus on seafood and cocktails. **Known for:** Cajun seafood dishes; weekend brunch; historic setting. *$ Average main: 28 ✉ 196 N. Castell Ave., New Braunfels ☎ 830/629–3474 🌐 www.mcadoos.com.*

The River House

$$ | SOUTHERN | The name of the game here is playful, modern Southern cuisine made with local Texas ingredients. You can choose from corn fritters with hot honey and jalapeño ranch, chicken-fried chicken with duck-fat cream gravy, Wagyu meat loaf, and so much more. **Known for:** elevated Southern cuisine; Sunday fried chicken supper; regular live music. *$ Average main: 18 ✉ 1617 New Braunfels St., New Braunfels ☎ 830/608–0690 🌐 theriverhousetx.com ⏲ Closed Mon. and Tues. No lunch Sat.*

Hotels

The Lamb's Rest Inn

$$ | B&B/INN | Getting a little rest is easy to do at this spot on the Guadalupe River. **Pros:** rooms have an up-to-date look; tiered decks have wonderful river views; excellent staff. **Cons:** small bathrooms in some rooms; on the pricey side; over-the-top decor in some rooms. *$ Rooms from: $203 ✉ 1385 Edwards Blvd., New Braunfels ☎ 830/609–3932 🌐 www.lambsrestinn.com 🛏 7 rooms 🍽 Free Breakfast.*

Float In

BARS | If the name wasn't enough of an indication, this riverside hangout fills up at sunset with tubers and paddleboarders cooling off with frosty beers and frozen drinks, plus snacks during happy hour. ✉ *462 E. Mill St., New Braunfels* ☎ *830/213–2355* 🌐 *thefloatin.com.*

Moonshine & Ale

BARS | This rock-and-roll piano bar, which is usually packed and raucous, is certainly not what you'd expect to find in a quaint German town like New Braunfels. But then again, what better activity to take part in after a day of tubing than a massive group sing-along with waterlogged strangers? ✉ *236 W. San Antonio St., New Braunfels* ☎ *830/608–0087* 🌐 *moonshineale.com.*

Sidecar

BARS | Cocktail connoisseurs head to this subterranean lounge beneath the Prince Solms Inn for both classics and the bartenders' unique creations. A tapas menu offers savory snacks to accompany your tipples. ✉ *295 E. San Antonio St., New Braunfels* ☎ *830/255–7432* 🌐 *www.sidecarnb.com.*

The Guadalupe River runs from the western points of Kerr County and stretches down to the Gulf of Mexico through Victoria. The upper river near Kerrville and Boerne is a wide, meandering centerpiece to the Texas Hill Country shaded by pecan and cypress trees. Below Canyon Lake, the Guadalupe River serves as a major recreational spot. White-water rafting and kayaking are both popular, but the more relaxed activity of tubing down the river trailing a cooler of beer is the main attraction in summer.

Below the Canyon Dam, the Gaudalupe is also considered one of the top 100 trout streams in the country. The state stocks the river with trout each winter, attracting anglers from miles around. While casting for beautiful rainbow and brown trout, you'll likely get a few hits from native Guadalupe smallmouth bass (the state fish of Texas), largemouth bass, and Rio Grande perch.

River outfitters are easily found dotting the banks of the river, where tubes, rafts, and kayaks can be rented for the day.

Gruene Outfitters

FISHING | For referrals and to stock up on fishing gear, visit Gruene Outfitters. ✉ *1629 Hunter Rd., New Braunfels* ☎ *830/625–4440* 🌐 *www.grueneoutfitters.com.*

Gruene

3 miles north of New Braunfels, 38 miles north of San Antonio.

Gruene is purely Texan. Ask most any Central Texan if they've ever two-stepped in this little town and you'll see a nostalgic gleam in their eye. Just north of New Braunfels, Gruene stands as a pristine portrait of Texas history and is revered as a place of Texas legends. After all, the entire town has been added to the National Register of Historic Places, and many of the buildings hold a medallion from the Texas Historical Commission.

Settled in the late 1840s by German farmer Ernst Gruene and his sons, the town gained most of its prosperity from the family's cotton business. Gruene's second son, Henry D. Gruene, built a Victorian-style home that is now the landmark Gruene Mansion Inn. Then in the late 1870s, he built the Guadalupe River–powered cotton gin, which now houses the famed Gristmill River Restaurant & Bar and Gruene Hall, a dance hall and saloon that served as *the* social venue for the community before becoming a live music venue in the 1970s.

Though the attack of the boll weevil on cotton crops in the late 1920s and then the economic impact of the Great Depression all but shut down the little town, this Texas star rose again in the 1970s with the restorative support of Pat Molak and Mary Jane Nalley. The two poured their boundless energy into preserving Gruene's original turn-of-the-century feel, an effort that's been rewarded today by the many visitors who stop by to appreciate it.

Restaurants

★ Gristmill

$$ | **AMERICAN** | Dining at the Gristmill is as mandatory as shuffling your boots along the floors of Gruene Hall when visiting Gruene. On a sunny day, request a seat on the multitiered deck that climbs the side of the cliff overlooking the Guadalupe River. **Known for:** charming riverside dining; famous Gristburger with spicy chili con queso; historic setting. *$ Average main: $18 ✉ 1287 Gruene Rd., Gruene ☎ 830/625–0684 🌐 www.gristmillrestaurant.com.*

Gruene River Grill

$$ | **AMERICAN** | Behind the Gruene Mansion Inn, this riverside grill draws quite a crowd. People seem to frequent this locale for the famed rib eye pan-seared in butter and balsamic vinegar, but a cup of the creamy jalepeño corn chowder brimming with fresh crawfish tails makes a notable impression as well. **Known for:** lovely views; rustic atmosphere; elevated homestyle cuisine. *$ Average main: $16 ✉ 1259 Gruene Rd., Gruene ☎ 830/624–2300 🌐 www.gruenerivergrill.com.*

Hotels

Gruene Homestead Inn

$$ | **B&B/INN** | This collection of historic farmhouses features rooms and suites dating from the 1850s to the early 1900s, renovated to reflect the ambience of their era while still providing modern-day comforts—perhaps the best one being the outdoor pool with a hot tub and swim-up bar. **Pros:** friendly and accommodating staff; rooms are impeccably clean and well-maintained; quiet and privacy despite music from nearby tavern. **Cons:** breakfast is very simple; noise from frequent Harley-Davidsons passing on the main road is unavoidable; close to a new housing development, which takes away from its quaintness. *$ Rooms from: $185 ✉ 832 Gruene Rd., Gruene ☎ 830/606–0216 🌐 www.gruenehomesteadinn.com 20 rooms Free Breakfast.*

★ The Gruene Mansion Inn

$$$$ | **B&B/INN** | If you can stay in Gruene for an evening or two, this historic inn is the place to be. **Pros:** cool history; riverfront rooms have nice views; close to shopping and restaurants. **Cons:** breakfast not included; very expensive; big shows at Gruene Hall can be heard in the rooms. *$ Rooms from: $430 ✉ 1275 Gruene Rd., Gruene ☎ 830/629–2641 🌐 www.gruenemansioninn.com 30 rooms No Meals.*

Nightlife

DANCE HALLS

★ Gruene Hall

BARS | What really puts Gruene on the Texas map is legendary Gruene Hall, known as the oldest continuously operating dance hall in the entire state. Many famous musicians owe their success to performances on this fabled stage, including Willie Nelson, Lyle Lovett, George Strait, Garth Brooks, Jerry Lee Lewis, and the Dixie Chicks. A trip to Gruene isn't complete without a turn on the old hardwood floors of Gruene Hall. *✉ 1281 Gruene Rd., Gruene ☎ 830/606–1281 🌐 www.gruenehall.com.*

Visit Gruene Hall to experience the oldest continuously operating dance hall in the United States.

Shopping

Cotton-Eyed Joe's

SOUVENIRS | Grab a souvenir T-shirt, bumper sticker, or cap at the downtown mercantile known as Cotton-Eyed Joe's. The aforementioned fanfare comes in a variety of styles and colors, and the shop is open until 9 or 10 pm, even on Sunday. ✉ *1608 Hunter Rd., Gruene* ☎ *830/620–1995* 🌐 *shop.gruenetexas.com.*

The Grapevine

WINE/SPIRITS | If you're heading out into the Hill Country for a wine tasting, stop here to get a sampling of what's ahead by the taste or glass. Or you can hit this store up on your way back to pick up bottles of your new favorites. ✉ *1612 Hunter Rd., Gruene* ☎ *830/606–0093* 🌐 *www.grapevineingruene.com.*

Gruene Antique Company

ANTIQUES & COLLECTIBLES | Antiques lovers should duck into Gruene Antique Company, where more than 8,000 square feet of antiques and collectibles await. It's open until 9 pm. ✉ *1607 Hunter Rd., Gruene* ☎ *830/629–7781* 🌐 *www.grueneantiqueco.com.*

★ **Gruene General Store**

GENERAL STORE | If Gruene Hall is king of the town, the Gruene General Store is its queen. Parts of the building date to the 1850s; the soda fountain is a 1950s time warp. You can find all sorts of unusual Texas gifts, cards, and foods. The store closes by 6 pm on Sunday. ✉ *1610 Hunter Rd., Gruene* ☎ *830/629–6021* 🌐 *www.gruenegeneralstore.com.*

San Marcos

19 miles northeast of New Braunfels, 30 miles south of Austin.

The largest town between Austin and San Antonio on I–35, San Marcos is home to former president Lyndon B. Johnson's alma mater, Texas State University; the Southwestern Writers Collection at the university's Alkek Library; and crystal-clear Aquarena Springs, which feed the San Marcos River. For the most part it's a college town, but most visitors to San Marcos buzz right by downtown to hit the state's best outlet-mall shopping at Premium Outlets and Tanger Outlets.

 Restaurants

Grins Restaurant

$$ | **AMERICAN** | Located just up the hill from Texas State University, Grins has been a favorite among students and tubers alike since 1975. They're known for their burgers (and have 12 different kinds to choose from) and crispy onion rings, as well as heaping, sizzling fajitas and frozen margaritas in several different flavors. **Known for:** diverse burger menu; casual atmosphere; excellent margaritas. *Average main: 18* ✉ *802 N. LBJ Dr., San Marcos* ☎ *512/392–4746* 🌐 *grinsrestaurant.com.*

North Street

$$ | **INDIAN** | This modern curry shop is putting out some of the tastiest Indian food in the Hill Country, served alongside a massive and diverse list of global craft beers. While they offer more classic plates of dishes like *saag paneer* and butter chicken with coconut rice and *papadam*, they also feature Indian-Mex mashups in the form of curry tacos stuffed with toppings and folded into paratha tortillas. **Known for:** massive global craft beer menu; Indian-Mex fusion dishes; plenty of outdoor seating. *Average main: 18* ✉ *216 North St., San Marcos* ☎ *512/667–7094* 🌐 *www.northsmtx.com.*

Pie Society

$$ | **PIZZA** | This breezy, red-toned pizzeria, located a quick jaunt from downtown, is the premier spot for a New York–style pie in San Marcos. They use all fresh ingredients and have a solid menu of specialty pies, plus salads, calzones, and meatball subs. **Known for:** New York–style pizzas; great calzones; plenty of vegan-friendly options. *Average main: 16* ✉ *700 N. LBJ Dr., San Marcos* ☎ *512/805–8900* 🌐 *www.piesmtx.com.*

The Root Cellar

$$ | **AMERICAN** | This café and art gallery has earned its bragging rights as San Marcos's best restaurant throughout the years. And yet, you'll find no pretense or stuffiness here, just a cheerful staff and bright, eclectic art–filled walls that make for a very comfortable atmosphere. **Known for:** farm-to-table cuisine; extensive wine list with local options; attached art gallery. *Average main: $15* ✉ *215 N. LBJ Dr., New Braunfels* ☎ *512/392–5158* 🌐 *www.rootcellarcafe.com* ⏲ *Closed Mon.*

 Shopping

For years, Texans anywhere within a 200-mile radius have flocked to the outlets here for back-to-school, Christmas, and spring and summer shopping. During these times, patience and dumb luck finding a parking space are virtues. But really, the endless variety of shops at the two adjoining locations draws a steady crowd year-round. For either, take the Center Point Road exit off the interstate.

San Marcos Premium Outlets

OUTLET | The sprawling mall on the north side of Center Point Road is host to such fashionable shops as Crate & Barrel, J. Crew, Pottery Barn, Giorgio Armani, and Gucci. The better part of a day can be spent strolling through the more than 130 stores. ✉ *3939 S. I–35, New Braunfels* ☎ *512/396–2200* 🌐 *www.premiumoutlets.com/outlet/san-marcos.*

Tanger Outlets

OUTLET | On the southern side of Center Point Road, more than 100 stores, from Old Navy to Le Creuset kitchen store, await. ✉ *4015 I–35 S, San Marcos* ☎ *512/396–7446* 🌐 *www.tangeroutlet.com/sanmarcos.*

Showdown

BARS | Although its Austin counterpart closed years ago, Showdown is still a mainstay in downtown San Marcos. The dark dive bar has a neighborly vibe, made stronger by the numbered mugs hanging above the bar for regulars. The cozy space manages to pack in two pool tables along with several pinball machines and plenty of tables for mixing and mingling. In addition to cold, cheap bottles and pitchers of beer, locals flock here to indulge in their jalapeño poppers, hash browns smothered in cheese and jalapeños, and sloppy-good burgers (you can even replace the bun with a quesadilla if you'd like). ✉ *207 E. Hutchison St., San Marcos* ☎ *512/392–7282.*

Zelick's Icehouse

BARS | Set in a 1930s service station, Zellick's Icehouse features plenty of modern touches like craft beer, cocktails made with fresh-squeezed juices, and a food truck serving burgers, tacos, and more. The rustic interior is certainly a draw, but so is the spacious exterior, which wraps around the building with plenty of space for groups, live music, and other fun events. ✉ *336 W. Hopkins St., San Marcos* ☎ *512/757–8787* 🌐 *www.zelickssmtx.com.*

Lockhart

18 miles east of San Marcos, 34 miles south of Austin.

Lockhart may be best known as the "Barbecue Capital of Texas" (as proclaimed by the Texas House in 1999 and the Texas Senate in 2003), but there's more to this quaint small town than brisket. The historic square built around Caldwell County's three-story 1894 courthouse has been coming to life in recent years, thanks in part to the many chefs, artists, musicians, and other entrepreneurs who have been leaving Austin and San Antonio for a slower pace of life.

★ Black's Barbecue

$$ | **BARBECUE** | Although Black's now has locations in Austin, New Braunfels, and San Marcos, there's nothing like a visit to the original location in Lockhart, where pitmaster Ken Black still smokes the meat just like his grandfather did in 1932. The brisket here is thick and juicy and the 9-inch beef ribs are memorable, but the sides also stand out, with less-common offerings like Mexican street corn, green beans, black-eyed peas, and extra-cheddar mac 'n' cheese. **Known for:** massive beef ribs; thick juicy brisket; inventive sides. Ⓢ *Average main: 18* ✉ *215 N. Main St.* ☎ *512/398–2712* 🌐 *www.blacksbbq.com.*

Chaparral Coffee

$ | **CAFÉ** | More than just a coffeeshop, Chaparral is truly a community hub. Owners Taylor and Austin Burge have developed the breakfast and lunch menu of the tiny space to fit the town's growing needs, and they throw DJ-fueled dance parties and other events here, too. **Known for:** some of the best coffee in Central Texas; community events; tasty breakfast and lunch offerings. Ⓢ *Average main: 10* ✉ *106 E. Market St.* ☎ *512/668–4274* 🌐 *chaparralcoffee.com.*

Commerce Cafe

$$ | **SOUTHERN** | From Sarah Heard and Nathan Lemley, the chef-owners behind Austin's Foreign & Domestic, comes this modern interpretation of a country café. Their famous popovers can also be found on the menu here, and the golden-flaky layers are perfect balanced with the seasonal salad of the moment. **Known for:** excellent chicken-fried steak; famous popovers; great cheeseburger. Ⓢ *Average main: 15* ✉ *118 S. Commerce St.*

At Smitty's Market in Lockhart, you can watch them smoke your meats as you wait in line.

☎ 512/359–4993 🌐 www.commerce-lockhart.com ⏲ Closed Sun. No lunch Mon. and Tues.

★ Kreuz Market

$$ | **BARBECUE** | This sprawling landmark barbecue spot is another must when touring Lockhart for barbecue. Like Smitty's, this one has pits, so you can watch while you wait, but unlike Smitty's, they have more rules here: no sauce and no forks (so don't try asking for any!). **Known for:** dry-rubbed meats smoked over post oak; historic building; no barbecue sauce or forks. *$ Average main: 18 ✉ 619 N. Colorado St. ☎ 511/398–2361 🌐 www.kreuzmarket.com.*

★ Smitty's Market

$$ | **BARBECUE** | If you're coming to Lockhart to experience its barbecue, a stop at Smitty's is an absolute must: it's still housed in the original 1948 Kreuz Market, which Edgar A. "Smitty" Schmidt started (it's a long story), and you can scope out a good look at the historic building while you queue for your 'cue. The line moves quickly here as you watch their team in action cutting meat and tending the live fire, which is said to have been burning for more than a hundred years. **Known for:** live-fire cooking; smoked prime rib; long lines that move quickly. *$ Average main: 18 ✉ 208 S. Commerce St. ☎ 512/398–9344 🌐 smittysmarket.com.*

Nightlife

Load Off Fanny's

BARS | If you're looking for a place to do some day-drinking in beautiful weather, this is your spot. Take a load off on the back patio, order food from a menu of wings, burgers, and snacks (all made with high-quality ingredients), and sip by the pint or pitcher. It'll be time well-spent, especially if you catch a local singer-songwriter's set. *✉ 202 E. Market St. ☎ 512/668–3131 🌐 www.loadofffannys.com.*

Lockhart Arts & Craft

BARS | This women-owned bar was started to bring together the things the three partners love the most: beer, art, music, reading, and spending time with friends. True to its name, this is an "art bar," where the activities are just as important as the drinks, featuring a schedule full of game nights, live music, crafting workshops, book club meetings, and more. In addition to beer and wine, they offer a menu of specialty cocktails made with beer and wine. ✉ *113a N. Main St.* ☎ *512/668–3113* 🌐 *www.ltxac.com.*

★ Old Pal Bar

BARS | From the owners of Austin's popular Nickel City comes the Texas tavern Old Pal Bar. Much like its predecessor, Old Pal gives off vintage dive vibes, but it has an incredible whiskey selection and a well-curated cocktail program. You'll reach peak Texan status when you enjoy a frozen Dr. Pepper alongside a beer-can chicken. Come hungry because this is better than your average bar food, and the fried chicken and jojos (seasoned potato wedges) are not to be missed. More nights than not you'll find live music or karaoke on stage and end up staying much longer than planned—just like you would at the home of an old pal. ✉ *100 E. Market St.* ☎ *No phone* 🌐 *oldpalbartx.com.*

The PEARL

BARS | Situated in an 1896 building just off the historic courthouse square, the PEARL looks like it could be the set for a Western movie. Locals and visitors alike flock here for the small-town Texas vibes and hospitality, plus the craft cocktails. There's often live music on the small back stage and, if you're lucky, it might just be a well-known blues legend, which has been known to happen from time to time. ✉ *110 N. Main St.* ☎ *512/668–3100* 🌐 *www.facebook.com/MainStreetPearl.*

Shopping

Bluebonnet Records

RECORDS | This local musician-owned record store features a wide variety of albums, plus equipment, books, movies, and more. ✉ *112 E. Market St.* ☎ *512/668–4489* 🌐 *www.bluebonnet-records.com.*

Grounded Soul Goods

OTHER SPECIALTY STORE | This rejuvenating shop is filled with light and greenery, all the better to showcase the candles, bath products, herbs, tinctures, teas, crystals, and more they have to offer. ✉ *106 N. Main St.* ☎ *512/829–1545.*

Rollfast Ranchwear

OTHER SPECIALTY STORE | This boutique features a well-curated collection of Western-inspired clothing, accessories, hats, boots, and gifts. ✉ *107 E. San Antonio St.* ☎ *512/797–3029.*

Wimberley

14 miles northwest of San Marcos.

Wimberley's windy little roads, shady oak and cypress trees, and compact town square give it the feel of an English village. Established in 1848 with only a small trading post to its name, Wimberley's first industries were lumber and shingle-making. The Blanco River and Cypress Creek, which run through the city, fueled the Wimberley Mill. But the Great Depression left the town stagnant, with the exception of a few working ranches.

The 1980s saw a revitalization in Wimberley as it began to gain notice as a retirement and artists' community. Galleries and shops selling local artists' Hill Country creations, from oil paintings to crafts, are found throughout the village square.

Restaurants

Creekhouse
$$ | **AMERICAN** | This modern kitchen and lounge, located right on Cypress Creek, is breathing new life into downtown Wimberley. There are several different bars on the property, making it easy to grab drinks and snacks, take in the amazing views, and enjoy the live music likely playing. **Known for:** beautiful creek views; shareable snacks; hibiscus margaritas. *Average main: 20 14015 Ranch Rd., Wimberley 512/722–3394 www.creekhousewtx.com Closed Mon. No lunch Tues.–Thurs.*

The Leaning Pear
$$ | **AMERICAN** | What started as a quaint farm-to-table restaurant inside an old house has become an institution in Wimberley. Though the look is much more farmhouse-modern these days, the menu still features the same delicious food they've been known for, like their farm-fresh soups, salads, and sandwiches. **Known for:** classic farm-to-table cuisine; wood-fired pizzas; rotating soup-and-sandwich specials. *Average main: 18 111 River Rd., Wimberley 512/847–7327 www.leaningpear.com Closed Mon. and Tues. No dinner Sun.*

★ **Longleaf Craft Kitchen + Bar**
$$ | **AMERICAN** | Named for the longleaf pine lining the interior of the dining room, this craft kitchen and bar lets local and seasonal ingredients drive the menu, so the offerings may change, but they are always incredibly fresh and flavorful. Offerings might include dishes like Hill Country quail stuffed with mushroom and apples and served with caramelized brussels sprouts, paired perfectly with local Hye-fig cider. **Known for:** craft cocktails; garden courtyard; farm-to-table food program. *Average main: 21 314 Wimberley Sq., Wimberley 512/842–3044 longleafwimberley.com Closed Tues. and Wed.*

Hotels

Blair House Inn
$$$ | **B&B/INN** | There's a lot to experience at this lovely little compound, where you can unwind with a rejuvenating massage, take a dip in the refreshing pool, or roll up your sleeves for one of the hands-on cooking classes. **Pros:** lots of privacy; beautiful grounds; comfortable rooms. **Cons:** limited dining options on-site; pretty pricey for a B&B; traffic noise from nearby highway. *Rooms from: $310 100 Spoke Hill Rd., Wimberley 512/847–1111 www.blairhouseinn.com 11 rooms Free Breakfast.*

★ **Collective Retreats**
$$$$ | **HOUSE** | Sitting on 224 acres of organic farm- and ranchland in Wimberley, this luxury getaway features spacious tents with amenities like king-size beds with 1,500-thread–count linens, wood-burning stoves, over-bed chandeliers, and private decks. **Pros:** lots of unique activities offered; luxurious amenities; impressive culinary options. **Cons:** a bit understaffed; Wi-Fi can be spotty; very expensive. *Rooms from: 400 7431 Fulton Ranch Rd., Wimberley 970/445–2033 www.collectiveretreats.com/retreat/collective-hill-country Free Breakfast.*

Creekhaven Inn & Spa
$$ | **B&B/INN** | Though you're only a short walking distance from Wimberley Village Square, the meandering dirt road to the inn makes this feel like a true hideaway. **Pros:** beautiful grounds and landscaping; very friendly staff; close to downtown Wimberley. **Cons:** some bathrooms are small or awkwardly laid out; on the expensive side; some rooms have less attractive decor. *Rooms from: $210 400 Mill Race La., Wimberley 512/847–9344 www.creekhaveninn.com 14 rooms Free Breakfast.*

Sage Hill Inn & Spa

$$$$ | **HOTEL** | A little less than 10 miles from Wimberley is a little weekend escape set on a 100-acre plot with rolling hills and enchanting vistas. **Pros:** incredible food with breakfast and dinner included in the price; views of the Hill Country from the west-facing decks are spectacular; most rooms have jetted tubs. **Cons:** some rooms have much better views than others; spa a bit on the small side; beds aren't as comfortable as the rest of the accommodations. *Rooms from: $399 4444 W. FM 150, Kyle 512/268–1617 www.sagehill.com 10 rooms Free Breakfast.*

Nightlife

Casa Vindemia

WINE BARS | This unique wine bar feels like hanging out at the house of a very cool friend. Browse all the art for sale inside, go on a wine-tasting adventure, or relax outside at one of the umbrella-shaded tables. *15555 Ranch Rd. 12, Wimberley 512/722–3092 www.facebook.com/casavindemiawineshop.*

★ **The Shady Llama**

BARS | It's not just a cute name, this bar is actually home to llamas and donkeys who roam the 35 acres and visit with guests who are seated in the modern-rustic beer and wine garden. You might not always experience a visit from a llama, but at least you can be guaranteed a beautiful Hill Country view, incredible sunsets, and a fun time with friends playing yard games while sampling craft brews. *18325 Ranch Rd. 12, Wimberley 512/539–7407 theshadyllama.com.*

Social On The Square

WINE BARS | This sleek, modern wine bar set in a renovated house brings a whole cosmopolitan vibe to Wimberley, thanks to its Pinterest-worthy subway tile and living wall sculpture. This is the perfect spot to stop for a glass and a charcuterie board when walking around town shopping. *107 Henson Rd., Wimberley 817/733–5771 www.socialonthesquare.com.*

Market Days

From April to December, the first Saturday of each month brings a surge of visitors to Wimberley for the famed Market Days at Lions Field on RR 2325. (It's about a quarter of a mile from the junction with RR 12.) Here bargain hunters shop to their heart's content among the 450 booths of art and crafts, gifts, furniture, and more. Gates open as early as 6 am and close whenever vendors decide to pack up. You will almost certainly get excellent deals on items you won't be able to find anywhere else.

Shopping

Ceremony Botanical Studio

OTHER SPECIALTY STORE | One of the newer additions to downtown Wimberley, this botanical studio entices you to enter with its collection of beautifully curated plants and succulents displayed outside the entrance. Inside, you'll find more rare and unique plants and handmade pottery, plus an array of incense, candles, bath and beauty products, and other lovely items. *14000 Ranch Rd. 12, Wimberley 512/842–3360 ceremonybotanical.com.*

The Old Mill Store

OTHER SPECIALTY STORE | The Old Mill Store has all the knickknacks of an old-fashioned trading post toward the front, but if you stroll to the back, you'll find paintings, sculptures, and handmade furniture. *314 Wimberley Sq., Wimberley*

☎ 512/847–3068 🌐 www.oldmillstore.com.

Wild West Store

SHOES | Step inside this quaint little shop, filled floor-to-ceiling with vintage boots and Western accessories, and you'll come face-to-face with the Boot Whisperer, who has made a name for herself by not only guessing your boot size at first glance, but also finding you a pair you're sure to love. *✉ 13709 Ranch Rd. 12, Wimberley ☎ 512/847–1219 🌐 www.wildweststore.com.*

Wimberley Glassworks

ART GALLERIES | Technically in San Marcos proper, take a detour to Wimberley Glassworks, one of the art community's most impressive contributors, to watch artisans blow and shape gorgeous glass creations. *✉ 6469 Ranch Rd. 12, Wimberley ☎ 512/393–3316 🌐 www.wgw.com.*

Dripping Springs

24 miles east of Austin.

Known as Austin's gateway to the Texas Hill Country, this small town just a half-half hour east of the city has risen in popularity in recent years, thanks to its nearby wineries and outdoor adventures. In 2014, it was named the first Dark Sky Community in Texas due to a town ordinance that limits the amount of light produced at night.

Sights

★ Dreamland

OTHER ATTRACTION | This unique outdoor entertainment and arts venue is spread across 64 fun-filled acres, with plenty to do, no matter your interests. You'll find sculptures and murals scattered throughout the property as well as the world's most extreme miniature golf course, pickleball courses, a beer garden, and multiple stages for live music and films. *✉ 2770 W. Hwy. 290 ☎ 512/827–1279 🌐 dreamland.us 🎫 Free; activities and events from $8.*

Duchman Family Winery

WINERY | Founded by doctors Stan and Lisa Duchman, this bucolic vineyard features Italian-inspired gardens, a central villa, and food-friendly grapes like the deep-purple Sangiovese and tart Dolcetto sourced mainly from the Texas High Plains AVA. Sample the award-winning Vermentino white while you stroll the gorgeous grounds before enjoying lunch next door at Trattoria Lisina, where chef-owner Damian Mandola serves up house-made pasta and wood-fired pizzas. *✉ 13308 FM150 W, Driftwood ☎ 512/858–1470 🌐 www.duchmanwinery.com.*

Fall Creek Vineyards

WINERY | In 1975, Susan and Ed Auler planted a test plot of grapes in the corner of their ranch, and it quickly grew from one-fourth of an acre to 7½ acres, and is now the oldest winery in the Hill Country. They source Texas-grown grapes from their two estate vineyards as well as a handful of local vineyards, each with its own distinct terroir. On your visit, taste the fruits of their labor in highly rated ExTerra single-vineyard labels, and be sure to check out the winery's namesake twin waterfalls on the north end of the property. *✉ 18059 Farm to Market Rd. 1826, Driftwood ☎ 512/858–4050 🌐 fcv.com 🎫 Tastings $20.*

★ Hamilton Pool Preserve

BODY OF WATER | **FAMILY** | About 30 miles southwest of Austin off Highway 71 is this small nature preserve that is home to one of the Hill Country's most beautiful natural pools. The continuously flowing Hamilton Creek spills over an enormous limestone outcropping, creating a beautiful 50-foot waterfall that gently plunges into the crystal waters of Hamilton Pool. A popular swimming spot for decades, recent rock fallings have

While currently closed to swimmers, Hamilton Pool Preserve is still lovely to visit on a nice day.

closed the pool to swimming for the foreseeable future; it's still a lovely place to explore and walk. Reservations to visit are required in advance. Entry fees are cash only. ✉ *24300 Hamilton Pool Rd., Austin* ✣ *13 miles southwest on Hamilton Pool Rd. from Hwy. 71 W (about 20 miles from Lakeway)* ☎ *512/264–2740* 🌐 *parks.traviscountytx.gov/parks/hamilton-pool-preserve* 🎟 *$12 per vehicle, $8 per person.*

Restaurants

★ Salt Lick BBQ

$$ | **BARBECUE** | Drawing Texans and visitors alike out to the Hill Country since 1967, at Salt Lick you can order barbecue plates a la carte, but most folks opt for the family-style option, which comes with unlimited brisket, sausage, pork ribs, potato salad, coleslaw, and beans. You can BYOB or head to the adjacent Salt Lick Cellars space to purchase beer and wine made from the estate's own fruit (including a BBQ Red designed to accompany the food). **Known for:** fun group dining; family-style Texas barbecue; BYOB policy. $ *Average main: 18* ✉ *18300 Farm to Market Rd. 1826, Driftwood* ☎ *512/858–4959* 🌐 *www.saltlickbbq.com.*

Hotels

★ Camp Lucy

$$$$ | **HOTEL** | Ignore the "camp" in its name—this plush hotel offers well-appointed guest rooms, spacious suites, and standalone cottages, all outfitted with luxurious amenities like exquisite mattresses, private balconies, deep soaking tubs, and fire pits. **Pros:** gorgeous interior design; delicious on-site restaurant with stunning decor; impeccable hospitality from the hotel staff. **Cons:** prices are much higher than average for this area; restaurant wait times can be lengthy; restaurant staff can be inattentive when busy. $ *Rooms from: 389* ✉ *3509 Creek Rd.* ☎ *512/894–2633* 🌐 *www.camplucy.com* 🍽 *No Meals* *36 rooms.*

Marble Falls

48 miles northwest of Austin.

Only 45 minutes from Austin, bustling Marble Falls has become a popular destination for a quick weekend getaway. Three lakes—Marble Falls, LBJ, and Buchanan—are the primary summer attractions here, but a number of other spots in and around town stand out, including nearby Krause Springs and Quarry Mountain and the renowned golf courses of Horseshoe Bay Resort.

Though the sides of Highway 281 running through Marble Falls are littered with your typical retail stores, the town's 19th-century Main Street offers much in the way of gift, home-decor, and apparel shops as well as excellent restaurants. And if you happen to be in the area around the holidays, Marble Falls is noted for having some of the most amazing Christmas lights along the lake.

Marble Falls was named for the natural falls formed by a shelf of limestone that ran diagonally across the Colorado River that flowed through the area. At the time, the water over the limestone created a bluish appearance that gave the impression of naturally occurring marble. However, visitors won't find marble here, and with the formation of the Highland Lakes, the falls are now completely under water and only visible on the rare occasions when the Lower Colorado River Authority lowers the lakes for repairs to the dams and boat docks.

Marble Falls has since gained fame for the amazing granite outcrops resulting from ancient formations in the Llano Basin, the most obvious marker being Granite Mountain, a monolith rising 866 feet above ground and spanning more than 180 acres. In the late 1800s, much of the economic growth of Marble Falls was due to the quarrying of this rock.

Highland Lakes

The Texas Highland Lakes are six lakes in the Hill Country region formed by several dams along the Colorado River. The dams were constructed in the 1930s and '40s to provide flood control for the river. As a result, six lakes were created: Lake Buchanan, Inks Lake, Lake LBJ, Lake Marble Falls, Lake Travis, and Lake Austin. Though built for river control and to help generate hydroelectric power, the lakes now provide main attractions for the neighboring towns of Marble Falls, Horseshoe Bay, Burnet, Lakeway, and Austin.

Sights

Krause Springs

BODY OF WATER | **FAMILY** | If you need a little relief from the Texas heat, a trip here will certainly cool you off. Just a few miles east of Marble Falls in Spicewood, the springs are actually two separate swimming holes on a private ranch opened to the public. From Highway 71, splash through a low-water crossing and up to a hilltop bluff with hypnotic views of rolling grasslands, sprawling oak trees, and an undisturbed horizon. Park your car near the main house and stroll down a flight of outdoor stairs to the spring-fed pools. Be prepared for the biting chill as your toes hit the water. ✉ *404 Krause Springs, Marble Falls* ☎ *401/236–7554* 🌐 *krausesprings.net* 🎫 *$9* 🕑 *Closed Nov.–mid-Feb.*

Restaurants

Blue Bonnet Cafe

$ | **DINER** | Don't even think about coming to Marble Falls without taking a seat at this small-town diner. There's a sign above the hostess stand that commands you to "eat some pie," and you'd be a fool to not listen and sample one of the at least 10 different types made fresh daily. **Known for:** famous pies; classic diner dishes; pie happy hour. *Average main: $9 211 Hwy. 281, Marble Falls 830/693–2344 www.bluebonnet-cafe.net No credit cards No dinner Sun.*

River City Grille

$$ | **AMERICAN** | On a nice evening, dining on the deck is the thing to do here. The views are amazing, and the food holds up its end of the bargain. **Known for:** huge prime rib; river views; good for groups. *Average main: $15 700 1st St., Marble Falls 830/798–9909 www.rivercitygrilletx.com.*

Hotels

Horseshoe Bay Resort

$$$ | **RESORT** | The breathtaking views of Lake LBJ spreading its glimmering fingers should be your first clue that this isn't your typical Texas resort experience. **Pros:** comfortable rooms; excellent activities for kids; top golf and tennis options. **Cons:** staff can be a bit too laid-back; hallways can get noisy; caters more to families. *Rooms from: $228 200 Hi Circle N, Marble Falls 877/611–0112 www.hsbresort.com 442 rooms No Meals.*

McKenzie Guest House

$$ | **B&B/INN** | This stately manor just off Main Street opened in 1907 as the Bredt Hotel and now has been brought back to life as a Texas Historic Landmark. **Pros:** historic vibes; excellent access to Main Street shopping; lovely farmhouse design. **Cons:** antique decor may be a little much for some; host communication can be improved; rooms are somewhat small. *Rooms from: $175 910 3rd St., Marble Falls 830/299–3530 mckenzieguesthouse.com 6 suites Free Breakfast.*

Moriah

$$$$ | **HOUSE** | If you have a large group and would like a little privacy, try Moriah, a small collection of three restored historic buildings on a picturesque 3-acre property with a private boat dock on Lake Marble Falls, just 8 miles from town. **Pros:** lots of amenities and activities; perfect for large groups; beautiful decor that feels like home. **Cons:** very expensive for smaller groups; pretty event-focused; not convenient to town. *Rooms from: $1200 1741 County Rd. 343, Marble Falls 512/598–4776 www.moriahin-hillcountry.com 5 rooms No Meals.*

Activities

Lake LBJ Yacht Club and Marina

BOATING | In the warmer months, if you want to know where the good time is, you'll have to get out on the water. Most of the recreational activity centers on Lake Marble Falls and Lake LBJ in the

Granite Mountain

One of the economic foundations of Marble Falls is Granite Mountain. The great granite dome rises 866 feet; its more than 180 acres of exposed granite serve as the largest granite quarry of its kind in the United States. Although visitors are not admitted to the quarry itself, you can get a great view of the mountain from J Street toward 2nd Street.

Krause Springs is the perfect place to cool off on a hot Texas day.

spring, summer, and early fall. These two lakes are known for being more family-friendly than Austin's wilder lakes, Travis and Austin. Lake LBJ Yacht Club and Marina can assist in outfitting you and your crew with the perfect watercraft. ✉ *200 S. Wirtz Dam Rd., Marble Falls* ☎ *830/693–9172* 🌐 *www.lakelbjmarina.com.*

Burnet

13 miles north of Marble Falls.

During most of the year, Burnet is a sleepy little town best known as a stop for people heading south from the Dallas area or east from Llano. But in late March through late April, the place comes alive with visitors from all over Texas who come to celebrate the state flower, the bluebonnet. Named the "Bluebonnet Capital of Texas," Burnet is famous on the Hill Country Wildflower Trail for having some of the best natural crops of bluebonnets anywhere in the state. (The Brenham area comes in a close second.) The second week in April is the annual Bluebonnet Festival.

Sights

★ **Longhorn Cavern State Park**

CAVE | FAMILY | Formed over thousands of years from water cutting and dissolving limestone bedrock, Longhorn Caverns are a fantastic exhibit of Texas natural history. With a history of Comanche tribes seeking refuge in the caves and calcite-crystal beds, the caverns are a perfect destination for families interested in how the limestone caverns in the Hill Country were formed. Be sure to wear rubber-sole shoes; it gets slippery down there. ✉ *6211 Park Rd. 4 S, Burnet* ☎ *512/715–9000* 🌐 *visitlonghorncavern.com* 🎟 *Park grounds free, cave tours from $19.*

A walk through the limestone caverns of Longhorn Cavern State Park is always fascinating.

Hotels

Canyon of the Eagles Nature Park & Resort
$$ | **HOTEL** | **FAMILY** | While driving the winding road to the hilltop lodge here, it's easy to believe you've taken a wrong turn, but after a few glimpses of sparkling Lake Buchanan, you dead-end right into the state-managed nature preserve and its low-frills guest lodge. **Pros:** panoramic views; close to hiking trails; great bird-watching. **Cons:** accommodations are somewhat primitive; pricey for what it is; outdoor dangers on trails, like bugs, snakes, and poison ivy. *Rooms from: $180* *16942 RR 2341, Burnet* *512/334–2070* *www.canyonoftheeagles.com* *62 rooms* *No Meals.*

Llano

36 miles northwest of Marble Falls.

The greatest attraction in Llano is the drive out there. Whether you're heading north from Fredericksburg on Highway 16 or east from Mason on Highway 29, you'll see some of the most beautiful panoramas of rugged hill country in the region. Perhaps the most inspiring features of the scenery are the dramatic granite outcrops that burst from the landscape in pink, speckled domes.

Llano's history is a rather slow and quiet one, which has translated into a refreshing personality trait of the town. Established in 1856 in compliance with a state legislative act to establish Llano County, the city was a frontier trading center that didn't experience much economic growth until the late 1880s, when the discovery of iron deposits in the northwest part of the county drew financial interest from

Dallas and northern states. The discovery spurred a number of charters for a dam, an electric power plant, and an iron furnace and foundry in anticipation of what many saw as the next "Pittsburgh of the West." But the mineral resources, with the exception of the perpetual granite quarries, soon proved too shallow to sustain economic growth, and Llano's small blip on the industrial map soon faded.

Much of the town's identity today rests in the ranching, farming, and granite industries. Visitors are often attracted by the relaxed atmosphere and activities along the picturesque Llano River. The town square has a historic feel; it's sprinkled with galleries, antiques and gift shops, and a museum of Hill Country wildlife.

 Restaurants

Chrissy's Homestyle Bakery
$ | **BAKERY** | At this tiny little bakery housed in an old building, the enchanting aroma of fresh-baked pies and pastries envelops you the second you walk in the door. The question of what to order then immediately overwhelms you as you scour the glass cases showcasing pies, sweet and savory kolaches, and cookies. **Known for:** excellent kolaches; delicous baked goods that sell out fast; history setting. *Average main: $7 ✉ 501 Bessemer Ave., Llano ☎ 325/247–4564 🌐 chrissyshomestylebakery.business.site ⏲ Closed Mon. and Tues. No dinner.*

Cooper's Old Time Pit Bar-B-Que
$ | **BARBECUE** | This Texas legend is serious about barbecue, and it expects no less from its clientele. The menu is literally what's on display in the open pits that greet you at the entrance: pick your meat from brisket, sausage, smoked turkey, ribs, or whatever else they have on hand for the day and step in line for the typical barbecue sides that include coleslaw, potato salad, and plenty of doughy, white bread. **Known for:** authentic Texas barbecue; picnic table seating; serve-yourself condiment bar. *Average main: $13 ✉ 604 W. Young St., Llano ☎ 325/247–5713 🌐 www.coopersbbq.com.*

Tumlinsons Smoky Top
$$ | **BARBECUE** | If Cooper's is the big-name barbecue spot in town, Tumlinsons is the understated gem that the locals love. Order by the pound and load up a tray of meat or choose a simple platter combination to enjoy in the pared down dining room. **Known for:** underrated Texas barbecue; good for groups; low-key atmosphere. *Average main: 16 ✉ 810 San Antonio St., Llano ☎ 325/423–3924.*

Hotels

1890 Karcher Haus
$$ | **B&B/INN** | The comfy rooms in this historic farmhouse are Victorian-theme, with details like claw-foot tubs and antique furniture and findings. **Pros:** excellent hospitality; walking distance of Llano's square; delicious homemade food. **Cons:** mattresses a bit too firm; rooms on the small side; decor could use a bit of a refresh. *Rooms from: 140 ✉ 1307 Wright St., Llano ☎ 512/591–3182 🌐 www.1890karcherhaus.com Free Breakfast 4 rooms.*

Shopping

Llano isn't quite the shopping hub that Fredericksburg or Boerne are, but near and along the town square you can find a number of gift and antique shops such as the Stuffology Store (507 Bessember Avenue) and Whimseys Antiques (305 Bessember Avenue). If you have time, be sure to stop in at the famed Fain's Honey (3744 S. State Hwy. 16), where you can choose from a selection of natural raw honey, creamed honey, sorghum molasses, and cane syrup.

If you're here from late March through late April, head out to Burnet to see the beauty of Texas bluebonnets.

Mason

35 miles west of Llano.

You don't just find yourself in Mason; you have to want to get there. Nestled in the rolling hills at the very northwest corner of this region, this pristine town was once a bastion of civilization for hunters on their way to or from various excursions, but today it's one of the Hill Country's best-kept secrets.

Originally established as a fort in 1851 by the United States government as one of many posts from the Rio Grande to the Red River, the town of Mason endured a tumultuous history for the better part of the Civil War under Confederate control. Following the federal government's reoccupation in 1866, the town began to see a resurgence through cattle ranching that remains a major part of the town's industry today.

Sights

Eckert James River Bat Cave Preserve

CAVE | One of the largest Mexican free-tailed bat colonies in the world is found in the hills of Mason County. Managed by the Texas Nature Conservancy, Eckert James River Bat Cave, a maternity bat cave, is home to more than 4 million. Only females inhabit the cave, where they bear and rear their young each spring; they depart in mid-October. You can watch in the evening and morning as the entrance to the cave swarms with female bats leaving and returning from an evening hunt to feed their pups. Stand clear of the entrance, unless you don't mind bat guano or having thousands of female bats buzz by. The best way to glimpse this phenomenon is from a safe distance a few hundred yards away. ✉ *James River Rd., Mason* ☎ *325/347–5970* 🌐 *tpwd.texas.gov/huntwild/wild/species/bats/bat-watching-sites/*

eckert-james-river.phtml 🎫 *$5* ⏲ *Closed mid-Oct.–mid-May and Mon.–Wed.*

Restaurants

Cooper's Original Pit Bar-B-Q
$$ | **BARBECUE** | This legendary Hill Country barbecue joint still uses the same recipes the late George Cooper developed when it opened in 1953. Though they have now grown into a regional chain, with locations spread throughout Texas, there is something to be said for visiting this humble original for the famed brisket, sausage, and ribs—and be sure to visit the well-loved pits outside, too. **Known for:** iconic barbecue joint with a long history; lively atmosphere; delicious brisket. *$ Average main: 18* ✉ *810 San Antonio St., Mason* ☎ *325/347–6897* 🌐 *www.coopersbbqmason.com* ⏲ *Closed Tues. and Wed.*

Lea Lou Co-Op
$$ | **AMERICAN** | The vibe is just right at Lea Lou Co-Op, whether you're taking in the beautiful exposed-stone wall interior or kicking back with friends in the spacious yard of the classic 1800s hardware store and lumber yard. The braided-crust pizza is famous here, but the juicy steaks and seafood platters shouldn't be overlooked either. **Known for:** historic setting; breaded-crust pizza; live music and dancing. *$ Average main: 16* ✉ *114 San Antonio St., Mason* ☎ *325/347–1234* 🌐 *lealoutx.com* ⏲ *Closed Sun.–Tues. No lunch weekdays.*

Hotels

Mason Square Hotel
$ | **HOTEL** | Each of the four well-appointed rooms in this boutique hotel is themed as a room you'd find in a large Texas house—the Library, the Farmhouse, the Shop, and the Ranch—and they're all beautifully decorated with thoughtfully chosen antiques. **Pros:** excellent location; beautiful decor; lots of privacy for a B&B. **Cons:** shower water pressure could be improved; no staff on-site; some rooms get a lot of street noise. *$ Rooms from: 115* ✉ *122 Fort McKavitt St., Mason* ☎ *208/220–2135* 🌐 *www.masonsquarehotel.com* 🍽 *No Meals* 🛏 *4 rooms.*

Performing Arts

The Odeon Theater
FILM | Located in the town square, The Odeon Theater is a Texas landmark. In continuous operation since it was built in 1928, the Odeon serves as both a movie theater and a venue for live shows. ✉ *122 S. Moody St., Mason* ☎ *325/347–9010* 🌐 *theodeontheater.com.*

Activities

Though the Guadalupe River has received much acclaim for its vast angling opportunities, the Mason County side of the Llano River is a little slice of heaven for fly-fishers. It's one of the longest remaining wild rivers without flood control or electric generation in the country. Anglers will delight in the copious amounts of largemouth bass, blue gills, and Guadalupe River smallmouth bass. And if you're lucky, you'll get a hit from the beautiful Rio Grande perch, a dark-gray perch dotted with brilliant sapphire spots.

Large outcrops of granite protrude from the river depths, creating easily navigable rapids and deep pools. Some of the river is wade-able, but a kayak or canoe is advised.

Index

A

ABC Kite Fest, *117*
ACL Live at the Moody Theater, *142*
Air travel, *32, 44*
Austin, 118–119
San Antonio, 50
Texas Hill Country, 209
Alamo, The, *53*
Alcohol, *30–31*
Allens Boots (shop), *177*
Altdorf Biergarten ✕, *215–216*
Amusement parks
San Antonio, 58, 92, 104–105
Texas Hill Country, 240
Aquariums, *60, 62*
Art galleries and museums
Austin, 127, 130, 143, 145, 154, 155, 162, 177–178, 189
San Antonio, 53, 56, 57, 59–60, 83, 92–93
Texas Hill Country, 227–228, 251
Auditorium Shores at Town Lake Metropolitan Park, *163*
August E's ✕, *216*
Ausländer Restaurant and Biergarten ✕, *216*
Austin, *16–17, 114–204*
Central Austin and the University of Texas, 114, 143–153
dining, 120–121, 132–135, 148–149, 159–161, 164–165, 168–171, 178–179, 182–185, 189, 192–194, 200–201
Downtown, Sixth Street, and Rainey Street, 114, 125–143
East Austin, 114, 177–188
festivals and seasonal events, 117–118, 140, 187
Greater Austin, 114, 197–204
lodging, 121, 135–137, 149, 151, 161, 171–173, 185–186, 195, 201, 203
nightlife and the arts, 121, 124, 137–142, 151–152, 161–162, 173–175, 186–188, 195–196, 203–204
North Austin, 114, 188–197
price categories, 121
shopping, 124, 142–143, 152–153, 162–153, 175–177, 188, 196–197
South Austin and South Congress District, 114, 163–177
sports and the outdoors, 153–154, 163, 164, 187, 189, 197, 204
tours, 124–125
transportation, 118–120
visitor information, 125, 131
West Austin and Zilker Park, 114, 153–163
when to go, 116–118
Austin City Hall, *125–126*
Austin City Limits Music Festival, *117*
Austin Fire Museum, *126*
Austin History Center, *126*
Austin Motel, *171*
Austin Nature & Science Center, *153*
Austin Proper, *135*
Auto racing, *197*

B

Ballet in the Park, *49*
Bandera, *206, 231, 233–234*
Barley Swine ✕, *189*
Bars
Austin, 137–138, 151, 161–162, 173–174, 186–188, 195–196, 203–204
San Antonio, 72–73, 80, 81, 88, 97
Texas Hill Country, 220, 227, 229, 230–231, 234, 238, 242, 246, 247–248, 250
Barton Creek Greenbelt, *153*
Barton Springs Pool, *153–154*
Baseball, *111*
Basketball, *76*
Bat-watching
Austin, 163, 164
Texas Hill Country, 258–259
Better Half ✕, *159*
Bicycling, *32–33, 44*
Big Top Candy Shop, *176*
Biga on the Banks ✕, *64*
Bird-watching, *104*
Black's Barbecue ✕, *246*
Blanton Museum of Art, *143*
Blue Bar Box, *80*
Blue Star Arts Complex, *83*
Boating, *254–255*
Boerne, *206, 234–239*
BookPeople (shop), *142*
Books and films, *27–28*
Brackenridge Park, *46, 89, 92*
Bremond Block Historic District (Austin), *127*
Brick's River Cafe ✕, *233*
Briscoe Center for American History, *143–144*
Briscoe Western Art Museum, *53, 56*
Broken Spoke (dance club), *174*
Buckhorn Saloon & Museum and the Texas Ranger Museum, *56*
Bullock Texas State History Museum, *144*
Burnet, *206, 255–256*
Business hours, *30*
Bus travel, *33, 44*
Austin, 119
San Antonio, 50

C

Cabernet Grill ✕, *216–217*
Cactus Cafe, *151*
Camp Comfort, *230*
Camp Lucy, *252*
Cap City Comedy Club, *196*
Car travel and rentals, *33–35, 44*
Austin, 119–120
San Antonio, 50–51
Texas Hill Country, 209
Casa Navarro State Historic Site, *56*
Cascade Caverns, *235*
Casino El Camino ✕, *132*
Cave Without a Name, *235*
Caves
San Antonio, 105
Texas Hill Country, 235, 255, 258–259
Chase's Place Cocktails + Kitchen, *220*
Christmas Store, The, *222*
Churches, *60, 101, 104*
Cibolo Center for Conservation, *235*
Circuit of The Americas, *197*
Clark's Oyster Bar ✕, *159*
Clay Pit ✕, *148*
Clyde Littlefield Texas Relays, *117*
Collective Retreats, *249*
Comedy clubs, *138–139, 196*
Comfort, *206, 228, 229–231*
Comfort Antique Mall, *231*
Commodore Perry Estate, *195*
Congress Avenue Bridge, *163*
Contacts, *44.* ⇨ *See also Visitor information*
Contemporary Austin–Jones Center, *127*
Contemporary Austin–Laguna Gloria, *154*
Contigo ✕, *179*
Continental Club, The, *174*
Cotton Gin Village, *219*
COVID-*19, 37*
Creek Restaurant, The ✕, *236*
Crowson Wines, *224–225*
Cruz de Comal (winery), *239–240*
Cuisine, *20–21, 150*
Culinary Institute of America, San Antonio, *76–77*

D

Dai Due ✕, *179*
Dance, *142*
Dance clubs
Austin, 174, 187, 188
San Antonio, 71–72
Texas Hill Country, 243
Darrell K. Royal–Texas Memorial Stadium, *144–145*
Deep Eddy Cabaret, *161*
Deep Eddy Pool, *154*
Dining, *36*
Austin, 120–121, 132–135, 148–149, 159–161, 164–165, 168–171, 178–179, 182–185, 189, 192–194, 200–201
cuisine, 20–21, 150
San Antonio, 51, 63–65, 68, 77, 79–80, 85, 88, 95–97, 104, 108–110
Texas Hill Country, 209–210, 215–218, 226–227, 228, 229–230, 233, 236–237, 240–241, 243, 245, 246–247, 249, 252, 254, 257, 259
Dirty Martin's Place ✕, *148*
Donn's Depot (bar), *161–162*
DoSeum, The, *92*
Dreamland, *251*
Dripping Springs, *206, 251–252*
Driskill, The, *127, 135*
Driskill Bar, The, *137*
Duchman Family Winery, *251*
Dude ranches, *232*

E

Earl Abel's ✕, *79*
East Austin Hotel 🏨, *186*
Easy Tiger ✕, *182*
Eckert James River Bat Cave Preserve, *258–259*
Elephant Room (jazz venue), *139, 141*
Elisabet Ney Museum, *189*
Elizabeth Street Café ✕, *168*
Emma S. Barrientos Mexican American Cultural Center, *127*
Emmer & Rye ✕, *132*
Enchanted Rock State Natural Area, *211*
Esquire Tavern, *72*
Esther's Follies (comedy club), *138*
Exotic Resort Zoo, *225*

F

Fairmont Austin 🏨, *135*
Fairmount, The 🏨, *69*
Fall Creek Vineyards, *251*
Feliz Modern POP (shop), *82*
Fest of Tails Kite Festival and Dog Fair, *49*
Festivals and seasonal events, *39–40*
Austin, 117–118, 140, 187
San Antonio, 49–50
Texas Hill Country, 227, 228, 250
Fiesta San Antonio, *49*
Film, *175, 259*
Fisher & Weiser's Das Peach Haus, *222*
Fishing, *242, 259*
Floods, *225*
Flying L Ranch Resort 🏨, *233–234*
Fonda San Miguel ✕, *189, 192*
Food Hall at Bottling Department ✕, *79*
Football, *76, 189*
Fort Sam Houston Quadrangle and Museum, *92*
Four Seasons Hotel Austin 🏨, *135*
Fourth of July Celebration at Woodlawn Lake Park, *49*
Franklin Barbecue ✕, *182*
Fredericksburg, *206, 210–223*
Fredericksburg Herb Farm, *211*
Frontier Times Museum, *231, 233*

G

Gardens
Austin, 155, 158, 200
San Antonio, 83, 85, 92, 93
Golf, *98, 111*
Government buildings
Austin, 125–126, 127, 130, 131
San Antonio, 62–63
Governor's Mansion (Austin), *127, 130*
Granite Mountain, *254*
Gristmill ✕, *243*
Gruene, *206, 242–244*
Gruene General Store, *244*
Gruene Hall (dance hall), *243*
Gruene Mansion Inn, The 🏨, *243*
Guadalupe River State Park, *235–236*
Guenther House, The 🏨, *85*
Guided tours, *52–53, 124–125*

H

Hamilton Pool Preserve, *251–252*
Harry Ransom Center, *145*
Health concerns, *31*
Hemisfair, *56–57*
Herb farms, *211*
Highland Lakes, *253*
High's Cafe & Store ✕, *230*
Hiking and walking, *204, 222–223*
Hill Country. ⇨ *See Texas Hill Country*
Hill Country State Natural Area, *233*
Historic Market Square (San Antonio), *75*
History, *24–26*
Hoffman Haus 🏨, *219*
Honky-tonks, *234*
Hoover's Cooking ✕, *182*
Hopscotch (gallery), *57*
Hot Joy ✕, *85*
Hotel Contessa 🏨, *69*
Hotel Emma 🏨, *80*
Hotel Havana 🏨, *70*
Hotel Saint Cecilia 🏨, *172*
Hotel San José 🏨, *172*
Hotel San José Courtyard Lounge, *173*
Houses of historic interest
Austin, 130, 189
San Antonio, 56, 59, 62–63, 83, 85
Texas Hill Country, 255
Housing, *31*
Hyatt Regency Hill Country Resort and Spa 🏨, *110*

I

I Love You So Much Mural, *163–164*
Institute of Texan Cultures, *63*
Iron Cactus Mexican Grill and Margarita Bar, *72*
Itineraries, *40–43*

J

Japanese Tea Garden, *92*
Johnson City, *206, 224–227*
Jo's Coffee ✕, *168*
Juan in a Million ✕, *182–183*
JW Marriott San Antonio Hill Country Resort & Spa 🏨, *110*

K

Kalasi Cellars, *211*
Kendall, The 🏨, *237*
Kerrville, *206, 227–229*
Kerrville Folk Festival, *227*
Kerrville Hill Winery, *227*
Kiddie Park, *92*
Kimpton Hotel Van Zandt 🏨, *136*
Komé ✕, *192*
Krause Springs, *253*
Kreuz Market ✕, *247*

L

La Barbecue ✕, *183–184*
La Cantera Resort & Spa 🏨, *110*
La Fonda on Main ✕, *96*
La Gloria ✕, *79–80*
La Panadería ✕, *65*
La Villita Historic Arts Village, *57–58*
Lady Bird Johnson Municipal Park, *211, 214*
Lady Bird Johnson Wildflower Center, *200*
Lake Austin Spa Resort 🏨, *203*
LBJ Presidential Library, *145*
LEGOLAND Discovery Center, *58*
Lenoir ✕, *169*
Liberty, The (bar), *186*
Libraries, *126, 145*
Little Longhorn Saloon, The, *196*
Llano, *206, 256–257*
Lockhart, *206, 246–248*
Lodging, *36*
Austin, 121, 135–137, 149, 151, 161, 171–173, 185–186, 195, 201, 203
San Antonio, 51–52, 68–71, 80, 88, 110
Texas Hill Country, 210, 218–219, 228, 230, 233–234, 237, 241, 243, 249–250, 252, 254, 256, 257, 259
Lone Star Court 🏨, *203*
Long Center for the Performing Arts, The, *164*
Longhorn Cavern State Park, *255*
Longleaf Craft Kitchen + Bar ✕, *249*
Lora Reynolds Gallery, *130*
Louis Tussaud's Waxworks & Ripley's Believe it or Not! Odditorium, *58*
Luckenbach, *206, 223–224*
Luckenbach Texas (saloon), *223–224*
Lustre Pearl (bar), *138*
Lyndon B. Johnson National Historic Park, *225*
Lyndon B. Johnson State Park & Historic Site, *225*

M

Main Plaza (San Antonio), *58*
Majestic Theatre, The, *75*
Marble Falls, *206, 253–255*
Mardi Gras Festival & Parade, *49*
Marijuana, *30–31*
Market Days, *250*
Marktplatz von Fredericksburg, *214*
Mason, *206, 258–259*
MASS Gallery, *177–178*
McKinney Falls State Park, *200*
McNay Art Museum, *92–93*
Medici Roasting ✕, *160*
Menger Bar, *72*
Menger Hotel, The, *59*

Mexic-Arte Museum, *130*
Mi Tierra Café and Bakery ✕, *65, 68*
Midnight Cowboy (cocktail lounge), *138*
Mission Concepción, *101*
Mission Espada, *101*
Mission San José, *101*
Mission San Juan, *104*
Missions, *46, 101, 104*
Modern Rocks Gallery, *178*
Mohawk (music venue), *141*
Mokara Hotel & Spa 🏨, *71*
Money matters, *31*
Morgan's Wonderland, *104–105*
Mount Bonnell, *154–155*
Mozart's Coffee Roasters ✕, *160*
Murals, *163–164*
Museum of Western Art, *227–228*
Museums. ⇨ *See also Art galleries and museums*
Austin, 126, 127, 130, 143–144, 145, 153, 154, 155, 162, 177–178, 189
San Antonio, 53, 56, 57, 58, 59–60, 63, 83, 85, 92–93, 94–95
Texas Hill Country, 214, 227–228, 231, 233, 251
Music
Austin, 139–142, 151–152, 174–175, 188, 204
San Antonio, 73–74, 80–81
Texas Hill Country, 223–224

N

National Museum of the Pacific War, *214*
Natural Bridge Caverns, *105*
Nelson, Willie, *131–132*
New Braunfels, *206, 239–242*
Nightlife and the arts, *36–37*
Austin, 121, 124, 137–142, 151–152, 161–162, 173–175, 186–188, 195–196, 203–204
San Antonio, 71–75, 80–81, 88, 97
Texas Hill Country, 220, 223–224, 227, 229, 230–231, 234, 238, 242, 243, 246, 247–248, 250, 259

O

O. Henry Museum, *130*
Oasis on Lake Travis, The ✕, *200–201*
Odd Duck ✕, *169*
Oge House 🏨, *88*
Old Bakery and Emporium, *130*
Old Pal Bar, *248*
Old Spanish Trail (San Antonio), *59*
Opera, *175*
Otto's German Bistro ✕, *218*

P

P. Terry's ✕, *170*
Packing, *31*
Paramount Theatre, The, *142*
Parks
Austin, 153, 158–159, 163, 200
San Antonio, 46, 56–57, 63, 89, 92, 101, 111–112
Texas Hill Country, 211, 214, 225, 233, 235–236, 251–252, 255
Parkside ✕, *133*
Peach farms, *221*
Pecan Street Brewing ✕, *226–227*
Pecan Street Festival, *117*
Pedernales Falls State Park, *225*
Peggy's on the Green ✕, *237*
Pinthouse ✕, *194*
Pioneer Museum Complex, *214*
Price categories
Austin, 121
San Antonio, 52
Texas Hill Country, 210

Q

Q*2 Stadium, 189*
Quack's *43rd Street Bakery* ✕, *194*

R

Ramen Tatsu-Ya ✕, *194*
Republic of Texas Motorcycle Rally, *117*
Ride-sharing, *35*
Ripley's Believe it or Not! Odditorium, *58*
Riven Rock Ranch 🏨, *230*
Roadrunner Inn, The 🏨, *219*
Rodeo Austin, *117–118*
Rodeos, *49, 117–118*

S

Safety, *31, 37*
St. Patrick's Day River Parade & Festival, *49–50*
Salt Lick BBQ ✕, *252*
San Antonio, *16, 46–112*
Alamo Heights and Brackenridge Park, 46, 89–98
dining, 51, 63–65, 68, 77, 79–80, 85, 88, 95–97, 104, 108–110
Downtown and the River Walk, 46, 53–76
festivals and seasonal events, 49–50
King William Historic District, 46, 83–88
lodging, 51–52, 68–71, 80, 88, 110
nightlife and the arts, 71–75, 80–81, 88, 97
North and Northwest, 46, 104–112
Pearl District, 46, 76–83
price categories, 52
shopping, 75, 81–83, 97–98, 110
Southside and the Missions, 46, 98–104
sports and the outdoors, 75–76, 98, 104, 111–112
tours, 52–53
transportation, 50–51
visitor information, 53
when to go, 49–50
San Antonio African American Community Archive and Museum, *59*
San Antonio Botanical Garden, *93*
San Antonio Missions National Historic Park, *101*
San Antonio Museum of Art (SAMA), *59–60*
San Antonio River Walk, 60
San Antonio Stock Show & Rodeo, 49
San Antonio Zoo, *93–94*
San Fernando Cathedral, *60*
San Marcos, *206, 244–246*
Schilo's ✕, *68*
Schlitterbahn Waterpark & Resort, *240*
Sea Life San Antonio, *60, 62*
SeaWorld San Antonio, *105*
Shady Llama, The (bar), *250*
Shopping, *22–23*
Austin, 124, 142–143, 152–153, 162–153, 175–177, 188, 196–197
San Antonio, 75, 81–83, 97–98, 110
Texas Hill Country, 221–223, 231, 238–239, 244, 245, 248, 250–251, 257
Signature ✕, *109–110*
Six Flags Fiesta Texas, *105*
Slate Mill Wine Collective, *214*
Smitty's Market ✕, *247*
South by Southwest (festival), *118, 140*
Southerleigh Fine Food & Brewery ✕, *80*
Southold Farm + Cellar, *214–215*
Southwest School of Art, *62*
Spanish Governor's Palace, *62–63*
Spider House Ballroom, *151*
Sports and the outdoors, *30, 36.* ⇨ *See also specific activities*
Austin, 153–154, 163, 164, 187, 189, 197, 204
San Antonio, 75–76, 98, 104, 111–112
Texas Hill Country, 222–223, 242, 251, 254–255, 259
Sternewirth Tavern & Club Room, *81*
Steves Homestead, *83*
Stubb's (music venue), *142*
Susanna Dickinson Museum, 130
Swimming, *153–154*

T

Taxis and ride-sharing, *35, 44*
Tesoros Trading Company, *177*
Texas Capitol Visitors Center, *131*
Texas Chili Parlor ✕, *134*
Texas Folklife Festival, *50*
Texas Hill Country, *17, 206–259*
dining, 209–210, 215–218, 226–227, 228, 229–230, 233, 236–237, 240–241, 243, 245, 246–247, 249, 252, 254, 257, 259
festivals and seasonal events, 227, 228, 250
lodging, 210, 218–219, 228, 230, 233–234, 237, 241, 243, 249–250, 252, 254, 256, 257, 259
nightlife and the arts, 220, 223–224, 227, 229, 230–231, 234, 238, 242, 243, 246, 247–248, 250, 259
price categories, 210
shopping, 221–223, 231, 238–239, 244, 245, 248, 250–251, 257
sports and the outdoors, 222–223, 242, 251, 254–255, 259
transportation, 209
when to go, 208–209

Texas Independence Day Celebration, *50*
Texas Jack Wild West Outfitter, *221*
Texas Memorial Museum, *145*
Texas Military Forces Museum, *155*
Texas Ranger Museum, *56*
Texas State Capitol, *131*
Texas State Cemetery, *178*
Thai Fresh ✕, *170*
Theater
Austin, 142, 162, 175, 187
San Antonio, 74–75
Thinkery (museum), *178*
Tiki Tatsu-Ya (cocktail lounge), *173–174*
Tobin Center for the Performing Arts, *74*
Tours, *52–53, 124–125*
Tower of the Americas, *63*
Toy Joy (shop), *143*
Train travel, *35, 44*
Austin, 120
San Antonio, 51
Transportation, *32–35, 44*
Austin, 118–120
San Antonio, 50–51
Texas Hill Country, 209
Travis Park, *63*
Treaty Oak, *155*
Trinity University, *94*
23rd Street Artists' Market, 152–153
Twig Book Shop, The, *83*

U

Uchi ✕, *170*
UMLAUF Sculpture Garden + Museum, *155*
Uncommon Objects (shop), *176*
University Co-Op, *152*
University of Texas at Austin, *145, 148*
UT Tower, *148*
UTSA Institute of Texan Cultures, *63*

V

Vaudeville ✕, *218*
Veloway, The, *200*
Veracruz All Natural ✕, *185*
Via *313 Plaza* ✕, *134–135*
Vietnam Veterans Memorial, *63*
Villa Finale Museum & Gardens, *83, 85*
Visitor information, *37, 44*
Austin, 125, 131
San Antonio, 53

W

Waterloo Records (shop), *162–163*
West Chelsea Contemporary, *155*
When to go, *30*
Austin, 116–118
San Antonio, 49–50
Texas Hill Country, 208–209
White Horse, The (dance club), *188*
Wild Basin Wilderness Preserve, *158*
Wildlife-watching
Austin, 163, 164
San Antonio, 104
Texas Hill Country, 223, 258–259
Wildseed Farms, *215*
William, The, *237*
Willie Nelson Statue, *131–132*
Wimberley, *206, 248–251*
Wineries, *211, 214–215, 224–225, 227, 239–240, 241, 251*
Witte Museum, *94–95*
Wright Bros. Brew & Brew ✕, *185*

Y

Yard Dog Art Gallery, *178*

Z

Zilker Botanical Garden, *158*
Zilker Park, *158–159*
Zoos, *93–94, 225*

Photo Credits

Front Cover: America / Alamy Stock Photo [Description: Abandoned building ruins with bluebonnet wildflowers in the hill country at Pontotoc, Texas, USA.]. **Back cover, from left to right:** Willard/iStockphoto, Sean Pavone/iStockphoto, Sean Pavone/iStockphoto. **Spine:** CrackerClips/iStockphoto. **Interior, from left to right:** Richard A McMillin/Shutterstock (1). Dean Fikar/Shutterstock (2-3). **Chapter 1: Experience San Antonio, Austin, And The Texas Hill Country:** Roschetzky Photography/Shutterstock (6-7). Cheng cheng/Shutterstock (8-9). Rolf52/Dreamstime (9). Pierce Ingram/Travel Texas (9). Richard Mcmillin/Dreamstime (10). Courtesy of the San Antonio Museum of Art (10). Zoryanchik/Shutterstock (10). Chris Zebo/Travel Texas (10). Sean Pavone/Shutterstock (11). Roschetzky Photography/ Shutterstock (11). Victoria Ditkovsky/Dreamstime (12). Kushal Bose/Shutterstock (12). ShengYing Lin/Shutterstock (12). Blanton Museum of Art, The University of Texas at Austin (12). Travel Texas (13). Travel Texas (14). San Antonio Stock Show & Rodeo (14). Jason Risner/Travel Texas (14). Charles Reagan (14). Pierce Ingram/Travel Texas (15). Texas Athletics (15). Joshua Resnick/Shutterstock (20). Elena Eryomenko/Shutterstock (20). Martha Graham/Shutterstock (20). Barre Kelley/Shutterstock (20). Lesya Dolyuk/Shutterstock (21). Cavan Images/iStockphoto (21). Zeytun Images/Dreamstime (21). Blake Mistich/ Travel Texas (21), RobertMPeacock/iStockphoto (22). TeddyandMia/Shutterstock (22). Jason Risner Photography (22). Courtesy Travel Texas (23). Courtesy Travel Texas (23). **Chapter 3: San Antonio:** Bpperry/Dreamstime (45). Crackerclips/ Dreamstime (57). Noamfein/Dreamstime (61). F11photo/Dreamstime (62). F11photo/Dreamstime (66-67). Crackerclips/Dreamstime (73). Chinklephotographer/Dreamstime (74). Moab Republic/Shutterstock (77). Joshuaraineyphotography/Dreamstime (81). Randall Runtsch/ Shutterstock (86-87). Strekoza2/Dreamstime (89). Moab Republic/Shutterstock (93). Koolaidpapi/Shutterstock (94). f11photo/Shutterstock (99). Photofires/Dreamstime (102-103). Pierce Ingram/Travel Texas (108). **Chapter 4: Austin:** Roschetzky Photography/Shutterstock (113). Sean Pavone/Shutterstock (122-123). Asterixvs/Dreamstime (126). LMPphoto/Shutterstock (131). Fotoluminate/Dreamstime (134). Chad Wadsworth (139). GSPhotography/Shutterstock (141). John Muggenborg/Alamy (144). Kruck87/Dreamstime (149). Roschetzky Photography/ Shutterstock (154). Roschetzky Photography/Shutterstock (158). Amanda Stronza/Bat Conservation International (165). PiercarloAbate/ Shutterstock (174). Wyatt McSpadden (183). Kushal Bose/Shutterstock (193). Keeweeboy/Dreamstime (202). **Chapter 5: The Texas Hill Country:** Emily Marie Wilson/Shutterstock (205). Steve Rawls (215). Marc Bennett (216). Malachi Jacobs/Shutterstock (220). Marathon Media/Shutterstock (224). EWY Media/Shutterstock (226). Rick Mcmillan/Dreamstime (235). Shutterdo/Dreamstime (240). Kellee Kovalsky/ Shutterstock (244). Noamfein/Dreamstime (247). Keeweeboy/Dreamstime (252). Fotoluminate/Dreamstime (255). IrinaK/Shutterstock (256). Bnorris309/Dreamstime (258). About Our Writers: All photos are courtesy of the writers.

*Every effort has been made to trace the copyright holders, and we apologize in advance for any accidental errors. We would be happy to apply the corrections in the following edition of this publication.

Notes

Notes

Notes

Notes

Notes

Notes

Fodor's SAN ANTONIO, AUSTIN & THE TEXAS HILL COUNTRY

Publisher: Stephen Horowitz, *General Manager*

Editorial: Douglas Stallings, *Editorial Director*; Jill Fergus, Amanda Sadlowski, Caroline Trefler, *Senior Editors*; Kayla Becker, Alexis Kelly, *Editors;* Angelique Kennedy-Chavannes, *Assistant Editor*

Design: Tina Malaney, *Director of Design and Production*; Jessica Gonzalez, *Graphic Designer;* Sophia Almendral, *Design and Production Intern*

Production: Jennifer DePrima, *Editorial Production Manager*, Elyse Rozelle, *Senior Production Editor;* Monica White, *Production Editor*

Maps: Rebecca Baer, *Senior Map Editor*, David Lindroth, Mark Stroud (Moon Street Cartography), *Cartographers*

Photography: Viviane Teles, *Senior Photo Editor;* Namrata Aggarwal, Payal Gupta, Ashok Kumar, *Photo Editors;* Rebecca Rimmer, *Photo Production Associate;* Eddie Aldrete, *Photo Production Intern*

Business and Operations: Chuck Hoover, *Chief Marketing Officer*, Robert Ames, *Group General Manager*, Devin Duckworth, *Director of Print Publishing*

Public Relations and Marketing: Joe Ewaskiw, *Senior Director of Communications and Public Relations*

Fodors.com: Jeremy Tarr, *Editorial Director;* Rachael Levitt, *Managing Editor*

Technology: Jon Atkinson, *Director of Technology;* Rudresh Teotia, *Lead Developer*, Jacob Ashpis, *Content Operations Manager*

Writers: Julie Catalano, Ramona Flume, Debbie Harmsen, Veronica Meewes

Editor: Amanda Sadlowski

Production Editor: Jennifer DePrima

2nd Edition

ISBN 978-1-64097-492-0

SPECIAL SALES
This book is available at special discounts for bulk purchases for sales promotions or premiums. For more information, e-mail SpecialMarkets@fodors.com.

PRINTED IN CANADA

10 9 8 7 6 5 4 3 2

About Our Writers

Specializing in the arts, design, and leisure and business travel, **Julie Catalano** is a freelance writer whose work has appeared in the *Dallas Morning News*, *DeSoto Magazine*, meetings and events publications, and AAA magazines in Texas, California, and Florida. She is a member of the American Society of Journalists & Authors, the Authors Guild, and the Austin Pastel Society. When not exploring her native Texas, she enjoys artistic destinations in New Mexico, Washington D.C., Wisconsin, Tennessee, and many more.She updated the San Antonio chapter this edition.

Ramona Flume is an Austin-based freelance writer and editor, specializing in travel. Her work has appeared in publications such as *National Geographic Traveler*, the *Guardian*, and *Texas Highways*. She updated the Austin chapter this edition.

Debbie Harmsen is a Dallas-based freelance writer and editor. She updated the Experience and Travel Smart chapters this edition.

Veronica Meewes studied creative writing and sociology at Sarah Lawrence College before moving to Austin, where she now writes about food, beverages, and travel for a number of media outlets. Her work has appeared in *Forbes Travel Guide*, *Food & Wine*, *Texas Monthly*, *Travel & Leisure*, *Austin Monthly*, *Texas Highways*, the *Austin Chronicle*, and more. In 2015, she published *The Fish Sauce Cookbook: 50 Umami-Packed Recipes From Around the Globe*, to demystify fish sauce and its many uses. She also served as editor of a 'zine-inspired community cookbook called *The Odd Duck Almanac* in 2019. She is a member of the Austin branch of Les Dames d'Escoffier and serves on the board of Slow Food Austin, planning community events to showcase the farmers, chefs, and producers who embody the nonprofit's mission of promoting food that is good, clean and fair. She updated the Texas Hill Country chapter this edition.